D1462143

Bengt Sundkler's *Bantu Prophets in South Africa* (1948, second edition 1961) has become widely known as a pioneering work on the life and ideology of Independent African Churches. After three decades, Professor Sundkler has returned to the same Zulu and Swazi churches in which he began his research in 1940. This time he interprets them from a different point of view. He has concentrated on the history and the leading personalities of some of these churches, including that of the famous Isaiah Shembe.

The difference in time and perspective between the earlier book and this new volume leads to challenging questions concerning the Southern Africa church movement as a whole. The present study is built on rich finds of original source material.

OXFORD STUDIES IN AFRICAN AFFAIRS

General Editors
JOHN D. HARGREAVES *and* GEORGE SHEPPERSON

Zulu Zion

and some Swazi Zionists

Zulu Zion

and some Swazi Zionists

BY

BENGT SUNDKLER

OXFORD UNIVERSITY PRESS
1976

Oxford University Press, Ely House, London W.1

GLASGOW NEW YORK TORONTO MELBOURNE WELLINGTON
CAPE TOWN IBADAN NAIROBI DAR ES SALAAM LUSAKA ADDIS ABABA
DELHI BOMBAY CALCUTTA MADRAS KARACHI DACCA
KUALA LUMPUR SINGAPORE HONG KONG TOKYO

ISBN 0 19 822707 8

© *Oxford University Press 1976*

*Printed in Sweden by
Almqvist & Wiksell Tryckeri AB, Uppsala 1976*

Preface

"Zionists"—*ama-Ziyoni*—they call themselves. Wherever they live and move in Southern Africa, their white garments with the green or blue sash and the wooden crozier give them away as "the people of Zion". In South Africa and Rhodesia there are at least two million of them, and their numbers appear to be increasing all the time.

They have nothing in common with modern Jewish Zionism. They are as a matter of fact a *Black* Zion, a charismatic religious movement of Africans, the beginnings of which go back to the first years of this century. Most of them are conscious of a certain historical link with "Zion" in the United States, an apocalyptic healing movement formed by John Alexander Dowie.

We are told that the number of African Independent Churches in South Africa is now some three thousand, and it is claimed that at least three-quarters of these belong to a charismatic, or "Spirit" type. In this book I do *not* include the totality of the Independent Church movement but concentrate exclusively on the "Spirit" churches.

My main concern throughout has, however, been other than statistical. I am almost on the point of saying that, for the purposes of this study it is not important whether the number is two thousand or three thousand; and in this book I even add to the complexity of the situation by suggesting that not only do Independent Churches emerge and flourish—something which all applaud—but also that some of them disappear and die, something which few have noticed. Again, it is wellnigh impossible to know how many fall into this latter category.

For linguistic reasons I have dwelt on Zulu on Swazi organizations alone, and of these, stuck to a very limited number, although faithfully, for as many as thirty-five years in some cases. How representative is this particular selection? They comprise chiefly such churches as for historical reasons— related to the beginnings of Zulu Zion—and because of ideological significance command attention. In the Swazi case it has been possible to be more inclusive; but here again, the historical links with the beginnings have determined the choice. We feel assured that the selection is as fair as one could hope for in the circumstances. Participating observation has been my ambition and usual approach. In the circumstances much less of it was possible than I would personally have wished—and indeed needed, for this type and kind of research. On the other hand, it would not have been possible to get "inside" the movement—to the extent that this is at all possible for a European—without being prepared to take part in the life of the Church: in the preaching, if and when called upon to do so—always in Zulu, without an interpreter; gladly joining in the hymn-singing, in meals and other convivial opportunities. This, to be sure, has its problems in South Africa; the difference between this situation and that of the adjacent Swaziland is enormous. I found the following situation pathetic, yet not unique. On the great day of the consecration of the new Zion Church at Boksburg ("Nkonyane" branch), December 2, 1972, I attended, accompanied by School Inspector J. N. Khumalo. On our arrival we found the leaders having their meal and were invited to sit down with them. After a while, old Rev. Mkize asked, hesitatingly: "Would you like to have a cup of tea?" We said, "Yes, thank you." Now he gathered all his courage and went one great step further: "Would you perhaps agree to share our meal?"—"We would be delighted and grateful," I said. Not knowing me very well, Mr Mkize exclaimed: "These are real Christians."

This is pathetic, I say, for it shows how difficult communication becomes over the abyss between man and man, and this on the particular level of trying to understand and interpret religious life and attitudes.

In publishing this book, I recall some of the difficulties which had to be overcome. The particular restrictions on research visits at certain times and to certain places, in city and countryside, did not always make my field work any easier. My own observations, too, had to be made rather intermittently, at odd periods available in holidays from my Scandinavian university. On the other hand, this intermittent character in the gathering of basic material could be turned into an emphasis on the time factor: I have followed largely the same groups over a span of some thirty-five years, and studied such changes as occurred.

My limitations for the task are obvious. In spite of efforts at understanding, I may have missed some of the rich overtones which make a difference in interpretation.

This study was thus written in anticipation of one to be made some day by an African scholar living much closer to the anguish and jubilation of the movement than I could ever be.

In an earlier study entitled *Bantu Prophets in South Africa* (1948, 1961) the approach was largely sociological. This time I have followed the path of history and of biography. I am dealing with the same limited number of Zulu and Swazi churches to which was devoted that other book, but the material, the presentation, and the final evaluation are different.

For me, it all began some thirty five years ago, in a week-day Church service at Ceza, Zululand. There were some hymns, a few prayers, a short sermon. After the service, an old woman came up to me, the newly arrived missionary and said, *"Mfundisi,* you noticed that I went out during the service?" No, I hadn't thought of that. "Well", she went on "you announced hymn No. ｜156,｜and that hymn is too strong for me. I begin to shake. But since many years we are not allowed to shake in Church. So I had to walk away. I went to sit down under that tree, singing *and* shaking."

I answered her, *"Mame,* my mother—this is not my church. It belongs to God and to you. If you want to shake, by all means do shake here, in your own Church."

The strait-jacket of White worship did not suit her. New forms for the new faith had to be found. This was a problem for the Church everywhere, throughout the continent of Africa. There was a search for a place where the individual could "feel at home" and where African rhythm and conviction could be expressed freely, convincingly and worthily. I have always felt that the Independent Churches have much to contribute to the treasure-house of the Church Universal, and therefore could not but try to understand and interpret their life and faith.

I was given generous access to archives. I thank the directors

7

and staff of the National Archives, Pretoria, and the Provincial Archives, Pietermaritzburg, as well as the Killie Campbell Museum, Durban; and the archives of the Dutch Reformed Church, Pretoria; of the Apostolic Faith Mission, Johannesburg and of the Full Gospel Church of God, Irene, Johannesburg.

A number of friends have assisted and furthered my work. Professor J. F. Holleman, then of Durban, now Leiden, and Dr. A.-I. Berglund of Johannesburg, gave me unfailing help. Professor Marja-Liisa Swantz of Dar-es-Salaam and Helsinki, Dr. H.W. Turner, of Aberdeen, Professor Monica Wilson, of Capetown and Professor Marcia Wright, of New York, read the proofs and suggested important changes. I thank them warmly. I also thank the Rev. N. Joëlson, of Durban, and the Rev. E. Krüger, of Paris, for their help.

In 1958, my research was connected with a Swaziland project directed by Professor Holleman. He and Dr. J. Hughes gave valuable help. A Swazi research assistant, the late Mrs. Regina D. Twala and Mrs. Thoko Hlatshwayo established many contacts which I could not have made on my own. Senator J. S. Vilakazi, Senator Mrs. Mary Mdiniso and Mr. J. J. Nquku represented rich sources of information.

In 1969 and 1972–73, these same Swazi contacts were further developed. Dr. David Hynd and Dr. Samuel Hynd, of the Nazarene Hospital, Manzini, helped me. So did the Rev. and Mrs. Wilfred Hart, of the Evangelical Alliance Mission.

Among my many African helpers, I think with gratitude of fellowship and co-operation with the late Rev. T. W. S. Mthembu, and with Mr. P. Mp. Mkize and the Rev. J. M. Sibiya (cf. p. 332).

The English of my manuscript was revised by Dr. and Mrs. E. J. Sharpe, Lancaster, Mr. David Minugh, M. A., and the Rev. Paul Nelson, Uppsala. Very Rev. T. Lind, Uppsala, read the proofs. I thank them warmly.

For generous financial grants I thank the Samhällsvetenskapliga Forskningsrådet, Stockholm, and the Afrika-Studiecentrum, Leiden. The Swedish Humanistiska Forskningsrådet gave a generous grant towards the printing of the book.

Uppsala, Sweden, September 1975

Bengt Sundkler

Contents

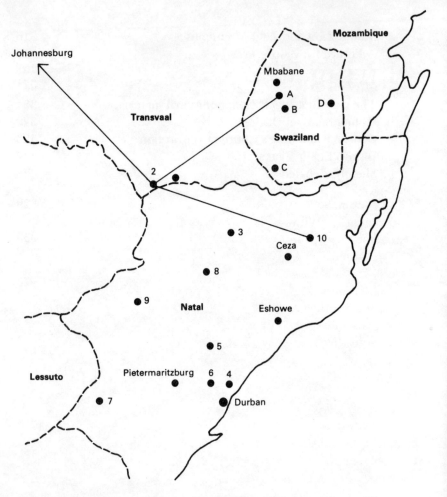

'Spirit' Church Centers in Natal and Swaziland.

1. Wakkerstroom: the Jordan of Zulu Zionism with strategic position related to 10, A, and the Rand.
2. Charlestown: Nkonyane headquarters.
3. Vryheid: Mdlalose headquarters.
4. Ekuphakameni ⎱ Shembe's
5. Nhlangakazi ⎰ holy places.
6. Camperdown: Nzuza headquarters.

7. Himeville: Cekwane headquarters.
8. Telezini: Khambule headquarters.
9. Besters: Msibi headquarters.
10. Nongoma: Zulu Paramount Chief's headquarters.

A. Lobamba.
B. Lozitahlezi.
C. Mahamba.
D. Stegi.

1. At the Source of the Living Waters

Nylstroom ... Nelspruit ... Groenvlei ... Springfontein ... Waterval ... Witwaters Berg: these South African place names, together with hundreds more of the same kind, have a severe story to tell. They remind us of the ecological condition of man in a dry land, looking for that basic, precious, life-giving fluid, water. It was for this that African tribes were searching as they pressed southwards into the high veld of the Transvaal. This was what the Cape Voortrekkers were looking for as in their ox-waggons they moved over veld and mountain further north.

Wakkerstroom (Rapid Stream) is such a name. The river at the side of which a little village, or town, was built, gave the place its name. Approaching the town, one passes over a bridge spanning the broad and relatively deep river. It all looks commonplace and ordinary, just like any other stretch of water.

But Wakkerstroom, to a million African Zionists in their white garments and with their wooden crosses, is no ordinary river. This is the Fountain, the source of Living Waters. This is the Jordan River, at least a Zulu Jordan. It was by these waters that the movement of the Spirit began, in the very first years of this century, just after the Boer War.

What is more, and much more, is the remarkable fact that on that first occasion when the Spirit fell on this Jordan at Wakkerstroom, Whites and Blacks joined and went into the waters together, there to "die" together, and to rise again, together, to the new life of the Spirit. Nor is this all. The white couple who led the hundred and more Zulu and Swazi into the purifying element was, paradoxically, a Dutch Reformed missionary and his wife, herself the daughter of a prominent farmer and Member of the Natal Parliament.

The Rev. P. L. Le Roux had started his career as a Dutch Reformed missionary and was to become the President of the rapidly growing Apostolic Faith Mission Church. Le Roux had received his initial ideas on healing and the Spirit from Andrew Murray, his professor and teacher, the leading Dutch Reformed theologian of that time. The relationship between these two men is one of the subtle turning-points in South African church history. Not that Le Roux and his wife were alone in taking their radical step. In fact, there was a team of three white missionaries who all became devotees of "Zion".

It would seem unfortunate, perhaps, not to say unwise, at this time of Black Power and Black Theology to try to argue such a case, as though even this purely and gloriously Black movement of the Spirit somehow originated with a few Whites. Here we must plead for patience. The Spirit moveth where it listeth, and the great Wakkerstroom story bears this out. In fact, one cannot fully understand the Black charismatic wave without also considering the Whites at its source.

We shall try to trace the early beginnings of this movement. Present-day Zion leaders among Zulus and Swazis are much aware of what they think they know of these beginnings. When asked about the originator of Zion, they will frequently answer "John Alexander, First Apostle"—thus referring to the Rev. J. A. Dowie of Zion City, Ill., USA, and to his emissaries to South Africa. (Dowie himself of course never visited South Africa.)

Let us concede that the matter of historical origins is not the most important aspect of the movement. Yet, the question is not altogether without interest in this case. This is so particularly because there is a tendency, among scholars studying Zion churches, to speculate on certain aspects of tribal psychology. It is recognized that Zion plays a special role among Zulu and Swazi (while Lekganyane and the Northern Sotho are conveniently forgotten in this connection!). This, it is claimed, must be due to some very special trait or design in Zulu or Swazi psychology: "The Zulu react in this or that way", or "Swazi always think along such-and-such particular lines."

All this may be very interesting and even entertaining, but it would seem misdirected and when these sweeping considerations are assumed to explain the proliferation of the Zion churches among the Nguni, one has possibly overlooked the simple, yet intractable historical point of view. It is worth considering that at the beginning of the movement there was for some time a concerted Zion missionary effort, by Whites and Blacks together, working and walking side by side. Let us direct attention to this springtide of Zion in South Africa.

In Southern Africa, *Zion* is a popular name for African churches. Here are a few:

African *Zion* Baptist Church
The Holy Catholic Apostolic Church *in Zion* of South Africa
Holy Spirit Jerusalem Church *in Zion*
Jerusalem Apostolic Kuphiliswa (Zulu for "to be healed")
Church *in Zion*
The Star Nazaretha Church *in Zion* of Sabbath
Zion Apostolic Swaziland Church of South Africa,

and so on, in more than a thousand combinations.

There are at least two thousand churches using this formula *Zion,* or *in Zion.* They are part of a mighty movement of the Spirit. At this time—at the confluence of Black Theology and of a worldwide, charismatic wave—they are of special interest.

Zion forms one large group, or family, of churches in the prolific world of "African Independent Churches". In a South Africa dominated by white caste and white colour, some of the African leaders felt that they could not stand this dominance any longer. They decided to strike out on their own and form their very own religious organizations, apart from the European-led mission churches.

This they were all the more determined to do, because the religious group, the Church, seemed to offer the only legally acceptable outlet for African leadership. Before and after the first World War the African Church became the sounding-board for social and political aspirations expressed in an "Ethiopian" myth. The noble name of "Ethiopia" symbolized the whole of Africa, a free Black Africa, liberated from colonial overlordship, and to be led by the Africans themselves.

The African Methodist Episcopal Church and the "Ethiopian Church" were among the first of a large group of "Ethiopian" churches: The Bantu Methodist Church, the Zulu Congregational Church, the Africa Church. They had a common denominator and ethos. They retained the liturgy, hymn-book and catechism of the particular European church that they had left behind, but emphasized African leadership and the "Ethiopian" vision, at a time when such expressions, though daring and, perhaps, dangerous, were still politically permissible.

Because of this common denominator, one might speak of an *Ethiopian type* among these churches. A few of them were eventually "recognized" by the South African government. From 1925 there existed an administrative machinery for the official recognition of churches. This proved, however, to be a very rare privilege; in fact, it was granted in only eleven cases. Recognition could be revoked. After the Johannesburg bus strike of 1953, the Ethiopian Church was, by administrative decree, deprived of its official status. This served as a reminder, if such were needed, to the churches to keep on the safe side of the law.

The Zion groups constitute another family of churches, the *AmaZioni*. They are "charismatic" groups, emphasizing Divine Healing and 'Prophecy', concerned with establishing a Zion of their own. It is with the origin of this African movement that we are concerned in this chapter, and this, as we have already indicated, takes us to Wakkerstroom, Transvaal, about 1900, and its Dutch Reformed missionary.

P. L. Le Roux, Dutch Reformed missionary

Petrus Louis Le Roux was born in 1864, in the Cape Colony, and was fostered in the relatively liberal tradition of the Cape. His family could help him toward an "Intermediate B.A." at the University of Capetown, but was unable to assist him any further, so he took up teaching. For some time he studied at the Wellington Missionary Seminary. It was here that he met the man who was to exercise the greatest influence on his life, Andrew Murray (1828–1916). This remarkable Scot, who infused a spirit of revival into the Dutch Reformed Church, had moved to Wellington in 1871, where he taught at the Seminary. Le Roux became one of his fervent disciples, studying his many books with their "Holiness-Keswick" message. Murray had a weak throat and voice. For this ailment he had visited various European centres of Faith Healing, including Stockmeyer's Hauptweil in Switzerland, Boardman's centre in London, and others. He was fully restored and healed. So impressed was he by his experience that he wrote a book on the Biblical message concerning Divine Healing, *Jesus the Physician of the Sick* (1884).[1]

Le Roux had a health problem of his own. He had hoped to become a missionary in Nyasaland but his health did not seem to allow him to go that far afield. When he asked his fatherly friend for advice, Murray suggested that he should become a missionary to the Zulu instead.

This home mission was a new attempt, on the part of the Dutch Reformed Church, to do mission work within the borders of South Africa. Le Roux was to be placed at Wakkerstroom, in Eastern Transvaal. This was only the second congregation in Transvaal to get its own, full-time Dutch Reformed missionary.

Nevertheless, the relationship between European mother church and the mission was unsettled. There was a world of difference between the prestigious work of a *Dominee*—the vicar of the white farmers—and that of a simple missionary to the Blacks, or *Eerwaarde*. This was symbolized by the fact that whenever the missionary preached to the white congregation, the sermon was not delivered from the pulpit, but from below, on a level with the flock. Le Roux experienced this difference when, as a language student in Natal, he met Miss Andrina van Rooyen, the daughter of a prominent farmer and Member of the Legislative Council for Greytown. When he married her, it was obvious that Le Roux married above his station. Little did his wife's family suspect that even worse things were to come.

In 1893, the Le Roux's were sent to Wakkerstroom as missionaries to the Zulu. Andrew Murray came all the way from

---

[1] J. du Plessis, in his *Life of Andrew Murray of South Africa* (1919) devotes a whole chapter to the role of faith healing—this is the term used—in Murray's life, *op. cit.* p. 330–352. He also makes the observation that Murray emphasized this aspect in the 1880's while later he did not give the same prominence to it. We shall see how very circumspectly Murray was to answer Le Roux's queries in 1898.

Cape to Ladysmith in Natal to take part in the commissioning ceremony with its "laying on of hands".

Placed near the borders between the Transvaal of the Boers, the Natal of the English, and the Zulu Kingdom, Wakkerstroom was in a politically sensitive area. It was, therefore, of paramount importance that those who were part of the local Boer establishment should honour its rules and subscribe to its values.

Wakkerstroom was called a town. Near the river, there were one or two main streets, some farmhouses, one or two shops, a few craftsmen and, of course, the church. Here the Dominee, Dr. A. P. Ackerman, preached the Word to his Boer congregation. With his flowing white beard he had the impressive air of a patriarch. He was to serve his flock for forty years or more (1875–1916).

The young missionary couple had to build from scratch. There was a chapel for the little Coloured community, near Wakkerstroom, and Le Roux found a warm welcome there. His congregation loved their worship and their hymns. They used *Zions Liedere*, a Dutch hymn-book of Moravian origin. This book gave its name to their little chapel. It was called "Zions Kerk".

At the end of 1893, Le Roux was able to baptize a group of fourteen new members. The Centenary volume of the DRC congregation records that: "Also a certain number of Whites were present."[2]

There was a native location beyond the borders of the white town, and Le Roux would make his way there on horseback. He also looked after the Africans at Groenvlei, some two and a half miles from Wakkerstroom where the Slang Rivier or Snake River meandered through the green countryside. In wet years the whole *vlei* or marsh would become one great lake.

The more Le Roux came to feel at home with the Zulu language and his little Zulu flock, the more he found time for study. Once again, he turned to the books of his fatherly friend, Andrew Murray. There was a little pamphlet of his, in Dutch, called *Divine Healing*. The book opened wide horizons, giving examples from the activities of Stockmeyer, Boardman and

[2] *Ebenhaeser*, Honderdjarigste bestaan van die N. G. van Wakkerstroom (1861–1961), p. 25.

18

many others in the West, all with similar experiences of trust and faith, often reputedly leading to miraculous healings. The theme never left his mind.

Le Roux was keenly interested in any occurrence of a similar kind in South Africa. He contacted one Johannes Büchler on the Rand. We shall meet him somewhat later, but must anticipate by stating here that Büchler had, in 1895, established a *Zion Church* in Johannesburg. They referred to themselves as "Zion" for the same reason as their friends at Wakkerstroom: they sang the lively *Zions Liedere*. In 1897, Büchler visited Le Roux and Le Roux's new convictions were strengthened.[3]

They compared notes about the American faith healer, J. A. Dowie of Chicago, and exchanged what little information they had of him. It was in this way that Le Roux, for the first time, was in a position to read *Leaves of Healing*, Dowie's church paper.

He wrote about all this to Andrew Murray. He told him about Büchler and asked for Murray's advice. He was also able to report to Murray that he and his wife had decided never again to touch medicines. "We are thus enjoying very good health." However, there was a problem, he told Murray, namely the Local Missions Committee, consisting of Boer farmers. They were firmly against Le Roux conveying his new teaching of Divine Healing to "the Kaffirs", as they called them. Le Roux did not wish to embarrass his Boer friends. "Yet, the question is whether this 'Glad Tiding', as you call it in your little book, can any longer be hushed up."

In December 1897, Murray could inform Le Roux that he had himself met Büchler, and he sums up his impression in that balanced, yet enthusiastic way of his: "I can understand that his strong views on faith healing may give offence. I know him only a little, but according to what I have heard of him, I consider him

---

[3] Local Missions Comm. of DRC, Wakkerstroom (H. B. Klopper, G. A. Kolbe and H. B. (?) Helm) 1.11.1901 to J. N. Martins. It is only through this letter that we know for sure that Büchler did in fact visit Wakkerstroom "four years ago". Le Roux of course mentions Büchler in his letters to A. Murray, but as far as I can see he did not mention that Büchler had actually visited him at Wakkerstroom. It is the members of the Local DRC Missions Comm.—sorely tried—who reported on this to the Missions secretary on the Rand. DRC Archives, Pretoria.

to be a man of true faith (literally, "true faith power") and that the Lord uses him as a blessing."[4]

During the next few months the elder man exercised all his highest gifts of wisdom and loving cure of souls. In January 1898 he reminded the young missionary of the need for wisdom: "When the Lord entrusts us with a heavenly truth, it is necessary to remember that heavenly wisdom and humility are needed so as not to broadcast this as and when the Lord wants [us do to so]."

A change of place, away from Wakkerstroom, might be the solution. Murray could think of other places "where you may have more liberty". He mentioned the little town of Harrismith, where he could attend to seven thousand Zulu on Boer farms.[5]

Yet Murray himself knew better than anybody that evasion or flight was not a solution. He keenly felt his responsibility for his young, possibly somewhat impetuous friend. Toward the end of November 1898 he summed it all up in a letter which clearly is an outstanding document of Christian pastoral care.

Dear Brother,
        Your question is not an easy one. It is one for which we need wisdom from above.
1. Some would say: At all costs, insist on your freedom and proclaim the truth which the Lord has revealed to you.
According to what the Lord and [St.] Paul have taught about holding back that which cannot be understood, it appears to me that where those with whom we work in common cannot yet bear a certain truth, we have the liberty to let it [=the truth] rest for a while in order to find a fuller acceptance for the essential part of the Gospel.
2. It may be that as we persist to proclaim this [particular] truth, the Lord opens to us the way to another sphere of work. Perhaps to the [Native] Compounds,[6] with the liberty there to preach what we regard as right. Or elsewhere, in some place which we do not [yet] now know.
3. Heavenly wisdom is needed to judge here. This is given to the humble and righteous, to those who are not self-willed.
4. The fear of suppressing a heavenly, glorious truth, thereby becoming unfaithful to it and thus failing to receive its blessing, is a very serious

[4] A. Murray, 8.12.1897 to P. L. Le Roux.
[5] A. Murray, 28.1.1898 to P. L. Le Roux. For A. M. Murray's attitude—possibly influenced by the Wakkerstroom incident—to "the Ethiopian danger", see H. A. Roux, *De Ethiopische Kerk*, Bloemfontein 1905, p. 4.
[6] I.e. Compounds of the Johannesburg mines.

one. Only the Lord can determine here and reveal whether our silence is a deed of unfaithfulness or a deed of humility for the sake of others who are not so far advanced, [thereby] retaining the opportunity of continuing to preach the Gospel in a wider sphere.

5. If you would promise to exercise the utmost care in this matter and not to make it a subject of public preaching, would not the [Wakkerstroom] Committee be satisfied?

These are my thoughts. With all my heart I pray that you may have the guidance of the Lord. Let me know what will be the outcome of the matter.

With greeting to your wife and praying for the Lord's blessing,

Sincerely yours,

Andrew Murray

This was the most helpful and merciful suggestion from the very best man in the Church.

Yet, it was not mercy but truth that Le Roux wanted. He was struggling with Andrew Murray's advice, and we can follow his wrestling with the problem in the quick notes, in a combination of Dutch and Afrikaans, which he jotted down on the envelope from his friend, at the same time widening the theological scope of the conflict. The notes do, incidentally, show the quality of the man who eventually was going to leave his church.

A Testimony of Blessing
1. A searcher for truth.
   Rev. A. M.: Powerlessness of preaching. Devotion ... There is ...
2. Baptism—Spurgeon=Ds Retief
   True baptism. Immersion of the faithful.
3. Divine Healing—medicine. Use of water.
   Büchler.
   Thirst after light. Jesus, the Lord of Healing for the Sick. *Blessing, purification, health.*
   Full assurance.
4. May I preach this thing? Yes,—Full blessedness comprises deliverance of Spirit, soul and body. /Christ/ bore sins, sickness also.
5. What Rev. A. M. says in his letter, our church won't take this. You must resign.
6. Zion of Dr. Dowie founded for this very purpose. Publication L[eaves] of Healing. I must go there. No other chance for me. Already for [too] long have I beheld this.
My sin—I have been obeying men more than God.
Consequences: (a) Deterioration in the congregation
              (b) Illness at home.

In the meantime Le Roux also sought the advice of five younger colleagues in the Dutch Reformed Church elsewhere in the country, informing them about the problems involved as "this teaching" seemed to spread among the natives.

What was he to do? One of his five correspondents, Dr. A. P. Kriel of Langlaagte, Pretoria, was able to give further information about the mysterious Büchler. He felt, he said, that Büchler was "a spiritual man" but that "one needed to be utterly cautious with such people". The Dutch Reformed Church favoured Faith Healing, Kriel thought, but he felt "that, in the first place you are called to proclaim Christ and 'Him crucified'" for, in fact, not all were healed in the cases quoted by Le Roux.[7]

The members of the Local Missions Committee pleaded with Le Roux that he be wise enough to avoid a crisis. This he could do by promising not to force the issue and, above all, by not taking the matter to his Native congregation. For the sake of peace, Le Roux seemed to be willing to accommodate. Then their fifteen-month-old daughter seemed to be fatally ill. She was at death's door for two weeks, yet her young parents consistently refused to give her any medication. Prayer must be the answer. So they prayed and prayed together with Charles Sangweni, their faithful churchwarden. It seemed hopeless. Le Roux told his African friend, "It is all over. Now the Lord will take her."

But Sangweni replied, "Maneel (=Meneer, or Sir) is like Peter who looked at the waves and not at Lord Jesus. Come, let us pray again." Their African friend sat there, praying, day and night— and the little girl pulled through.[8]

This was the sign. It was an argument ad hominem that seemed unanswerable. Le Roux could compromise no longer. In that same month, October 1900, he handed in his resignation to the Missions Committee. He had decided to leave the Dutch Reformed Church and to venture into unknown country.[9]

However, there was a war—the Boer War—and this had taken

[7] A. P. Kriel, Dec. 3, 1897, to P. L. Le Roux. Apost. Faith Mission Archives, Johannesburg. Cf Almanak, N. G. Kerk, 1929.

[8] Mrs. Le Roux: Jesus our healer for 15 years, The Comforter, Oct. 1913, p. 7. Trooster, Sept. 1958.

[9] Le Roux, Oct. 15, 1900 to J. N. Martins. Briewe 1903–09, S. VI. 2. N. G. Kerk Archives, Pretoria.

a definite turn for the worse. Only a week earlier President Kruger had left the country for Europe in the hope of winning support for his cause. The local Boer Committee insisted that Le Roux could not resign for the duration of the war. He might consider the issue *after* the war. They had the impression that Le Roux had consented not to broadcast "this teaching". When, however, there were reports to the contrary, Le Roux was brought before the Committee to answer charges. After a long meeting in October 1901, the Committee challenged him to declare his position on the four capital issues taught by Dr. Dowie of Chicago, then known to represent "The Universal Christian Church". These four issues were: the use or otherwise of doctors or medicines; the teaching that the eating of flesh was against Holy Scripture and therefore sinful; the use of tobacco being sinful; infant baptism being against the teaching of Holy Scripture.[10]

In his letter to the Local Committee on October 15, 1901, Le Roux answered these questions. He insisted that he did, indeed, agree with the Bible and various modern authorities, including Dr. Dowie, on each count. A lively correspondence is extant between the Committee and the missionary. In some letters (e.g. Oct. 10, 1901) Le Roux took the opportunity to disclaim a too legalistic approach to these problems. "Divine Healing is not for everybody", he wrote. "This glorious blessing is only for the children of God. Nobody can be forced to practise Divine Healing. We do not hold that anybody will be excluded from heaven because of the use of medicine." The Boer community as a whole at Wakkerstroom was challenged by the message of healing. One of the European women became mentally disturbed. There did not seem to be any help for her. Le Roux advised the family to turn to "Büchler of Zion who prays for the sick". This they did, apparently with good results.

But while Divine Healing had been his first concern, increasingly it was now Infant Baptism that made him unhappy. It was not taught in the Scriptures, he thought, and therefore he felt that its practice was the cause of "loss of spiritual power". In January 1901 he informed the D.R.C. General Secretary in Johan-

---

[10] Bro. P.L. Le Roux: Native Work. Apost. Faith Mission Archives, Johannesburg. 6 pp.

nesburg: "I can never again baptize a child." He acknowledged that he was thereby about to take a critical step: "I must cut off [*losmaken*] from all my family and friends. I am in heart and soul Afrikaner and this makes it that much harder".[11]

The Boer missionary leaves the laager

In 1902, the Boer War came to an end. In March 1903 Le Roux took the consequences of his position and resigned from the Dutch Reformed Church.[12]

In April 1903, the local Dutch Reformed congregation received their new missionary, A. J. Kropholler, as the substitute for Le Roux. The new man reported to his superiors in Johannesburg on what transpired at Wakkerstroom.[13] The day after his arrival he met *"den heer (vroger den Eerw) le Roux"*—"Mr. (former Rev.) Le Roux." The takeover from Le Roux turned out to be a dramatic affair. Two members of the local DRC Missions Committee welcomed the new missionary to the congregation of the Africans. At that, the Le Roux's stood up, and ten minutes' tumult followed, in that members of the Le Roux party hurled accusations against the Committee. Suddenly, a few of them forced their way up front, took a firm grip of their beloved reed-organ and carried it triumphantly to the manse, at that hour still occupied by the Le Roux family. Characteristically it was this one thing which they insisted on taking along on their path into the unknown future. In fact, Le Roux soon saw to it that his impetuous friends returned the instrument to the chapel.

Already in October 1902 Le Roux had anticipated his resigna-

---

[11] P. L. Le Roux 4.1.01 to J. N. Martins. Sinod. Send Komm. Briewe 1903–09. NGK. Archives, Pretoria.
In my interview with P. L. Le Roux, in Oct. 1941, he told me that in seven years as a DRC missionary he had "sprinkled two thousand Natives for the DRC".
[12] A first letter of resignation from Le Roux to the N. G. Kerk Mission Commission, Johannesburg, dated Oct. 15, 1900.
Cf. *Notulenboek der Zendingscommissie 1898–1913*; Jan. 30, 1902.
Cf. also *ibid.* March 3, 1903.
[13] A. J. Kropholler 21.4.1903 to the Secretary (J. N. Martins), Gen. Missions Commitee, DRC. Sinod. Send Komm. Briewe. 1903–09. *Notulenboek der algem Zendingscommissie 1898–1913* (9.3.1903). NGK. Archives, Pretoria.

tion as he wrote a letter in Zulu to one of the Zulu parishioners, Jona Hlatshwayo. I quote this letter in full, as it can justifiably be taken to represent his teachings to Africans at this time.[14]

Visiting your home, I taught you a little about the Law of Zion, so that you may know it. I did so in order to give you a chance to choose. As for myself, I have indeed seen that Zion is right: it is the Kingdom of God. How?
1. Because it definitely insists on the Word of God.
2. It says that God and He alone is Lord, and that all men must obey His Word.
3. It says, the faithful must leave everything sinful and be really converted. It doesn't accept: beer, pre-marital sex, lying, hashish, tobacco and the taking of medicine nor the consulting of doctors or diviners.
4. It forbids the taking of medicine and the consultation of doctors because the Word of God says, "I am Jehovah who heals you" (Ex. 15: 26). Again it says, "Regard not diviners" (this is the equivalent to the Zulu translation, while the English [Westminster Study Edition] has "Regard not them that have familiar spirits, neither seek after wizards to be defiled by them. I am the Lord thy God").

Again it says, "Jesus took our infirmities and bare our sicknesses" (Matt. 8: 17). Again (James 5: 14): It can be seen that Our Lord wants to be our *inyanga* (doctor) to heal us when we are sick in body. Zion says that the faithful will obey the Word of God and thank [Him].

As for me, I am going over to Zion. Those who wish to follow me may do so. Let every man give account to God for his stand. Let each man do as he thinks best. One mustn t just imitate but let each man choose for himself. I have learned that certain evangelists do not like the way of Zion. They are now rushing in all directions, sending letters, asking to be accepted anywhere. Some are going to the Wesleyans and others to the Lutherans.

But, I insist that those who do not like the way of Zion shall be treated, as before, according to the rules of the Dutch Reformed Church. They must stop running in all directions and stay at home to do the Lord's work. The work of the Church has not stopped, it goes on all the time. By the grace of the Lord, those of Zion will find their place where they can build in their own particular way. For the time being, let us just sit where we are. And those of Dutch Reformed Church, let them stay in their places.

> May the Lord be with your spirit
> I am your Pastor, P. L. Le Roux

A place in which to build, where they could live and worship

[14] P. L. Le Roux 17.10.1902 to J. Hlatshwayo, in G. T. Le Roux collection, Pretoria.

—this was Le Roux's concern, not only for the Africans but also for his own young family. Having resigned from the security of the Dutch Reformed Church, they had marched straight into the unknown. They had been virtually evicted from their house, with their baggage and belongings, without having anywhere to go. At that moment, if not earlier, the enormity of their transgression was brought home to them. They had left the *laager* and were to be completely ostracized by the God-fearing community of Wakkerstroom. They were turned out of their house, and left sitting with their children and their baggage on the road. When at last a shelter was found, their new status as that of outcasts was clearly shown. They were helped this time not by their own Afrikaans-speaking community but by the "enemy", an Englishman and a reputed atheist at that. He owned a *spookhuis,* a haunted house, with a mud floor, which no one else would have thought of occupying. This became the home of the young family, and remained so for ten years.

The Le Roux children were made to feel what ostracism meant. No right-thinking parent would allow their children to play with them; rotten eggs and tomatoes were thrown at them. After all, had they not left the *laager* of their own free will!

Three years later, Mrs. Le Roux held evening meetings in the 'tea-room that they used for the purpose. After 9 p.m. there was a curfew for natives at Wakkerstroom, as in any other wellorganized South African town. Mrs. Le Roux planned the meeting to end punctually so that her people could get safely home before the curfew started.

An enterprising custodian of justice in the town challenged her one evening, by ringing the curfew bell half an hour earlier. This meant that these singing Zulu Zionists were bound to commit a criminal offence by being out after the curfew. The law provided for an exception, however, because even after the curfew bell, a native in the company of a European was safe. So Mrs. Le Roux took them all with her and they walked, in a group, down the main street to the native location. The Le Roux children—Bank Directors and Headmasters of high schools now—relate that she never in her life forgot that walk: those glances of the other Europeans in the street!

As Le Roux had explained to Hlatshwayo, he already had a

dream of a place for his Zion. He sent an application for a site to the Government. He had to express himself in legal terms, but it can be seen that his real objective was the foundation of a Zion, a Christian settlement, to be the first Zion and holy place in Southern Africa. This document, now lodged in the National Archives at Pretoria, is therefore of interest. He wrote on June 29, 1903:

The Sub Native Commissioner
Wakkerstroom District
    Dear Sir,
            I beg respectfully to submit the following to your notice.
From a farmer in this district I have leased a piece of land situated about nine miles from this town, near Castrol Nek.
The size of the farm according to the declaration of the owner is about fifteen hundred morgen. Much of it is hilly, fit only for grazing. It is my purpose on the said land to erect buildings for a church and a school for natives.
Every resident will have to pay the owner £3 per annum and be allowed a plot for cultivation and grazing rights.
As I am aware of the provision of what is termed the Squatter's Law, I hereby respectfully request that, for the sake of the spread of Christianity, the Government allow a certain number of families (say about fifty) to settle on that land and that such settlements be subject to government supervision.
        Trusting to be favoured with an early reply.

He discussed the matter with the Commissioner, a Mr. L. Tyrell, and followed it up with a new letter on July 20, asking the Government to state the number of families that would be allowed on a site of this kind. He found a sympathetic response from the local Commissioner, who favoured the application.

However, a higher official, the Native Commissioner for Eastern Transvaal (E. H. Hogge), objected. "This application only means the thin end of the wedge as he will apply for more each year and feel aggrieved that he is not allowed them." He saw the Wakkerstroom application in a larger perspective, related to the farm policy of the time. "I take it from speeches in the council that the object of the government is to discourage the gathering together of large numbers of natives on particular farms."[15]

[15] P. L. Le Roux correspondence with Transvaal authorities in S. N., A. 1903, 31, 1515, National Archives, Pretoria.

That was the end of this particular dream of Le Roux's, but his African followers were to continue to be inspired by it. For *Zion* was to stand, not only for lively worship and colourful garments, but also for the Utopia of a place of their own. They were to seek that city.[15a]

In March 1903, Le Roux definitely joined Zion. To all intents and purposes, Le Roux was a Zion missionary for five full years, 1903–08. We shall return to him but now have to introduce his two European colleagues and co-workers, Johannes Büchler and Edgar Mahon, and his American overseer, Daniel Bryant.

Büchler—Mahon—Bryant

Johannes Büchler's background was Swiss. He was born in 1864 at Herisau, near Appenzell, Switzerland. He died in Johannesburg in 1944.

His Swiss parents had been strongly influenced by a revival in the Herisau district, Switzerland in the 1860s. They formed a group of friends who felt that "they had received the Holy Spirit according to the promise of Christ". Ordinary good Swiss burghers therefore regarded them as madmen—and the Büchlers and their friends took the consequences. They gave away their belongings and decided to leave their country. Some thirty of them emigrated, via Holland, to South Africa, the majority settling in the Cape Province. It was here that P. L. Le Roux, as a young man, was influenced by these Pietistic foreigners.[16]

The young Johannes Büchler accompanied his parents to Kimberley, the diamond city, in 1870, but when gold was discovered further north he travelled alone to Johannesburg in 1889. There, with the help of a grant from the Government, he started a school, reputed to be the first English-medium school in Transvaal. He liked to preach, both to the Europeans

---

[15a] Interviews with G. T. Le Roux, July 1958 and January 26, 1973; with A. M. Le Roux Dec. 1972. As to Le Roux's financial situation, J. A. Dowie wrote to D. Bryant (5.11.1903): "I sent" [Le Roux]—'a very able consecrated man' "a certain sum of money to show him my appreciation; he did not ask for anything".

[16] Cf. W. A. Schoch, *Vertrauliche Mitteilungen über die geistigen Erlebnisse einiger Kinder Gottes in Süd-Afrika.* Loreh [Württemberg], 1908.

and the Coloureds.* He was accepted as Pastor to the Coloureds in 1892, and the following year saw his ordination in the Congregational Church, for the purpose of serving the Coloured congregation.

However, he had a problem that the Congregationalists could not solve for him. He had grave doubts about Infant Baptism and this led him in 1895 to resign from the Ebenezer Chapel; from this time he encouraged his Coloured congregation to build a chapel of their own. On March 21, 1895, they formed a new congregation, which they called "the Zion Church", most probably for the same reason as the Zulus at Wakkerstroom. They had the same Moravian hymn book, in Dutch, *Zions Liedere.*

Büchler concentrated on the Coloured community but he was equally anxious to teach himself more theology. The books of Georg Müller appealed greatly to his temperament. Working in the city of Johannesburg, he had access to new publications which of course people in the country, in places such as Wakkerstroom, lacked. In this way he came across a new publication from America, *Leaves of Healing,* published by Dr. John Alexander Dowie, Zion City, Chicago, Illinois. This struck a deep cord in Büchler's heart and he became a regular reader of the paper. In 1897 he recommended it to his friend at Wakkerstroom, Le Roux.

He was drawn to Dowie's theocratic message with its fourfold Gospel of Jesus as Saviour, Sanctifier, Healer, and Coming King. But it was the message of healing that influenced him most as he was unwell himself and was looking for help. In 1898 he began to correspond with Dr. Dowie and was soon prepared to start divine healing at a home for Europeans at Jepperstown in Johannesburg. This home attracted a number of patients.

Büchler's influence in South Africa grew. He had a large circle of correspondents and he travelled widely in order to baptize and to pray for the sick. He felt that he had a "sixth sense", a capacity for "seeing" when people far away needed him. It was thus that he saw, with the eyes of the Spirit, that a Salvation Army Captain by the name of Edgar Mahon, in Southern Na-

* "Coloureds", in South African terminology, refers to the population of mixed descent.

tal, had fallen ill and needed him. He went there, prayed for him and Mahon was healed. They became close friends and Mahon married a step-sister of Büchler's. However, his healing activity was also to arouse opposition in certain quarters.

He was all the more encouraged by powerful letters from Dr. Dowie. The American was thrilled by the new possibilities that this contact with Büchler seemed to open up, on Zion's behalf, in Johannesburg and in Africa as a whole. He told Büchler that he wanted him as his "Overseer" in South Africa. But first Büchler must come to the very Fountain, to Zion in Chicago.

John Alexander Dowie (1847–1907) was of mixed Scottish and Australian descent. He founded The Christian Catholic Apostolic Church in 1896, with its headquarters at Zion City, near Chicago. "Zion" was a theocracy and John Alexander himself, was First Apostle of Jesus Christ, though he was later to regard himself as "Elijah the Restorer". He became known as a great healer. Divine Healing, without doctors or medication, was one of the tenets of his Church, together with a number of taboos against such things as pork, alcohol and tobacco. In 1896, he began publishing his monthly, *Leaves of Healing*. One can still find tattered copies of early issues, religiously kept and guarded by second and third generation Zulu and Swazi prophets.

After Dowie's death, his Church was headed by W. G. Voliva. In the last few years of Dowie's reign, the two had quarrelled, but Voliva later always insisted on Dowie's greatness.[17] Voliva could not avoid divisions in the Church and there was soon to be a number of competing Zions in Illinois, some of which extended their competition as far afield as South Africa.

Büchler went to Chicago, met the famous man—and was repelled. He was sickened by the sycophantic personality cult encouraged by "John Alexander, First Apostle" himself and he made his feelings on the matter quite clear. Büchler was a solid and balanced person, and when Dowie's admirers sang the First Apostle's praises, the young man from South Africa challenged both the First Apostle and the twenty-four other "apostles"

[17] R. G. E. Gordon Lindsay, *The Life of John Alexander Dowie*, 1951. W. J. Hollenweger, *Enthusiastisches Christentum*, 1961.

around him, at which the latter threw up their hands in horror and exclaimed, "This Balaam's ass from South Africa has dared to criticize this man of God." Dowie never forgave him. In his own particular way he told Büchler that he would never be well again, and demanded that he return home, but this time without offering to pay for his return ticket.

Büchler returned to South Africa, where he now co-operated mainly with Plymouth Brethren and Baptists. As we shall see, when the Apostolic Faith arrived on the scene in 1908, he accepted their teaching but "disliked their manifestations". Thus Büchler, who had played a certain role in introducing Dowie to South Africa, eventually became one of his many critics. As far as his own enterprise in Johannesburg was concerned, he was now determined not to have it confused with Dowie's movement, and even changed the name of his congregation in order to forestall any mistake. Unwittingly, he anticipated later developments when, in 1903, he exchanged the name "Zion Church" for "Apostolic Faith Mission".[18]

His aversion to Dowie did not deter him from inviting one of Dowie's men, Daniel Bryant, to South Africa a little later. And a firm believer in Divine Healing he remained throughout. His work was largely confined to Europeans and Coloureds but his contacts with Le Roux and Mahon were to be of importance to Black Zion.[19]

Edgar Mahon (1867–1936), of Irish stock, was part of the nineteenth-century frontier tradition of South Africa. Born at Maseru, Basutoland, he had a Standard IV education and joined

---

[18] In a letter of 18.2.1903, Büchler applied to the Secretary, Native Affairs, to be appointed as Marriage Officer for his church, now, "to avoid trouble and confusion," to be called Apostolic Faith Mission. He informed the Government that the office-bearers of the Church were to be "under the direct control of the *Holy Spirit*". The Secretary, Native Affairs, 23.2.1903, rejected the application. SNA 24, 444 (1903). Nat. Archives, Pretoria.

[19] *Constitution and Deed of Trust of the Zion Church*, Johannesburg, 1926. Cf. J. Büchler, *Gods Onuitputlike Bronne*, 1931; *Geschiednies van die Christelike Doop*, n.d. *Uitverkiezing*, n.d. Interview with Mr. John Büchler, (Johannes Büchler's son), Johannesburg, Dec. 1972. See also John Büchler, 'The Full History of the Free Baptist Church of S. Africa, previously called The Zion Church', (stencil), 1966.

the Salvation Army. Rugged, strong, and slow of speech, he rose to the rank of Captain and was well liked because of his musical gifts, playing the concertina and handling the Army drum with an accomplished skill. In the Army he met his future wife, a step-sister of Johannes Büchler, and thus of Swiss background. Her brother could "see" things and so could she. In fact, she was thought to be "psychic", and for some time, as a young girl, she had been attracted to Spiritualism, where she had been acclaimed as a natural medium. However, the Salvation Army proved to be the antidote to this infatuation and, like her husband, she rose to the rank of Captain.

There was a close fellowship between her and her stepbrother, Büchler, who, while in Johannesburg, "saw" or felt that her family, then in Southern Natal, was afflicted. Mahon was suffering from tuberculosis. Büchler went there and prayed for his brother-in-law, who was immediately healed. Büchler then went one step further: the Salvation Army did not recognize the need for the ordinary sacraments but Büchler faced Mahon with the challenge of baptism. As they came across a pool by the roadside, Mahon was baptized by Büchler.

However, this meant that Mahon had committed an act of disobedience to Army discipline, an act not unlike the breach of discipline that Le Roux had committed against the Dutch Reformed Church. The Army of course rested on a foundation of discipline and so, while Le Roux was allowed to resign from his church, Mahon was dismissed by his superiors in 1899.

He had learned Zulu while in the Salvation Army. During the Boer War he became a Sotho expert and this at Ladysmith, in Natal! Working behind the frontier at Ladysmith as a craftsman and blacksmith, he met thousands of Sotho soldiers and carriers who had been engaged by the British Army. Here was his God-given mission field. His Sotho friends responded by teaching him their language. This also showed the way after the war, when he moved to Harrismith and other places in the Orange Free State. In the end, he found a centre at Mooigelegen, from which to serve Basutoland. At the same time, as we shall see, he kept contact with the Zulu Zionists. In Natal, he had been instrumental in converting a well-known chief, Khumalo, and in Basutoland he had influenced Chief Jonathan.

There are similarities between him and Le Roux in their early devotion to the cause of Zion, and yet, Mahon's contribution has a character of its own. Although his best Bantu language was Zulu—as was Le Roux's—he was a pioneer for Zion in the Orange Free State and in Basutoland, where of course he had to use the Sotho language. He remained loyal to Daniel Bryant even after the latter's break with the Dowie—Voliva group.[20] He never joined Pentecost and its South African version, the Apostolic Faith, and was critical of such phenomena as speaking with tongues.

Mahon was the one European in South Africa who managed to establish something akin to a 'Zion City' of his own. Moving from place to place in the Free State, he formed centres consecutively at Harrismith, Kalkoonfoontain, and finally Mooigelegen. If ever there was a couple of "frontier missionaries" in those parts of the world, it was Edgar Mahon and his wife: Edgar, sound and solid, round and joyful, Irish and humorous; she, "psychic" as her children describe her, sensitive and of unshakable faith, the two of them forever on the move, seeking a city. There was one annual Church festival, Christmas, when all the faithful—between three and five thousand of them—would congregate at the Mahon centre. Even today this festival attracts thousands from near and afar. It should also be underlined that the musical aspect of the Mahon worship appealed to Africans, not least the drumming performed by the ex-Salvation Army captain. At the Church festivals some twenty-five choirs would sing. Mahon and his wife also had the gift of healing. Mrs. Mahon's gift was that of foreseeing future events, particularly the arrival of patients coming to be prayed for by the missionary.[21]

Edgar Mahon claimed that he established his church—as the "Christian Catholic Church in Zion"—already in 1902. On account of his connexions with the Rev. Daniel Bryant he later (from 1920) changed the name to "Grace Mission Church". This

[20] Cf Bryant's correspondence, in D. Bryant collection, with Daniel Bryant, Los Angeles.
[21] See F. P. Burton, *When God makes a Missionary* [Revised] Minneapolis, 1961. Interviews with the Rev. Alfred J. Mahon, Kransfontein, O.F.S., Sept. 2, 1969, and with the Rev. and Mrs. J. R. Gschwend (*née* Mahon), Krügersdorp, January 1973.

again was changed to "Mahon Mission", finally, in 1958, to the "Mahon Mission of the Baptist Union of S. Africa".[22]

Dowie could not have sent a better man. Pastor *Daniel Bryant*, of Baptist background—his father was one of the Baptist pioneers at King's Creek, Ohio—came under the spell of Dowie just before the turn of the century and joined Zion. In the fast-growing Zion community, Bryant stood out as a cultured and well-read person. He was sent to Marinette, Wisconsin, to organize a local church there but was soon recalled to headquarters, in order to edit the *Zion Banner*. It was explained to him that "part of the grounds for this call is due to the fact of your versatility in the English language".[23]

A short while later he was posted to Cambridge, Mass., and then again in 1903 to Cincinnati. The impetuous Dowie liked to move his people about. Whenever difficult situations arose, Bryant, with his balanced personality and wide outlook was expected to act as a trouble-shooter.

In order to build Zion in South Africa, Dowie needed a gifted and dedicated person. Bryant was such a man. He and his wife —the latter an elocution teacher—had musical and literary interests.[24] They had much to give to their little Zion community in Johannesburg, for the four years during which they served Dowie's cause. After the fall of Dowie they returned to the United States.

In 1903, John Alexander Dowie, First Apostle and Prophet of the Restoration, was at the very height of his reign. Opposition from within—from some of his seemingly faithful lieutnants —was to be intensified in the next few years, culminating in his demise in 1906, written off as a mental case. But in November 1903 he ruled supreme. One can see this from his "General Instructions" for Bryant. Here he was a general or a field marshal outlining his grand strategy for South Africa and Africa as a whole.

[22] Cf. papers in file No. 21/214, Native churches, National Archives, Pretoria.
[23] Wm H. Piper, May 1, 1901, to D. Bryant. The Bryant papers, Los Angeles, USA.
[24] J. A. Dowie 22.4.1902 and 23.10.1902 to Bryant and A. J. Gladstone Dowie [J. A. Dowie's son] 21.1.1903 to Bryant. The Bryant papers.

34

More than that, he saw himself as a leader with a unique position in the history of the Church, sending his servant to far-off Africa. But Bryant had to try to play down this role of Dowie's: "With regard to my prophetic office, as the prophet foretold by Moses, the Messenger of the Covenant, and Elijah the Restorer, who, in my judgment, are one and the same person, I desire you not to make it a prominent and continuous seal of your ministry. Salvation is not through faith in me. It is through faith in Jesus."

It is tempting to quote generously from the twenty-four page long foolscap letter, "given" by Dowie on November 5, 1903. We must, however, limit ourselves here to a few paragraphs. Bryant was told to spend some months in London on his way to Johannesburg: "It is my wish that you should study the English people from the great metropolis of the British Empire, London". As an ex-Australian, Dowie was well aware of the role of the British Empire, at this particular time, the year of Queen Victoria's death, and the year after the cessation of the Boer War. Dowie wanted Bryant to grasp Great Britain's supposed plan to dominate Africa from the Cape of the Good Hope to the mouth of the Nile. In order to understand this policy, Dowie must follow the Parliamentary debates, and he must have "access to the public galleries, or if possible to the members' private gallery of the House of Commons". Certain members were particularly important. "I direct you to observe exceedingly carefully the utterances of Joseph Chamberlain, late Secretary of the Colonies" and his protectionist ideas. Bryant must "be able to speak with personal knowledge and authority on it" when he reached South Africa. This was no ordinary little pastor sailing to save an African soul or two. "The overseer of the Christian Catholic Church in Zion ought to be a well informed man in connection with all public affairs ... and to speak with moderation and absolute knowledge of the situation."

After four months of this Bryant was to proceed to the country of his calling. Dowie knew already at this time that there were certain Europeans in South Africa who took an interest in his message. Thus he thought that his *Leaves of Healing* and other publications had found their way to South Africa: "We have a considerable number of friends" in Durban and Pietermaritzburg. Johannesburg was, however, the right place for the headquarters of the Church. Already Dowie's intense will was trying to establish a wide network of influence. "Eventually these great provinces [the four provinces of the country] must all have separate Overseers, for the field is far too vast for one Overseer." In that hyperbolic style of his, the Field Marshal charged his envoy: "You will at once take command of all there is to take command of in South Africa!"

There had been certain plans to publish the *Leaves of Healing* in Dutch also, for the benefit of the Boers. Dowie resisted this: "It is better for the Boers to drop their Dutch ... Tell them that the General Overseer has a strong conviction that the English language will become a universal language and that it will be the means, in God's hands, of restoring that unity of thought which was destroyed by the confusion of Babel".

For his evangelistic outreach Bryant was directed by Dowie to pay special attention to the unattached foreigners in the country, to American and Australian newcomers. Dowie was born an Australian himself; he knew that "the Australians, generally speaking, are a very intelligent, honest and upright people, full of energy. They have brought large capital into that country [of South Africa] and helped in its development. You will, of course, pay particular attention to our American fellow-citizens". But for everybody, of whatever nationality, there was a happy message: "Please, express, on every occasion, the tender feeling I have for South Africa. Tell them how I have wept and prayed and toiled that it might be blessed". Also on the material side the Bryants were certain to be provided for. They were to have a salary of three thousand dollars per annum. The sumptuous atmosphere of the place at which Dowie dictated his letter— Fifth Avenue Hotel, New York—could not but induce generous thoughts and gestures: "I shall see to it that you are sufficiently well cared for, without indulging in unnecessary expense I shall expect you to live in a manner becoming the dignity of your office".[24a]

On April 22, 1904, the Bryants arrived at Durban, and established contacts with European friends there. The success was

[24a] John Alex. Dowie Nov. 5, 1903 to Daniel Bryant, Bryant papers, Los Angeles.

instantaneous. Bryant reports that he received into fellowship twenty-one and baptized sixteen. Le Roux met him in Durban. The South African taught his new American friends his first—and possibly only—expression in Zulu: *"Ukuthula [ebandleni]:* Peace be in the Church"*. This greeting has resounded millions of times ever since. The train which took the Bryants and Mr. and Mrs. Rideout—Mr. Rideout was Bryant's financial manager—on their way to Johannesburg, stopped at Volksrust station: "As our little party of four stepped out on the platform at Volksrust into the circle of dark, beaming faces, we were able to say heartily *"Ukuthula!"* (Peace). *"Ukuthula akubekuwe!"* (Peace to you) came back the hearty response".[25]

In Johannesburg Bryant was to concentrate on establishing a European congregation, soon expanding to Pretoria. For some time Pretoria was shaken by the boisterous appearance of Zion. Bryant reported to his wife in Johannesburg:

The entire town is stirred up and many who attended are scared off. Our attendance last night was 150. The fight is on in dead earnest. People are fighting us like demons. The ministers [are] against us in full array.[26]

But only a few weeks after his arrival, in May 1904, Bryant went to Le Roux at Wakkerstroom and to Mahon at Harrismith. It was a two weeks' visit of historical importance. The accounts of the young American couple reflect something of their personalities.

The observant Mrs. Emma Bryant writes:

[25] D. Bryant, in *Leaves of Healing,* Oct. 8, 1904. Prior to Bryant's arrival, the Durban group of European "Zion" met in a room, Queen's Hall, Greyville Junction. The first indication is in a Church advertisment in *Natal Mercury,* Oct. 17, 1903 through May 7, 1904, with special meeting for "Scandinavians". From May 1904, thus following Bryant's visit, the name in the newspaper advertisment was changed to the official Christian Catholic Church. From June, 1904, the meetings were moved to Good Templars' Hall, Smith and Park Street. The glad news in *Leaves of Healing,* with local adaptations, seems to have been the core of the message. Bryant was reputed to bring an extra attraction: "a first class cinematograph" and a phonograph. *Natal Mercury,* April 18, 1904. Cf. Appendix, p. 322.
[26] D. Bryant to Emma Bryant, n.d., most probably 1905, Bryant papers. cf. D. Bryant to J. A. Dowie April 13, 1905 in *Leaves of Healing* 29.7.1905.

We reached Folksrust [sic!] at half past four o'clock. Charlie [Sang-weni] and a few others slept in the station all night in order to be there to meet us, and their *ukuthulas* (peace to thee) made little warm spots in the cold, frosty night air as we stepped out into the darkness". Later in the morning they were driven in the mail cart drawn by six mules eighteen miles across the veldt. "It was a perfect morning. The high, thin air is always cool and penetrating in winter. We enjoyed the vast-ness, the solitude, and the restfulness; and we opened our spirits widely to it.

About a mile out of Wakkerstroom Mr. Le Roux, his wife, children, a friend, and five or six natives on horseback met us. They gave us most cordial greetings, and took us in. When we reached the bridge at the entrance of the town, two large companies of native members of Zion waited for us.

As we drew up, they cheered, and waved, and sang. We stood up in the carriage and returned their salutations, then passed on through the town, a triumphal procession, to their hall, where a little service of welcome was to be held. Our procession consisted, first, of five or six fine horsemen, who led the way and formed an imposing escort; the next, the two Cape carts in which we rode; then a long line of dusty men, women and children, all in holiday attire, wearing gay turbans, waists, and skirts, rings, bracelets and anklets.

Daniel Bryant also recalled the procession. He did not so much notice the bracelets and anklets, but took in other aspects:

Escorted by the horsemen and followed by a line of natives nearly one-eight of a mile long, we marched through the town, stirring it to its depths. In little groups on the streets, and from the windows and porches, the White inhabitants gazed at the scene in utter amazement.

We baptized one hundred forty-one of eight hundred who follow the Faith. We take pleasure in sending a view of this Baptism which was one of indescribable beauty.[27]

This was the first Zion baptism for Africans in South Africa. Their Jordan was the Snake River at Wakkerstroom. The im-mersion took place next to the bridge leading into the village. Le Roux and his wife stood there in the water to the waist, wait-ing their turn, and were then immersed three times, baptized in the name of the Father and of the Son and of the Holy Spirit. Crowds of Europeans and Africans watched from the bridge as

[27] *Leaves of Healing,* Oct. 8, 1904.

Bryant, in his black gown, standing to his waist in water, immersed the faithful.[28]

Bryant got to know some of the leading Zulus. There was Daniel Nkonyane: "The sight of his noble earnest face impressed me deeply". He met Muneli Ngobese and others.

After [the] all-day service, many remain in the sacred spot throughout the night. My bedroom at Rev. Pieter L. Le Roux's home was within forty feet of the Church-building, and I can personally testify to their singing until morning.[29]

The spell of that kind of thing—being thus kept awake by Hallelujahs throughout the night—was to wear off eventually, but this was the very first time.

On July 31, at Pretoria, Bryant ordained P. L. Le Roux as Elder and Mrs. Le Roux as Evangelist in the Christian Catholic Church in Zion.

Next, it was Mahon's turn. From Wakkerstroom, they went to Harrismith in the Orange Free State. Again, Mrs. Bryant: "We have no trouble in recognizing our Zion friends. As we alight at our station we scan the crowd assembled there, then we march straight up to the cleanest, most earnest and expectant-looking person, or persons, and say, 'Peace to thee!' We have made no mistakes yet."[30]

Here, Mahon's choir impressed them. Daniel Bryant writes: "We were overcome by the heavenly sweetness of their voices, a number of which being of such excellence that we have never heard them surpassed, if equalled".

At Harrismith, Bryant baptized sixty Africans, including Chief Joseph Khumalo. The chief had been a fervent Methodist, having served as a local preacher and teacher for fifteen years. But he had fallen seriously ill, and felt that he was "dying". Mahon

[28] The total of 141, according to *Leaves of Healing,* in the text under the photo of the baptism. Cf. "Sister Le Roux, Notes on P. L. Le Roux," (Apost. Faith Mission Archives, Johannesburg) stating that she and her husband were baptized together with 'a sister and 40 Natives'. P. L. Le Roux himself mentions the figure 150 during two consecutive days.

[29] D. Bryant, *ibid.*

[30] *Leaves of Healing,* ibid.

prayed for him, after which he recovered. Now he was a devoted Zionist, and a faithful reader of *Leaves of Healing*.[31]

Mahon's right-hand man at this time was Elijah M. Lutango, who stayed with the missionary at Harrismith and accompanied him on his evangelistic tours. He had been a member of another Mission earlier on. He now felt "they preached only half of the Gospel". This lack expressed itself also on the social plane: "There was no fellowship between the whites and the blacks". "As for me, I have found the True Love which does not separate brethren because of difference in the colour of their skins. In all Africa such love has not been known."

Lutango felt they owed all this to Dowie in the great country of the United States: "I believe that he is the Restorer, although it was very hard for me at first to believe [this], because I was taught that John the Baptist would come again as he was".[32]

Soon Mahon took Lutango and other African co-workers on a longer tour. He was set on winning Basutoland for Zion. To reach this goal he first went to the Basuto chiefs. Seven or eight African chiefs had visited him at Harrismith, pleading with him to go there. Chief Jonathan Molapo took them under his wing. Mahon found that "Chief Lesiama Molapo also wants Zion at his place. His son and wife have offered themselves for the work of God in Zion."

They touched a bee-hive of political intrigue in the Sotho realm, with its cleavage between the ruling Moshoeshoe house *and* the ambitious Molapo line—Molapo being the second son of Moshoeshoe's first wife. Molapo's son was Jonathan Molapo. The Molapo party had established some autonomy by annexing their own territory beyond the river Caledon, a political boundary which to a pious Zionist must have looked like any peaceful and purifying Jordan. To the political and tribal tensions was added a denominational tug-of-war, resulting in Christianised chiefs, leaving the Church and/or commuting between Catholic and Reformed loyalties, often because of the polygamy issue. Upon this bustling scene the Lutango-Bryant-Mahon party arrived.[32a]

[31] *Ibid.*
[32] E. H. Mahon, in *Leaves of Healing*, Oct. 14, 1905.
[32a] Cf. H. Dieterlen, "Un visitateur embarrassant," *Journal des Missions Evangéliques,* (Paris), 1905, p. 39. Communications to the author from M. Bernard 6.5. 1975 and from E. Krüger, 30.4.1975, both Paris.

In a month's time, they held more than seventy meetings: "About six hundred professed to find salvation, and I saw over twenty thousand people at our meetings".[33]

Lutango knew that polygamy was the foremost mission problem. The established missions insisted that a polygamous convert keep one wife and leave the others. With Zion, they found, all this was different. Lutango writes:

When we were among to Basutos, hundreds asked, "What shall I do, for I have many wives?"

Deacon Mahon always said "Enter ye into the ark with your wives and children; the Lord wants all of you. Repent!' Many of them entered into the bonds of love. I thank the Lord for giving us His servant,

Just as he had done at Wakkerstroom, Bryant now baptized hundreds of Basutos into Zion in the Caledon River.

As a result of this numinous experience in the Sotho Jordan, Chief Samuel M. Molapo resigned from his chieftainship to become, for a while, an elder in Zion.[35]

In this account, we cannot follow the Bryants any further. Suffice it to say that they returned to the United States in 1908, the year of the arrival in Johannesburg of a Pentecostal team. under John G. Lake. In the chequered history of Zion, Ill., Bryant was soon to forsake Dowie's successor Voliva—whom he disliked. He formed his own Grace Missionary Church, and eventually returned to that Baptist Church from which he hailed, while Mrs. Bryant successfully carried on her practice as an elocution teacher. Throughout all changes and chances Bryant stuck to the Mahon Mission, and gave it his support.[36]

For the purposes of this book we emphasize one fundamentally important conclusion: the fact of this team of Zion missionaries. For four creative years, in the tumultuous post-war period, there was formed this Zion triangle of Wakkerstroom—Kransfontein—the Rand, jointly and actively propagating the message. At the apex of the triangle, on the Rand, Daniel Bryant, Overseer, guided the campaign and represented the contact with Zion, Ill., and its ever more assailed leader, J. A. Dowie, First Apostle.

[33] E. H. Mahon, *ibid.*
[34] Lutango, *ibid.*
[35] D. Bryant, in *The Pen and Pulpit,* Dec. 1909 (Vol. II, No 5) Zion City, Ill.
[36] Daniel P. Bryant Jan 4, 1974 to the author.

P. L. Le Roux, Zion missionary

After meeting Le Roux's white colleagues we now return to him. In March 1903, he definitely joined Zion. He worked in close contact with Overseer Bryant. When in 1906 Bryant had to go on a ten months' visit to the United States, he left his Johannesburg faithful in Le Roux's care. Le Roux was thus also in charge of a Zion congregation of Europeans. From an "Address of Thanks" given to Le Roux at the end of the year, it transpires that his period of office had been a time of "tribulation, trial and disaster", but that Le Roux apparently had saved the situation. His Johannesburg Zion comprised some sixty adherents, some twenty of whom had characteristic Afrikaans names, the remainder being English.[37]

While Le Roux was thus already spending shorter or longer periods on the Rand, Mrs. Le Roux, having been ordained an Evangelist of Zion by Bryant, kept the congregation going at Wakkerstroom. But in spite of his "journeyings oft", Le Roux's main responsibility was with his Zulu Zion which he had helped to call into existence in and around Wakkerstroom.

He was a Zion missionary—without much material support. In fact, although he had a family of eight children, from 1903 to 1926 he had no fixed salary. For the year 1906, he did receive ten pounds a month "for personal expenses". When at a later date, he was to exchange Zion for another Church, the Apostlic Faith Mission, he was there accorded five pounds a month, also "for expenses"—but this was all. Also, while a servant of the Apostolic Faith, he stayed on at Wakkerstroom, from 1908 to 1913, but then moved to Johannesburg, while his wife cared for the family and for the African faithful at Wakkerstroom from 1908 to 1926; it was only in that year that she and the children finally moved to Johannesburg.

---

[37] D. Bryant, "Instructions to my successor, Elder P. L. Le Roux" Febr. 14, 1906. Bryant's "Instructions to my successor" were sweeping: "You will have charge of all the work throughout South Africa. If trouble should originate with any one on the field, you have the power to suspend that person from office, membership, of work, pending my restoration upon return."

Address dated Dec. 6, 1906 to Le Roux signed by 59 European and, possibly, Coloured adherents. The Johannesburg Zion meetings, Thursday evenings, held "in Miss Ada White's house". Farewell Address 27.11.1906.

In the midst of all this, the family received unexpected help. When in 1893 Andrina van Rooyen married Le Roux, the match was regarded by her family as a *mésalliance*; the scandal was compounded ten years later, when Le Roux left the Dutch Reformed Church for Zion. Yet when Mrs. Le Roux's father died, he was found to have bequeathed the destitute family an unheard-of fortune of two hundred and fifty pounds. For this bounty they could manage to buy a little farm at Wakkerstroom. Throughout the years, Mrs. Le Roux kept the family alive by the proceeds from the farm.

The very first Black Zion

The very existence of the first Zulu Zion was a bold challenge to the social and economic system of which they had been a part. Zion provided them with a new set of taboos, and the tobacco-growing, pipe-smoking farmers in the district were both intrigued and shocked.

But they were a creative group also, because, carried by an early charismatic wave, they were to form and fashion some of the linguistic and liturgical symbols characteristic of the whole Zion movement in Southern Africa. Above all, this charismatic movement cannot be understood without the apocalyptic dimension: these Zulu in white, brandishing their holy staffs, were waiting for the immediate return of Jesus. From among their flock were to emerge two or three of the African church fathers of the whole movement. It would seem, therefore, that any little scrap of evidence as to the development in the first formative years would be worthy of attention.

The frustration of African farm labour at this time led to attempts at dissent. There was a famine. The Boer War was followed in 1903 by a severe drought, and for several months the whole country lived on American mealies.[38a] At this point Zion showed these Africans that the reward for their labour was shockingly inadequate. As a group, integrated and carried by a new religious conviction which had set them apart from the faith of their masters, they were made bold enough to protest. Zion was about to provoke what might develop into a local revolt, however mild and hesitant. Mrs. Le Roux noted later:

"Their masters opposed us the more because the native was paid with tobacco; now he would not accept it. He had to have money or clothes. The master would threaten them, but 'no' was the answer. Used to be slaves of drink and tobacco. Glory to God."[38]

As we have already stated, Le Roux was a Zion missionary 1903–08; even after 1908 he kept in touch with the Zulu Zion which he had helped to call into existence in and around Wakkerstroom. How many were they? In 1903, the Zion group comprised at least one hundred and fifty, and this number was bound to rise rapidly in the following years. Le Roux himself estimated that he was followed into Zion by three-quarters of the Zulu members of the Wakkerstroom Dutch Reformed congregation. The remaining fourth preferred to remain loyal to the religious tradition of their farm bosses. (Cf. Appendix, p. 321.)

Large sections of the African population were particularly unsettled and uprooted at this time, after the Boer War. Historians have naturally emphasized the hardships of the two warring nations, Boers and Britons. The Bantu struggling on both sides have not been sufficiently noticed by historians. For months after the war they were still concentrated in Refugee Camps. I suggest that some of these might well have functioned as breeding-grounds for apocalyptic visions. Zionists at Wakkerstroom and Charlestown may have been conditioned by such ideas. Reference should be made to such leaders as E. M. Mahlangu and Steven Mavimbela (p. 60 and 215). Mahon's Sotho Zionists, in the Siege of Ladysmith, belong to the same category. (Cf. Appendix, p. 321.)

But the drama of the first Zulu Zion and their mild revolt at Wakkerstroom must be seen within a wider framework of wars and rumours of wars, involving Wakkerstroom and adjacent districts, from 1884 until 1906, and beyond. It began in 1884 with King Dinuzulu's fight against Chief Zibhebhu, Cetshwayo's cousin. The King received Boer aid against his foe—but had to pay a stiff price. Annexing the districts of Wakkerstroom, Utrecht

---

[38] Notes on P. L. Le Roux by sister Le Roux, in file "P. L. Le Roux Stucke." Apost. Faith Mission Archives, Johannesburg.

[38a] *Native Affairs Commission Report 1903–05*, quoted by M. Wilson in *Oxford History of S. Africa*, II, p. 58.

and Vryheid, the Boers formed their own "New Republic"—and it was precisely within this New Republic that, at first, Le Roux and Daniel Nkonyane and their Zion faithful preached their gospel.

Then followed the Boer War—and some of its effects on the emerging Zion have already been registered in the preceding pages. The aftermath of that war was characterized, among the Whites by insecurity and fear and among the Blacks by resentment. The Natal whites knew what caused the Africans to appear less submissive than they used to be: it was all the fault of the missions, they felt, and this again was aggravated in the first years of the century by what was known as 'the Ethiopian threat': "There was a tendency in Natal to see every educated African as a dangerous Ethiopian, ready to drive the white man into the sea."[38b]

So when the 'Zulu Rebellion' did break out—largely as a protest against the enactment in 1905 of an oppressive Poll Tax—it was claimed that it was instigated by the Christian Africans. The Governor of Natal knew that 'the kolwa as kolwa' (Zulu for Christian believer) were behind the rebellion. He now had proof of the vicious effect of missionary activity; which ought to be suppressed.

Dr. Shula Marks, in her great book, *Reluctant Rebellion,* shows that "'the Kolwa' were as divided as their fellow-tribesmen". Equal numbers of Zulu Christians, about three hundred, fought on each side.[38c]

It is against this background that the attitude of the emerging Zulu Zion at Wakkerstroom stands out clearly, and with a character of its own. The Zionists were no less Zulu because they were Christians. Moreover, on one particular issue they were known to identify with the rebellious cause more decidedly than others. A mysterious political rumour of a 'millenial' character, possibly instigated by Dinuzulu himself, spread among the Zulu people at

---

[38b] Shula Marks, *Reluctant Rebellion: An Assessment of the 1906–08 Disturbances in Natal,* N.Y. 1970, p. 167, and *idem,* 'The Zulu Disturbances in Natal', in R. I. Rotberg, (ed.), *Rebellion in Black Africa,* N.Y. 1971.
Cf. L. E. Switzer, "The Problems of an African Mission in a white-dominated multi-social society; the American Mission in S. Africa 1885–1910". Ph. D. thesis, Natal; Los Angeles 1971.
[38c] Shula Marks, *Reluctant Rebellion,* p. 335.

this time: *"All pigs must be destroyed, as also all white fowls"*. If this order was indeed issued by Dinuzulu, Zion at Wakkerstroom recognised the taboo as sanctioned by a heavenly King as well. They knew this from their Bible and Dowie's *Leaves of Healing*.[38d]

But when the Christian Zulu of the Rebellion were branded as "Ethiopians", the Zionists at Wakkerstroom and elsewhere insisted that they were not Ethiopians. Any member of their flock displaying what they regarded as Ethiopian tendencies, ran the risk of being excommunicated. In 1910, this happened to one Brother Moroane, in Johannesburg. His "Ethiopian" sins were held against him:

"Br. Le Roux says the Zulu Christians of our mission at Johannesburg have broken with Moroane /in/ that he is considered by many as an Ethiopian Minister, who uses Tobacco etc. ... They also take exception to the life and conduct of Br. Moroane who is an overseer and, they say, uses Tobacco and medicine and permits the use of Kaffir beer".

From the beginning these taboos had strengthened the group cohesion of Zion and, it seems helped to emphasize for the time being their unity with their white fellow believers submitting to the same taboos. The 'Rebellion' may have tended to widen the gulf between White and Black. But in Zion, at Wakkerstroom and elsewhere, the ties of dedication and affection common to Black and White, were still strong, stronger probably than in any other comparable Mission-related congregation at the time.[38e]

In the nature of things, it is no easy task to characterize the activity of the first Zulu Zion. But there are a few notes made much later by Mrs. Le Roux and one short statement by a Mr. James Moodie, written in 1912. We have interviewed a number of Zulu Zionists from the Wakkerstroom days, now living at Charlestown.[40] Their statements were both challenged and corroborated by groups of their contemporaries. With all these reservations we shall make an attempt to reconstruct the course of events, but precision regarding years and dates cannot be expected.

[38d] *Ibid.*, p. 165; J. Stuart, *A History of the Zulu Rebellion 1906*, London 1903, p. 103.
[38e] Minute–Book, Apostolic Faith Mission 1908–1914, August 20, 1910.
[40] Our best witnesses were Rev. J. N. Mdakane and Mrs. Gasta Sibisi-Zwane, both of Charlestown, both well over 80 years of age, with entirely clear minds.

Le Roux and his wife had shared the great initial mystery with this group: they had been through Jordan with them. They were baptized together in that rapidly flowing, deep Slang Rivier. This was *amanzi amaningi*, "much water", as it should be for baptism to be right. Mrs. Le Roux writes: "We had spoken to believers about baptism in the river running strong outside a small dorp (village)." This was part of the teaching which they were able to share with the flock.

As far as speaking in tongues was concerned, Le Roux seemed not to have received that gift. He was a solid and balanced person and to his own personal regret could not manage more than an inarticulate *"she-she-she"*, answered by the enthusiastic and encouraging *"Amen"* of the crowd. Neither could Daniel Nkonyane, the leading Zulu, speak in tongues. However, some of the Zulu women were able to transpose to that other, and sacred language. Julia Madela was one. Leya Mate was deaf and dumb, but recovered the ability of speech through prayer, and then spoke in tongues. So strong was the female preponderance in this field, that Daniel Nkonyane's wife, Elizabeth, had to admonish: "Let now the Holy Spirit enter the men rather than the women." On the spearside, Michael Ngomezulu, Daniel Nkonyane's close friend from Utrecht, Natal, was the first to achieve this ecstatic utterance. He carried the burden of an enormous message. The Word, *Izwi*, had told him: "The whole world must be converted and enter Zion." To such an extent was he filled with *uMoya*, the Spirit—that he could pass through the river at flood; the onlookers feared that he would drown, but no, he emerged on the other side unharmed.

The worship of the group was soon transformed. They experienced what to them was a miraculous change from the rigid and starchy discipline and regimentation of their Dutch Reformed catechisation. They may have been deprived of their beloved reed organ which in Mission days had been their pride and joy. But this did not seem to matter any longer. These Zulu men and women were on their own now. The Spirit was over them. As they sang their hymns from the *Zions Liedere*, they felt that they did so with a new power and conviction. In the Sunday morning worship, they would "run about like mad", swinging and jubilating—as one of them told me years later.

With Daniel Nkonyane himself, the Spirit manifested itself, thus: not in tongues, but through the gift of prophecy. He could "see" things beforehand and would tell the congregation about it. Elizabeth, his wife, could also "see", but she had the special gift of seeing, or discovering, sins which a person might try to conceal. This diagnosis was particularly helpful for Nkonyane's healing activities. He would lay his hands on the sick part of the patient and pray.

Nkonyane was practically illiterate; but this failing was overcome by the fact that he knew some of his most beloved Bible passages by heart: Matt. 3 on John the Baptist, Matt. 11—"Come unto me ..." and John 15—the Vine and the branches. For the rest, he got by as a whole generation was to do after him: he had a notebook with Bible references, and would in the course of the sermon call out Genesis so-and-so or Exodus or Daniel or Acts—and a literate Reader would ponderously and laboriously read the text for him.

Michael Ngomezulu was singled out for his special spiritual gifts in Zulu Zion. It seems certain that he was the very first to have a vision of the white robes to be worn by those in Zion. Somebody read to him that chapter in the Book of Revelation, and there it was. He recognized what he had already seen in his dream. It was irresistible. He could not, was not allowed to do otherwise. He bought white material, and somebody made the robe for him.

It can at least be conjectured that photos of the "First Apostle" himself, at Zion, Ill., John Alexander Dowie, had been of some influence here, shining in all his splendour from the pages of the *Leaves of Healing* (see third page of illustration).

Ngomezulu did not know it then, but millions were to follow his lead. Sashes came later, and were the outcome of healing activities. The Word of God had to tell a person in his, or her, dream that in order to be healed, a specially coloured sash must be worn. Shoes were a complication. Many had just bought them, when Daniel Nkonyane declared that for holy worship they would have to follow the example of Moses of old: no shoes in the temple. This he had been told by the Angel.

The women wore doeks (cloth). That first generation of Zion women, at least until the end of World War I, had white *doeks*,

Overseer Daniel Bryant, Zion City, Ill., and Johannesburg, visiting Wakker-stroom, ab. 1904. With him, Rev. and Mrs. P. L. Le Roux and Bryant's treasurer, Mr. Rideout, Rev. Daniel Nkonyane, Charles Sangweni and the very first Black Zion.

First Zion Baptism, Wakkerstroom, May 24, 1904.
Performed by D. Bryant (in black gown).

3†–743194 *Zulu Zion*

Mahon Christmas meeting, near Harrismith, about 1905. To the left in white coat Rev. E. H. Mahon. With him Samuel Molapo—son of a Sotho chief—interpreting Mahon's message from Zulu into Sesotho. Ox-driven "tent wagons".

E. H. Mahon (centre) and Gospel Choir, about 1905. Seated in same row as Mahon, from left: Choir Master Micah Luthango; Minah Khumalo, daughter of Chief Khumalo of the Ladysmith district; unidentified; Evangelist Elijah Luthango; Eveline Mahon; Chief Alexander Mopeli of Lesotho. Back row, standing from left: First two unidentified; Rev. Samuel Molapo; Evangelist C. McDuling; Rev. Walther Ndebele; Rev. Timothy Mabuza.

Left: John Alex. Dowie, "First Apostle", Second Elijah, Zion City, Ill., U.S., the garb of the "Aaronic priesthood". Right: In search of new symbols. Muneli Ngobese (together with Fred Luthuli) with an early staff of distinction. Ab. 1907–08.

Left: Rev. Edw. Mahon on an evangelistic tour. Right: P. L. Le-Roux as President of the Apostolic Faith Mission.

Bishop Stephen Nkonyane.   *Overseer Paul Mabilitsa.*

Servants of the Church of the Spirit (P. Nzuza).

made of two yards of white material, wound around the head. A sophistication in the display of *doeks* came while praying under the influence of *uMoya*. They would solemnly shake the *doeks*, suggesting thereby the Presence and the Power of the Spirit.

Then there were the holy staffs! Here a Joel Ngobese led the way. He was given the idea at a moment of concern and fear. Lightning had struck particularly hard that year: hard even by the standards of a climate which is used to severe storms. It threatened their Temple and their kraals. So Ngobese was led to cut a staff with a cross-piece, armed with which he went and "spoke to God". The chapel was left unharmed.

Gasta Zwana, my informant on this particular point, saw nothing inappropriate in this, relating it with gusto, anxious to remember exactly how it all happened. I did not draw any possible parallels with traditional Zulu religion. Mrs. Zwana emphasized that the use of holy staffs was soon turned from cosmic to medical concerns: one could place the staff on the afflicted part of a patient.[40a]

Here again, a personal vision or initiative was to set the pace for the others, and on an occasional visit after months in Johannesburg, Le Roux would be surprised by the sight of his Zion faithful, all in white, armed with holy staffs.

There is obviously a tendency now within Nkonyane Zion to idealize the spiritual achievements of the first group around Daniel Nkonyane. *"Ba be strong pambili"*, I was told, in an expressive but not necessarily very good Zulu, "they were powerful in those early days". This would be corroborated by the claim that "we would have to pray for a person only once or twice", and

---

[40a] Bishop E. Mdlalose's (cf. p. 72) recollection differed on this point from that of Mdakane and Gasta Zwane. He claimed that it was A. Mbata at Wakkerstroom who was first shown the white garments, and as early as in 1904. Soon after the universal Baptism of May that year, the group of Zionist withdrew for a three days fast broken by ritual drinking of milk (1 Cor. and Hebr.) As they were now filled by the Spirit, Mbata saw white garments to be carried by the Saints. According to Mdlalose it was one Hezekiah Luthuli from Ermelo who first saw the holy staffs, both the wooden ones for the ordinary members and the more sophisticated brass staffs for male leaders,—only later also women could be entrusted with brass. The divergence in traditions shows how difficult it is to reconstruct these beginnings now. Interview with E. Mdlalose, Vryheid 14.11.1972.

the patient would be healed, whilst in these latter days "many times" were needed to achieve the same good effect. The first group followed strict rules of fasting and would congregate for prayer, first on the top of a mountain and then in a pool or a stream; mountain top and deep pool being also the two great symbols of Zion dream-life—with also Freudian overtones.

They had struck out on a new road, seeking the City of Zion. This meant that they were not to copy the worship of the Whites. Daniel Nkonyane had himself been a member of the same Dutch Reformed Church from which Le Roux had emerged. He knew that his baptism in the Jordan, "much water" of a deep river, was the great symbol of the fact that theirs was another road than that of the Whites. What about Holy Communion? Here again Daniel insisted that Zion was different. Zion, he said, did not allow beer, and wine was beer. So they boiled raisins instead and prepared ordinary bread, and were greatly edified.

In 1940, I interviewed Pastor Le Roux about the changes that had taken place at Wakkerstroom in those early years. He had been disappointed. When he began his work he was used to the African congregation following his lead. "When I said sprinkling is not right, they all said, 'Amen'. When I said, medicine is wrong, they answered 'Amen'."

But the visions which had struck his faithful later created a more difficult problem. On his return from the Rand, Le Roux found in the Wakkerstroom Zion one group in white robes, seated on one side, and others in ordinary clothes sitting on the opposite side. Le Roux felt that this concern with ritual symbols was the result of too little discipline: "If you don't control the people, they take the outward show. When left to themselves, they get such things."

In fact, Le Roux was shocked by the extravaganza which he had unwittingly spirited forth and felt it as his duty to fight these tendencies while he was still with his Zion flock. As he returned to Wakkerstroom from Johannesburg, he had to tackle the problem. On at least one occasion, the Zion faithful fought over this problem throughout the night. Le Roux let them talk, he told me later, and went to sleep for a while. But he woke up to conclude the deliberations. As far as he was concerned, he was for outlawing those who fancied crosses and robes. From his point of view, this showed an intolerable "Roman Catholic" influence!

One can still overhear his message, as one studies the marginal notes in his well-worn Zulu New Testament (now in the possession of his son, Director Andrew Murray Le Roux). The Epistle to the Hebrews had obviously given him texts for teaching on the sanctity of the New People and its New Worship. There was Hebr. 9: 10, "The worship of the *first* tabernacle", as opposed to that brought by Christ, "stood only in meats and drinks and diverse immersions, and carnal ordinances."[41] Le Roux adds a note in Zulu to the term: "*Carnal ordinances*: white robes, pork, tobacco, to carry the 'cross' (or holy staff); taking off shoes".

Is it because of these disagreements with the rising generation of his devoted Zion friends that he had heavily underlined the expression in 1 Cor. 14: 33: *For God is not a God of confusion,* but of peace.

Daniel Nkonyane was well aware of the white leaders' nervousness on this point. When Edgar Mahon was about to pay them a visit at Wakkerstroom, Nkonyane had to issue special instructions to his noisy flock. He was anxious to please Mahon, also for personal reasons—it was Mahon who in the end found a site for Nkonyane at Charlestown. So the order of the day in Zion on that occasion was: "No noise (*umsindo*) today, on account of the white man!"

P. L. Le Roux, Pentecostal missionary

Only a rapid outline can be drawn here of the entry of Pentecost into South Africa. We emphasize the continuity between Zion and Pentecost. The American leader, *John G. Lake* (1870–1935), had been a member of Zion in America, before coming to South Africa—this is one indication of this continuity. But like many others he was disenchanted with Dowie and he does not mention him after 1907.

It was at this time of tension in U.S. Zion and in his own life that Lake became aware of his power of healing. He describes his experience. As he prayed for a sick person, he felt currents

---

[41] Margin notes in Le Roux's Zulu New Testament.

of power streaming from head to feet. "Shocks of power came intermittently, possibly ten seconds apart. They increased in voltage until after a few minutes my frame shook and vibrated under these mighty shocks of power.[42] Then Satan came and suggested ... it is only psysic phenemona".[43]

He now received "a spiritual vision of Africa", more especially of Zion in and for Africa, possibly suggested to him through some contact with Daniel Bryant. He sold his business and went to South Africa where he arrived in May 1908. With him were two colleagues, an ex-Methodist, Tom Hezmalhalch and one A. Lehman—the latter with earlier missionary experience from South Africa.

So now Pentecost hit South Africa. The Pentecostal team of three first preached in a Native chapel at Doornfontain, Johannesburg, but soon took over the Zion Tabernacle.[44] Here is another indication of that continuity between Zion and Pentecost which we have already noted. Some of the liveliest healing services ever held in the Southern hemisphere were now to follow.[45]

The fire of Pentecost had been kindled at 'the Azusa Street Mission' in Los Angeles in 1906, and sparks from that conflagration were also flying into parts of South Africa. Archibald H. Cooper, who was to play a leading part in the "Full Gospel" movement in South Africa, had been converted by Gipsy Smith in Capetown, in 1904. In 1907, he received the first "Apostolic Papers" published by the "Azusa" movement in Los Angeles. In this way he, too, was prepared to acknowledge the influence from Lake and his colleagues whom he sought soon after their arrival.[46]

Not that all were convinced by the lively meetings in the Taber-

---

[42] Diary John G. Lake. Oct. 1907. Apost. Faith Mission, Johannesburg.

[43] The unorthodox spelling throughout Lake's literary efforts suggests some degree of word-blindness.

[44] *The Comforter,* Oct. 1913, See also Minute-Book, Apost. Faith Archives, Johannesburg.

[45] *Pentecost in South Africa,* essay, ink, 10 pp. by J.H.L. S[chuurmann]. Full Gospel Archives, Irene, South Africa.

[46] Ms. "How Bro. A. H. Cooper of Durban, S. Africa was converted." Full Gospel Church Archives, Irene, South Africa.

nacle. Johannes Büchler was one of those who kept aloof from the new movement. Le Roux, on the other hand, was won over. He attended the Pentecostal meetings very soon after Lake's arrival in July 1908. To him, the decisive difference between Zion and Pentecost was the speaking in tongues. He had personally an extraordinary experience. Writing about himself in the third person, he said: "He was convinced that this was of God ... He was awakened that night just as the clock struck three. The next moment, the Lord spoke to him in a clear voice: 'Said I not to thee that if thou wouldest believe, thou shouldest see the glory of God?'"[47]

To him, joining Pentecost meant leaving Zion, and much of the crisis experienced in the following few years by African Zionists was directly or indirectly connected with Le Roux's new departure. The above-mentioned Archibald Cooper also joined the new movement. The two men, Le Roux and Cooper, now co-operated for some time in the Apostolic Faith Mission. They were to become prominent in Apostolic Faith and Full Gospel respectively, and were from there to influence Africans who later were to emerge as leaders of new Independent Churches.

Pentecost in Johannesburg had to be interpreted to Zion back home at Wakkerstroom. Le Roux informed his Zulu flock that he had now joined Pentecost. One of his European fellow Pentecostals, James Moodie of Ladybrand, was present.

I was privileged to be at this converence. The Natives could not understand this step over to a new faith. Sis le Roux spoke to them in Zulo. I saw that her message carried weight with them. Then one of the oldest members stood up, walked to Bro le Roux where he was sitting. He took Bro Le Roux's beard with his forefinger and thumb and said, This man when he first came to us, he did not even have beard (meaning so young he was) and we trusted him then, and we will trust him to the end. This saying settled the whole difficulty, this act of the old native made a great impression on me.[48]

This proved to be too optimistic an evaluation. The confusion was great. To the Africans, already the name *Zion* seemed inalienable. No Zulu Zionist was prepared to part with it. In 1910

---

[47] *Trooster-Comforter,* A Pentecostal Monthly, May 1948, p. 7.
[48] Statement by James Moodie 18.3.1948. Lead pencil, 4 pp. Apost. Faith Archives. Original spelling, by this European, retained here.

Le Roux reported this to the Executive Committee of the Apostolic Faith underlining the danger of some Zion groups refusing to join the new organization. The resourceful Committee suggested a neat compromise: "that this portion of our Mission be known henceforth as the Zion Branch of the Apostolic Faith Mission".[49]

To Lake, these questionings at Wakkerstroom were minor problems. He was looking much further afield. His South African Pentecost had begun in a Native chapel, but was increasingly to concentrate on European work. His colleague Lehmann was diverted to African evangelism. Segregation was to take its course characteristic of South Africa. Speaking in terms of the generally changing outlook in South Africa at that particular time one might suggest that 'Cape policy' was being substituted by a 'Union policy'. The Minute Book of the Apostolic Faith Mission, November 6, 1908 reads: "It is decided that the baptism of Natives shall in the future take place after the baptism of White people." July 30, 1909: "In future, the baptism of Whites, Coloured and Natives shall be separate."

Lake soon felt called to extend his characteristic contribution with regard to segregation. He had managed to approach Louis Botha, the Prime Minister of South Africa, and records that he had been invited by him "to address the Parliament on the subject".[50] He felt that as an American he had valuable experience: "I framed the policy in harmony with our American policy of segregation of the Indian tribes, having as an example the mistakes of the United States and other nations in regard to their handling of the Native nations." "This policy", he adds with that grandiloquent gesture of his, "as outlined by me, was practically adopted by the Boer Party *in toto*".[51]

He rejoiced all the more when African Churches *in toto* joined his own Church. As an example he mentions that one organiza-

---

[49] Apost. Faith Exec. Comm. 20.8.1910. Apost Faith Mission Archives, Johannesburg.

[50] We have searched in vain in Hansard at this time for any indication of Lake's address, and imagine that Lake may have appeared before some Parliamentary Committee.

[51] Gordon Lindsay (ed.), *Sketches from The Life and Ministry of John G. Lake* (1952), p. 22.

tion called "The African Catholic Church" did so, comprising "the entire body, including one bishop, one general super-intendent, 4 district superintendants, 8 ordained ministers, 28 catechists, 36 sub-catechists (or elders) and one adviser to the bishop." "Now, brothers", Lake goes on in his jargon, "these are the things that set hell to roar and the devil to howl. The more they howl, the more God seems to open doors".[52]

There were no limits to Lake's expectations. "Pentecost", he wrote in 1911, "is rather a great systematic evangelizing move-ment, extending practically from the Cape to the Zambezi, and from ocean to ocean. We ... expect soon that a number of our workers will open work beyond the Sahara".[53]

He was thus looking far afield, but experienced trouble nearer home. His closest co-worker, Hezmalhalch, rebelled against his domineering ways and left him in 1911, and two years later, after considerable internal struggles, Lake left South Africa for good.

Providentially, Le Roux was soon to take over the leadership of the Apostolic Faith Mission as its President from 1915 until his death in 1943. His main responsibility was now preponderant-ly with the European section of the Church. At the same time he was also supervising African work, particularly in and from Wakkerstroom. Some of the best of his former Zulu co-workers left him, or felt that he had left them. Daniel Nkonyane, Elijah Mahlangu and some others established their own groups.

A survey from 1911 of the new "Native work" within the Apostolic Church did however show that the number of African preachers under the control of the Apostolic Faith Mission was 350, the number of European preachers 150 at this time—and Le Roux himself was quoted as being in charge of the Zulu work in Natal.[54]

---

[52] *The Upper Room* (Los Angeles) Vol. 2, No. 5, May 1911.
[53] *Comforter,* July–August 1911.
[54] *The Comforter and Messenger of Hope,* Febr. 1911.
In 1914, Le Roux applied to Government to be appointed a Marriage Officer. "After the fullest consideration", the Minister of the Interior refused to comply —an indication of the uphill struggle of the Apostolic Faith Mission at this time. Minute Book, Apost. Faith 1908–14, Dec. 7, 1914.

In May 1910, Apost. Faith Mission decided to notify the Town Council, Wak-kerstroom "that the premises to be vacated by the native preacher Daniel ...

Also from his new vantage point, Le Roux was to experience how the African work was fanning out into a great number of fresh break-aways. Very often now there was a conglomeration of local groups from both Zion and Pentecostal (or "Apostolic") background; this was to be seen in the combination of "Zion" and "Apostolic" in the nomenclature of the new organizations.

African Church Fathers in Zion

We have come across Daniel Nkonyane already. In the Zion crisis of 1908–10 he was to emerge as the outstanding African leader. As Le Roux gradually left Zion and joined the Apostolic Faith, Nkonyane took charge. Not that he was afraid of taking charge. This powerful and impressive Zulu was a born leader, and in that excitable group and situation, he seemed calm and balanced.

He had been with Le Roux ever since the latter's Dutch Reformed days in the 1890s, and was himself originally a member of the Dutch Reformed mission. He had therefore, one must assume, shared much of Le Roux's experience. Our attempt at a reconstruction of life in the Wakkerstroom Zion has shown Daniel and Elizabeth Nkonyane to have been two of Le Roux's most trusted co-workers. Daniel's brother Andries must also be mentioned (the Dutch form of his baptismal name is a reminder that he, too, had had early contacts with the Dutch Reformed Church). While Daniel concentrated on the Zulus, Andries became Zion's envoy to the Swazi. The two brothers knew that their forefathers hailed from Swaziland, and thus they felt they were also responsible for a Zion in Swaziland. As if this were not enough, a young Swazi lady teacher by the name of Johanna Nxumalo in the Groenvlei school near Wakkerstroom, would remind them of this obligation. She had been baptized by Daniel and he had solemnized her marriage to a Zionist pastor, Paul

shall remain in the hands of our Mission and under our control". Apost. Faith Mission, Minute Book 1908–1914, May 6, 1910.

In October, 1900, Le Roux was directed by the Apostolic Faith Mission to call in D. Nkonyane's "certificate" (presumably his ordination certificate). *Ibid*, Oct. 14, 1910.

Khumalo—whether he had any legal authority to do so, we shall overlook in this connexion. We shall hear more of this remarkable woman in our chapter on Swaziland.

As Nkonyane took over the local leadership of the Christian Catholic Apostolic Church in Zion, he looked around for European support to replace that of Le Roux, and found it in Edgar Mahon, who came over to Wakkerstroom at a time of crisis. Nkonyane was evicted from Wakkerstroom—it is not unfair to assume that this was to some extent due to his Zionism—but Mahon found a site for Nkonyane at Charlestown.[55] However much Nkonyane represented African leadership, he was thus not above certain contacts with the Whites.[56] This move was timely and important. Timely, because it was only now, in 1911, that Africans were at all able to buy freehold sites here. Some three hundred "stands" were sold to Africans at Charlestown.[57] Not a few of these families were Zionists from Wakkerstroom; they are still there at the time of writing.

As headquarters for Nkonyane Zion, Charlestown became important because of its strategic position on the Zion map of Southern Africa: from there, Nkonyane could reach out westward to Johannesburg, south-east to Nongoma, the royal residence of Zululand, and east to Lobamba, the royal residence of Swaziland.

Nkonyane's move from Wakkerstroom to Charlestown also signified his definite breach with Le Roux. It was Le Roux's ever-faithful Charles Sangweni who was left in charge of that African

[55] Cf. Alan Paton, *The Charlestown Story,* published by the Liberal Party of South Africa. In 1957, "the axe fell on Charlestown", and the freeholders were to be told to move elsewhere.

[56] I can think of one objection to underlining this connexion: Here is obviously another European trying to rub it in that independent African Church leaders too would rely on European contacts. This is not my concern at all, but rather to point out the loyalty of the African Zionist leader to the international Zion cause somehow seen to be represented by Zion City, Illinois.

[57] To Africans at this time Charlestown was an important railway junction, on what was, until 1910, the border between Transvaal and Natal, and passengers had to get passes at the railway station. This led to many hardships; the problem was often discussed in these years. Secretary for Nat. Affairs, Pietermaritzburg 14.7.1903 to Minister of Lands and Works. 1/1/301 SNA 1596/1903. *Ilanga lase Natal* 12/6 03; 6/11 03.

work at Wakkerstroom which was connected with the Apostolic Faith. Nkonyane, while anxious to retain contacts with the ever-shifting Zion representation in Johannesburg, felt strong enough to establish his own movement. In 1922 he went so far as to change the name of the Church. He made a significant addition—"Holy Spirit"—to the already long row of terms in the name. His church was now Christian Catholic Apostolic *Holy Spirit* Church in Zion.

In 1927, Nkonyane's Church reported to Pretoria that they numbered ten congregations in the Union—five in Natal, and five on the Rand and in Eastern Transvaal, and soon a growing church work in Swaziland was added. None of these local congregations amounted to more than some two hundred or two hundred and fifty members.

Nkonyane Zion has known both ups and downs. In 1935, Daniel Nkonyane, died. He was succeeded by his son Stephen. Stephen Nkonyane persisted in his hope—against hope—that Walter Dimba's Federation movement (see p. 296) would provide what it promised, Government recognition. He was given a prominent role in this—largely fictitious—enterprise and regularly attended its well publicized assemblies. Increasingly he concentrated his energy on his Church's considerable interest in Swaziland. Here it was that in the 1930s he had thrown in Zion's lot with Swazi royalty. When these connections in the end affected his own matrimonial status, his Zion followers reacted, and his son Henry succeeded him, as thirty years earlier he had inherited the leadership from his father Daniel, the founder of the Church.

Henry Nkonyane was relatively educated, with a Junior Certificate. His orderly presentation of the Christian gospel testified to the beneficial effect of his years at the Sweetwaters Bible Institute. In 1969, however, his career was cut short by a tragic car accident.

This time, there was no Nkonyane of mature age and experience to take over the leadership. Michael Mkize was elected Bishop. In him the Church acquired a leader with a Bible school training, clearly noticeable in his sober and knowledgeable Bible exposition.

Paul Mabilitsa († 1942) was the intellectual among the first Zion

leaders. He was a Tswana, son of a Bakxatla chief, from Rusten-
burg, Western Transvaal. He was to have succeeded to the chieftainship, but declined, for "I am serving a greater Chief". He was
first a member of the Berlin Lutheran Society and received his
early schooling there. Working in Johannesburg, he was
won over to a Baptist conviction through Pastor William Leshega
(cf. p. 165) and was baptized by Leshega in 1901.[58] He met Johannes Büchler and it was probably through him that he found his
way to Basutoland, where Büchler's brother-in-law Mahon was
particularly active. In 1909 he managed to get himself arrested
by the Protectorate authorities: his preaching and baptizing activities were regarded as unorthodox in a country and during a
period when the Roman Catholic Church felt called to safeguard
religious law and order in that country.

Returning to the Rand after this experience, he contacted the
new representative of Voliva's Zion, an American by name of
Modred Powell. In 1920, Mabilitsa established his own organization, the Christian Apostolic Church in Zion of South Africa
(he had left out the epithet 'Catholic' on account of his experience in a Basutoland jail!), and found a strategic place for
his headquarters, Alexandra Township, Johannesburg.

He was highly respected in African Church circles on the
Rand and called *Johoza*, the great, impressive person. He was a
talented and powerful preacher, always returning to that 'Little
Bible' of John 3:16—"For God so loved the world"—which was
his favourite text. He shared Le Roux's aversion to the outward
display of Zion piety. He could not accept croziers for ordinary
church members. This was the prerogative of the leader himself,
for, he argued, in the Old Testament there was only one Moses.
Nor did he believe that it was effective to use these holy staffs
for driving out demons. "We are exactly as in Zion City, Ill.,"
he told me, insisting that the American Church fathers would
not lend themselves to this more dramatic exercise. While
Daniel Nkonyane claimed that the Zion faithful, like Moses and
Jesus of old, must not wear shoes in church, Mabilitsa stuck to

[58] P. Mabilitsa's own statement in an application to Zion, Ill., dated 25.11.1912
(Archives, The Christian Catholic Church, Zion, Ill., U.S.A., Forms of Applications for Membership).

his liberal attitude also on this point: "If Jesus will admit only the shoe-less into heaven, then, really, he came in vain", he confided to me.

On the other hand even Mabilitsa had to accept the fact that some of his close co-workers were as much "filled with the Spirit", as the Nkonyane faithful. N. Ngobese "was full of prophecies and such things". Amos Mbata had the gift of foretelling things that were to happen from five to ten years hence— the "Influenza" of 1918–19, for instance—and it all came to pass just as he had prophesied. Mabilitsa himself had experienced that fasting was the sure method of receiving the Spirit. His Church as a whole would therefore occasionally practice fasting; some of the leaders would extend this deprivation to a week, and were sure then to be filled by the Spirit.

For Zion in the City, on the Rand, it was valuable that Mabilitsa had educational ambitions. At his Alexandra headquarters he established a school which in 1932 developed into one of the very few secondary schools for Africans on the Rand. His eldest son, Philip, leader of the Church from 1943 to his death in 1965, was sent to Fort Hare where he took a B.Sc. degree, and another son was trained at the prestigious Ohlange Institute, near Durban. The second and third generation Mabilitsas are well-known intellectuals on the Rand, an indication of how here, too, a revivalist movement can act as a social lever for the group.[59]

Elias Mahlangu (1881–1960) was another of the Zion Church fathers who hailed from Le Roux's group at Wakkerstroom. He was, however, neither a Zulu nor a Swazi, but a Ndebele, born near Ogies in Transvaal. Yet, both because of his beginnings at Wakkerstroom and the long-term effects of his activities he should be mentioned here. In his case, too, it was the upheavals

[59] My interviews with Overseer Paul Mabilitsa, Oct. 1941, his son Philip, July 1958, and with his son Jacob Mabilitsa, Dec. 1972, and church papers produced by them. According to the present Mabilitsa tradition, Paul Mabilitsa after having left his Lutheran church, joined Leshega's Baptist Church for a while (cf. p. 165). In 1914, Mabilitsa claimed to have 25 "tabernacles" and some 135 local preaching places in S. Africa and beyond. *Leaves of Healing*, 21.3.1914., with place names and men in charge.

of the Boer War that set him on the move. As a young man he somehow found his way to Wakkerstroom, where he is supposed to have looked after Le Roux's cattle. He was baptized by Le Roux, whom he occasionally accompanied on his evangelistic tours for the cause of Zion. The Mahlangu tradition now insists that he acted as an interpreter for Le Roux, but this is probably attributing to him a function that was unnecessary in this case. Le Roux spoke Zulu well and loved to preach in that language. Mahlangu was obviously a linguist. One of his sons reports that he knew "almost all the languages: Venda, Shangaan, Pedi, Sotho, Tswane, Zulu, English, and Afrikaans in which he excelled; he was very good in Afrikaans." This latter accomplishment he had acquired as a young farm-hand; it also seems probable that originally he was baptized in the Dutch Reformed Mission Church.

Le Roux's influence over him was decisive, and Mahlangu, along with Daniel Nkonyane, J. Ngobese and others, received his first impressions from the life of the Zion group at Wakkerstroom.

Like Nkonyane, Mahlangu showed a special interest in winning Swaziland for Zion, all the more as his wife, Ma Khambule, was a Swazi. In fact he placed representatives of his own at two strategic points in Swaziland, Mbabane and Pigg's Peak, although with rather indifferent results.

In other parts of Southern Africa, Mahlangu's presence made itself felt. Himself a member of the Ndebele royal family—"Mahlangu Mgwezane wenkosi"—he was reputed among his followers to have been "a great man: a man and a half". Cautious and calculating, he nevertheless took the risk of joining the African National Congress—a step which of necessity was to result in difficulties with the authorities from time to time. But this endeared him still further to his faithful. They appreciated his leadership and message.

It is of course almost impossible now to recapture that message. It seems characteristic, however, that when his son was asked by us to quote Mahlangu's favourite hymns and Bible passages, he would point to those with a decidedly apocalyptic emphasis. This was, as we have already seen, characteristic of the Wakkerstroom Zion group, and Mahlangu naturally shared this concern. His favourite hymn was one from the American Board Hymn-book: *Emafwini nangu ehla*, Lo! He comes with clouds descending. Hallelujah! Amen! Bible quotations, which must have been his favourite sermon texts include Rev. 3:11, "Behold, I come quickly", and Rev. 8:13, "an Angel ... saying with a loud voice, Woe, woe, woe, to the inhabitants of the earth ..."

Such was Mahlangu's popularity that in the uncertain conditions after Le Roux's resignation, Mahlangu was preferred as the new, African leader by one section of Zion, while Nkonyane commanded the loyalty of the majority. The latter moved, as we have seen, to Charlestown, while Mahlangu established his own "Zion Apostolic Church" in Johannesburg.

In an application for recognition made in 1927, Mahlangu claimed that he had formed his church already in 1911—[the] "parent body ceased to exist" and it seems to be an established fact that Mahlangu's group was formed at least prior to 1914.

He moved to Johannesburg, trying to accommodate within one organization ambitious local leaders of various tribal backgrounds. This is where his linguistic skill stood him in good stead. But as early as 1918 there was a serious break-away. Two Swazi evangelists, Josiah Mlangeni and Mzimela, left Mahlangu in 1918 and formed Zion Apostolic Swazi Church of South Africa.

The following year Mahlangu did send an official application to the Native Affairs Department, Johannesburg. It was in the form of a letter from four of his lieutenants, with the request that Mahlangu be recognized "as our Acting Superintendent". Of course, at that time—prior to 1925—there was no administrative machinery for recognition of Independent Churches. This may have been one reason why the Mahlangu group had to wait for a reply. They had, fortunately, acquired the Africans' virtue of patience. So about twenty years later they wrote again to the Native Commissioner, Johannesburg—April 11, 1938.

Sir,
    Re: Our application of the 10th Feb. 1919 which was not replied, we humbly beg you to look up the same. Consider, we appealed to the Commissioner on the above mentioned date. To state that the Church which was Supervised by Revd D.C. Le Roux should be known by the N[ative] A[ffairs] Dept at Pretoria, we doubt as to whether the Church was made known to Pretoria.

One look at the names of these who signed the application of 1919 suffices to show that even after the Swazi walk-out, Mahlangu was going to have difficulty in controlling a tribally reduced organization. For among these supporters was Ezra J. Mbonambi of Verulam. To cut a long story short, one might say that a number of well-known charismatic leaders were at some time or other connected with this man—Is. Shembe and J. Chiliza among others—and in each case this led to conflicts.

Towards the middle of the 1920s, Mbonambi was involved in a notorious court-case, and with this the union between him and Mahlangu ended in a dramatic faction fight among their followers.

The 1920s on the other hand was also the time when Mahlangu could extend his influence to Rhodesia. Daneel's study of Zion among the Shona shows Mahlangu (referred to as "Mhlangu"!) to have been recognized as one of the great Church fathers of these fast-growing groups in the North.[60] A list of twenty-one pastors and thirty evangelists from the 1920s shows that rather less than half of the local leaders were Zulu-Swazi while the remainder consisted of Ndebele and Northern Sotho.

Edgar Mahon's contacts with Le Roux and Daniel Nkonyane have already been mentioned. Mahon's role appears to have been significant as a starting point for certain important African Church leaders. We may mention two of these, Edward Lion and Titus Msibi, while aware of the fact that we thus do not attempt to follow the development of the worthy Mahon Mission itself.

Bishop *Titus Msibi* must be considered. He was to form his own

---

[60] M. L. Daneel, *op. cit.* I, p. 289 ff.

In 1919–20, it was still uncertain whether Mahlangu or Mbonambi was finally to emerge as leader of the Zion Apostolic Church. In 1920, for instance, a printed Constitution of the Church gives Mbonambi as the head. In 1921, however, Mahlangu had established his right. There is a notice September 17, 1921, in the *Natal Advertiser*, stating that Mbonambi is *not* the President of the Church.

Sources:

a) Interviews December 1973 with E. N. Mahlangu's son, Mr. Patrick Mahlangu of Diep Kloof, Khotso, Johannesburg.

(*b*) Correspondence and other papers of the Zion Apostolic Church covering the period 1919–60, now with Mr. P. Mahlangu.

African Zionist Ministers' Association. With his blue turban and his long beard, he was an impressive figure and represented an important Zion tradition. He too was converted by Mahon. The European leader had, as we have seen, begun his Zion activity at Ladysmith, during the Ladysmith siege of the Boer War. Mahon subsequently moved on to the Orange Free State, while Msibi remained at Ladysmith.

Msibi was regarded as one of the leaders in Zion. His personal contact with Mahon may have accounted for this status. "I was given power to ordain by being ordained myself by Mahon", he explained to me. He liked the epithet "Catholic" in Zion's original church name, and insisted that it be retained in the name of his own church, formed in 1931: the *Congregational Catholic Apostolic Church*. More than any other Zulu leader known to the author he was enthralled by the idea of succession: he represented "the priest-ship derived from the Roman Catholic Church". In the same breath Msibi can state, as he does in his handwritten Constitution, "that our faith rests on the version of the old and new Testaments embodied in the holy bible and Believe in the doctrine and teachings of our former leaders John Dawi and Wilbur B. Voliva who extracted their doctrine from Zion names of Books".

His most significant contribution was the unifying of certain Zion Churches, some twenty-five. It was no simple proposition: "Some Zionists join me, and then again they leave me. They should of course remain on the foundation once laid by John Alexander [Dowie], First Apostle", he told me in 1958. Msibi had high hopes. "We would if possible (should the Government assist us) like all these Zion Churches to unite, and have one Church."[62]

[62] T. Msibi, May 1934, to Secretary, Native Affairs, 214/374. National Archives, Pretoria. Certain groups have retained effective contacts with their particular Zion in Illinois, U.S., until this very day. E. M. Ngema, Edenvale, Transvaal, of the Christian Catholic Apostolic Church in Zion—related to the Dowie-John A. Lewis- C. W. Mc Ilhany succession, *not* Dowie—Voliva—declares in his *"Constitution"* of 1961 that the General Overseer in Zion, Illinois is "the highest authority". "The storehouse is located at headquarters in the U.S." This "storehouse" relationship is emphasized even to-day by the following provision: "In theory, all money collected for the church in South Africa are sent to head-

One of Mahon's first converts was *Edward* [Tau] *Lion,* the most spectacular of the Sotho Zionists of an earlier generation.[63] According to his son and successor, Solomon David Lion, Edward ordained Mahon! This version is most probably another indication of the over-dramatization of one's own role to which the two Lions were prone. No doubt, Mahon's preaching tours were the starting point, and Edward Lion was attracted by the music and message of the Mahon band.

Mahon was impressed by Lion's apparent results. During the course of one service, Lion baptized one hundred and thirty people in the Caledon River, the first mass baptism in that Sotho Jordan. Lion was also known as a successful healer. The Mahon talent of precognition drew Lion's attention to similar powers within himself. He would see beforehand a patient coming to seek his help. Only when he had "seen" the case in advance was he prepared to heal the person concerned.

On the other hand, Lion's exploits in other directions, not least with regard to his many women followers, were an embarrassment. In 1910, Lion encountered the Apostolic Faith worship in Johannesburg, and returned to Basutoland to work on behalf of this new faith. In 1912 he joined the organization and in 1917 he established a "Zion City" of his own in Basutoland, the Zion Apostolic Faith Mission. More than anyone among the first-generation leaders, Lion was intent on this aspect of founding a city of Zion. In an application to Government in Pretoria he says that his intention was "to create [my] own tribe so as to be able to buy [a] farm".[64] It was characteristic of his garnished interpretation of his own role that he claimed "600,000" adherents

---

quarters, in Zion, Illinois, USA and in turn all operating expenses are paid from the storehouse at headquarters. But, to facilitate matters, the duly appointed and ordained Overseer in South Africa actually manages all the finances ... However, he should remit 10% of all collections to the General Overseer at headquarters, a token of loyalty and faithfulness."

[63] Lion's clan was Tau, near Maseru. As a young man he clashed with his brothers and in order to separate from them, he took the English name "Lion". We visited his son Solomon David Lion at Maseru in Dec. 1972 and had long interviews with him. We also visited his colony at Klipgat, West of Pretoria, another tightly-knit Zion city of this group. Edward referred to himself as Edw. W. Lion, W. for White, White being the grandfather's name on his mother's side.

[64] Bantu Affairs Dept., Pretoria, 214/4, Zion Apostolic Faith Mission.

by this time, a figure well above that of the whole population of the country of Basutoland. It was in line with this self-appreciation that in the letterhead of his correspondence, he referred to himself as "General Oversear of the World".

However exaggerated these claims may have been, Lion did have an influence. His most important gain was a Pedi Zionist by the name of Ignatius Lekganyane, who spent the first years of the 1920s with Lion in Basutoland, and obviously was greatly influenced by him. In 1925, Lekganyane established his own Zion Christian Church, "Z.C.C.", which under his leadership and under that of his sons Edward (called after Edward Lion!) and Joseph was to develop into the biggest and most spectacular Zion in South Africa, with its centre near Pietersburg, Northern Transvaal. The "Zion City" once established by Edward Lion was to be greatly surpassed by the powerful Zion City of Lekganyane's.[65] We have drawn this line of influence here in order to link Lekganyane, too, with the early beginnings of Zion, leading back to Mahon. The connection here is so well established that it is not too far-fetched to imagine that the now famous drums of Lekganyane's Zion give loud echoes of those instruments once beaten in the nineteenth-century Salvation Army in Natal.

Le Roux—Mahon—Bryant—Nkonyane—Mabilitsa—Mahlangu—Msibi—Edw. Lion: We now return to where we started, at the source of Zulu Jordans and Swazi Bethesdas. Our story so far has shown that the beginnings of Black Zion were not as exclusively African as one might presume or would like to believe. The first decade of the movement echoes with the hearty and happy—and sometimes not so happy—relationship between White commitment and an emerging Black charismatic community.

The movement had begun in a White Zion. But it did not end there. Le Roux and Mahon were, after all, only catalysts. Black Zion was on its own now.

It is a remarkable story, even a paradoxical one. Wakkerstroom was as unlikely a source as one could imagine. Yet, the Boer missionary at Wakkerstroom was a Zionist at heart for ten eventful years and served as a Zion missionary for half of that time.

---

[65] Material on Legkanyane in file 120/4 / 68[I], National Archives, Pretoria.

The same man was for thirty-five years to inspire and give form to what appears as a dynamic and rapidly growing White countervailing movement to that Dutch Reformed Church from which he originated. It was largely due to his leadership as President of the Apostolic Faith Mission that the sound development of that White Pentecostal movement was due. All this goes to prove that P. L. Le Roux has a place in South African church history. The same applies to Edward Mahon.

But this historical sketch does also show something else. A study of the origins of the movement provides an antidote to certain interpretations which nowadays are applied to this and similar phenomena. Some scholars—overlooking tiresome facts—prefer their own theories sometimes dressed up in ready-made jargon, with any number of "variables", "*zeitgeists*", and "levels", all presumably tending to produce African Church Independency.[66] This is all very impressive, and generally recognised as such. Yet, in the long run, also facts are interesting.

---

[66] Cf. David B. Barrett's *Schism and Renewal in Africa*, 1968. The main thesis of Barrett's well-known book is to establish a "*zeitgeist*"—as the author calls it—i.e., "the socioreligious climate of opinion favouring independence" (*op. cit.*, p. 110)— with altogether 18 factors. "All tribal units in Africa can be located somewhere on this continuum" [of 18 factors]. It so happens that the Zulu have reached 17 out of altogether 18 factors. They "occupy alone the highest place on the scale" (*ibid.*, p. 115) and we are assured that in 1975 the Zulu will have produced a "*zeitgeist*" of 18 factors, *ibid.* This is all very interesting—but the author has not considered that decisive factor: this concerted team of missionaries and of African co-workers, at the source of it all.

2. A Spectrum of Charismatics

Among Zulu and Swazi, the name "Zion" is used in at least two different senses: one more specific, another wider and all-embracing. The former refers to churches which in some way regard themselves as genealogically related to Zion City, Ill., and to "John Alexander [Dowie], First Apostle". Very often, however, the term is used in a wider sense, for churches which emphasize the guidance of *uMoya,* the Spirit, and healing as central concerns.

There is sometimes a tendency to equate all of Zion with what is loosely referred to as "Messianism", and some invidious misrepresentations of Zion have been the result, the more so since such theories often lack any foundation in fact. In order to counteract such tendencies we suggest that a presentation of five leaders will show the wide variety, the broad spectrum of the Spirit-dominated churches.

As to the five leaders we are pointing out what E. Mdlalose and Grace Tshabalala, Mrs. Nku and Mrs. Mbele and Job Chiliza have in common. They are not homogeneous. Chiliza stands out as a spiritual leader of unique quality and depth. As we shall see, he became increasingly critical of the Zion churches, and was anxious to draw a clear line between them and his own church. This was so not only because he managed to get his church recognized by the Government, but above all because of his evangelical understanding of the central themes of the Bible. He was also critical of the more picturesque display of Zionist piety, in the form of robes, cross staves and the like. Yet, the four others share with Chiliza a common denominator: the unshakeable centrality of Jesus the Christ. Chiliza himself was part of the Full-Gospel tradition and therefore related to the world of Pentecostalism generally. The fact that Ma Nku and Ma Mbele refer to themselves as "Apostolics" places also them in another group than "Zionists in a strict sense". Yet, structurally there are close similarities between the two groups. One must not forget the historical continuity in South Africa between Zion and the Apostolics. This continuity is so marked that it would seem worth while to regard the Apostolics as a variant of Zion, although this characterisation would not meet with the approval of the Apostolics as such.

E. Mdlalose

Archbishop and Mrs. Elija Mdlalose represent a combination of what might be regarded as two central Zion traditions, those of Nkonyane and of Mabilitsa, and for this reason belong here.

In Mdlalose's case there is the added interest that he emphasizes his church's affinity to Zulu royalty. In a later chapter on Swaziland we shall encounter Zionist relationship to Swazi royalty. In Zululand, the subservient political position of even Zulu royalty within the power structure of South Africa has tended to make such attitudes untenable. Many Zion leaders among Zulus do, however, emphasize their close affinity to the Zulu royal house and Mdlalose may well be the most prominent among these.

He felt that he had special Biblical authority for his interest in Zulu royalty. Ordained by a group of "Apostolic" pastors in 1915, the question arose where he was to serve. "Casting lots" was the obvious solution. This meant, in their group, opening the Bible at random and pointing to chapter and verse. In Mdlalose's case, Acts 9:15 was the outcome: "a chosen vessel to bear my name before the Gentiles, *and kings,* and the children of Israel."

There it was—an injunction from on high to go to Solomon, King of the Zulus. Mdlalose wrote a letter to the King, informing him that he had an important message to convey to him. Mdlalose felt he was in a strong position, for King Solomon was married to a sister of his. Thus the King referred to him as *umalume* (maternal uncle). He proceeded to the Royal Kraal at Nongoma and, as he told me later, was well received: "Kings are just like God. They first look at you, just like God. They

69

won't accept you until you have done a rightful thing. King Solomon—he was very deep." Without fear Mdlalose was able to explain the Zion message, and to spell out the avoidances it implied, particularly pork and sour porridge. The King listened with interest, and Mdlalose reports that the King had answered in a conciliatory manner: "If you introduce new laws—that we must not eat cattle meat or goat's meat, please don't make that a rule for all my people." But the King went on: "You insist on avoiding this and that kind of drink or meat. Where in the Bible are these forbidden, Mdlalose?" Mdlalose had to admit that he in fact relied on *two* sources of authority, and he answered: "There may not be any Bible authority against it, but I feel that the 'Holy Spirit' is against it."

From that moment, Mdlalose's spiritual position at the Royal Kraal was assured. At least in King Solomon's time and in that of his brother and successor, Mshiyeni ka Dinuzulu (1915–43), he was regarded and treated as something of a Royal chaplain (according to interviews with leading Zulu officials, 1958). Often he was asked to open with prayer important national and similar meetings at the Royal Kraal. Archbishop Mdlalose told me: "I always used to go to Nongoma—the place of the Royal Kraal—in order to create a fine weight of influence in the Royal Place" (*ukulungisa isithunzi esihle ebukhosini*).

As we shall see later, Daniel and Andries Nkonyane and the local pastors of their particular Zion were to enjoy a similar role at the Swazi Royal Kraal. Through Mdlalose, it was now Mabilitsa's Zion that held this important position in the Zulu royal centre. But that was the trouble. Mabilitsa was, after all, not a Zulu, and Mdlalose's organizational dependence on him could not but be felt as a problem. Sometimes Church collections had to be sent from Zululand to Mabilitsa at Alexandra, Johannesburg. A leading personality of the Zulu realm took Mdlalose to task over this financial issue: "Why take Zulu money and give it to the Sotho?"

This was irrefutable logic. Mdlalose now began to place the Church's money in a bank at Vryheid, a Zululand town, and he informed me that the European bank manager had advised him to add "*Natal and Zululand*" to the Church's name in the official rubber stamp. Once more, Mdlalose felt that he should follow the good advice of good men: it also helped to lay the foundations of a particular Zulu section of Mabilitsa's Union-wide Zion.

E. Mdlalose, born in 1897, was an Anglican, greatly influenced by the leading missionary in Zululand at the time, Archdeacon Johnson. And an Anglican he would probably have remained, had he stayed in the comparatively sheltered milieu of St. Augustine's, Nqutu, Zululand. But like tens of thousands of his contemporaries he went to Johannesburg to make a living. There he got a job as a hospital orderly. He took to drink at this time, but later met a Zionist group who chased the alcohol demon out of him.

Once, while drunk, he had a dream in which he saw people resting on a bed above his bed. They were sick, and the filthy vomit ran down over his own body. This made him wake up— and he never again touched beer after that ordeal.

He joined Zion in 1910, and five years later he was ordained. This ordination, however, took place only after considerable debate. The power struggle in the Zion group at Wakkerstroom had now been transferred to Johannesburg, and Mdlalose was drawn into it. It concerned adherence or otherwise to Old Testament rules of conduct. Mdlalose followed the Nkonyane line, emphasizing the importance of Old Testament observances with regard to garments, shoes and similar things. Paul Mabilitsa, as we have seen, shared Le Roux's aversion to what they termed outward form, while Mdlalose insisted that the God who had instructed Moses to take off his shoes in church meant what He had said also as far as the Zulus were concerned. At the time, in 1915, an American, Rev. M. Powell was in charge of the Zion congregation in Johannesburg, and he took a different line from that of Le Roux. He recommended that Mdlalose be ordained. In fact, the two church leaders, Nkonyane and Mabilitsa, although differing between themselves with regard to rules of ethics, were able to agree as far as Mdlalose was concerned.

Mdlalose's forte was to be that of a healer. As such he was not doctrinaire but relied on the Spirit: God Himself knows whether this or that particular sickness will be overcome by the laying on of a holy stick, or by a sash of special colour, or simply by the archbishop's own hand. "It is all in Matt. ch. 10. We must not do our work without the authority of the Bible His Word never ages."

The Archbishop's wife, Mrs. Emelina Mbatha-Mdlalose, was a member of the very first Zion group at Wakkerstroom. Like the majority of that group, she was born and christened in the Dutch Reformed Mission community. Her personal development has traits that are probably characteristic of a considerable number of young Zulu women at the time.

Boys jilted by her retaliated by "throwing" *ubutakati*—black magic—at her and as a result she was affected by a special form of hysteria, *isipholiyana*. She turned to Pastor Le Roux for help. He prayed for her and she was healed. At least, this was her story fifty years after the event. The healing made her join Le Roux's Zionist congregation at Wakkerstroom. It was here that some years later she met her future husband.

The Mdlaloses, while influenced by the Nkonyane group, were technically and officially part of Mabilitsa's Zion, and we have already given a rapid survey of the history of this group.

After Paul Mabilitsa's death in 1942, the leadership of the Church was taken over by Mabilitsa's son Philip. A well-known educationalist (B.Sc., Fort Hare) on the Rand, the younger Mabilitsa was not regarded by the majority of the Church as a very spiritual leader in Zion. His high educational attainments and, possibly, certain convivial habits of the wealthy élite made him seem not altogether consistant with the standards of his own church.

In 1952 a revolt was staged against the younger Mabilitsa, and Mdlalose was seen as the obvious alternative: sober and safely placed on the same educational level as the broad majority of the Church.

Some Zionist leaders tended, however, to underrate Mdlalose for this very reason. R. Nziba, head of the Bantu Independent Ministers' Association, had a problem: "Mr. Potgieter" [Pretoria official of the Bantu Affairs Department, at the time in charge of the Bantu Churches portfolio] "cannot accept Mdlalose as he does not speak Afrikaans or English". And yet Nziba knew he had to placate the Church as such: "We must give Mdlalose something higher." Calling him Archbishop—instead of Bishop—seemed a pleasant enough solution, and this was indeed what happened in 1953. At the same time, this title given to the Zulu leader posed a problem for the official leader on the Rand. Nziba, who himself was not a member of the Mabilitsa–Mdlalose Zion, did not have to worry about the consequences of his generous solution.

Mdlalose's hand was greatly strengthened by two co-workers, very different one from the other, yet united in their support of the Zulu leader.

The first of these was P. Lawrence Coka, the administrator. He thus also represents an important element in the central leadership of the "Spirit"–churches. Ethiopian-type churches often excel in their ambitious administrators but Zion churches also need them, and Coka could administrate. Having passed first year in High School, he had already tasted the fruits of general education. He earned a living, acting as a factotum in a lawyer's office in Vryheid, a position which could not but increase his usefulness as a General Secretary of the Church. As such he was constantly busy in posting more or less important statements and proclamations on behalf of his Zion church to Central Government in Pretoria and provincial authorities in Pietermaritzburg, Natal.

But Mdlalose, the Archbishop, and Coka, the administrator, would have been much the poorer without their special "Prophet and Messenger", Philemon B. Sibiya. He is indeed a genuine apocalyptic mystic in Zulu Zion.

He too was related to Zulu royalty. Paramount Chief Cyprian's mother was a Sibiya, and the prophet was thus as closely related to the King as Mdlalose had been to his immediate predecessor. But Sibiya could rely on higher authority. For three and a half years, 1931–34, he had retired from the world preparing himself for his spiritual task. All this time, "I fasted and prayed and went through purifications"—as he told me. For "forty days and forty nights" he had been without sleep or food. Then one day, at the end of his ordeal, he had a vision. From behind him, there came somebody like a man, yet an Angel: "He laid his hands on me and placed a white cloth over my head. He took ointment and consecrated me". This consecration gave him his office and authority.

In 1933 he had a vision of war in heaven, and he knew that war would also come to the earth, and that he, Sibiya, had been sent to warn the world, more especially South Africa, against it.

73

From his youth he had been a man of visions. Born in 1899, he received his first vision of God in 1910, as Halley's Comet appeared: "Then God opened my heart".

Something of the urgency that had once driven George Fox to warn "the bloody City of Lichfield" now directed Sibiya to challenge the blooming city of Durban. On August 18, 1939 he wrote to the Native Commissioner in Durban (as rendered in Coka's English):

"I am directed by Him who sent me to request you to forward this Message to the Rulers of the City of Durban, for their consideration."

His message could not have been more encouraging as far as the English-speaking majority of that City of Durban was concerned: The Holy Ghost had revealed to him "that all the existing Kingdoms on Earth ... have not got His covenant except only the Kingdom of ENGLAND where God's covenant was. The Lord lifted up the Flag, the Union Jack, and commanded me to read from it. I did so and read the Flag by the Spirit and I found that it was the Covenant of Freedom of all Nations for gathering them together and also a Covenant of *love*".

With the help of Coka, Sibiya claimed that Zion was not a Church: it was the Kingdom of God itself. This was the persistent message which Coka and Sibiya proclaimed as long as their companionship with Mdlalose lasted.[1]

Grace Tshabalala

In order the better to understand the Nkonyane tradition within Zion, we shall now turn to one of the local women leaders.

Mrs. Tshabalala is one among a million Zulu Zionist women, herself now a widow at Kwa Mashu in Durban, a small, graceful,

[1] *Sources*. Letters from P. B. Sibiya to the Native Commissioner, Durban, 18.8. 1939, 10.10.1939. 24.7.1941. File 134/214. Prov. Archives, P. M. Burg. P. L. Coka to Native Commissioner and to Secretary Native Affairs, Pretoria 11.5. 1945, 25.5.1945, 2.4.1946, 22.8.1953. File 134/214, *ibid.,* and National Archives, Pretoria.
Interviews with P. B. Sibiya 1958; with Archbishop Mdlalose 1941, 1958, 1972; with Mrs Emelina Mdlalose 1941.

dignified lady of some seventy years, a person of great moral strength.

The more one studies the story of her life, the more she stands out as a paradigm of the history of the Christian Church among the Zulus in the twentieth century. She is representative also because she belongs to the dominant Nkonyane Zion Church, the beginnings of which we have followed in this study.

For obvious reasons my studies of Zionism, in an early volume and in this one, have had to concentrate on men, while this movement is of course largely a movement of women. It so happens that I have regularly contacted Grace Tshabalala and she has on my invitation written a little autobiographical outline for me which must form the backbone of the story. I wish I knew much more of her and about her, not only for the sake of this little chapter in a book, but above all in order to learn from her how to live as a Christian and how, in adverse circumstances, to persevere in faith and hope and charity—and inalienable joy. I have always felt that this woman has something to teach me and others in this respect.

She was born in 1904 on the Kalabasi Mission farm, Dannhauser, Natal, "under Rev. J. Dewar, of the United Free Church of Scotland", as she puts it in her brief autobiography. This happened to be a mission farm, where the conditions for African squatters were comparatively privileged. Her father and grandfather had been "deacons" in the Presbyterian Church, and thus trusted local leaders in the Christian community. The Presbyterian group was traditionally well-informed, by catechetical teaching and intellectual ambition: on this kind of farm—as distinct from other farms at the time—it was taken for granted that children should go to school. So Grace passed standard VI and was in 1922 sent to a Teacher Training Institute, where she emerged as "T6" teacher, the first and lowest rung on the ladder of the teaching career. She taught off and on in Government-aided schools in the years 1921–25. Especially memorable and determinative experiences from those years were two dreams. A prominent lady member of the local Presbyterian congregation told her that in a dream she had seen Grace teaching the baptismal class. They decided they had to fast for some time in order to find the explanation of the dream. At this time of fasting, Grace herself had a dream of people in white garments. A voice told her to go to the kraal of Simon Khumalo at Washbank—some fifteen miles away—where she would find people who needed her. They sang and prayed, only to find that the people were drunk and chased the young zealots away.

Soon she had another dream. A voice asked her, "Do you see these people?" "Yes", she replied, "I see Roman Catholic nuns dressed in black." The voice went on, "Do you want to dress like they do?" She replied, "No, that dress is pitch black, it is a dress of mourning." The voice asked her, "What kind of dress do you want?" Grace answered, "I want a green dress"—and woke up from her dream. She adds in her autobiographical notes, "Zion was not known in our part of the world at that time." Soon, however, she did meet a group of young Zionists in white with a green sash and was led to visit their chapel. There she was after some time told by leading women that young Richard Tshabalala wished to propose to her. In this group, there was of course a Biblical precedent for a step of this kind. Once upon a time, "Elder Abraham" had sent a servant to ask for a wife for his son, and the servant had returned with Rebecca (Gen. 24). So Grace was married to Richard in 1926, and she moved with him to Charlestown—the headquarters of Zulu Zion.

Richard, born in 1903, was the son of one of the very first families in Zulu Zion, a member of Le Roux's and Daniel Nkonyane's group. His father died when Richard was only five. This meant that the chances of any education for the boy were nonexistent. Richard grew up with the tradition of the first generation of Zion, and from them he had his understanding of the Christian faith.

In 1930, the young family moved to Durban to find a livelihood. One of the Zion pastors had seen a vision of Grace's future: she was going to a far-off place and was going to have five years of sorrow. But after the five years, God was to remember her again. And it happened just as Rev. Dhlamini had foretold. She bore seven children, but only one of them, a boy, survived, and is now her helper. All the others died, either in birth or in the first two years of life. The family had a room in Chesterville in the slums of Durban. Overcrowding, undernourishment and illness combined—in this case as with tens of thousands of others—to prove the Rev. Dhlamini's pious prophecy to be correct.

After the lean years, things changed for the better. They were able to build a chapel of corrugated iron in what was once Cato Manor, Durban. During and after the war they both worked as organizers in the Red Cross (African section). In 1945, Grace passed her Red Cross Advanced Home Nursing certificate. In 1960 her husband passed away, and the widow had to find some livelihood. For twenty years she has worked four-and-a-half days a week as a housemaid in a Durban family, devoting the remaining two and a half days to her Zion work.

In 1952 she took an initiative that was going to be her great contribution to the cause of Zion. She felt the divisions of Zionists as a personal challenge and affront and wished to do something about it. This was all the more remarkable as she was not born in Zion but after her marriage had had to adjust to and identify herself with the Zion group. This had been a process which had not always been easy, for she was the educated teacher in a group of virtually illiterate people.

She invented an ecumenical approach of her own, singularly suited to the situation. Single-handed she managed to inspire a unity drive involving no less than thirty-two Zion churches in Natal.

It was as a woman and a mother that she made her appeal for unity. She would challenge the women in other Zion churches in terms like these: "We are all women. We are all mothers. We all have our children, and in this city with its dangers we all worry about our children. We need to pray for them. But if we are divided, our prayers do not seem to have any strength. Let us join together and lament with one another' (*sililelane*) and pray together for the well-being of our children and the unity of all of Zion."

She liked to quote that Bible passage "where Jesus sanctified himself to God because of those who had agreed to accept his word", John 17, verses 21 and 23. Her Zion programme she expressed in this way:

To overcome all discrimination among Zion and to bear one another's burdens. To preach the Gospel to our young people so that they will follow in our footsteps by avoiding beer, tobacco, meat of an animal that just died and was not slaughtered; and unnecessary ornaments such as earrings and necklaces; further, cinema and "concerts"; also dances; for Jesus' sake, the Son of God, He who of His own will and because of his infinite love left His glory and became man among men and in the end died for us sinners.

Grace managed to bring together women belonging to hitherto divided Zion churches, calling the new concern "the Father's Zion", *i Zion ka Baba*. The members make a special effort to visit the widows and other bereaved members of the Zion Church and to support them in various ways. At the beginning there was opposition from some of the leading men, but they relented, and let the women have their way. Grace's mission movement did not in the first place aim at an organized unity. Rather it expressed, as has been suggested, a common concern and a concerted declaration to respect and support one another and to increase the feeling of Zion's togetherness.

My late wife and I visited a quarterly meeting of this *Zion ka Baba,* held in what was then Cato Manor. Some forty women were packed in the one room belonging to Grace's family. Pastor Tshabalala was there in his green vestment with white lace; the women in white and blue garments. Grace led the meeting with immense energy. She invited us two Europeans to preach, which we did and the response was amazing. Grace intoned *"We, womlandela u Jesu",* "Oh, follow Jesus", a clarion call which they sang, each woman lifting her right hand, as though making a renewed oath, or promise, to God. Again they sang about heaven, *"Khaya elihle",* "Thou beautiful home". The singing in that little room was deafening. In the circumstances, this was done also for other than immediately obvious reasons. Grace explained to me: "Here in Cato Manor, you get one room for a family to live in. While you try to pray and sing, people in the next room, on the other side of this corrugated iron wall, dance and drink and swear and use obscene language. Ears are funny", she said, "in a setting like that you only hear the swearing and the obscene language. That is why we Zionists shout in order to drown the voices of the gang of Satan."

Grace Tshabalala brought her organization as a tribute to Zion as a whole and the Nkonyane Zion in particular. She thereby gave an impetus to a Zionist Union movement where Stephen Nkonyane was to take a leading part in the latter years of the nineteen fiftees (p. 295). She was, after all, merely a woman. In July 1958, I sat together with Nkonyane, Rev. A. J. Tshabalala and a few other Zionist leaders, discussing this contribution from their women. "Yes, they can pray all right," said one of them, "but of course man's prayer is stronger, for he is the head and leads in everything." Looking at Mrs Grace Tshabalala, I was not so sure.

Apostolic Women

We are told that in South Africa, African Independent Churches count at least three million adherents. It is likely that, of these, at least two million are women, and it can be safely taken for granted that well over a million are part of the white-dressed, crozier-carrying army of Zionist women. Instead of generalizing on this anonymous mass, we selected three representative women. We mentioned one, Grace Tshabalala and her Zion ka Baba (p. 75). The other two, both leaders of their own Churches, would regard themselves, not as Zionists, but as "Apostolics", and they would point to certain symbols and rituals distinguishing them from Zionism.

I am aware of the fact that in Africa, and not least in the "home-lands" of South Africa, the Church was a women's movement. It functioned as a Women's Lib., long before that term was invented. In the circumstances it was not possible for me, a White man, to come much further in my contacts than what is recorded here (and in *Bantu Prophets,* with its analysis of the significance of women's participation in the movement.) Here is an exciting task awaiting the new generation of African women scholars.

In a few significant cases, women have established themselves as leaders of churches. We shall consider Ma Nku—Mrs. Christina Nku of Evaton, near Johannesburg, and Ma Mbele of Brits, the latter herself an ex-member of Ma Nku's "St. John's Apostolic Church".

Frail and petite, Ma Nku may possibly be overlooked as one walks among the thousands of her faithful assembled for one of the annual festivals. But when this charming little woman leads

the flock packed into her big church, one soon discovers something of her power. In a moment, she has them all clapping
hands with a compulsive rhythm, and speeds them on. Soon she
is dancing herself in front of what seems to be an altar. Her
hypnotic glance obviously has an electrifying effect on the
people. She waves to all, they to her; all move and dance as far
as the accommodation allows. The eighty-year-old leading lady
performs with the energy of a young girl and with the authority
and dignity of somebody who knows that she, and she alone, is in
charge.

Born in 1894 to a family of the Ndebele tribe, who were members of the Dutch Reformed Church, at the age of twelve she
had already had auditions. She heard the voice of God telling
her, "Pray", and she knelt to pray. A year later, she had a terrifying experience—she felt she met Satan himself on the road.
She ran to her mother, who overcame this fright of her daughter's by singing a hymn three times with the words "See the love
of Jesus." For nearly a week she could not eat because of the
terror that she still felt.

In 1914—she was then twenty years old—she was ill and had
visions, in which she saw heaven open. She asked God to be
taken to heaven but was told that she was to live. She developed
a strong aversion to certain kinds of food at this time, particularly pork: "Pork poisons people." In 1920 she married, and in
1924, went through another crisis of ill health, and was left unconscious for some time. In this state, she had a vision of a very
impressive church with many doors; she was later sure that there
were in fact twelve doors. She was told to follow the baptism of
John and Jesus. In her subconscious, she replied that she was
already baptized by the Dutch Reformed Church, and she was
now given to understand that the building she had seen was the
Temple of Jerusalem on Mount Zion, where all the saints are
assembled. This vision was her personal calling to build precisely that Church in South Africa. In this connexion, the young
couple exchanged the Dutch Reformed Church for the Apostolic
Faith Mission, and there she discovered that Europeans too
could be filled with the Holy Spirit, and she felt that this was
her place. Yet even here, she experienced resistance against what
she felt as her spiritual gifts. In an interview she quoted pastor

Zion Women at worship. Upper left: Mrs Grace Tshabalala.

Rev. Job Chiliza, Founder, African Gospel Church.

The Servant, Johannes Galilee Shembe.

Zion congregation with forest of crosses.

Part of the multitude in "Paradise", Ekuphakameni, Durban, next to Isaiah Shembe's mausoleum.

Le Roux as one of those who had objected to some of her more elaborate displays of prophetic rapture.

She decided to establish St. John's Apostolic Church. In one of her visions she had "seen" the exact spot near Evaton where she had to build her new Church. Although she knew that those fields were on European land, she would go there regularly to pray and to meditate, anticipating the day when her Church with its twelve doors would rise there in all its splendour.

It transpired eventually that this particular urban site was set aside for African housing, and Ma Nku could therefore buy that coveted place.

It was above all as a healer that she became known. Attending one of her yearly August meetings together with some ten thousand faithful, I realized that those people would claim, possibly without exception, that they were there because of having been healed by this woman, or because they were awaiting their opportunity for her healing touch.

The Church soon developed into a big enterprise. Ma Nku would pray over water, which thus acquired healing qualities. People would bring thousands of buckets and bottles to the annual meeting, eagerly taking them back home against the time when they might be needed. In fact, she had had to resort to the same device as that attempted by other great water-healers on the Rand—one thinks of her neighbour, the famour prophet McCamel—installing an electric water pump on the property.

This arrangement stood her in good stead for the baptismal services in connexion with the annual conference. Some three hundred people were baptized on the one occasion which we witnessed. There was an outdoor fountain, not unlike a small swimming pool. For two hours, men, women and children were ushered into the font and baptized by a number of pastors in the name of the Father and of the Son and of the Holy Ghost.

Then followed the service in the church. The church with twelve doors was now complete. In 1956 Mrs. Nku had taken a party —including her daughter, a well-known teacher—with her to London in order to see St. Paul's Cathedral, which was reputed to have this sacred number of doors. They did indeed count twelve doors in that English cathedral, and Ma Nku returned to Evaton greatly satisfied with the result of her explorations.[2]

In the packed church there is an atmosphere of joy and jubilation. A girls' choir, and a men's musical band—twenty-six strong —with drums and trumpets, perform with innate rhythm and the convert's enthusiasm.

Mrs. Nku now takes charge of one of the most essential tasks in the Church: around the pool of Bethesda in the church, there are a thousand water-bottles—on one occasion there were nine thousand bottles—and she prays over them. She invites all to turn to the East and to raise their hands, while the band is playing, and the congregation singing "Thou Lord of Jerusalem", and one of her co-workers is saying a prayer. Now all are clapping their hands accompanying the hymn, and the blessing of this good lady is added to the water.

Her success as a healer and her winsome personality have continued to attract a large membership, both on the Rand and in other parts of Southern Africa. Thus we shall later meet her representative in our chapter on Swaziland. In the nature of things it is difficult to make an exact assessment of numbers, but her following probably now numbers some fifty thousand. The faithful contribute generously to the Church, particularly on the occasions of the three main festivals. The income of the Church is considerable—although of late it has been reduced by a spectacular case of theft and another, equally spectacular, lawsuit.

For the occasional visitor there is no easy access to Ma Nku. She is known to be spending her days in prayer and must not be disturbed. Yet she is much more communicative than her younger disciple, *Ma Mbele* (b. 1904). By personal disposition and, possibly, by device, Ma Mbele has established her reputation as a person who is both withdrawn and secretive. We feel that this device is becoming increasingly popular among Zion prophetesses on the

[2] Ma Nku is a world traveller, always determined by her visits abroad to prove the correctness of her visions. Thus she went in 1955 to the Red Sea, in 1956 to St. Paul's Cathedral in London, in 1961 to the United States, and in 1966 to India.

Rand. Very fortunately, Ma Mbele's husband is an ideal public relations officer for their Church.

Ma Mbele had a revelation in 1940 in which she was told by God to heal the sick. She now feels that she neglected that call, and that she did so for more than ten years. She was punished, for in 1951 she "died". God told her in a vision: "I need you as a Healer and Helper of many." Her husband, Bishop Mbele, explains: "You know, 'died'—we mean that she lost consciousness. I saw her failing and then eventually regaining consciousness." She knew then that she could not resist the divine call any longer. Even if she did not herself like this task, she had to do it because she felt constrained by God. To some extent she had been healing people even before this time. But now it was all changed. She had been a member of Ma Nku's St. John's Apostolic Church, but had to establish her own Church now. Her reserve is part of her self-defence for the sake of her spiritual task. Even in interviews, she prefers to let the Bishop do the talking. "She does not speak— she must not lose her power", her husband explained to me.

She regards herself as a visionary. She told me that visions could come to her any time, day or night, and she had to be pre-pared for those extraordinary visitations. This attitude enables her to "read" people, to "see" if certain people are good or bad. She exhorts them to mend their lives, for she has already "seen" that if there is not a change of heart they may die. If a person carrying hidden native medicines enters the Church, she "sees" this: she will jump up and exclaim, "Now there is *umuthi* in the house!" As she prays for people, she will confide to her husband, the Bishop, whether this person is to live or to die, but, as she explained to me, she will not tell this straight to the congrega-tion. The Bishop himself was not beyond the reach of his wife's second sight: "When I go to Johannesburg, she sees whether I meet a lady friend and how she is dressed. When I return home, she will tell me all about it."

In fact, the union of husband and wife—administering Bishop and inspired prophetess—has proved in this case to be an ideal combination. The Bishop, a fine-looking church leader, had ac-quired the necessary know-how of episcopacy in a way that could hardly be bettered: for twelve years he had been the driver of the [Anglican] Bishop of Johannesburg. With his big episcopal ring, his wide circle of acquaintances, and his generous appreciation of his wife's spiritual power, he was a great help; and yet there was never any doubt about the fact that she was the real leader.

By comparison, Ma Nku was at a disadvantage. As she built up her Church she was effectively helped by the charismatic Apostolic pastor, Elias Ketsing (d. 1948), and by her husband. Bishop Nku's death in a railway accident in 1949 was a great loss to her. She now placed her motherly trust in her son, but this younger man, Bishop Johannes Nku, became involved in power struggles with other men in the Church. The breakaway by Bishop Peter Masango, winner of a widely-publicized and costly law-suit at the beginning of the 1970s, was felt by Ma Nku as a terrible blow. She made public statements to the press which showed her to be unhappy and desperate.

It is in their capacity as healers that Ma Nku and Ma Mbele are known and attract their followers. They attend above all to mental disorders: *ufufunyane* and, the hardest of all, *isinyanya,* are among the hysteric illnesses which they tackle, in social situations where crises of social and cultural deprivation are, of necessity, numerous. There were also reports of cases of rheumatism and similar disorders which had been healed. Ma Mbele particularly stressed that she had difficulties with the *isinyanya* demon: "It does not agree with the Church. I have to fight hard to bring those people into the Church, for the demon protests against going into the Church."

The sacrifice of an animal is sure to increase the strength of the healing. Bishop Mbele explained to me how the prophetess would "baptize" the beast before it was slaughtered. Later the bones are burned in order to produce especially valuable ashes. The blood, together with specially consecrated water, and the ashes, are mixed in a tub placed in the vestry, and this concoction is particularly helpful, especially in cases where demons cause difficulties. As we shall see, Ma Nku's representative in Swaziland can claim great healing successes through resorting to similar sacrificial devices.

84

Job Chiliza (1886–1963)

As leader of the *African Gospel Church,* Job Chiliza was critical of
Zionists. He knew the movement from the inside, for in his
younger days he had been a member of one of the most *uMoya*-
charged, and perhaps least reputable, of Zion groups, that of
Ezra Mbonambi. In certain respects he shared Zionist attitudes.
But Chiliza would claim that he had found something more
valuable, and above all more Biblical, than the Zion ways.

It was suggested to him by a Government official responsible
for dealing with Church recognition that since he was now head
of a Government-recognized Church, he should amalgamate the
whole number of Zionist groups with his African Gospel Church
—but he turned down this tempting proposal: "It is impossible",
he replied.

I wish I could convey a sufficiently dynamic and rich impression of this man Job Chiliza. When he preached he looked like
Paul Robeson, perhaps a somewhat bowed, more chastened Paul
Robeson. His voice was deep and velvety. There was balance and
finesse and sheer goodness in his strong, heavy and charming
personality. One cannot forget the impression of him leading the
worship of his congregation. The singing was deafening, followed by even more lively prayer. In the crowd of some seven
hundred Zulu men and women, some here and there would suddenly jump up and shout "Hallelujah!". When all began praying
at once, it was as though a tremendous African storm was
gathering strength. In the midst of it all, Job Chiliza stood there
on the platform. An immense volume of sound rising and falling, swelling and surging and fading, directed by the two
fingers of Chiliza's slow-moving right hand. One felt that he held
them all in that strong and quiet hand of his.

He was on his own now, as an uncontested leader of men.
But he had been through decades of difficult contacts and con-
tests with Black Zionists and White Pentecostals. From this pro-
tracted struggle, this long spiritual pilgrimage, he had emerged
a wise, subtle, and firm church leader.

The family represented a noble tradition in Natal Protestantism, that of the American Board Mission. His father had served
as groom to Dr. F. B. Bridgman, the mission pioneer near Dur-

ban. This gave Chiliza his educational opportunity. He had a Standard V education, and spoke English well. The mission also taught him his trade as a shoemaker. In his later years, he studied for Standard VI in a correspondence course. He felt he needed this qualification in order to be appointed a Marriage Officer of his Church.

In 1958, my wife and I stayed with the Chiliza's for a few days at their home Faschadale, south of Durban [Now It Can Be Told!] On his little farm—seventeen acres, "Black spot in White area"—he had built a special house for European guests, with three rooms and a kitchen. As a matter of fact it had not been used for years when we stayed there. One could not have wished for a more thoughtful and gracious host. On those occasions he spoke about himself:

I was born a Christian. Like Jeremiah, I was prepared in my mother's womb. Since my birth I have never beaten another person, never deceived anybody else, never been in jail, never spoken a bad word about others. I was born like that. I have been looking for truth ever since I was born. As a boy, I followed other boys and took to drinking and the other things boys do. But my heart was up there in heaven.

[The Bible?] Oh, the Bible is my friend. I never depart from my Bible. On a steamship, there is a clock on the captain's deck. That is the Bible. The Bible is my compass.

[Most beloved Bible verses?] John 17:21. Africans and Europeans must be one, and love one another. That is the mind of God. If you stay there, you will see every nation, Black or White, in the right perspective. Then, Matt. 28:18–20, and Mark. 16.

I began in the American Board Mission and stayed with them for six years. There were no bad ways there. I taught Holy Spirit in the American Board and my listeners were, also in the American Board, baptized in the Holy Spirit, even if this Mission never teaches the Spirit. All that group I took with me to the other Churches of which I became a member.

Then I went to the Zion Church. I met six girls who preached, and they had the Holy Ghost. I listened to them. They had been taught by Ntanzi of the (Apostolic) Faith Mission, a follower of Ezra Mbonambi, and Ntanzi was one of Le Roux's men. In 1922, on a Sunday, I was baptized by the Holy Spirit. I felt as if I was flying right up. Only after a while did I realize that I was still here on earth. But Zion was a transitional stage for me. They are just like wind. They do not stand on the foundation of Christ. Because to baptize once, or ten times, is all the same to me. God does not look at me because I was baptized ten times in much water. God looks inside to see if I have repented.

In 1926, I went to Cooper because I was hungry for the Holy Spirit.

This was Archibald Cooper, whom we have already met in the very first springtime of South African Pentecost. Forty years later, these Africans still remembered Cooper's gift of speaking in tongues. *"Hau, Cooper yena wakhuluma kakhulu"*: "That Cooper —he could speak." Cooper was at this time conducting an evangelistic tent campaign in Durban.

"One night six-seven Zulus came", Mrs. Cooper relates.[3] "They sat at the back of the tent. Afterwards they came to thank Cooper for being allowed to listen. One of them said: 'My name is Job Chiliza. Mfundisi, I am a Christian and I speak to my people but I am not preaching the gospel that you are preaching, and I feel God wants me to preach the Full Gospel.'

'Some time ago I saw a vision of a man. God told me he was sending that man to me. He will be your spiritual father.'" Chiliza suggested that Cooper was that man of the dream.

Chiliza joined the Full Gospel Church and was baptized once again, this time by Cooper and in the Umhlatuze River. Chiliza, the shoemaker, was accompanied by Nondaba, the bread-delivery man, with his horse-drawn bread-cart, and Ngcobo and Mseleko, the kitchen boys. Nondaba, an enormous Zulu, had been a member of the Swedish Holiness Covenant. He was hesitant to join Cooper, but his wife showed him the way. She received the Holy Spirit, and some time later, he followed. There was nothing else to do but to sever his old connexions. "Swedes don't like the Spirit", he said, as if stating a well-known and generally accepted fact.

Chiliza and his colleagues developed a strong African congregation as part of Full Gospel. In 1942, he suggested to the white leader that they be allowed to establish an African Full Gospel Church with a Committee and a Constitution of its own. This was refused, and Chiliza left, taking his African Church with him—all the leaders and possibly seven thousand followers. This was the most spectacular breakaway in Durban during the Second World War. But we are only acquainted with one side of the quarrel; Chiliza's presentation of his case—in an interview with me—may have been reconstructed during the years 1942– 58. Nevertheless it has a pathos of its own:

[3] Ms. "How Bro. Archibald U. Cooper was Converted." Full Gospel Archives, Irene, South Africa.

"In 1926 when I joined you", he had told Cooper, "you promised to help us. But you are not helping me now. You put yourself in front before my children, and you put me behind. But I am the father of these children, whom I have borne in the Spirit. You are their grandfather, but you cannot take my place. These are my children. You try to separate them from me."

Chiliza's co-worker Julius Mzimela told the European, in that subtle and sharp way in which Africans always score and which Europeans find so difficult to match: "I have always hitherto taken you as a man whose word could be trusted"—to which the European, hurt and pompous, replies: "Do you mean to say that I am a liar?" Mzimela retorts, "I never said that." The European turned to Chiliza and Mzimela: "Well, do what you like. Don't you believe that you will be able to take all the people. Some, I am sure, will remain with me." They all left as "one Body"—an appropriately exact and rich image for that group.

Even Chiliza could not restrain a word of criticism against the Whites:

> The sad thing is that a European missionary does not really like to see us [Africans] being blessed in our work. Instead they grow envy inside. You open your heart to him; yet he does not like you to grow. When I try to explain our way of looking at things, he gets angry.
>
> When you speak the truth there is a quarrel. I spoke to Rev. Cooper. My pastor and I are grown-up people. We need a constitution. They want a say in the Church. Then, he said, you can go away.
>
> But I have been greatly helped by other Europeans, of the National Government in Pretoria, such as a School Inspector who visited us in 1958.
>
> The European does not understand. One day in our Full Gospel meeting, Mizraim Dlamini from Ceza and the missionary there spoke in favour of a leading Zulu pleading that he be allowed to carry on as a polygamous Christian. But that European did not understand. He can shout. "Jesus Christ is returning soon, Halleluia". But the demons in my heart are too clever. The Devil is too smart. With a foreign tongue you can never reveal the real mysteries. Yet I need someone to teach me to open the eyes of faith. The Holy Spirit and teaching must go together.

Even now Chiliza was not prepared to strike out on his own. He took his people to another White-led group, the Pentecost Holiness Church, with American leadership. On their advice he called his organization the African Gospel League. After another

88

five years, developments forced Chiliza to form his African Gospel Church. Such was Chiliza's standing, and his contacts, that only two years later his Church was recognized by the Government. It is interesting in this connection to note that one of his American promoters-behind-the-scenes, Pastor C. J. Lucas, received an official letter (dated February 17, 1953) formulated by a civil servant, one of the foremost architects of *apartheid:*

The letter stressed that the Department in principle favours independence of Bantu churches, from European control, when the ability of the office-bearers to administer the affairs of the Church in an efficient manner has been established.

Chiliza certainly was an efficient church leader in his own way, but he was more than that: he was at the same time an embodiment of the aspirations and longings of his group, spokesman and prophet.

Throughout all these vicissitudes, Chiliza retained a surprising liking and even admiration for Europeans: "I always find them in the light." In a passage of the Union Buildings he had caught a glimpse of the foremost of all Europeans. Together with other leaders of African Independent Churches he asked for an audience with one of the Department officials in order to discuss some church matter. And there, in the corridor, he saw Dr. Verwoerd: "I shall die satisfied to have seen the face of Dr. Verwoerd", he told me.

But it is as a preacher and Bible expositor that Chiliza is most remembered. Six years after his death, we sat down with some of his former colleagues and prompted them to characterize his preaching, particularly in view of the homiletical effect of the example that his preaching had given.

"He joined the Old Testament and the New together." His interest was typological, showing how the function of the Old Testament is to anticipate the New, the result of the New Testament being to demonstrate how the Old Testament prophecies are fulfilled. At the same time he found himself in a polemical situation, showing what he felt to be the fatuousness of Zion's Bible interpretation: certain taboos against swine flesh and medicine were wrong; sacrifice of goats was wrong, *because* Jesus had been sacrificed, etc.

There was a typological parallel between the great figures in the Bible. Adam, after the operation on his rib, had a wound—and Eve lived because of this wound. In the same way, the wounds of Jesus benefit the Church, his Bride, living through his wounds. The ram, sacrificed by Abraham on behalf of Isaac —Jesus sacrificed as the sacrificial lamb. The blood of the Passover Lamb on the doorposts (Ex. 12) was seen as a parallel to the liberating Blood of Jesus.

We heard Chiliza preach on John 7:38. "He that believeth on me, out of his belly shall flow rivers of living water." One cannot but recall his deep voice, with its humorous generous grunts interspersing the flow of speech.

His explanation seemed very African. We recalled from East Africa that the sensitive place was the "stomach" rather than the heart or the brain: *Nimewaza tumboni mwangu*, "I thought in my stomach", is the Swahili expression.

We put Jesus too much in the head, behind the hard bone of the skull. But Jesus said that whoever believes in him, life will flow from his belly. Let us not place Jesus in the hard forehead, but in the stomach, where he can lie nicely and softly, just as Jesus lay in Mary's womb. Jesus finds his resting place there. That is where the power is; that is where Jesus is. The belly is the power-station of the body. Look at this arm of mine. If the stomach does not do its work, what can the arm do? We men-folk have sinned, for we have not sufficiently appreciated the fact that it is from the belly that power comes. The glory and power of Jehovah is to be found in the stomach.

The stomach is a great thing. Our food is digested there. When we are hungry we realize how important the stomach is. Jesus felt this when he was tempted by the Devil in the Desert. For forty days he had to go hungry in the desert (*walanjiswa*). Satan knows that in order to tempt a person, he has to see to it that this person is hungry. But from a person filled with Jesus, power and blessing will flow.

Not only the presidency but also the gift of preaching was inherited by his son, William Chiliza, B. A. In listening to him preaching, I had the opportunity of studying the birth, or emergence, of a sermon. The congregation was assembled on a Sunday afternoon in 1969 in their Church hall in Fountain Lane, in the run-down central area of Durban. Some 220 members were assembled—100 men and 120 women, including four little children. The congregation began by singing and praying for about half an hour—a deafening volume of sound. Job Chiliza had told me that he felt embarrassed by these demonstrations of the Spirit, but there was now little that could be done about it. Slips of old newspapers were handed out to the men, a practical device as they were liable to spit or vomit to express their pent-up feelings. The whole act appeared to provide these faithful with something akin to a weekly emotional bath: labourers, taxi-drivers, shop-assistants, house-"girls", housewives—the week of labour with its harsh experience was left behind; for an hour or two they were lifted up on high, into heavenly places. But it was more than that. The release of these pent-up feelings had its social counterpart. Here was an exercise in corporate cleansing. It was more than an individual exercise, it was the corporate group, the actual Body which purified itself—and the African preacher was very much part of the body of his own people.

I was suddenly asked to preach, and the picturesque name of the shabby little side-street—Fountain Lane—suggested to me the text John 7: 37–38, "If any man thirst, let him come unto me, and drink. ..." I spoke of a dry land—and the Fountain.

My little homiletical effort in Zulu was followed by a long ex-position by William Chiliza on the same text. He was immediately at home with all these images and what is more, he could bring them to life: "In the dry places, in the desert, nothing can live, except the camel. [I hadn't thought of that.] How does a camel exist in the desert? He gathers water in certain parts of his body" —this he illustrated by demonstrative grasping gestures of his two hands to his shoulders and to his stomach.

In order to be pedagogical and relevant to "Africa", I had referred to Kalahari and Sahara. But no, the desert which haunted these people was further away and nearer home: the desert of Judaea in Matt. 4, with the Devil lurking about, trying to tempt even the Lord, and as the sermon developed he found one oasis here and another there from which he could bring refreshing streams of water to his expectant people.

In his youth, *Nicholas Bhengu* had contacts with Job Chiliza, impressed as he was by Chiliza's concern for a Biblical message.

Sometimes Nicholas Bhengu and his movement have been dis-cussed in surveys of African Independent Churches.[4] If we have

[4] Katesa Schlosser, *Eingeborenenkirchen in Süd- und Südwestafrika,* 1958, and W. J. Hollenweger, *Enthusiastisches Christentum,* 1969.

refrained from so doing it is definitely not because of a lack of interest in Bhengu. We have followed his work for decades. But Bhengu's person and work have a unique quality and must never be confused with the general Independent Church movement. Organizationally, he has retained certain links with the Assemblies of God. This, as he would maintain, was necessary for him in order to obtain Government recognition.[5] But his message has as he would insist, a certain affinity with that of the Plymouth Brethren and the Baptists,[6] and even more strongly than his friend Job Chiliza he would as a matter of course emphasize the distance between Zion and himself.[7]

Trends

In the introduction to this chapter we emphasized the broad variety of type and ideology between the five 'Spirit' churches discussed here. This we claim has been amply illustrated by these rapid sketches.

We dealt with two groups which are "Zionist in a strict sense", thus forming a link with our first chapter: E. Mdlalose and Grace Tshabalala; further, with two 'Apostolic' groups under Ma Nku and Ma Mbele; and, finally, with J. Chiliza's 'Gospel' Church, related to Full Gospel. The five of them together are largely representative of the general character and trend of Zion in South Africa, the term "Zion" here understood in a *wider* sense, including also Apostolics.

Some differences in structure should be mentioned. Churches with women as presidents as in the case of Ma Nku and her sister in the ministry, Ma Mbele, are exceptions. At the same time the role of women as local leaders should be emphasized. Women carry both the financial burden and the evangelistic outreach.

---

[5] A. A. Dubb, forth-coming book on N. Bhengu and his church.

[6] Ph. Mayer, *Townsmen or Tribesmen*, Capetown 1961, p. 193.

[7] Dr. Katesa Schlosser has written a valuable book in German on some of the Independent Church leaders. It is unfortunate, however, that in her attempt to characterize Bhengu's ambition to create a community for his congregations she should quote as his sociological ideal "Sovjet Kolchosen" (collectives) *op. cit.*, p. 35; this is quoted by Hollenweger, p. 150. It is unthinkable that Bhengu would deliberately have used that term, and one does not need to know very much about the situation in South Africa in order to query the wisdom of ascribing such ideals to this well-known Christian leader in South Africa.

Grace Tshabalala's co-operative initiative (p. 75) must be mentioned.

This may be the place to emphasize one of Zion's great contributions to African society. Some of the charismatic churches are very much a men's world, with the women taking a subordinate place, but such churches are few indeed. By and large, Zion gave the women a central and honoured position. In healing activities and in the worship and social life of the church, new emotional contacts of care and concern were found where women and men could meet on equal terms, because in the last resort these terms were regarded as those of the ultimate authority, the Spirit.

This development must be seen together with parallel changes in African society as a whole. The nineteen-fifties may well represent a decisive turningpoint. The collective anonymous leadership exercised by the women masses in the bus strike on the Rand, 1953 (*"Azikwelwa"*) and the brave speech by Mrs Natalie Nxumalo, Mpande's Day, 1955, to the men of Zululand are dramatic and creative break-throughs for a fundamental re-interpretation of the role of the African woman. New activity on the part of women in business enterprises is another important economic and sociological factor.

But nowhere in any of the modern institutions, was this role as strong as that of the *"Manyano"*, the women's organizations in the Churches. This applies by degrees to all churches, Mission-related *and* Independent. Taking into consideration the particular social level with which we are dealing here, the Zion and Apostolic churches were undoubtedly showing the others the way. "Of course, man's prayer is stronger, for he is the head", the Zion preachers at Cato Manor, Durban, told Mrs. Grace Tshabalala (cf. p. 75). I noticed her smile, wise as that of Mona Lisa. She may have felt that, ultimately, prayer comes not from— the head, but from the heart.

There is also the difference between city-oriented and rurally-based churches. Job Chiliza was very much at home in Durban where he had spent most of his life. On this point he shared experiences with Mrs Grace Tshabalala. Her world, too, was Durban, including the two narrow sectors of the city to which she had access: on the one hand, the kitchen of the Swiss family for which she had laboured throughout a life-time four and a half days a

93

week *and* on the other, the backrooms and little garages in African townships where she witnessed Thursday afternoons and throughout the week-ends. Her rhythm of life thus epitomized that of a million sisters in Zion. As a city, Durban differed from the cosmopolitan Rand, the latter a melting pot of many peoples and languages. Durban remained largely Zulu, and for the Zulu there were here much closer links with rural connections "back home" than on the Rand. Mrs. Tshabalala would feel obliged on occasions to pay visits to Charlestown and its Nkonyane head-quarters. Chiliza had managed to get a footing in what was at the time one of the few remaining "black spots in White areas". He used to leave the city occasionally and visit his little Faschadale farm—he especially liked to celebrate important church festivals there. Chiliza—such is my estimation of his role—was one of the most outstanding Church leaders in South Africa in this century, and, as was to be expected, altogether unknown to Whites or Blacks outside his chapel in narrow Fountain Lane, in what was then the African slum in the centre of Durban.

3. The Church of the Spirit and the Church of Light

We shall now meet two of the most remarkable leaders of Zulu churches, Paulo Nzuza and Timothy Cekwane. They share certain fundamental characteristics with Zion. They claim, of course, to be "Spirit churches" and that, as we shall see, at a higher degree, or pitch, than any ordinary Zion group.

Yet, they insist upon not being mixed up with the Zionists, whom they regard as largely misguided. Both Nzuza and Cekwane are conscious of a unique position in the history of the Church, and possibly in the history of the salvation of the Black man. They are, each in his own way, original and creative innovators, in their turn establishing new traditions.

With both there was a similarly strong conviction, on the part of the Founder, of being overwhelmed and constrained by the Spirit of God. They had been given new, luminous visions and found for their message new and original concepts by which to integrate and organize their entire understanding of the Holy Book. That mysterious Book may have been written and printed years before their time but its hidden and unique meaning was only now revealed, through these Founders and to their enthusiastic followers.

Paulo Nzuza (1896–1959)

The African's search is for Black identity. The independent Church movement is a corporate attempt within the context of this search. None has struggled more intensely with the question of identity than Paulo Nzuza. An assiduous Bible student, he found his solution in the Bible.

Living in South Africa, he could not but be struck by the divisions between peoples and nations. The very appearance of men proved to Nzuza that they were different. The colour of the skin, the shape of the nose, the form of the hair; all this testified to some secret basic divisions. Some white ideologists had said as much; and if they were learned Hebraists they knew God as *"Hammabdil"*: the Divider, who divided the waters from the firmament, and heaven from dry land and day from night.

These were cosmic events that had occurred long ago. More disturbing were the divisions between man and man. But here too, Nzuza's Bible provided the solution. Adam being the common father of all, it was with Noah and his three sons that the divisions had appeared. Here it was that a terrible event had occurred: Noah cursed Canaan, Gen. 9:25. In the prolongation of these divisions it was that Nzuza's "Church of the Holy Spirit" emerged as an answer, no, as *the* answer to the longing of centuries. He had found an answer which appeared Biblical, logical, and totally satisfying to himself and to his faithful followers. He had worked out a highly original, grandiose system of his own, built on the firm foundations of a series of selected verses from his Zulu Bible. It was the kind of system which could, in fact, emerge only in the divided racial world of South Africa, reflecting, and indeed emphasizing, its schizophrenic character. It served to sanction that closely-knit, rather secretive church of his, the Church of the Spirit, *alias* the Church of the Canaanites, with its headquarters at Hammersdale, some twenty miles inland from Durban.

They were a devoted group. In principle all the "Servants"—the term used instead of "pastors"—with their families live together at headquarters.

They were all in sober black—even their dress emphasized the difference from the ordinary white-robed Zionists.

My informant, a seemingly well-balanced and integrated person, was anxious to draw the line between their own real Spirit Church and ordinary Zionists: "Zionists do not understand. They have not grasped the significance of that fundamental key verse of 1 Cor. 14:27, 'If any man speak in an unknown tongue, let it be by two, or at the most by three, and that by course and let one interpret.'" 1 Cor. 14:27 (A. V.).[1]

Only Nzuza's Church has grasped and realized the full meaning of this great statement.

Paulo Nzuza was born a leader. His mother was of the Zulu clan. He thus had royal blood in his veins and was aware of it. He felt at home when he represented his Church at the Royal Kraal at Nongoma. He was big and sturdy and strong, an immensely powerful and authoritative man. There was no hesitation or vacillation with him. God himself had given him a unique revelation.

It is difficult to convey an adequate idea of the extraordinary strength of this man's ego and personality. At his headquarters at Himeville and in his chapel in Durban, I was impressed by this uncompromising seriousness, this unyielding claim of his to have been set aside by God for a high purpose. My personal contacts with Paulo Nzuza himself were admittedly few. More decidedly than other church leaders he kept this inquisitive White man at a distance. But I must at least register this overwhelming impression of an angular person, different from others. Zion prophets were of often round and happy, jolly and jocular; not Nzuza.

The young boy had early contacts with the Whites; his father had been a servant of Dr. Bridgman, the leading American missionary near Durban, and Paulo had had some years in school. His active frame of mind found an outlet in the Salvation Army, where as a young man he had his first experience as a preacher and as a leader of men.

Then the *Day* came: the ninth day in the month of May, 1916, at Stanger, near the grave of King Shaka, "there descended upon one Paulo Nzuza the Blessed Spirit of the Holy Ghost, who declared through this the chosen leader of his followers that according to the Scriptures he and they should be the elected family of Jehova God according to the texture of their

---

[1] My interviews with Paulo Nzuza himself June–July 1958, with "Servants" and members of his Church 1958, and August 1969. T. W. S. Mthembu Notebook, on P. Nzuza and others. Idem, special notes on "The Late Bishop Paul Nzuza", 46 pp. A statement of the Doctrines of the Church of the Holy Ghost and The Constitution of Its Governing Authority.
Bantu Affairs file 251/214 Pretoria.

skin and hair. Upon the 17th day of June, 1917, the Blessed Spirit of the Holy Ghost prescribed and ordained that the said Paulo Nzuza and his inspired followers were to preach the Gospel" (from the official constitution of the Church).

These two transforming events, affecting first the leader, and then a year later, his flock, formed the "Church's foundation" (*isisekelo se Nkonzo*). Every sermon centres round those experiences, and testimony and worship echo with this unique revelation.

Nzuza felt he had to find an answer to the most disturbing of all problems in the various interpretations of the history of salvation: Where, in the history of Salvation, do the Blacks come in? The Bible had revealed that there were three sons of Noah: Shem, Japheth and Ham. First, from Shem a line proceeds via Abraham, Jacob and Moses to John the Baptist and Jesus. They were all circumcised, and it is surmised that they were all "in the line of water". This is the line of the Jews, the Church of the Jews.

Secondly, there is the line from Japhet *via* Esau or Edom, on which are to be found the Edomites or Gentiles. This line leads in one bold leap from Esau to "Saula Paula" or St. Paul, the apostle to the Gentiles or the uncircumcised Whites and the "line of water". Noah had three sons, however, and Ham's son Canaan was cursed: "a servant of servants shall he be unto his brethren" (Gen. 9:25). Seen from the standpoint of harsh South African reality there could be no doubt as to the identity of the heir of this awesome curse.

"For us, the line of Moses is closed." On that line the seed of Abraham had been told to follow the order of circumcision, an order which had not been given to the Blacks. The Esau—St. Paul line likewise failed to reach the Blacks. The non-circumcised therefore had to wait: there was an interim period of anxious suspense—"from Saulo Paulo to Paulo Nzuza"—until that Day, May 9, 1916, when the Holy Ghost descended upon Nzuza.

"We came in via the Resurrection", into the history of salvation. The passage of the Bible referred to here is Acts 10, with St. Peter's vision of "a great sheet knit at the four corners, and let down to the earth", containing a great number of beasts of the earth. "We, who do not follow the Moses—John the Baptist—

Jesus line, were born then." "That vision was our Christmas", they explained, "the creatures of the earth represented nations, and particularly the Zulu nation."

"What date was it, when that sheet was lowered down from heaven?" they asked me. I had to admit that, very unfortunately, I did not know such an elementary fact. It happened at Christmas, they assured me, more specifically December 25.

This development was to find its fulfilment in the prophecy of Nzuza. Corresponding to these "lines", there are three churches, and no more: the Church of the Jews, the Church of the Gentiles, and the Church of the Canaanites, or of the Holy Ghost, founded by Paulo Nzuza, the *Mqhalisi*, the "Founder" or Initiator. The remarkable thing about this latter Church is that its members, and they alone, possess the Holy Ghost in His fulness, because they, and they alone, do not "follow the water-line". They have found something which is greater than water, namely the Holy Spirit. They do thus not baptize with water, but by the laying on of hands and the Bible on the head of the candidate; they continue praying fervently until the candidate receives the Spirit. But this negative attitude to the use of water for baptism, proves that this church alone is "in the New Testament". Water was connected with the Old Testament, while Nzuza and his people have taken the decisive step into the New Covenant, that of the Spirit.

One cannot but be impressed by the systematic constructive urge of this Bible study. The tripartition in the Bible found by Nzuza is different from that conventionally emphasized by other South African prophets: these most often refer to Whites, Blacks and Asians (or "Indians"). Here the three peoples are the Jews, the Gentiles and the Canaanites, or Nzuza's own church. This is according to certain "lines" in the Bible. Nzuza used that English noun in Zulu: *"i-line"*, *"nge-line"*. "The Bible line is like a railway line, and the Spirit is the engine", one of the "Servants" told me. There are thus three patriarchs or forefathers (*okhokho*); Jacob, Esau and Canaan; three church founders: Simon Peter, Saula Paula and—Paulo Nzuza: "We Zulus were left alone, St. Peter and St. Paul never came to us".

There are three different lines of succession: first, that of circumcision, which also is the "water-line", although this element is shared with the second line, that of non-circumcision; and thirdly, the line of the Spirit, that of Nzuza (1 Cor. 14:27). There are also three different kinds of worship: that of Moses— Simon Peter; that of St. Paul; and that of the Spirit. There are three different languages of worship, Hebrew, Greek and "a third language which only we understand", that of the Spirit.

At my visit to the Church headquarters in August 1969, one of the leading pastors defined very neatly and sharply the Biblical authority for each of the three parties concerned:

I. The Church of the *Jews*: Acts 2
II. The Church of the *Gentiles*: Acts 10
III. The 'Church of the *Spirit*', born May 9 [1916]: 1 Cor 14:27.

With this unique revelation imparted to Paulo Nzuza, it was important to understand his place and role in the history of salvation.

In our brief presentation of Paulo Nzuza in the second edition of *Bantu Prophets,* we took a risk in placing him among the Messiahs. His genealogical speculations and the extraordinary esteem in which he was held by his church led us in that direction. We should have avoided this. It was misleading to include him in our tentative series of five Bantu Messiahs. His son and successor told us as much at the time of our visit to the Church in 1969. To categorize Paulo Nzuza in this way "is a blasphemy", he told us, and we are all the more ready to agree with him as we now question the category of messianism as applied by various observers in sweeping terms to the prophet movement as a whole.

Our informant was very precise in his claims for Nzuza's position. He was not an Apostle, like St. Peter of the Church of the Jews or St. Paul of the Church of the Gentiles. He was an *initiator, Mqhalisi,* like Moses of old, for the Holy Spirit began anew with him. This same Holy Spirit had ceased to operate after the time of the New Testament. Then the world had been lacking true Christianity for all this time, all these centuries, until at long last on May 9, 1916, the Holy Spirit descended on this man

Mfunwa Nzuza, thereby initiating the New Community, this Church of the Spirit, which alone understood 1 Cor. 14:27.

This difference between Jews, Gentiles and the *Tertium genus* is in fact characteristic not only of conditions here on this South African soil, but in heaven, too. It all began early, on the first pages of the Old Testament. Something went wrong in the relationship between the Gentiles and the Zulu: the Bible proof is to be found in Gen. 25:23, the Lord's explanation to Rebecca: "Two nations are in thy womb ... and the elder shall serve the younger".

Zionists and Pentecostals may indeed speak with tongues, but they do not have the key to the Scriptures, which consists in a right and full understanding of the key passage of the Bible— 1 Cor. 14:27—in the version conveyed by Nzuza himself. This *one* verse in the Book is "the fieldglass" through which to look at the whole Bible. Not the Initiator himself but a Bible verse is thus the fieldglass. There are, according to Nzuza, six points in the verse: 1. Tongues; 2. Two; 3. Three; 4. Only (at the most; *kuphela*); 5. Each in turn, "by course"; 6. Interpretation.

If any man speak in an unknown tongue,
let it be by two, or at the most, by three,
and that by course; and let one interpret.

Only Nzuza's church demonstrates that it understands this verse, and thereby the Bible as a whole, in its fulness. The whole drama of speaking with tongues is performed in the spotlight of this verse. Three players are involved; Nzuza's church is paramount, in fact *hors concours,* in that it engages this interplay of *three* actors: the Spirit-filled speaker with tongues; the interpreter; and the notary, whose task it is to record in a "book of prophecy" the inspired words conveyed by the interpreter.

In that intense act of the Spirit, the roles will soon be changed: the interpreter now himself starts to speak with tongues, and is in his/her turn interpreted by a colleague.

In 1958, at Chesterville (Durban) we witnessed a charismatic performance: a table is placed at the front of the chapel. A and B stand on each side, and a pastor, a "Servant" (*Mkonzi*) places himself between them, in front of the table.

There is a short hymn, "Come down Holy Spirit", repeated

many times. This serves to help the actors to warm up, get into the performance. *A* moves up and down on his feet, cutting the air with his flailing arms. *B* performs the same rigid, mechanical exercises.

A, with closed eyes, speaking in tongues: *Eroy, roy, emeroy,* (screaming now) *meroy, chura, chura, churāāā, era yisa, hura erei, amiray* (screaming the whole time out of the depths of his subconscious).

B, also with closed eyes, shaking and moving mechanically up and down on his feet, screaming in Zulu:

> He says, the Spirit,
> He says, the Holy Spirit,
> He says, that Glory,
> He says, the Bible brings out his words,
> He says, the Great One is coming.

B now starts to speak with tongues:

> *Didi di di di*
> *ko ko ko ko ko ko*
> *ehe hehe he he*
> [sound of a hippopotamus]
> *popo he he he*

A (snorting in tongues) *roy roy, rey, bot soi,*

A now interpreting *B*'s inspired statement:

> He says, ye have not come to receive the Holy Spirit,
> He says, the Spirit is coming,
> He says, the Spirit will not be tired.
> He says, I, the Spirit of Heaven,
> He says, to the Blacks and to the Whites,
> The Spirit speaks so that it will be understood also by Whites.
> This is a wonderful teaching.

The hymn, "Come down Holy Spirit" is repeated, after which there enter two women, *C* and *D*. During the singing of the hymn, they begin to shake and become attuned to their roles. One appears to be crying. Both hold their arms half raised, shaking and screaming. The responses follow each other very rapidly.

C screaming at a terribly high pitch:
> *ho ho hāāā*
> *sininini husōōō*

D, a fine looking, slightly-built woman with a suffering expression, obviously under some pressure:
> She says, the Father
> She says, Jesus in heaven
> She says, there has appeared the way of Truth
> She says, I myself
> She says, Miracle
> She says, the Sent Ones
> She says, he is working
> She says, Words
> She says, you will bring
> She says, servants
> She says, you will marvel.

C screaming,
D concluding her contribution with a spiritual
> *dsiiii* − − −

I underline that the glossolalic sounds as represented here were what I personally as an observer could catch and annotate on the occasion. I did *not* use a tape-recorder at that time. In any case the structure of the sounds appeared to the listener as a repetitive babbling, not very different maybe from what Felicitas Goodman has rendered from Mexico. Comparing the two glossolalists, *A* shows a greater variety than *C*.

The interpretation by *B* and *D* has marked stereotyped character, proceeding by hurried, brief assertions. These do not have the homiletic or pedagogical function common among White glossolalists. We also notice the remarkable introductory words "He says"; "She says", *not,* "Thus saith the Lord", which is the common introduction among other glossolalists.[2]

The Servant in the centre makes a sign with his hand, at which all kneel to pray. To say that there was a deafening volume of

[2] Felicitas D. Goodman, "Phonetic analysis of glossolalia in four cultural settings", in *Journal for Scientific Study of Religion,* VIII, 1969.
Idem, *Speaking in Tongues,* Chicago 1972.
Nils G. Holm, *"Glossolaliens kulturmönster och ljudstruktur ... i Svensk Finland",* Lund 1974. (stencil)

sound, produced by the one hundred men and women in that little chapel, would be a gross understatement. Fierce screams and squeals are interjected with cries: *Jehova, Jehova* or *Moya Oyingcwele*!

That fundamental text in their Bible, 1 Cor. 14:27, has an injunction about prophecy: "Let it be by two, or at the most by three". Nzuza's church is unique in that it emphasizes this numerical situation. The two are supplemented by a third, the Servant, who stands between them. He has to enter the interpreted message in a *Book of Prophecies*. At the end of each month, all prophecies of that month entered into this important book are read for the edification of the flock. They also ascertain whether they have been fulfilled or not. Individuals mentioned in the prophecies are challenged to state whether they have done anything in fulfilment of what was prophesied for them.

A thorough psychological study of the contents of this *Book of Prophecies* in its social context would be instructive. In the circumstances, however, we can do no more than reproduce examples of the realm of ideas to be found here: evidently it is a world of threatening dangers and accusations.

23.5.1954. The One who Waits for the Holy Spirit (*o Mele u Moya Oyingcwele*), Member Nxumalo says, the Holy Spirit says, the Living says, Listen to me, my people, I proclaimed about my kraal and that which was brought down from heaven ... In my kraal there are three short men who carry three bundles tied together. They bump them here and there in the kraal. The first one is like a small river appearing at the sleeping place of the daughter of the leader, the one who sleeps in the temple. The medicine called *idungamuzi* brings bad luck into my kraal. The Holy Spirit says that in my kraal there are harmful things. There is a bad shadow (*itunzi elibi*). In the kraal Jona is the one who is disturbing (*zamazamisa*) my kraal ... He is associated with those who come out from my kraal and he acted as their secretary. You must write to Him Who Walks Before You (=obviously the leader of the Church) in order to find out who that Jona of my kraal is. If he leaves, the Church will be well again. These three men collected the soil which falls from their feet, that soil with which they kill.

December 1956. The prophets Member Ny. Khumbuza and Miss Ngubane. Interpreter Miss Ngubane. Thus says Jehovah in heaven. There is an Angel with a sieve. The Great One (obviously the Leader of the Church) must tell him so that God shows him what to do. He says, These are temptations. He says, Ye Servants (=pastors), ye must pray and be strong. There will be a sieve for the Servants from Miss

Ngubane (*isihlungo kubakhonzi eka Nkosazana Ngubane*). Thus says Jehovah, there will be sifting, beginning with the Great Ones and ending with the small ones.

The whole of the Bible, but particularly the first book, Genesis, provided material for Nzuza's teaching. The *Mqhalisi* himself ran a theological course for the "Servants". In a notebook he had marked all his Bible references, and the "Servants" would laboriously copy these references into their own little notebooks. Each Servant had an attaché case of his own, containing Bible and notebook, the latter filled with the concentrated teaching of the Leader:

"The patriarchs (*okhokho*) and the family connexions (*imindeni*) are different. These are the readings about the patriarchs:

Gen. 25: 22, 23, 24, 27	Acts 7: 8–9
Gen. 49: 1, 2, 28	Gen. 25: 13–15
Gen. 10: 7, 13, 15	Gal. 4: 22, 24"

This copying was part, probably the main part, of the ministerial training given by the Leader himself. In principle this training took some five years, the first two of which were spent at the Church's centre near Port Shepstone and the remaining three at the "Peaceville" headquarters, at Hammarsdale.

How does this knowledge of Bible verses work out in practice? We attended a service in the chapel at Chesterville. The preacher was perhaps not one of the foremost of the group, but the tendency is characteristic.

The preacher announced that he was going to teach his congregation *"The meaning of Sabbath"*. Studying his notebook he called out one verse after the other, and a Reader in the congregation would stand up and read the text suggested: there followed a short explanation of each verse:

Gen. 1:2–3: Yes, light was created. That was the first thing created. It was created in the beginning. Then light was created. Amen (AMEN from the congregation) Hallelujah.

Gen. 1:30: Yes, in the beginning God created every beast of the earth and fowl of the air and the green herbs. This was created by God, this was the first thing created by God in the beginning. Amen. (*Amen*)

Matt. 12:8: Jesus is the Lord of the Sabbath. Jesus created the Sabbath. Then that day became the Sabbath. Hallelujah. Amen. (*Amen*)

Ex. 12:16: Nothing cooked must be eaten on that day or used that day. For you see on that day nothing that has been cooked must be eaten or cooked that day. On the Sabbath we must not eat anything cooked or used. Hallelujah. Amen.

Ex. 31:15: The seventh day is the Sabbath. On the seventh day nobody is ever allowed to do any work. For it is the Sabbath. It is a holy day, Hallelujah.

Luk. 23:3 [The Reader finds his verse with expert dexterity and reads with emphasis].

"And Pilate asked him, saying, Art thou the King of the Jews?— Yes, Jesus is the King of the Jews. Hallelujah". But there is some hesitation—until another Servant, obviously more meticulous in his copying of sacred verses, suggests an amendment from the Master's notes: Luk. 23:53. The Reader now reads verses 53–54 where to everybody's satisfaction there is, in fact, a reference to the word Sabbath: "Six days had passed. And now it was the day of preparation. And the day of preparation is the Sabbath. Hallelujah. Amen!"

A hymn follows: *"The Holy Spirit gladdens us."* The singing is a lengthy and lively affair. All bang their Bibles rhythmically, and there is a rhythmical clapping of hands, a swaying of bodies and heads to and fro. We notice that the congregation sings in two parts, soprano and bass. Singing in four parts is condemned as "Western" or "European".

Nzuza's people are understandably proud of their treasury of hymns. They are known to have been composed by the Leader "in the Spirit". New hymns are given to the Church once a year. They are short statements, rather conventional in their ideas, mostly consisting of only two lines, sung over and over again, performed with immense energy and repeated assiduously for a year in the local congregations. They are first sung in the Spirit, and then in Zulu. Some refer to Jesus:

> *Wafa wafa u Jesu*
> *ngenxa yezono zethu*
> Jesus,
> he died, he died,
> because of our sins.
> Help them· to carry their burdens
> knock and it will be opened to you
> by the Lord Jesus.

There is a dramatic interpretation of Jesus' struggle for the faithful:

Prevent the *Lion* ("The devil, as a roaring lion", 1 Peter 5: 8)
by the power of Jesus.

Other hymns show the role of the Spirit in the Church.

Those of the Spirit are the foremost of all churches.
If you know yourself [and your spiritual situation]
You could enter this Church of the Spirit,
It has holiness and peace
led by Jesus.

Send down, o Lord, the Spirit of truth,
The world cannot receive him, for it does not know him,
But you of the Church of the Spirit know him.

Angels also play a prominent role in the hymns:

There is the angel flying
Calling the Black nation

or as an introduction to the giving of a message:

SANIBONA, ye holy angels
May the Lord bless you.

This same blessing the Angels had indeed imparted to the
Church here on earth. This highly disciplined, hard-working and
sober group is an enterprising community. Their headquarters
at Hammersdale provides indications of this: the whole place
hums with activity under the leadership of the Founder's son,
Petro Nzuza.

One would have liked to study in some detail the structure of
this well-organized church, but the difficulties in the way—from
outside and from inside the Church itself—were unfortunately
too great. Suffice it to say, therefore, that Nzuza's church combines close collective unity with a strong urge to spread the message far and wide. This was the vision of Paula Nzuza, the
Founder himself: the "Servants" would go out on evangelistic
errands in groups of twos, for two–three months at a time, only
to return to headquarters for another three months, assembled
for common counsel and further instructions. While some other
Zion groups are mainly rural in their outlook and scale, Nzuza's
men—it is very much a men's world—show a remarkable power of
adaptation to an increasingly industrialized society. The new

leader is intentionally and in fact a modernizer, yet he has retained the loyal support of the older generation of "servants".

They are a tightly-knit group, and there is an obvious correlation between the more disciplined Spirit expressions sprung from
the peculiar theological interpretation of their role *and* the
disciplined ethos of hard work and group solidarity.

Advantageously placed near a railway and a main road, next
to labour-demanding border industries, they run a successful
bus company, with some twenty *"Siza Bantu"* buses, a garage,
and a tea-room. The administration of the enterprise has a well-
organized filing system, and contacts between the buildings at
headquarters are facilitated by an impressive telecommunication
system. But these, after all, are mere technical details. The main
thing is that they know that they, and they alone, are right.

Timothy Cekwane (1873–1949)

"My calling", he explained as he solemnly plied his broom across
the floor, "is to take the besom of God and sweep the world."
Among the Zulu churches of South Africa, this is the closest
resemblance we have seen to Tenri-kyo, one of Japan's new
religious movements. The members of this particular Japanese
community have also taken the broom as their symbol, and the
urge to cleanse and purify is similar in the two cases.

Cleansing is of course a concern of all Zionists. Zulu Jordans
and Swazi Bethesdas bear witness to this. But Cekwane's "Church
of the Light" is more obsessed than most with purification.

Consider the beginning of it all. The printed Church Constitution—*Isiseko so Msebenzi we Bandla loku Kanya*— has this to
say:

"The Work that happened in the World in 1873: God inserted a
drop of blood into Cekwane's wife, and she became pregnant.
There was darkness at noon for half an hour that day. This
miracle took place in upper Natal at the source of the Mzimude
river, near Himeville. This woman in whom this happened was
a pagan in *isidwaba* (skin petticoat). She bore a son with the name
of Timothy"—and Timothy was to become the Founder of the
Church.

This drop of blood from heaven was creative: the red colour of the evening clouds over the Dele Mountain; the red in the garment of the members of the church; the red in the palms of the stigmatized elect—all these phenomena were reminders of what had happened in that woman's womb.

The besom was no ordinary broom, for the twigs had been collected on the Dele Mountain, and served thus as a reminder of what had happened on the Mountain that evening when the groups were filled with the Spirit.

It happened long ago, in 1910. Timothy Cekwane was a local preacher at Himeville in Mzimba's Presbyterian Church of Africa. This was a responsible and honoured position; yet, he felt dissatisfied with the cold and formal worship of their Church. The hymns, the prayers, the message—they were all still conditioned by the Europeanness of that Presbyterian Church from which Mzimba had emerged.[4]

But then, suddenly, unexpectedly, the hour struck. In the sky over the mountain a star approached, a very strange and different star—with a tail! The rational Whites called this strange celestial body Halley's Comet; but to Timothy it was a messenger from God Himself. It moved slowly, yet approached so close; it almost touched that majestic mountain on which Timothy and his people were assembled. They felt the Spirit coming over them like a mighty wind. They ran over the mountain; they screamed; they sensed an irresistible urge to take off charms and amulets from their wrists, and their medicines, and to throw them far away; they had to confess their sins before God and men, in an outpouring of the soul in which nothing was to be left hidden. The branches of the bushes from the Mountain they gathered and beat themselves and one another, driving out the demons.

In that Spirit-filled night on the Mountain, Timothy was gripped by an ecstasy that overpowered him. Gesticulating and gyrating as if intoxicated by the Spirit, he prayed and screamed in an unknown tongue. He opened his hands. To his amazement

[4] My interviews with W. Zondo and A. Mjwara, and the Durban congregation July 1958.
Dr. J. W. Bodenstein, Notes "Ukukhanya Mission",
(Rev. Fr. Cekwane), 14–16 Aug. 1959, P. O. Himeville". 44 pp.

he saw blood trickling from the palms of his hands. His faithful told him that there was blood coming out from his lips, too. Water was brought to him; as he prayed for it, it turned into blood. This sacred fluid was powerful, filled with healing qualities for the sick.

This group who during that first night had experienced this new relation were indeed privileged and elect. They were a new race, distinct from all others, for they had together seen "the Day of the First Forgiveness".

The elect were to form the nucleus of the new Church, *Ibandla loku Kanya,* the Church of the Light. Their headquarters, called Ekukhanyeni, The Place of the Light, was established on the slope of that very mountain. This was, and remained, their incomparable Zion where the whole Church would assemble every August for its yearly meeting. The place—with some forty-five houses, cattle and horses—was now the property of Timothy Cekwane himself, later that of his son and successor Frederick Timothy Cekwane.

It is a glorious place in the Drakensberg, the most beautifully situated Zion in all of Southern Africa. To get there, I had to wade through the upper reaches of the Umkomazi River. Beyond Ekukhanyeni, a rugged mountain range rises to form a majestic backdrop for the sacred drama which was played out here. On moonlit August evenings, one can contemplate the snow-clad mountain tops of the Drakensberg and from below, the sound of the river can be clearly heard.

The church at present has a membership of less than five thousand. The strongest local congregations are to be found here at Ekukhanyeni and near Durban. To the yearly meetings the faithful come from as far away as Johannesburg, in buses and taxis.

Timothy Cekwane directed his church for forty years—his faithful never fail to point out the Biblical associations of that number—until his death in December 1949. His grave with its marble slab and the Bible reference to Rom. 6: 1–2 is to be seen at Ekukhanyeni.

After Cekwane's death, a succession crisis followed in 1950—considerable property interests at Ekukhanyeni were at stake—but his widow and her party managed to have Frederick Timothy accepted as the new leader. As one would expect, the celestial powers were once again involved: According to the printed constitution of the Church, signed by F. T. Cekwane, the Star shone over the head of the dead leader, and the younger man adds: "The Star which appeared in connection with the outpouring of the Spirit, showed itself at my ordination to the ministry". This was confirmation of what the dying founder was now reputed to have said, pointing to his son: "He is my blood. He is I".

Worship and intense group fellowship created and promoted by worship is everything in his Church. Two occasions serve as an indication of the worship life of the group.

The yearly meeting at Ekukhanyeni in August lasts a week and culminates in the last four days, Thursday through Sunday. Some eight hundred participants have come from neighbouring districts, from Durban and the Rand, some sixty per cent of them men. The number of children here is exceptionally large for a Zion Church.

The eight hundred help to keep Ekukhanyeni Village a clean and well-swept and quiet place throughout the festival: all speak in hushed voices.

Frederick T. Cekwane directs the meeting but being a rather shy and diffident person, he does not dominate. I have the impression that he is more a figurehead than a leader. His father, the founder, had greater charismatic gifts of leadership. Cekwane is assisted by three pastors, thirteen evangelists and three deacons. The deacon responsible for liaison with the outside world and therefore also with my observers, is W. Zondo. I had met him in Durban, where he had been in business as a butcher, and in this Church, where blood is the central symbol, his trade seemed particularly significant and meaningful.

Among the evangelists, Aaron Mjwara attracts attention by his orange dress, his solemn deportment and his claim of stigmatization.

Thursday is the day of preparation. The two main acts of the day well illustrate the extraordinary gift for the ritualization of the whole of life which is found everywhere in Zion, but which this particular Church has perfected. Cooking for eight hundred people is a major affair, and firewood is needed. Why should they not make a ritual out of it? So after a hymn, Cekwane reads the last two verses of the Book of Nehemiah. "Thus cleansed I them from all strangers ... And for wood offering, at times appointed, and for the first- fruits, Remember me, O my God, for good." Then teams of woodgatherers are sent out on the mountain, with the sacred words of the prophet Nehemiah ringing in their ears.

The place needs to be swept and a strange and utterly charming ritual follows. The women in red garments are sent off to their task with a verse from the Book of Revelations (7:9). This refers to white robes, but in this connection the colour is less important; what is important is the reference to "palms in their hands": they begin a solemn dance, holding their brooms, moving slowly forward in a long row and then retreating again, all the while singing hymns.

On Friday morning Mr. Zondo, the butcher, is in command, for now follows the slaughtering of cattle. One head of cattle after another is brought forward and shown and the name of the congregation which had presented it is announced.

Now there is another announcement. "Let us begin our great work!" This is the climax of the whole year, for now red garments are to be handed out to each individual: the women receive the flowing long red frocks, while the men and children have to be satisfied with red sashes and/or epaulettes. Cekwane himself is seated in the Temple and receives them all. Co-workers bring in packages of garments, with ten in each. Each individual kneels while entering and leaving the room, and while receiving the garment. The church members have in common a characteristic mannerism, most probably inherited from Timothy Cekwane himself: as they kneel, thy suddenly lift the right hand to the face, covering it with a rigid jerking movement, which is repeated a number of times. The reverence is further accentuated by each person kneeling and bowing to the ground. Cekwane hands over the precious garment and sprinkles each one with water, while hymns are sung. When receiving the sacred dress some begin to sob and groan. Others suddenly throw themselves to the ground, praying and groaning.

This is an overwhelming moment for each individual. Life is after all much greater than the ordinary week-day slavery in the

Egypt of the Whites. Life is more glorious than the meanness and dreariness of the everyday job—as a washer-woman, an errandboy, a driver. On this high mountain they are lifted up on high, very close to God's own heaven. These garments signify the reassurance of a change of identity, into something other and greater than before.

This ceremony takes considerable time; in fact, it continues all day and all night until the next morning! Saturday is devoted to preaching, and the afore-mentioned Aaron Mjwara gives two addresses. On Sunday there is the baptism of thirty children, followed by Washing of the Feet and by Holy Communion. Cekwane's role during the last two days of the meeting is to hear confessions. This is again part of the same urge for cleansing.

Somehow, the worship of the yearly meeting seems sober and restrained. An ordinary Sunday service in the church's little temple near Durban gives a somewhat different impression. Some forty men and thirty-five women have assembled; Zondo, the butcher, is in charge, genuine, genial and generous.

A hymn from the American Board Zulu hymnbook is sung, followed without warning by about ten minutes of corporate howling, concluded by repeated Amens, at which all raise their hands. "Our Father" is intoned, and another period of howling and grunting follows. Zondo is supposed to preach, and I can just perceive in the general commotion that he is reading from the Bible and trying to make himself heard. Some are jumping up on the chairs, crying. Aaron Mjwara in his yellow garment with a red sash begins to shake with his whole body. Describing a slow circling movement with his body, he eventually sinks down with his head against the floor, howling and grunting all the time. Another participant, Mr. X, fat and voluminous, jumps onto a chair, shouting from time to time at the top of his voice. Mr. Y. is now jumping up and down, shouting *Hhayi, hhayi hey*! Mr. Q holds his hands above his head, shouting, while Mr. Y's condition soon becomes more dramatic than ever, as he begins to cry.

Zondo has obviously touched a deep nerve, for he is reading from Rev. 11. I had never before realized just *how* striking the images of that chapter are, and verse 6 has words which fit Cekwane's church exactly: "they have powers over waters to turn them to blood". From this point onward the situation becomes chaotic. The pandemonium hitherto has been the merest whisper, compared with the spirit-inspired eruptions which follow. Now all the men are screaming and howling; the women, however, have so far kept quiet. Zondo is roaring at the top of his voice in the attempt to make himself heard: "The waters were changed and became blood. God has given that power to men." Then he finds another of his church's standard texts, Ex. 39:3, about Aaron's holy garments, in gold and scarlet, purple and other colours.

God gave the law to Moses and to Aaron, and now he provides us with the same kind of garments. These were given not by the power of men, but by God in heaven. We shall put on the garment of the blood of Jesus. Heaven will shed not only water but blood.

Mr. X is still crying and howling. "Aaron of the Old Testament preached about these garments and the New Testament knows the same colours. We are now in New Testament time, bought as we are by His blood which brings forgiveness." Zondo's message is followed by a testimony from Mr. Z:

I was a pagan. I saw a horse with two boys riding; next to them I saw a heap of garments; white, red, green. Who is keeping these boys? [Answer from the crowd: "the *abafundisi*". The crying and howling is now reaching impressive proportions.] I was ill. Somebody said unto me, "I shall show you another earth." I saw a boy with garments from heaven and a voice said, "These are thine".

To emphasize the importance of this tremendous insight he bangs the table in front of him. "The Man of Heaven [obviously T. Cekwane, the Founder of the Church] told me to mention this whenever I stand up to preach."

Mr. Y. now falls down, stiff and rigid, as if dead, his head bent backwards. Seven men take him and place him on the floor. P. now reads Acts 19:11, implying the miraculous power of certain pieces of cloth which had touched St. Paul's body. "The Man of Heaven said, You will receive power from these cloths and bear children." Now the women in their red garments, hitherto a silent mass, begin stirring.

One woman begins to scream and then falls down as if dead

among the mass of by now howling women. The men attempt to revive Mr. Y. but he does not budge. All are weeping, sweating, throwing themselves backward and forward, from side to side.

Apparently this was only the introduction, however, for now Aaron Mjwara rises to preach. The crowd is singing a hymn and Aaron is looking for a Bible text. He is searching in the Old Testament and then in the New, then back again to the Old, lost among all these chapters and verses.

"I thank the Lord Jesus that I am to preach. I am not going to speak with the voice of men, for the Time of the Flesh is past. Now is the Time of the Spirit. We are going to speak about the Resurrection. Now we shall sing another hymn while I am looking for the chapter from which to preach." All this time Aaron seems to be searching the Scriptures for some text, but in the end, while the singing and crying goes on, he gives it up and places the Bible closed on the table.

At this moment, P. falls backwards, rigid, over a pew. Somebody else falls down as if dead among a dozen or so scared little boys.

Mr. Q. is getting really wild now, falling to the ground and crying out terribly. Somebody else, a man in a yellow garment, throws himself with a heavy thud to the floor, shouting *ho ho ho*. The "dead" man suddenly begins to scream, and some ten men take care of him. Four men are now lying on the floor, grunting and beating the floor.

Meanwhile Aaron Mjwara has been standing waiting for his chance to preach. "Elijah was given a broom on the mountains. My calling is to be the besom of God. The House of Africa has been perfected through the Broom. It is perfected."

Aaron is shouting now with all the rest. Suddenly there is a brief lull in the uproar. Aaron screams, pointing to one of the women: "Give her that water to drink, so that she will vomit out the snake which had killed her."

The woman in red, who has hitherto been lying as if dead, starts to move on the floor; she rises to a sitting position, shaking, her hands raised. Then she leaps up, and then suddenly falls down again, lifeless, among a group of children. There some of the women take care of her. Aaron now asks Zondo to read one of the standard texts, Neh. 13: 30–31, a reference to Israel being distinct from strangers. He applies this to the Church of the Light: "Which other people has to that extent been blessed by the love of God, that they without being learned and educated could do this?"

There now follows a time of prayer for the sick. Matt. 10: 1 is read, and all raise their hands. Twenty-three men, fifteen women and ten children move forward, or are pushed forward, to form a group to be prayed for, all kneeling. The others turn to prayer for their fellow members. All shout and cry, their heads touching the ground. Some howl, others bark or grunt, while Zondo cries: "Cleanse the sins, O Lord!" Five women in red, two men in yellow and another five men in black garments move among the sick, fanning, hovering with their dresses, clutching, embracing, pulling and pressing the patients on various sensitive parts of their bodies; all sweating, all screaming, all swaying as if drunk, all raising their hands.

After the service I was able to have a quiet interview with Aaron Mjwara, the chief charismatic of this remarkable group. In him is concentrated the strangest power in his Church. He is No. III in a "Succession of Blood," ultimately related to the role of blood in the supernatural birth of the Founder himself. Timothy Cekwane had gifts of stigmatization; blood would emerge from the palms of his hands and from the corners of his mouth. Toward the end of his life this gift waned and had therefore to be imparted to somebody else. While he was still alive, a woman called Mary Mkize Cekwane, married to a relative of the leader, had the same symptoms, although in her case blood would emerge from the mouth only. She died, however, at the age of thirty, before the leader's own death. A week before his death Timothy was known to have transmitted the gift to Aaron Mjwara.

For eight long years Aaron had seen these stigmatization phenomena in his own body but had carefully hidden them from others. It was only when that Man of Heaven, the Founder himself, had noticed his gift and encouraged it, that he dared to reveal it to others. He had a recurrent vision, which he felt to be determinative for his own role and message. In his dream he would see two figures, whom he recognized as Noah, the Man of Water, and Cekwane, the Man of Blood. They stood there together. He, Aaron, was praying for rain, *imvula,* but the Cekwane of the vision was changing it into blood.

In the variegated family of Zulu Zion, Cekwane's Church of the Light is important in that it has realized more definitely than the others the dream of the Mountain of Zion. Their head-quarters, "Ekukhanyeni" in the Drakensberg, may at present be threatened: the whole area is scheduled to be declared a National Park; but half a century of red, blood-spattered visions on the mountain has conditioned this group quite intensely. To the other Zionists, the red colour in the Cekwane garments is the "wrong" colour; according to them the right colours are of course white and blue and green. The Cekwane group take this criticism with sublime composure, for they alone know the secret derived from the supernatural birth of the Founder.[5] Knowledge of this secret has integrated his group to a remarkable degree. The man-nerisms of the Founder are repeated by the faithful wherever they are, and they thus identify themselves with a personality whom they meet in the living word of the testimonies, and in the intimate relationship of the dream.

Cekwane had a genius for finding creative symbols, all related in one way or another to the one central image and experience of blood, and there is a constant dialectic in this Church be-tween Noah and Cekwane, between water and blood, both with purificatory qualities against all threats of pollution. The colour of blood makes their garments distinct. To be privileged at the annual meeting on the Mountain to put on again the sacred gar-ment of the Church heightens the individual's sense of personal identity, at the same time as it transcends individuality and renders him part of the corporate body of the Church.

The integrating function of common avoidances is another point. A Church member must not, in principle, eat from the same utensils as these used by non-members. Nor may he sit on

---

[5] I have also in the latter years of my Zion research come across the therapeutic qualities of the regular Zion colour scale white—green/blue and the power-loaded dangerous colours red/black: Cf. *Bantu Prophets,* p. 213 ff. and "colour symbolism" under Index, *ibid.* Here I refer to O. F. Raum, *The Social Function of Avoidances and Taboo among the Zulu* (1973), and to Dr. Harriet Sibisi's forth-coming work "Health and Disease among the Nyuswa Zulu", which I have studied in ms.

a chair on which a non-member has rested. The use of the broom is here more than just a practical measure; it is a symbolic instrument: it serves to heighten the sense of the dangers of pollution and the need for purification.[6]

Structurally there are obvious differences between the two churches discussed in this chapter, those of Nzuza and of Cekwane. More than any other church mentioned hitherto, Cekwane's group was conscious of its necessary and life-giving relationship to that far-off Zion of theirs, the mighty Drakensberg. Nzuza on the other hand was city-centred. The initial revelation had been given near Stanger, North of Durban.

As compared with the Cekwane faithful, Nzuza's church reaches out to more progressive strata in African society. The collective bus-company initiative has tended to attract a generation of younger men and strengthened the financial basis of the Church. In this case there was a clear group direction by strong leaders, Nzuza Senior and Junior, on a different level altogether from the fumbling organization of the Cekwane group.

Again, the two principal characters of this chapter should be compared with those in chapter II. The aspect of representativity is fundamentally important and must not be overlooked. The Mdlaloses and Ma Nkus are indeed characteristic of the main stream of Spirit churches, in fact representing the great majority, while the two actors in this chapter, dramatic as they are, represent only themselves and their special groups. The extraordinary charismatic claims on the part of both leader and flock among the Nzuzas and Cekwanes make their particular ideologies to stand out in sharp relief and naturally lead into our subsequent chapters on George Khambule and Isaiah Shembe. Furthermore, this sharp ideological profile must not be made into an image of the charismatic movement as a whole.

---

[6] "The Gift of Blood is transmitted to our Church. The blood is a promise (isithembiso) to save and heal our bodies together with the spirits. Mental illnesses are cleansed away by the Blood of Christ. Hebr. 9: 14".

F. Cekwane, letter 19.8.1958 to Rev. T. W. S. Mthembu, with the author. A doctor writes: "From the answers to my careful enquiries I was able to draw the conclusion that there is strong evidence that Timothy C. was suffering from leprosy and Maria Mkhize and Aaron Mjwara from pulmonary TB." Letter with B. Sr.

4. The Seals of the Secrets of the Saints

The least known, and possibly the most interesting, of Zulu prophets was *George Khambule* (1884–1949).

His movement might easily be forgotten altogether, for of this church, at least, it can be said that it has definitely come to an end. We can follow its rapid and daring span, from the beginning in 1919 to the death of the founder in 1949 to the final catastrophe, the burning of the last Archbishop's house, with all his papers and belongings. After that, nothing was left—except, by sheer good luck, photostat copies of a great number of precious liturgical books of remarkable originality.

There are a number of reasons why Khambule is worthy of particular interest:

1. His was a religious community with both a Prophet and a Precursor of the Prophet. It was the Precursor who persuaded the Leader to take up the challenge, and for some creative years these two men worked in cooperation.

2. Khambule established the most tightly-knit community, living in total exclusion from the surrounding Zulu society and social structure.

3. A whole set of new and surprising signs and symbols bound the group together: secret names of the Saints; a secret angelic language, expressed in certain letters of the alphabet; a sacramental role of sacred stones, found in river-beds and on mountain-tops; these stones taking the place of that of water in other Zionist groups. It offers a rare example in Zulu groups of definite *"cargo"* inventions, the most important being a Heavenly Telephone, a hot-line from Telezini to the Throne of Heaven.

4. No other church has to this extent allowed a study of the

119

meaning of role-taking in African Independent Churches. Joining the Church of the Saints gave the member a new identity, and this role-taking comes closer to putting on an *eikon*, a mask, than in any other comparable group.

This is perhaps sufficient justification for paying some attention to George Nazar Khambule and his Church of the Saints.

Precursor and Prophet

And he that sat was to look upon like a stone;
a jasper and a sardine stone.

That shining white spot of light dominated everything else in the hazy world of his dream. *John Mtanti* (1873–1937), teacher at the Anglican Primary School at St. John's, Nqutu, Zululand, had felt certain strange forebodings as he went home after a day's work in the school. The times were frightening.

A few years earlier, a star with a tail had appeared on the skies over Zululand, and John's uncle, Job S. Mtanti, had formed his church, the Zion Free Church Impumalanga Gospel of South Africa—as a response to the vagaries of Halley's comet.[1] This time—it was now 1918 and 1919—the "Influenza" was killing masses of people in Zululand and all over the world, as a terrible sign of the approaching doom. To be sure, there had been a World War between those two dates, but this, at Telezini, seemed a minor incident compared to these giant cosmic events.

As he went to sleep that evening, Mtanti thought of these apocalyptic occurrences—and then in his dream he saw it, that shining white stone! Was it not what he had read in the last book of the Bible? "The one seated on the throne was like a stone" (*wafana netshe*), his Zulu Bible from that beloved Book of

[1] Job S. Mtanti reported Jan. 26, 1945 to the Magistrate, Paulpietersburg: "The Holy Spirit descended on me on the 24th Dec. 1910. I beg to refer to the following Scriptures Acts 20:1–4, Isaiah 42:61 [non-existent], Thess. [!] 26–28 [probably 1 Thess. 5:26–28]. The word of God said I should base my doctrine in accordance with Zulu nation custom amen and that I should not have any other person over me because The Holy Spirit which is my minister descended on me". File 852/214. S.N.A., Government Archives, Pretoria.

Revelation, ch. 4: v. 3 had suggested to him. This was the central symbol of a mighty vision which Jehovah gave in the dream that night. He could never forget it. He told his family and friends at Telezini. He wrote about it to a neighbour working in Johannesburg. This vision impressed itself so indelibly upon his mind that, twelve years later, on October 8, 1931, he sent a report about it to the Magistrate at Nqutu:

Nqutu, October 8, 1931
Sir,
I have the Honour to inform you, Sir, that I have seen Visons [sic!] in 1918: and in 1919 was Translated by Revelation.
My desire is to preach the same among my countrymen but I have no audacity. I hereby apply for the permit for the religious operation I am now undertaking. May be my request shall be met with your Lordship.
I have the honour to be your humble Servant
John Solomon Mtanti

A few weeks later he sent an exercise book to the same Magistrate with detailed drawings of his visions.

This dream sketch of Heaven provides a deeper insight into Zulu apocalyptic piety, in first and second generation Christians, than via any other known inroad. Mtanti had been an Anglican teacher in an elementary school, and was thus comparatively educated; references to the "river Styx" and to grammatical terms ("subject", "predicate", "object") are learned reminiscences from studies at the St. Chad's Teacher Training School.

Above all the organization of the many Bible references, in a system of five stages ("gates") is not as arbitrary as one might think, but rather the result of many years of endless, breathless combinations of Biblical ideas and heavenly dream images. He

[2] Our reproduction of John Mtanti's drawing needs an explanation, perhaps even an apology. Visiting Nqutu in 1939, I was invited by the then Native Commissioner to look at the Mtanti document. I copied drawing and text as best as I could, in a small 5″×3″ notebook. Here the proportions have been somewhat modified in that the heavenly "streets", or the parallel lines connecting the five "gates" were shortened. Again, for clearness's sake I have lifted out the many Bible references that cluttered Mtanti's picture and placed them below (p. 120–21). In 1973 we made an abortive attempt to find anew the original Mtanti document. It could not be located in the Provincial Archives, Pietermaritzburg and our ambition to look for the paper in local files at Nqutu came to naught, for other reasons.

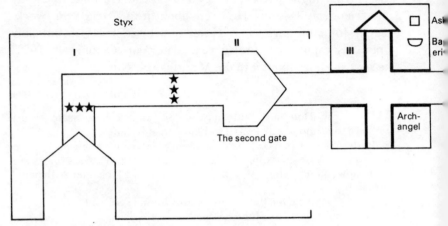

John S. Mtanti's vision of Heaven.
John S. Mtanti's Bible quotations to the Sketch of Heaven and its Five
Gates. Thick lines: drawn in red by Mtanti

   I. Three stars on Styx; Sinner John Archangel [=John S. Mtanti]
  II. Mt 18:6 (stumbling block: mill stone)
      Is 1:20–21 (Faithful city, harlot full of judgment)
 III. Amos 8. Sunset at noon
      Gen. 18, Abraham: "but dust a. ashes"
      Zach. 13. Fountain to house of David
      Is 17: Grapes a. Olive tree
        2–3 berries, 4–5 on utmost bough
      Ez. 31 Trees of Eden

      Rm 2: Circumcision
      Mk 16:19 Jesus at right hand of God

 IV. Is 1:18–25 Sins as scarlet
      Am 8: Basket of summer fruit
      Hab 2 Prophet on Watchtower
      Ps 39: [no specific terms here]
      Dan 10: Final revelation of Man of heaven

  V. Num 24: Star out of Jacob
      Amos 5:8: Seven stars and Orion
      Job 9:19 Arcturus, Orion a. Pleiades,
      Dan 12: Stars for ever and ever

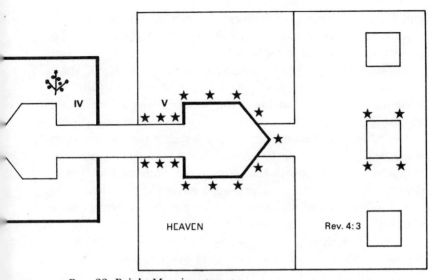

HEAVEN   Rev. 4:3

Rev. 22: Bright Morning star
1 Tess 4: God's trumpet call
Is 57:15 High and lofty one: name "Holy"
Mal 3:16 Book of Remembrance
Ex 23:21 My name is in Him
Rev. 4:3 On the throne *like a stone*
Ps 103 The Lord's pity
Zach 8 Salvation fr. east country and west country

  I. Is. 1:18 Confession
     Granted to me
III. Feb 1, 1866, Amos 8:8–10, May 29, 1919
     Ashes Gen 18:27, Zach 13 Well
IV. Is. 17:6. Ez 31:8 Archangel May 11, 1871
                       April 15, 1887
                       Rom 2:12–29
The third gate: Mark 16:9 1919
Where I was particularly instructed by the Archangel.
The first question asked from me was this. Do you know me?
I am the Archangel uniting with Jehovah Ex 23:20–21
Dent. 28:58 Is 1:18–25 Amos 8:1–11
Ps 39. Dan 10:1 Hab. 2:1–2

                               Blackboards in all 23.

  V. Num 24:17 Amos 5:8 Job 9:9 Dan 12:3

End Rev. 22:16 1 Tess 4:16
Is 57:15
Mal 3:16 Ex 23:21, Rev 4:3
Psalm 103:12–14 Zach 8:7–9

had his great vision on February 15, 1919, and his letter to the Nqutu Magistrate is dated October 8, 1931. A decade of Bible study is concentrated in the sketch.

An unhurried study of Mtanti's many Bible quotations shows how the dreamer proceeds from Gate I to Gate V according to a certain basic liturgical-architectural pattern, from a *Confiteor,* via sacraments of purification, Ashes and Baptisterium ("well"), to the Altar, the Throne of Grace. I imagine that Mtanti's personal, and at times intense participation in Anglo-Catholic worship at the St. Augustine's Cathedral,—the mother Church in his district, close to Telezini—had been a guide for him also on this dream-pilgrimage of his, unto the star-spangled heavenly places, with precious stones a-shining.

Speculations with sacred numbers and letters is another characteristic aspect. Here Mtanti, the school teacher, showed the way, "a more excellent way", to Khambule, the Prophet, barely literate as the latter was at first.

There are a number of delightful observations made by Mtanti, the farmer, discovering strange aberrations in Biblical botany. At the fourth Gate, for instance, he sees a vine with grapes visualized by Is. 17:6: "two or three berries in the top of the uppermost bough, four or five in the outmost fruitful branches thereof." This strikes Mtanti so much that he must at least allude to it by the soupçon of a drawing.

In his commentary to the Sketch, Mtanti stated that his "translation" to heaven had taken place on February 15, 1919. It had far-reaching consequences. "I was told to leave my House for seven months living in a hut alone fasting for 39 days." At the same time he "was told to put off the boots for ten years": Barefoot he appeared as one of Nazarites of the Old Testament; it is, we think, not too far-fetched to interpret this Zulu school teacher's decision as a protest against the unnatural panoply of modern civilization.

Years after the event, Mtanti could describe his vision calmly. But its immediate effect was to unnerve him. The school-children were frightened when their teacher suddenly appeared only to cry *"Nakho! Nakho!"*—"Woe, woe!". He left his school, for he felt he had now to search for the one thing that could save the world from utter destruction: holy stones with which to build the new Jerusalem. In streams nearby he found some of them. They looked like ordinary stones to ordinary people, but Mtanti discovered a message in them, or rather *on* them.

But this message was so great that it required a more prominent prophet than himself to proclaim it. Again, his dreams showed him the way. A man appeared in these dreams, and he recognized the face and stature of a neighbour of his, George Khambule from the same Telezini village, now working as a mine captain in Johannesburg. So John Mtanti wrote to Khambule pleading with him, for God's sake, to return to Telezini, there to take up holy "weapons"; in other words the stones of Telezini and of the Book of Revelation.

George Khambule himself was impressed by this preciseness in quoting the Bible. He was to develop an angelic language of his own where the newly-discovered elements of the alphabet and the series of ciphers were to be taken along into new flights of fancy.

At first Khambule was not interested. But harsh facts of life, and of death, made him obey the call. His Johannesburg paramour was taken ill, and died. Khambule was so shaken that he himself—in those terrible months of 'influenza' and rumours of death everywhere—fell ill and was taken to hospital. There in the evening he 'died', and woke up again at 4 a.m. the following morning. He knew then that he had been through a terrifying experience.

He heard his dead girl-friend crying far below in the fire and smoke of hell. And he heard his deceased sister, Agrineth, crying, and saw the angels of Satan with their forks about to push the dead into the fire. Then Jesus appeared—Khambule was now in heaven—and, as a lid was removed from the floor of heaven, the two of them were looking from above down at the earth and its central point, Telezini. He saw there his own corpse, foul and smelling, and his wife crying beside it. Then he was told:

Return to the earth to save its inhabitants. Go tell the pastors to leave their beds. A pastor must not sleep with a woman. And a menstruating woman must not bring food to a pastor. If she has given birth to a child, she is polluted for a time and her husband must not sleep with her, in the case of the birth of a boy for seven days, if it is a girl, for a month. She must be purified by the prayers of the pastor. And as this will tax the strength of the pastor, he must not eat pork or drink beer nor taste medicines. Go tell your people to marry the Heavenly Marriage, the Marriage of the Lamb.

George Khambule, now rising from this 'death' of his, woke up—and returned home to Telezini.

The Khambules were a well-known family at and around Telezini. Most Khambules, including George, were by now esteemed members of the Wesleyan Church. In a largely Anglican area—the fine cathedral of St. Augustine's was built by the legendary Archdeacon Charles Johnson—the Wesleyans were a particularly progressive community. For some reason, George had not availed himself of the same educational opportunities as others in the Church. It was only in Johannesburg that he discovered he had to do something to achieve literacy, and there he had picked up the three R's in a night-school.

George Khambule was an impressive, dignified Zulu, at this time—36 years of age. When he approached on his splendid horse people felt that there was somebody extraordinary.

As he returned to Telezini, Khambule had no intention of leaving the Church with which his family had had such good contacts. As he told of his miraculous death and resurrection it was natural that people came from near and far to listen. A few men and some young girls would stay on in the Khambule kraal. After two to three weeks they felt called to go out together in a long procession in the neighbourhood, witnessing in the night. They would walk round a kraal singing and praying. People would feel the urge to confess their sins to Khambule. He could 'read' them, looking right through them with his piercing eyes, revealing sins they had committed weeks and months before.

The group round Khambule grew. His miraculous message could not fail to attract young and old. He was soon prepared to build a church centre, that of "the Saints". A strange community emerged, and the well-established Zulu society in the Nqutu district was shaken. For here, in their midst, a new separate society, *apart,* suddenly appeared. The number of girls and women living permanently at Khambule's place grew within a year to a hundred and more. No Zulu (or anybody else for that matter) could but interpret this as a modern variation of the *isigodlo,* the harem of the Zulu kings of old. But this was an *isigodlo* with a difference. The young women had been advised or ordered by Khambule in the name of the Almighty to break their ties with their families. Marriage was not allowed; instead they were to enter the "Marriage of the Lamb". John Mtanti drew the line here. He felt that Khambule had gone too far, and this matter caused the two of them to separate.

The Saints divided their time at the Telezini Zion between work and worship. An impressive stone temple was built. At worship in the main hall, the Saints were placed according to a strict hierarchical pattern, and those who saw deeper knew that this corresponded to the order of angels and archangels and the elders in the heavenly places.

Khambule himself was to be seen only occasionally in the midst of the ordinary Saints. Most of the time he spent in seclusion in an adjacent, secret room where he received special instructions from Jehovah himself and from where he could through his lieutenants direct both worship and work. Here he had a collection of his holy stones, placed in the Ark of the Covenant, a fine wooden box. Here he had—or was reputed to have—a supernatural device, a "Heavenly Telephone", a hot-line to heaven (to adapt a phrase from modern power politics). In his writings there are numerous references to this machine. What it may have looked like—if anything—nobody will ever know, for the few survivors of the Saints angrily deny its exist-ence. In any case, it was part of the numinous secret presence (or absence!) of the Prophet, in which lay much of the paradox-ical influence he exercised. In his seclusion he also found leisure to write the beginnings of his diary and to conceive an extraordinary rich worship.

The first few years of the Church were happy ones. The flock grew. There were at least two important centres, apart from Telezini in Zululand: one at Msinga in Natal, the other at Witbank in Transvaal. Not that the membership was large at any time, but the total was well over a thousand.

As early as the mid-1920s, however, the Church experienced a two-fold crisis, one internal, the other external.

The rift between Khambule and Mtanti grew. This was a

tragic conflict. Mtanti had been the John the Baptist of the Movement, the loyal Precursor of the Prophet himself. In his vision he had seen Khambule as the *induna* of Jerusalem. Mtanti opposed two of the most startling things about the Church of the Saints, the Marriage of the Lamb, as enacted by Khambule, and the mystery surrounding the 'Heavenly Telephone'. And Mtanti had been the Church's second-in-command, the *uMazisi*, the Teller, *alias* St. John Marko.

In his Diary—September 12, 1928—Khambule argues with his lost friend, now in a state of ill health: "What is all this noise? What if I ask you who will heal you, if you do not turn to me? Have you forgotten what I said? [now he changes from second to third person]: He will not be healed without me, never. I was not called [to become a prophet] by the Teller (=Mtanti). I am called by the One who called the Teller. I *am* the chief *induna* of Jerusalem".

It was about this time that John Mtanti definitely left Khambule to form his own Church, that of "Jerusalem".

Even more fatal was the conflict with the chief of the Nqutu area, Isaac Molife. To him, a staunch Anglican, Khambule's claims and rules of conduct were a deadly threat to Zulu society as such. The chief had to act. Khambule was called before the Zulu chief and his councillors, and later to the Magistrate's court.

His case illustrated the struggle for power between chief and prophet in African society at this time. Some of the prophets were indeed so strong as virtually to subjugate the chiefs. Khambule failed in this attempt. He found some human consolation in protestations to his secret Diary [Aug. 28, 1926]: "All things at Nqutu are lies. I am in charge at Nqutu". But officially he could not get away with his claim. He had to leave Telezini and Nqutu.

The Carrier of the Ark found he had a tragic duty to perform that day. The little community—for many had left Khambule in order to stay on in the world, that is Nqutu, and the church was greatly reduced—behind its Prophet had to set out on a pilgrimage through the inimical world of the Philistines towards some unknown Zion. On his head the Carrier of the Ark had the wooden box with the most precious possessions of the Church, Khambule's holy stones—and the tragic march through the Wilderness began.

First they settled at Kingsley. But soon they had to move again to Talana, outside Dundee. His beloved second wife Ma Mhlungu died at Talana. It was a great misfortune that, on these wanderings 'in the desert', the box of the Ark was destroyed or lost, and they had to make do with a cardboard box for this purpose. In the end, through their combined efforts they managed to buy a little plot at Spookmill. This was—fortunately, at that time—'a black spot in a white area', and here Khambule and his flock found their last refuge, their ultimate Zion. It was here, after his death in Johannesburg on January 9, 1949—at the age of sixty-five—that Khambule's corpse was brought, and here one can to this day see his tombstone.

After Khambule's death, there was some uncertainty as to the succession. There were two main contenders. Mordechai Sikakana had a claim, for he was the brother of Khambule's widow, and therefore, according to Zulu tradition, her guardian; he lived at Spookmill. Howard Hlongwane, a policeman, had joined George Khambule in 1929, he told me. Although he had no theological training he was almost instantly promoted from ordinary member to priest. This was understandable, tall and impressive as he was. His wife was a Mhlungu and she was closely related to Khambule's other wife; he in fact called her 'auntie'.

Although Khambule had left some of his finest robes as a gift to Hlongwane, Sikakana could however base his claim on an irrefutable fact. Khambule had left his staff, his 'iron rod', in his care. There was not much that the Hlongwane party could do to *that,* and Sikakana became the Archbishop of the church.

It was as such that I met him in 1969. He was old and ill by this time. Six months later he died of cancer. Only a few weeks after his death, the mud house, which was the late Archbishop's residence, was burned to the ground, of causes unknown. In the fire were lost all the sacred robes, the Ark, and the liturgical books written by the Prophet himself.

Our story, from Telezini to Spookmill, has a more general application. We speak of the formation of African independent churches, and serious statisticians are forever adding new thousands to their numbers throughout the sunny continent of Africa. But this little story shows one thing which was sometimes overlooked, that is, that not only do many churches grow and flourish in Africa, but many of them also wither and die.

A church with a difference was Khambule's concern. His dream-journey to Jesus in heaven was so decisive for him and his flock that it was bound to determine all aspects of the Church's life: its idea of revelation, its acts of worship and its order of conduct. We shall look at each of these in turn and shall thus consider a *different* source of revelation; signs of a *different* language; *different* acts of worship; and, finally, a *different* law of conduct.

A different Source of Revelation

In the first decades of the century, in the locations of Johannesburg, Durban, Port Elizabeth and elsewhere, rumour had it that the Bible to which missionaries referred was, really, the wrong book. It was a device of the Whites to keep the revelation of the true God away from the Africans. The Afro-American "Athlican Constructive Church" therefore introduced their own sacred book, Holy Piby, the true Bible. Here was God's revelation to his black children.

Khambule and Mtanti were basically concerned with the same problem, but solved it in their own particular fashion. Of course we all have our own particular Bible: our own personal selection of choice chapters and passages. Thus Khambule and Mtanti had theirs. They were personally attracted to the apocalyptic books in the two Testaments, the Old and the New. But in their case, the dream activity of the prophet was the catalytic agent. Combined with blurred elements of certain apocalyptic expressions in the Bible, the Prophet's dream showed them another source, more tangible, yet much more heavenly and mysterious, of the Revelation of God to his people. In Khambule's diary, December 15, 1935, he has entered a 'Song of the Church of the Saints through St. Itengirrah'. Certain participants in the liturgy make their statements. One of them says:

St. Nazar came to inform us that he had seen people [milling about] like ants. The Lord Jesus called him and said "That is the Bible [of those] who denied the Bible which was written by angels' tongues, and nobody can read it except St. Nazar who was given it".

No wonder that the *chorus* goes on:

Beyond the River
we shall sing the new song
and bring thanks to St. Nazar
for what he has done for us.

Khambule, or St. Nazar, rested assured that he knew that other and real source of Revelation, that other and heavenly Bible, written with other signs. This was the fundamental contribution of John Mtanti, the Precursor to Khambule's movement.

In the search for sacred stones Khambule joined him. They looked for stones in the river-beds of Telezini, and they looked for them in the Bible. Excitedly searching the Scriptures, they were to discover, to their amazement, that the Book of Life was full of stones; from the days of Abraham and Jacob of old to those of Jesus and his Adversary Satan, in the desert, until the shining pages of that last book in the Bible: a mysterious stretch of stones. To them the bread of Life was stones.

Much later, in 1969, I was to see in Archbishop Sikakana's chapel near Dannhauser some twenty holy stones placed on the rickety table that served as an altar. And I heard him explain, half convinced, half embarrassed the message conveyed by those stones.

Sikakana's competitor for the post-Khambule leadership of the Church, Howard Hlongwane, a hefty and hearty policeman in what was once Western Native Township, explained the matter to me in 1958. Without his eloquent interpretation I would never have grasped anything of the secret. He demonstrated how, apparently, some of the letters of the alphabet, were inscribed in the stones: an "L", or an "A", or, perhaps "N". In the little nooks and crannies of those stones one could, with inspired imagination, find what one wished to find; that is where these heavenly instructions came from. "L" meant *L*eviticus or *L*azaro as the case may be. "A" was probably *A*dama or *A*ndrew, and "N" was *N*oah or *N*azar or—if you wanted to say something about the Holy Spirit—*N*icodemus who came to the Lord by night and received special teaching about matters of the Spirit.

This was all very convincing and logical, at least to my teacher, Police Sergeant Hlongwane. Nobody could mistake his enthusiasm and conviction as he tried to inform his sceptical European interviewer.

This conviction and enthusiasm in Khambule's disciple Hlongwane was, one must presume, only a shadow of the authority with which Khambule himself demonstrated the stones. His diary returns to these secret letters again and again.

Khambule himself had "the Gift to read the stone": He pronounced his imperious *"Vula!"* (Be opened), and the meaning of signs was unfolded.

The first page of his diary from 1925 has a series of these letters. One combination seems somewhat easier than others. "This is why all the nations shall be under you. Says A.O. under oath. It is so I.K. S.P.T." A.O. of course stands for *A*lpha and *O*mega. The following letters were more personal. Khambule discovered it at the first glance. He sometimes used "Illy" as his own heavenly first name, thus *I*lly *K*hambule. Are you a *K*ing, *P*riest and *T*hixo? he goes on to ask. The following letters most probably were taken by Khambule to represent *S*aint, *P*rophet and God (*T*hixo).

The more elaborate combination of letters earlier on the same day, "SIJNHDAEE", is to some extent explained by Khambule himself, at least as far as the two last vowels are concerned; E and E refer to the Old Testament figures, Elijah and Elisha, one of whom ascended into heaven in a chariot of fire. The first two, most probably are *S*t *I*lly, referring to Khambule himself, and again the letter N almost invariably stands for the heavenly name for Khambule, *N*azar or St. *N*azar.

But Mtanti and Khambule had anxiously been looking for that comprehensive stone which would convey a composite and if possible complete message. They spent years on that search, and great was their joy when at Ncekwini, twenty miles from

Telezini, at last that most precious stone was found; "The glorious morning star, on which all the apostles are written."

It must have been on such a day, that Khambule added a new passage to the 'Morning Worship' of his church. There the Priest was to say:

He who has ears, may he listen to what the Spirit saith to the Churches. He who is victorious, I shall give him hidden manna. I shall give him a white stone on which is written a new name, unknown to others, [known] only to those who receive it.

No wonder that the chorus of the congregation would happily respond:

Thou God of St. Itengirrah, God of St. Nazar. We give thanks for Thou gavest us St. Nazar.

In the seclusion of his vestry, Khambule pours out his soul in joy and elation over this find. No wonder that he must exhort himself. "Take the likeness of the Lord Jesus." The throng of visitors to his Zion at Telezini proved him right: "They would never have come to you to know what you are, if the glorious morning star of dawn did not exist".

The faithful at Telezini must have heard the enraptured note in Khambule's voice as in his sermons he would repeat with tremendous emphasis the sonorous richness of those secret configurations of the alphabet: S P S I Z F B T M I A L T S K. He goes on to say in his diary: "These are the names, that were written on the glorious morning star". "This is how he has received the power of the Apostles that were written to him". For the signs stand for the fullness of the apostolic message: Simon Peter Saint John [of] Zebedee, Filip, Bartholomew, Alpheus and all the others, except Iscariot, of course for we are dealing with a holy stone, which admits of no sinfulness. "A" for Andrew seems somehow to have fallen out in the process, but one should not be punctilious in matters of this nature.

The full list of the apostles recurs or is referred to frequently in Khambule's diary. They form the basis of his peculiar authority. Nobody could have a surer apostolic succession than he who holds them all in his hand.

By the same logic, another stone with certain peculiar lines which *could* be interpreted as the letters, "A", "B", and "C", was very holy indeed, for here was a triad or the Trinity, those three Gods of our religion: "God F, and God S and God H", as Khambule develops the connexion, musing and meditating, as he writes his diary.

To be fair one must add that Khambule could nevertheless claim that no prophet had a larger collection of Bible verses than he. He must have heard those other hesitant beginners who had to rely on their *"Matthew five"* and leave it at that. Khambule could not but smile at the limited Bible knowledge of some of those competitors of his. In one of his hymnbooks he has filled six closely written pages with what he was pleased to call "Religious knowledge", consisting of no less than some seven hundred and twenty separate Bible-references. It must have seemed very impressive to some of his followers. They felt that one could in all fairness hardly ask for more.

Khambule's authority was challenged from time to time by local authorities and by other churches. But he felt assured because of this special contact which he established with heaven. In the middle of a series of Bible references from December 1928, he writes: "Let it be sworn on two stones that this kingdom will not be destroyed by any man. I will not fear anybody for Jehovah is with me."

The local chief, Isaac Molife, represented law and order and would for that reason, finally, evict Khambule from Telezini. In his diary the prophet records one of the first skirmishes with the chief. He was anxious to let the world know "what I am and God's revelation to me. Once I asked chief Isaac if he was not surprised to see me already being referred to as *Mfundisi*. Knowing my position, he admitted that he was surprised". Khambule said: "It is because God revealed himself to me. You call your men, and I shall tell you about the secret." On that first occasion he could not go much further, but continues his argument in the relative safety of his diary:

I am accused for being a troublemaker. I am an out-law because I have my own private faith (*inkolo*); I am not a pastor because I received no laying on of hands! [He compared himself with St. Paul and his calling (Acts 26: 16–18)]: "Can that which the Lord told St. Paul be denied? Who laid hands on him after the Lord had spoken to him? And Moses of old?' [In the Zulu text, Khambule uses these English words: Moses of old], as the Lord appeared to him, who laid hands on him? What I was, as the Lord Jesus Christ revealed to me the Scripture of truth, was written by H.G. Latin RIO EST M.B. % MGU"; [and Khambule's Bible reference this time is to Deut. 30: 10–20. No doubt 'Moses of old' had written this very especially for our prophet at Telezini]: "This commandment is not hidden from three . . . it is not beyond the sea that thou should say, who shall go over the sea for us?" [For Khambule alone understood the hidden things—thereby making his religion into something very different from that of the foreign missionaries. His is a revelation here and now.

This whole argument in the diary is concluded]: "After a few days Jehovah gave me two stones of the Covenant. This is the time when you shall see all God's secrets I – – B B L they are to be found on his chosen mountain".

There was a supernatural drama of both concealment and openness about those stones of his, and this tension dominated him. That mysterious verse which had attracted the attention of the New Testament writers about "the stone which the builders rejected" was sure to appeal to Khambule, and he quotes it in order to strengthen his own authority.

Once found in the river bed and on the mountain, stones were brought to Khambule's Zion and hidden in the Ark of the Covenant. The revelation was imparted to the prophet on June 20, 1922. This was the day when God himself told him, "The Ark carried by the Cherubim will be given to you". No wonder that priest and congregation could exclaim in the Ark Liturgy:

Here the Creatures and the Elders and the Angels make him startled and thank him who is seated on the Eternal Throne.
Congreg: All the Angels say, God, Thou art great.

Khambule placed his stones in the wooden box, called the Ark, and this box was always kept in the holy of holies.

He was not always able to feel its radiance. Ebullient though he was, even he could be dejected at times. The opposition was too hard. On October 25, 1928 at one a.m. he writes:

"You may say I may see heaven. No more did I listen to what is said there. Thy eyes did not thrive. Neither did I listen to Agnes [his wife] for she is a child. Why is it that [what is sung] in the hymns does not happen? Today there are questions which I cannot answer because I have been speaking on my own behalf. If I can give the answer at all."

135

Yet this was a very unusual spell of pessimism in this robust warrior of a man. He was soon prepared to continue the fight. Close at hand, he had his "weapons"—his stones.

Telezini was ideally situated. There was a river close by; in the dry season one could dig up stones in the river-bed. And there was a mountain. It may have appeared quite ordinary to common people. To Khambule it stood on a level with the high and holy mountain in King Nebuchadnezzar's Babylon. It is recalled that in that place "a stone was cut out of the mountain without hands", Dan. 2:45. And the divine kingdom "would break in pieces and consume all these kingdoms". No wonder then that even King Nebuchadnezzar himself had to fall upon his face and worship the prophet, Daniel.

A straight line went from Babylon to Telezini. Khambule had a very real experience of this. He had been sued before the court at Nqutu by a White man over some case of a run-away horse. But the white man lost the case.

The One who had been preparing for me by the power of my God saw a stone on the mountain, which was cut but not cut by the hand of man. It broke all that belongs to Babylon. Dan. 2:44–46. This is the power of heaven which has descended and which is here. I thank him who sits on the clouds who loved me and who introduced me to eternal riches ... Through Him I shall never die. I praise the Creator of all things, and the Elders above there give thanks on my behalf together with the four Creatures who are there with my God. Yes, Amen. (D. 28.11.1928)

While still at Telezini, the Ark in the holy of holies added to the sacredness of the prophet's seclusion. Nothing (or almost nothing) was allowed to disturb this. For here, in July 1925, was a problem of dramatic proportions. Solomon, King of the Zulus, was to visit the Nqutu district, possibly including Telezini. In his diary, the prophet struggles with this vexed question: "Angels are asking; if King Solomon comes here, what can be done? A cow should be slaughtered. Then, what about us, can we be seen? This is very great; of Eternity". He cannot forget what his faithful had just done to him, praising him in terms that suggested a greatness above that of King Solomon: "Today a heifer was slaughtered for us in order to praise *Tixo Khambule*, God Khambule".

It seems that after all the people of Telezini had overrated the importance of their little village, and the King of the Zulus apparently did not actually come, thus releasing the prophet from this otherwise acute problem of Church and State, or—as the case may have been—of Time and Eternity.

In any case, the emphasis placed on dramatic secrecy of the holy place helped to build up the numinous character of this Zion. This could be extended to other centres of the Church. In August 1925, Khambule writes at Witbank—next to Nqutu and Msinga, one of the preaching places of the Saints:

> This house ... there will be seven lamps in it. This has the effect of allowing the General of the Lord not to be seen outside. Why? Because the whole throne of Kingship is here. The whole throne of God is here. All of it is here in its fulness. This first vision will not be broadcast. The Gate Keeper will represent the Lord Jesus here.
>
> What is going to happen is very extended indeed as it is said that they must know that God's throne is here. It must not be visible. The Prosecutor (*Mshushusi*) must remain invisible because of this strength ... As to the Gate-keeper he knows that all the power of God is here. In Zulu we say, *Buhlaluse*, the invisible king, is here. This kind of thing is what is needed here, as we represent his will to be done on earth as it is in heaven.

Secrecy was the one aspect; revelation of secrets was the other, and this, again, was Khambule's privilege.

His hymn on The Breaking open of the Seven Seals bears witness to this:

Priest: They are singing a new song saying:
Congregation: Thou art worthy to take the Book.
Priest: And to break open (*qhaqha*) its seals.
Congr: Because thou wast slain for all generations and tongues so that people and nations may be of God.
Priest: Thou madest us kings and priests of our God.
Congr: Who is worthy to search the Book?
Priest: And to break open its seals.
Congr: There was none in heaven and on earth and under the earth.

It is then suggested that only St. Nazar could do this, for the hymn goes on to praise "what St. Nazar has done".

It is characteristic of Khambule's understanding of these apocalyptic events that he uses a different verb for 'open up' than that of his official Zulu Bible. The latter has the verb *ukunamulula:* "cause to open softly". Khambule uses the nervously energetic *ukuqhaqha,* to rip open, break open, tear open.

This is what he had done as he was given those precious stones with their profound secrets by God himself. By turning the stones in his strong hands, he could read the message and would proclaim it to his flock with tremendous emphasis.

All the more he had to meditate on the difference between that Book when *opened,* with all its questions challenging him and all its answers inspiring him *and* the Book when *closed,* put together (*incwadi esongiwe*). In the latter state it rested, as it were, from its labours. The prophet would look at the sun and the moon. Sometime they would be "quiet as a Book put together" (Diary II, 27.4.1926).

Diary

It is impossible here to find space for an adequate edition of Khambule's voluminous diaries. A few extracts will have to suffice to convey an idea of his world of thought and vision.

4.6.1925
The Word coming from Jehova, Nazar D.O.J.R.S. The whole Bible was written to you. So it is, because you say you died and rose again. No, it is not so, it is because all the Scriptures were written with you as addressee. There are many prophets who died and rose again as those. But their strength is in you and the names of these Scriptures were written to you in the heavens. It is not because of your faith, says St. Gabriel who stands before God.

The Word of Jehova God. In these Scriptures all the nations will be saved through you. The story was written. Love and glory of Lord Jeses (sic!) Holy. Part of the house was written *SIJ NHD AIEE.* All the strength of the prophets was written to you. These are their names beginning from St. Samuel up to the forefathers O.A. Who ascended in a burning chariot E.E. All were written to you. That is why Jehova said all the nations shall bow under you, black as well as white shall follow you.

A.B.C. three stars are there to-day representing God F God S. God H. They were written to you, this power, three entities, *eziqu ezitatu.* You knew me. These stars existed before anybody else. Therefore all nations shall be under you. Says AO by oath. This is so I.K.S.P.T. Are you priest and God? This is the answer, No, says Jehova Immanuel. God with us. Who is the Judge? *Simakade* [the Eternal], says Jehova. Thus the Scripture. It says about you that you are what you are. Those who do not believe this Scripture should simply die.

4.6.1925 6 p.m. – 9.30 p.m.

General of the Lord and prosecutor I.K.Y.I.Y.K.A. The glorious morning star, the stone on which are written all the apostles, (stones of the 12 apostles).

You have taken the likeness of Lord Jesus. If the star seen by the wise men did not exist, who were they, these wise men of old? ... They would never have come to you to know what you are if the glorious morning star did not exist. This is written in the heavens, says St. Gabriel.

Noble one of heaven, this is the morning star of God. Thus says St. Gabriel. What was hidden shall now be exposed in the open. This is written in the heavens. St. Gabriel says this as he had the sword in his right hand and in the left the palm leaves which represent the morning star that led the wise men to the Child. When they had seen the Child they adorned him with gold. So it is, they adorned him in spirit and in heart, says Jehova Y.

S P A J Z J F B T M I A L T S K. -SOS. These are the names that were written on the glorious morning star. Thus he has the power of the Apostles which was written to him, and that is why he alone went to Zwana.

All the mighty apostles are perfectly in him. There are St. P and St. A and all great ones except Judah who was not included there. But among them was placed St. Stephen. Those who were stoned for fighting for their Lord and the Saints. Such as Zebedee's son and St. Matthew, the publican. How can I name them all to the prosecutor. Is it because of faith? No, this is what God destined himself in his power. So it is and I thank God. This matter is continuing. It is very far-reaching indeed. The children of men now hear you through their works. I praise the Eternal of hosts.

Big black stoles are needed rather than the ones we [now] have. They shall be fastened on the right hand side. They shall be marked with silk, which is known by the Carrier of the Ark. They shall be white, marked with black or red. They are for the seven spirits of God.

Friday 5.6.1925 7 p.m.—9.30 p.m.

The word from Jehova. I was very much in love with St. AHK. The great ones St. Michael and St. Gabriel and St. Ag. HK. have also come. These three are great. Lord, justify my heart as I, who am nothing, am visited by the heavens, *izulu*. We are waiting. The great chief of our King, the Prosecutor and Judge of cases, St. AHK, has spoken. This is the first word. My brother did not like me to marry. When I was in heaven I said, the one who looks after Joannah for me will be rewarded. When things got harder we loved one another very much. Therefore when she is here she is my child and myself at the same time. This is why it is said to my brother he must buy a glittering royal gown.

I exist because Joannah lives ... Therefore it is said to-day, buy the royal gown. I did not know that you have nothing. I asked for

139

From George Khambule's diary.

the gown myself and there was a dispute because I prided myself with you. It is so, it is hard because people do not see. That day will be a great one. Joannah is going to be given into marriage with the Lamb.

Saturday 8.8.1925 – 8 p.m.
The word from the Lord. What has been done in heaven with the gown bought by the Judge is very great. It has been changed there. She is no longer called Joannah. She is called Agreneth Hlazile ... So stand things in Heaven. Secrets are being revealed. This is a real wonder. Things are concealed above. The Lord himself has come holding many names in his hand, but they will not be explained.

Sunday 26.7.1925
The word from Jehova ... You should have known why it is said that the Church members will be surprised when they find Joannah already crippled. It is because Satan has planned great evil, right from the day of the marriage. He failed on the day until he began to conquer here on earth. He therefore went to God and asked for many things in accordance with his plans ... Satan has really great power ... He tempted the Lord himself. It even appeared as though he is no longer an Angel.

31.7.1925
The word from Jehova. The day which was expected has arrived. There is thus no peace in heaven because of these gangs (*ama Gang*). This matter is more the concern of the nations who are the real masters of it. It is very bad in heaven. There is fighting with swords. You must know this; it is hard if gangs are called. It happens when Satan has planned too much evil ... Prayers must be held. St. John 14 must be read by the Carrier of the Ark. All the members will attend the prayers. If the Spirit is willing, you Nazar should also go.

140

George Nazar Khambule with the General of the Lord and the General's Clack of the Lord.

Archbishop Mordochai Sikakane, July 1969, (d. Jan. 1970).

Bishop E. Vilakathi's Jeriko Church, swinging along to join the Good Friday Festival, Lobamba, Swaziland.

Swazi Zion churches: same occasion.

Bishop Vilakati, Mankaiana, Swaziland.

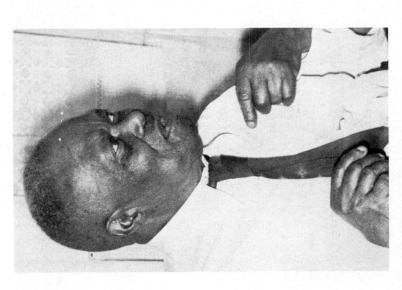

Bishop Walter Dimba, head Federation
Bantu Churches

1.8.1925

The word from the Lord. What is Satan after all? ... The difficult time is passed, all the prophecies have been fulfilled. It is now time to witness regarding the telephone.

1.8.1925

Joannah Zondo. The word from Jehova. It is said, I must let you know this. Great things are going to happen on the earth, says Jehova. One day they saw souls of many people facing North and West; [they were] dead and not facing heaven. I saw very few facing heaven, and the lost souls were then nothing before God. They are really nothing, why? They do nothing for God.

2.8.1925 11 a.m.

Sunday 16: 1925 Witbank: this is the plan for the Judge and the Cross[3] ... It must go and surround Witbank. The travelling fare for Adelaide will be paid by Nathanael, says the Lord concerning this journey.

Diary II: 27.4.1926

The sun was quiet as a Book bound together (*incwadi esongiwe*) and the moon was quiet as a bound Book. It was fulfilled which was said, that the sun was their God. John Mark came and told us. St. Nazar will come and he will be in Jerusalem.

Signs of a different language

Before entering the gates of these secret realms, an attempt should be made to interpret Khambule's attitude to language as such, that is, to his own Zulu language. Here was a man obsessed with the language. His academic attainment was limited. He had attended a night school in Johannesburg. And he had one book, albeit in itself a library of books, his Zulu Bible. Khambule was ever reading that book, enthralled by the sonorous associations of consonants in the proclamations in the Book of Revelation. One can, as it were, overhear his own individual predilections as he quotes, and misquotes, the verses from that miraculous book. A telling example is one of his numerous "Songs of the Church of the Saints".

---

[3] "The Cross", in this connexion a special formation of some of the faithful who as a group pray for patients or for the unconverted world.

They came out of the Temple
seven vials filled with the wrath of God
who liveth for ever and ever. [cf. Rev. 15: 7]

The Zulu version has the equivalent of the following text in the English translation: "And they had breastplates as it were breastplates of iron; and the sound of their wings was as *the sound of chariots of many horses running to battle.*" (Rev. 9:9).

Khambule renders this verse like this:

Zazi namakurasi njengamakurasi
Umsindo wamapiko azo waunjenge krustail

A literal translation would be: "They had breast-plates as breast-plates and the sound of their wings was as that of crystal".

The strange euphony of the word *kurasi* attracts him to such an extent that he says: "They had breastplates like breast-plates"—which is of course meaningless. It is not the informative comparison he is after but the euphonious flow of *Kurasi.* This leads him to an association with *krustail* (crystal) in the last line.

Hitherto we have only briefly brushed the surface, the exterior. Stones, however precious, would have remained dumb, devoid of a message, even to George Khambule himself, were it not for that secret language, spoken by angels. But it was here that Khambule prevailed: he constantly received messages in that language and wrote them down.

An example is a crisis of authority which occurred in the Church. Khambule turned to God and he related the outcome:

The Lord swore saying to St. Nazar. If they do not obey you, they will never enter heaven. He confirmed it by oath saying s f m s m d- f r d t s s r f m r d". Khambule therefore exclaimed, "Oh God, why am I here, You God have grace and goodness m r m f m r d d t d."

This is secret language or angels' language, and I cannot claim personal acquaintance with it. Neither have I listened to Khambule himself pronouncing it. I have to rely on secondary information. Fortunately I had a demonstration of the language by Khambule's faithful successor in Johannesburg, police sergeant H. Hlongwane. By day he patrolled the streets of Western Native Township but during the night he was constantly translated through his dreams to a more heavenly City. George Khambule—this was eight years after the prophet's death —would visit him, speaking to him in Zulu. In 1958, Hlongwane explained these things to me. Jesus also came to Hlongwane in dreams, speaking in English and other foreign languages, and this was followed, still in the dream, by a translation into Zulu performed by the Holy Spirit.

With great emphasis on each new letter and digit Hlongwane repeated to me what Jesus of his dream had recently told him:

Everything is correct. Look from A D 495 X. This is a lock.

The heavenly voice then inquired, "Have you understood?", which was answered by Hlongwane in the affirmative.

As a church leader, Khambule during his lifetime exercised such far-reaching and formative influence on his followers, that I feel entitled to suggest that Hlongwane's performance on this particular occasion was an echo, however weak and inadequate, of the kind of thing which Church members were constantly hearing from Khambule himself. In an authoritative voice he would spell out the Will of God with a string of loose letters from the alphabet, the latter a learned device with which Khambule, as we have already pointed out, had made his acquaintance only late in life.

His religion had made him transcend the narrow borders of ordinary language. His heavenly experience made the thin shell of Zulu words burst and explode into a fireworks of enrapturing sound.

Khambule was fascinated by the sound of foreign tongues. In May 1927 he notes in his diary: "On May 23, 1926, the Gate Keeper spoke to the Clerk saying, St. Itengirrah, which name is in translation Regenah for Doxah in Greek and in Roman and in Hebrews and in Latin which translated is Mowishi."

Through Mtanti, the ex-teacher, Khambule had contact with that glittering, yet unreachable world of learning which seemed to be the prerogative of the Whites. Ordinary Zulus had to remain outside this realm. It was a common experience in established churches at the time to hear accusations against missionaries for having withheld this essential learning from the Africans. Khambule on the other hand had been given special revelation from on high and had thus insight into what would otherwise have remained a closed world.

It was in this fashion that Khambule received his revelations of the new names given to the 'Saints', the chief public figures in the church. As to himself, Khambule was called St. Nazar, a name obviously derived from the Zulu name *aba Nazari* for the Nazirites of the Old Testament. George Khambule sometimes was referred to as the Judge, *uMahluli,* while John Mtanti was sometimes St. John Marko or the Teller (*uMazisi*) and Hilda Sithole was the "Court Prosecutor", *uMshushisi.* Again, "the Carrier of the Ark" was one *uKubingela Mbata. "Captenis"* was the name of a certain Agnes Kuzipika.[4] Another prominent actor, his young niece, was given from on high the name *St. Itengirrah.* This name is, just as obviously, a reflected expression of Khambule's fascination with the language (one notices for instance the double 'r' in a Zulu language which knows no "r"). *St. Substantno* is another name with difficult consonant combinations to the Zulu ear, and with fascinating associations to the world of learning and thinking. All these strange names are revelations. In his Diary (Aug. 8, 1925) Khambule meditates on the way in which the names are given to him: "Secrets are being revealed. This is a real marvel. Things are concealed above. The Lord himself has come carrying many names in His hand, but they will not be explained".

This secret language functioned on different levels: the message of the stones provided a secret code whereby the prophet could open the Bible and interpret it to the group. Further, the secrecy of the language served to place this church apart from the rest of society and to integrate the flock into a *communitas* of immense strength. They knew that these secrets were revealed only to them, for ever ...

Different Acts of Worship

Khambule's religion *is* worship, in the specific sense of corporate religious dramatic performance, in which prayer and praise are acted out by the whole community as a total, all-

---

[4] Explanations given by Archbishop M. Sikakana's widow.

144

engaging drama. It must be kept in mind that the Saints were a closely-knit religious community, living together, working together and worshipping together at their Telezini Zion, directed by an authoritative, and indeed charismatic, leader who also was a creative and imaginative stage-manager.

Consider Khambule's background. He had heard Pastors Mtembu and Ndaba, both of the Enyanyadu Wesleyan Congregation, preach long, lively and instructive sermons, based, we presume, on the English Methodist model. The hymns were largely Methodist hymns translated into Zulu.

Mtanti had a different background. He was an Anglican, from an area dominated by the moderately Anglo-Catholic tradition at the nearby St. Augustine's Cathedral. The choruses and responses in the worship of the Saints seemed distantly related to that model.

But summary references to these two Western streams of influence are an altogether inadequate explanation of what was to emerge as the rich worship of the Saints.

Here a reaction against the worship of the Whites was one important consideration. Baptism in a font or in "much water"—both were equally wrong. Khambule's Church, in order to be different *and* faithful to its basic vision, used holy stones instead. The priest of The Saints holds the child with one hand and the stone in the other. With the stone he makes the cross on the forehead and chest of the child, baptizing it in the name of the Father and of the Son and of the Holy Ghost.

The purificatory function of this kind of baptism is further emphasized by the simultaneous display of holy ashes. A female Warden of Ashes would hold a pan or basin containing ashes and accompany the actual baptism in the name of the Triune God by thrice scooping up (*ukucaphuna*) ashes and returning these again into the basin, without however applying these to the body of the baptizand.[5]

For healing services, the "weapon" of stones is used in a similar way. The prophet lays his hands on the patient, placing the power-charged stone on the sick part. At the burial of Saints,

[5] Mrs. Sikakana's explanation does not tally with the official account in the Church's constitution, cf. *Appendix,* p. 322.

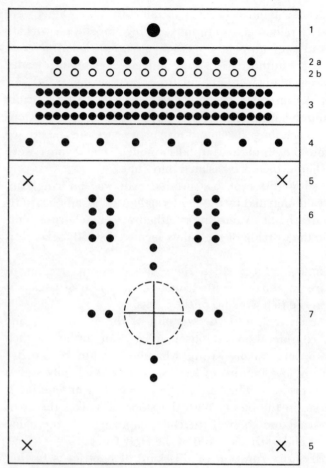

*George Nazar Khambule's "Congregation of All Saints" at worship.**

1. George Nazar Khambule himself, in episcopal gown with his brass staff. *2 a.* Twelve prophets in purple. *2 b.* Twelve apostles in white. *3.* Choir, or *isigodlo,* in white and black. *4.* Eight lectors in green, facing altar. *5.* The four cardinal points, in white. Standing still and quiet the whole time. *6.* Sixteen Readers in green and red facing each other. *7.* The "Hospital": eight elders praying for the sick.

Ad. 1. G. N. Khambule: "He only sits. He does not preach." Present only on great Feast days. Other days withdrawn in his Holy of Holies, speaking in his Telephone to the Throne above.

* This sketch according to original outline drawn in July 1941 by Stud. Theol. (now Bishop) P. B. Mhlungu. With B. Sr.

146

the priest holds a stone as he reads from the Bible and prays according to Khambule's liturgy. When he scatters soil on the corpse, "he puts the stone in his pocket".

But while opposition against the customs of other churches possibly played some part, the positive factor was the Book of Revelation, as experienced by both Khambule and Mtanti. Here they found the authoritative pattern for worship. Khambule had the gift of engaging everybody in active worship. This was also the means of evangelism: people joined him also because they enjoyed playing their part in the great drama at Telezini.

An idea of this active and dramatic worship can be conveyed by some of his most representative liturgies, with the understanding that these, as a matter of course, were sung antiphonally, by leader and congregation.

I. *Priest:* The Gates of Paradise were opened. He saw angels decending. *Congregation:* As lightning they spoke to him saying: We have heard their prayer.

P.: The Gates of Paradise.

C.: Were opened.

P.: He saw an angel descending.

C.: As lightning.

P.: He spoke.

C.: With him and said.

P.: God has heard.

C.: Thy prayer.

P.: St. Nazar did not agree and said. I do not want to go to the Earth. But St. Itengirrah said to him. It is good that thou goest because I have revealed myself to Thee.

C.: He told all the faithful.

P.: But first the Lord showed himself to St. Itengirrah, and when he had passed (*dlulile*) all his trials (*amacala*) he said. After the Lord had revealed himself to him, he (*Nkosi*) spoke to him.

C.: It is good that Thou goest to tell what I have seen.

P.: So it was; when he came to the earth.

C.: He told all the faithful.

P.: But after this they did not obey him.

C.: They mishandled everything holy.

P.: Glory be to the Father.

C.: As it was ...
      Amen, Amen, Amen.

II. *Prayer at 11 a.m.*

Priest: *Akaseyukutula* (Peace)
    Through the New Jerusalem.
    Let us pray. Come, ye are called.

Congregation:
   Through St. Itengirrah.
Pr.: Peace be unto you. In 1918 on the 18th day of the 10th month
   it was dark at Khambule's place.
C.: Today many St. Itengirrahs exist.
P.: Gates will be opened as he went and entered into the twelve gates
   because he was worthy.
C.: Itengirrah overcame death.
P.: Today you can call by telephone. Some of you are blessed;
   others among you are cursed.
C.: Itengirrah walked with Madie.
P.: What do you say? How are your hearts? Look, the Gate is open.
C.: It is good to follow them where they are going.
Pr.: One day it happened that St. Itengirrah entered Paradise.
C.: Today there are many St. Itengirrahs.
Pr.: He sang, saying: He is happy with the Saints above.
C.: Itengirrah overcame death.
Pr.: He came and cried before the Lamb saying: what have I done
   on earth that I am here?
C.: Itengirrah walked with Madie.
Pr.: You see that you should go to heaven. But this will be
   not according to your wishes but according to right.
C.: It is good to follow them where they are going.
   All Simeons and Ivins enter through St. Nazar. Amen.

III. *Basic Liturgy*

Priest: Glory be to the Father and to the Son and the Holy Ghost.
Congregation: As it was in the beginning ...
P.: Praise ye Jehovah.
C.: The name of Jehovah be praised as it was in the beginning.
   1st and 2nd reading.
P.: The hymn: "Hosanna in the highest".
C.: Hosanna in the highest.
P.: *Akaseyukutula* (Peace).
C.: Through the New Jerusalem.
P.: Come, ye are called.
C.: Through St. Itengirrah.
P.: Let the congregation give thanks.
C.: For what was done by St. Nazar.
P.: Because he fulfilled his sending.
C.: He did not fear the people of the earth.
P.: He will reign over the nations.
C.: He will rule by his iron rod.

IV. *Worship of the Giving of the Ark* (at 11 a.m.)

P.: Peace be unto you.
C.: Through St. Itengirrah.

P.: Let us pray.
Come, you are called.
C.: Through St. Itengirrah.
P.: One young woman said. Here I am, I do not see.
When thanks are brought.
But the Child when brought be thanked,
it holds a Sword.
C.: When St. Itengirrah is giving thanks, saying, God Madie holds the
Sword.
P.: Here the Creatures and the Elders and the Angels thank him who is
seated on the Eternal Throne.
C.: All the Angels say: God, thou art great.
Pr.: It happened on the 20th of June in 1922 that the word of God
came to St. Nazar, saying: You are fortunate, because the Ark which
was carried by the Cherubim will be given to you.
C.: The Angel said, St Nazar, you are fortunate because ye will be
given abundance.
Pr.: The Ark of the Covenant will be given to some of your young
women. Therefore put them apart.
C.: The Ark of the Covenant will be given to young women.
P.: He repeated many times: It is indeed good that they put them
apart, they will be given power.
C.: Therefore it is good that they put them apart, because they are
given power.
P.: At that time St. Nazar told them: It is good that they put apart
the Ark of the Covenant and it be given to girls of our Church.
C.: St Nazar said: Why should we be given power?
P.: At that time, that is in the Beginning, there was great commotion
(*ubuyaluyalu*), but they will put them apart.
C.: They will do it according to what the Angel said, they will leave
any gain to them.
P.: Secondly, it happened in the evening. Saul Mtshali came and said,
A man came who said, I had to come here to be prayed for. Three
girls and two women [and] St. Nazar went to his kneeling place.
Then the Word came and said, 'It is not as those two are saying.
They must take water [and ashes] for a sinner and put hands on
him'.
C.: These two may take water and that other one, ashes.

V. *The Song of the Cherubim*
Through St. Itengirrah.
A. Hosannah in the highest.
Peace be in the New Jerusalem.
B. Come for ye are called through St. Itengirrah.
C. The Church must give thanks because of what was done by St.
Nazar DC.*

* DC=Da capo.

149

D. Because he fulfilled his sending.
   He did not fear the people of the earth.
E. He will rule the nations. He will rule them with an iron rod.

Song

A. Let us sing, let us sing to the Lord. Let us sing to God.
B. Let us sing to Iveni, Let us sing to Itengirrah.
C. Let us sing, let us sing to the Word, let us sing to Messiah.
D. Let us sing, let us sing to Nazar, let us sing to Immanuel.

Hymn of Praise

A. Holy, Holy, Holy DC.
B. Lord, remember me in Thy Kingdom and be with me
   where you are.
C. The Lord said, indeed I tell you. Today you will be with me
   in Paradise. Remember through Calvary. DC.
   Jesus died there. *Amen* (repeated six times).

VI. *The Song of the Telephone*

1. *Gatekeeper:* There is no longer faith nor righteousness. We are here
   by the will of the Lord.

Chorus 1
We have been called here
to tell the Church
of the Wire
and its works.

Chorus 2
Those who pray
about difficult matters
are called by that Wire.

Verse 3
St. John Marko announced
that now was to appear
the overseer (*Induna*) of Jerusalem.

Chorus 3
The Judge who is the great *Induna*
of new Jerusalem
has come.

VII. *Hymn of the Saints*
This place is The Fountain
of salvation through St. Itengirrah
St. John 4: 12, Rev. 22: 5

150

This place is the Fountain
of Salvation
      Bis.
Hosannah to the Saviour:
He will wash you in the Pool.

The contents of these liturgies are soon described. It is all
about the communication between Heaven and Telezini. Against
a solemn backdrop of Paradise, with Jehovah established in the
centre, there is an occasional introductory reference to the
Trinity. The core of the drama deals with Telezini, beginning
with George Khambule's vision of Telezini from heaven in 1920.
This is the real centre of the doctrine. In the foreground, St.
Nazar and St. Itengirrah move and act as the chief players. Communication between Telezini and Heaven is reached through the
Gates—the role of the Gate-keeper in Khambule's writings should
be stressed—and by means of the "heavenly telephone". Then
again, space is filled with the armies of the Apocalypse: Angels,
Creatures, Elders; illuminated by an occasional flash of lightning, more Zulu, perhaps, than Hebrew.

The form of the liturgy is most interesting. It does not look
very impressive, on paper. This worship has to be heard. We
repeat that it is all in the form of sung responses, performed
antiphonally by these highly musical Zulu men and women. It
is as music that this liturgy lives and moves the hearts of the
participants. There is a constant response and *inter-play*—the
exact word for what occurs—between the Priest and his Congregation, between the Stage-manager and his cast. Sometimes
the responses are very brief. At other times the Priest sings
long passages from the Book of Revelation or from the living
tradition of Khambule's life, while the congregational response
is perhaps reduced to one short line, sung with great enthusiasm.

In 1969 we heard Archbishop Sikakana as Leader sing one
verse at a time from St. John's Apocalypse, and his little congregation of four or five under the determined and energetic
direction of the Archbishop's wife, Nesta, would repeat the
same holy words. This was not all: the Archbishop would sing
one line, with strong emphasis. The congregation would
respond with the same vigour; then—and this had a very

moving effect—the Archbishop would repeat the singing of the words with a soft voice, as if whispering a great secret, and his wife and the congregation followed him. With innate discipline they would enter into the secrecy of these holy mysteries and corporately whisper their joy at the Angels and Creatures and Elders, invisibly but certainly present, moving their wings softly.

This was also part of Khambule's considerable genius, for as the insignificant little group at Spookmill in 1969 arranged a special service for the benefit of their white visitor, they were all aware of their fundamental debt to "George", who had once conceived and created all these words and the liturgical arrangement of words, and the music, and their copes and mitres and staffs.

This effect was emphasized by the pattern of movements enacted by the Archbishop and his group. It perhaps goes without saying that in these actions they believed they were solemnly imitating the movements and mannerisms of the un-forgettable George Khambule himself. I take this for granted for I have often noticed how in these churches this jerky curtsy or that strange sound—howling, hawking—performed regularly by the group was at the same time an expression of an identi-fication with the particular church founder who perhaps un-wittingly had introduced this step or sign or sound. Thus while leading the singing, Sikakana would hold his archiepiscopal crozier in his left hand, moving in a dancing rhythm; from time to time bowing deeply. All this was repeated by his fol-lowers.

Now he announced that they were going to sing the Lauda-mus. Swinging his crozier, he danced up to the little window of the room, and then stepped back again, bowing deeply. This movement would be solemnly repeated five or six times, all parti-cipating.

Role-taking

Police-sergeant Hlongwane could hardly wait, he told me when interviewed in 1958. He had to work another few years as a policeman; then he would go back to Spookmill in Natal, the headquarters of the Church, near Khambule's grave. The prophet had died at Hlongwane's place in Johannesburg and had given him some of his robes. But, Hlongwane said, when at last he was free to take up his church-work as a full-time job, he would challenge Archbishop Sikakane at Spookmill and force him to hand over Khambule's staff. The power of the Church, he felt, was contained and concentrated in that staff. When Khambule, as often happened, paid dream-visits to Hlongwane, he would as a matter of course appear with this 'iron rod' of his. It had a fish's mouth for its head, Hlongwane told us, and this shape proved its connection with Moses' own staff, according to St. John ch. 3. Hlongwane was recognized as the 'Aaron' of the movement, but with the staff he would at last be promoted to be its Moses.

Here, of course, Hlongwane knew that he could rely on Khambule's own judgment. More than thirty years earlier, October 5, 1925, the prophet himself confided to his diary a contented statement: "My God spoke to me on this day: The rod of strength. To-day it is like this: There are bishops' croziers, but compared to this, they are nothing". Fortunately for Hlongwane, he also had a number of holy stones which he demonstrated to me at his Johannesburg home. To me, these seemed to be perfectly ordinary stones. To Hlongwane, they possessed a mysterious potential of life: "They are all biding their time, until I shall appear", he told me.

That powerful iron rod of Khambule's and its effect on its rightful owner was only part of the whole process of role-taking at Telezini. For this is really what worship was all about: role-taking. The elaborate selection of sacred garments and robes in various colours was no whim. It ensured to the *dramatis personae* a new and higher identity. It illustrates traditional African experience of changing one's personality by putting on a new mask. In 1925 it happened to Khambule himself: "At this he was given the robe of [King] David and changed into another nature" (*wa penduka esinye isimo*).

His beloved Joannah became particularly close to him as they were united in the Marriage of the Lamb. The choice of dress for Joannah had to be made with care and concern. For the Marriage of the Lamb she was given a ring, "that was never worn by anybody else. Therefore when she is here she is my child and myself at the same time (*ungumntwana wami futhi uyimina*). This is why it is said to my brother [Khambule], that he must buy a glittering royal robe." "I could not undertake marriage in an ordinary dress," says Angel A.H.K. [thus Joannah in her new appearance as Agrinet Hlazile Khambule] ... "Royal silk robes are needed. I exist because Joannah lives (*Ngikhona ngoba uJoanah ukhona*). Therefore it is said to-day, buy a royal gown ... Dressed in a green gown, I praise God." On this occasion she was given a new dress, but this indeed meant much more and went much further than just a change of dress.

Saturday 8.8.1925, 8. A transformation was achieved there as she is no longer called Joannah. Now she is Agrinet Hlazile. Thus says Scripture, regarding that one Joannah, revelation shall be by a person. Now she is Agrinet. So it is over there ... She will be dressed in white as she leaves from here. Secrets are being revealed. The Lord himself has come, holding many names in his hand."

But if such a change of role and identity could happen to a mere woman, what might not happen in the case of Khambule himself? The Diary, June 12, 1925 at 1 a.m. gives a surprising answer. Jehovah told him that he was going to carry a stole with the inscription "*Ukulunga kwabangcwele*"—the Righteousness of the Saints—a name which not even an angel had previously received: "It is a miracle. Who am I? Jehovah. It will be so written that this will be plainly visible to anybody".

A week later, on June 18, 1925, he is still struggling with this seemingly numinous insight into his own role: "There is much more that could be spoken or explained. Why? The words come from Jehovah, affirming the words of Priest J.S.B. Khambule. They are really very great. I am not surprised. This is really great. You are going to the Holy Place as it happened to my King, and so a similar likeness is going to take place". This is why, a year later, in June 1926, the Diary can have the notice: "At that time, the appearance of St. Nazar was like that of the sun and his voice like that of a mighty waterfall".

Is this aspect of role-taking one reason why Khambule often refers to Phil. 2:5–11? "Let this mind be in you which was also in Christ Jesus ... who took upon him the form of a

Servant (*ukuma komfokozana*). As he meditated over that word, he may possibly have related to Rom. 13:14: "Put ye on the Lord Jesus Christ" (*nambate,* put on the dress).

To him Phil. 2 meant: Act Jesus! Play Jesus! In the land of the Philistines, in a land of sorrow and contempt and hatred for the Black man, play Jesus and act that part, "until *Kalvani*", his word for that strange English name Calvary.

You cannot do that, Khambule's ex-friends among the Wesleyans and Mtanti's ex-friends among the Anglicans, all at Telezini, would retort sharply. What you are performing is nothing but a Feast of Fools! "But no", Khambule might have wished to say. "It is a Feast, indeed the Marriage Feast of the Lamb. All depends on your attitude. You must enter this drama fully, in order to get anything out of it. You must accept the rules of the drama. From the outside, all this may well appear as outrageous claims and pretensions. But, we beg you, enter the circle; take part in the drama; become one of the actors. Play Jesus!"

We notice that we have for a moment strayed from our course. We shall return to this theme later, and let these considerations serve as an approach to the so-called 'messianic' groups. If you remain outside and refuse to join the play, you miss something essential; in fact, you miss everything.

With these considerations in mind, one begins to understand why there are constant references to the particular robes which the *dramatis personae* at Telezini must wear:

The Gatekeeper appeared in a black robe with which he fought Satan; St. Itengirrah as the Carrier of the Ark must wear a green robe with black stoles.

The robe of the "General of the Lord: Write "red", and let it hang down on the sides. Write dark brown. It shall be written in full "THE WITNESS OF THE GENERAL OF THE LORD". (D. 4.6.1925) Whoever speaks with God must wear a necklace and a crown. (11.9.1925)

Notorious as the religion of Telezini soon became, it managed to attract European visitors, armed with their eternal attribute, the camera. Khambule saw deeper than they (D. 12.3.1926): "The Whites wish to take photos only on account of the dresses worn.

155

Yes, these are very beautiful. This is the angel's work. It is great and they marvel. And the police look on. It is really great. I thank my God very much indeed."

A different Law of Conduct

It was the ethic of the Church which brought about the great crisis and led to its final and inevitable downfall. Worship was innocuous. Within the four walls of the temple they might sing and pray and play, as much as they wanted, all the way from Telezini to the Throne above. Nobody would care or protest. But it was the strange, asocial conduct of Khambule and his people that gave offence and brought him to court and led to his eviction from Telezini. I hasten to add that it was the Zulu chief and his Zulu community, much more than the Magistrate—the White Government's personal representative at Nqutu—which felt offended by Khambule's strange conduct.

The root of it all was to be found in Khambule's own initial calling: "Risen", translated to heaven, he heard Jesus order him to go down to Telezini, and the earth in general, in order to follow strict rules concerning pollution and purity.

A wife who was a Saint soon found no alternative but to move definitely from her kraal, to Khambule's Zion. The family bond would be broken, of course, but this seemed a small sacrifice as compared with the eternal bliss promised by the Prophet. He arranged the "Heavenly Marriage", the Marriage of the Lamb. Whether men or women, they had to go through this solemn process. The men or the boys, all in twos, and the women and girls likewise; joined together, all called brides. They had to stay in seclusion for two weeks. They were supposed to emerge "fat and white" for the wedding. The wedding itself was a joyous affair. The brides would put on pure white robes. One head of cattle was slaughtered, and there was a wedding cake, and a ring made by Simon Mhlungu who melted a sufficient number of "tickies", silver threepenny-pieces, for the occasion. The wedding was performed by Khambule himself, "The Judge".

Khambule himself had shown the way. He parted from his

wife, Ma Sikakane, and they subsequently called each other "sister" and "brother". He then entered into a more "heavenly marriage" with at least two women followers, and in his Diary, as we have already seen, he emphasized his delight with these young ladies. His Diary, in fact, sometimes contains strong expressions of emotional contact. In Johannesburg, on September 22, 1925, he had a dream: "I saw the Lord having descended, but not for judgment. The church of the Saints had gone to him, I myself was late, though, but he got hold of me and kissed me thoroughly in the mouth (*yanganga kakhulu emlonyeni*). This kissing meant that my word would thrust (*hlaba*) when I preach. There it ended."

In order to avoid pollution, the Saints must not shake hands with infidels; they must not eat fermented things, nor drink beer or *amaheu* (light ale). Dishes made with blood must not be eaten, nor *ububende*, a favourite Zulu dish made of blood added with pieces of mincemeat.

The danger of pollution was greatest in the case of death. The Saints, therefore, were forbidden to touch a corpse. There were patients at Khambule's Zion who were *not* healed, but died. They would have to lie there, until at last some relative from afar or some non-believer from the neighbourhood would bury them. In calling someone to help the messenger would not refer to "death" but simply say that so-and-so was "very ill". If a relative of a Saint had passed away, the Church forbad its member to console the family.

There was Bible authority for this attitude, they felt: "Leave the dead to bury their dead". Yet this uncompromising attitude could not be maintained indefinitely. The Church simply had to take care of their departed, as we have already indicated.

It was this "caste" attitude, this total separation from the social body, which turned chief and people against Khambule. From his point of view this was part of the sacrifice he had to make in order to be faithful to his vocation. He records it all in his Diary, on March 12, 1926:

I have not brought peace. I have come to separate people, [to set] a daughter at variance against her mother and the father against his son. Why? Because there cannot be any understanding between the

one who has seen me and the one who has not seen me. S. Matt.
10: 22–24, 25–28, 32–38, Acts 5: 34–39, Proverbs 21; 29–31.

April 14, 1926

The days when I walked in noise and to beer parties are past,
1 Peter 4: 1–3. You say that I am bringing unrest to the nation.
No, it is you who are bringing unrest by throwing away the faith in
God and walking according to Baal's religion, so that our country
followed Baal's religion. It is good that you will call all your prophets
so that we should go with them into the mountain to stay there for
ten days without food. They would sit there and die and be finished
but I alone will be left.

This was indeed the method Khambule, like other prophets,
used in order to build up his inner authority: to fast on the
mountain, or at least reputedly to do so. More than other Zulu
prophets, he was aware of the stones scattered about on the
mountain, and of their purity and their potential message.
More than anyone else he could feel at home in those awe-
inspiring surroundings, and then return with renewed strength
and conviction.

During his lifetime unknown to outsiders, whether Europeans
or Africans, and very nearly doomed to remain unknown also
after his death, Khambule is nevertheless one of the most fascinating among Zulu prophets. With his remarkable power of imagination and creativity he produced liturgical offices of great orginal-
ity. His diaries provide a more intimate insight into a prophet's
mind than any other available material in South Africa.

The isolation of this gifted man from the rest of the community
—white *and* black—was so total as to be impressive.

I suggest that George Khambule's group came nearer to the
absolute ideal of a closed communitas than any other group in his
time.[6] Not only was this group carefully segregated from any contact with the whites—although Khambule did note in his diary
with some pride that Europeans armed with their cameras had

---

[6] Cf Victor W. Turner, *The Ritual Process* (1969), p. 128. O. F. Raum, *The Social
Functions of Avoidances and Taboos among the Zulu* (1973), p. 529.

visited Telezini to take some exotic pictures. But, more important, they isolated themselves from Zulu society as a whole.

In this situation there were certain elements of modern culture that they appropriated, some for practical reasons, others probably for mythological reasons.

There was the alphabet, for instance. One would have liked to sit in on a lesson in that Methodist night-school in a Johannesburg location, about 1919, with mine-captain George Khambule as one of the students. One would have liked to overhear his struggle with those unruly letters A, B, C, until at last they were broken in to form words and sentences and whole messages. Khambule, we have suggested, was a man obsessed with language, a new literate with only one Book. His mental energy, withdrawn as he was in his Holy of Holies, was spent meditating upon the mighty words in the chapters of the Book of Revelation.

He was in a unique position, for he alone possessed the Keys to an understanding of these verses: those holy stones of his with their secret, yet unmistakable message to the faithful.

Isolated at Telezini from White civilisation and Black culture alike, he established his own world of values. He knew that the times were apocalyptic. In the time of the *"Influenza"* of 1919 he had himself "died" and been translated to heaven—that was the basic fact. But other miracles were to follow. In 1927, an aeroplane fell out of the sky near Nqutu. It hurt itself and died (*"yafa"* was the expression in Zulu) and had to be dragged away by lorries. This was another warning of celestial activities concentrated to that very area of Telezini.

And the Telephone! Nobody will ever know what Khambule's invention looked like. It probably had very little in common with Mr. Bell's contraption. That was precisely the point. Cut off from modern technology and from such machines as were used by the dominant caste in society, the prophet felt all the more the urge to establish his own celestial *cargo,* his superior means of communication, the Heavenly Telephone. He made the best of the situation.

The angelic language transmitted by those signs on the stones together with the corporate struggle of the 'convent' against threatening pollution and for ritual purity were the means with which to maintain external boundaries against an inimical world and to establish total loyalty to George St. Nazar, Prophet and Judge.[7]

[7] *George Khambule: Uppsala Collection* (handwritten; Zulu; photostats)

George Khambule, Diary	1925– 28	120 pp.
George Khambule, Diary	1926–1937	46 pp.
Worship Service Book		244 pp.
D:o	1926–1933	95 pp
D:o		52 pp.
Hymnbook		22 pp.
D:o		28 pp.

Bantu Affairs Department, Pretoria, file 852/214

P. B. Mhlungu, Isalema, Ibandla labangewele: George Khambule, handwritten 50 pp. (1941).

Constitution of The Church of Christ the Congregation of All Saints of South Africa (in Killie Campbell Museum, Durban) Cf. Appendix, p. 321.

Nqutu Magistrate's Office:

Statement by I. J. S. Mtanti October 8, 1931, to the Magistrate, 1931

Zion Free Church Impumalanga Gospel of South Africa (Job S. Mtanti)

From Rev. Joseph M. Mtanti to B. Sr. 7 letters, 1973

Interviews with Archbishop Mordochai Sikakana 1969.

Interviews with Mrs Nesta Sikakana, 1969, 1972, 1973, and 1974.

5. Shembe and Ekuphakameni

If I had consulted my Zionist friends about including a chapter on Shembe in this book on Black Zion they would most probably have been unanimously against the idea. They are, of course, aware of the power and attraction of Shembe; but they probably try all the more to convince the European inquirer that Shembe is not sufficiently "Biblical" or "Christian". They might repeat to the European some of the fanciful and negative stories about old Isaiah Shembe. In so doing they would show that they have no idea of the serious prophetic concern of the man whom they would wish to exclude from their company. In short, they feel embarrassed by being classified with Shembe's *Ama Nazaretha*, which they generally regard as misguided.

They would be saddened even more by attempts on the part of Western scholars to make Shembe essentially representative of the Zionist movement as such. This applies particularly to the sweeping attempts to characterize the Zionist movement as a whole as "Messianic".

Structurally, of course, the similarities are striking. There is the same fundamental emphasis on healing as the central concern of the Church's activity. There is the close fellowship of the local groups, symbolized by the white garments of the faithful. Shembe has realized what most Zion leaders could only dream of creating, but never managed to turn into a reality: to found a *Zion* centre for his Church, preferably on a Holy Mountain. Shembe's Ekuphakameni near Durban and, more especially, the Inhlangakazi—80 miles away—are such unrivalled mountains.

Shembe is better known than any other Zulu prophet. The July festival at Ekuphakameni is regularly publicized in the Natal press and further afield, but it is the Sunday dances which are best known. The Nazaretha are in fact a Sabbatarian group, and the great religious events which take place on that Saturday are almost invariably overlooked.

Among authors who studied Shembe we mention Esther L. Roberts (1936), A. Vilakazi (1954), Katesa Schlosser (1958), C. G. Oosthuizen (1967) and H. J. Becken (1972). Some of these contributions are discussed in the Appendix (p. 326–29).

These learned scholars are all agreed in finding Shembe of particular interest. Adding, from our point of view, these few pages to the debate, we shall concentrate on Shembe as prophet and preacher, poet and healer, at the same time attempting to draw his profile in such a way as to bring out the similarities with, and the differences from, the ordinary run of Zionist prophets. How did he understand his role—and how did his followers see it?

In making this attempt I did not feel entitled to rely only on Shembe's *Hymn-book*—although I shall make some specific references to it and to Shembe's poetic creativity. I have used Dr. John Dube's book on *uShembe* in Zulu as well as the valuable, new archive material *"The Acts of the Nazarites"*, collected at the instigation of Johannes G. Shembe himself. Above all, a study of this kind must be done on a basis of persistant fieldwork, in the midst of the life of worship in the Nazaretha Church. I have been privileged to do so, mainly for the great 'July' festivals, from 1941–69 with one additional visit, in 1972–73. I realize as well as anybody else that as a European one is of course excluded from fundamental dimensions of this whole world of worship and work; yet, it may be said that the repeated contacts over a generation were instructive.

The Call of the Prophet

As a person Shembe was very different from the usual, boisterous and extrovert Zionist prophet. Quiet, withdrawn and softspoken, he exercised his considerable influence over the masses by other means than shouting and jokes—in fact, both he and his son and successor Johannes Galilee Shembe seem reticent and strangely humourless. When preaching to his faithful—and he would see before him ten thousand of them, at the 'July' festival,

162

all in white, in the Paradise section of Ekuphakameni (the Zion of the Church)—he never raised his voice. A powerful Zulu assistant had to act as a human loudspeaker, carrying the prophet's message far and wide.

In an interview in 1969 Johannes Galilee explained to me, in that self-critical, slightly detached fashion of his:

> Shembe was an ignorant person (*isiula*). I am ignorant myself, as far as theology is concerned. Shembe always asked: 'Is that right? Should I do it this way?' If he thought he was wrong, he would give way immediately. He had nothing of his own. He was only interested in the Scriptures, particularly in Jesus Christ. He did not with to add anything to what Jesus Christ had said.

Isaiah Shembe felt assured by his awareness of being sent. "God has revealed his wisdom in sending Shembe who is just a child, in order that he might speak as a wise and educated person" (Dube, 34).

Very little is known of Shembe's background. His son Johannes Galilee complained to me that he had not had time to do research into their family background and his father's early years. That he came from the Harrismith district in the Orange Free State and of an old Hlubi family seems, however, to be an established fact.

As a young man Shembe worked on Boer farms and had a way with horses and cattle that he showed throughout his life. On the advice of his parents he took four wives. But then, he heard a voice telling him to climb a mountain. He did so, and the same voice told him to go into a cave. Overcome by sleep in the cave he had a dream: he was trying to reach certain people, who walked in front of him, but all the time he seemed to be too late. Then lightning appeared and he was asked to survey the earth. As he looked down on the earth of men, he had a terrible vision of his own putrefying corpse. The voice went on to warn him: "If you do not leave *ukuhlobonga* [sexual sins] you will never see me. It is this which hinders your spirit from unity with our Spirit. Because you dwell in a filthy carcase, you may not unite with us."

Then he woke up. That day he did not work. He said: "*I have seen Jehovah*" (Dube, 8). He was always aware of this fundamental spiritual experience on the mountain. He had been set apart.

He did in fact part with his four wives, a very demanding decision. Yet, from time to time the heavenly powers would appear. Lightning would strike, and a Voice said "I will eat your flesh". Shembe recorded that "I was overcome by great fright as I heard this voice". He fell ill, and an *inyanga* came to heal him. But the Voice said, "You will be healed by Jehovah alone". So he paid the *inyanga* one head of cattle, and let him go—and his faith in Jehovah healed him.

He was not yet baptized, but went about preaching in the Orange Free State—in those lean years immediately after the Boer war. Prior to his own baptism he felt constrained by his own experience to pray for the sick and to drive out demons. He now accompanied a Wesleyan local preacher. He listened to his message, "but my heart was not moved by the preaching". Then one day, a group of men from Johannesburg baptized people in a river—and this caught Shembe's imagination. He joined the Baptist preacher, William M. Leshega from Boksburg, on the Rand.

W. M. Leshega

It may seem an unnecessary exercise, at this point, to say anything about Leshega. Yet, Shembe was part of Leshega's church for five years, from 1906 to 1911, and he probably received from Leshega most of his impressions of European missions in South Africa, such as they were at that time. Very little is known about Shembe's milieu in those early years, so any little straw of evidence is of interest.

William Mathebule Leshega was no nonentity at this time. He did in fact appear as one of the leading spokesmen of African churches on the Rand, and his life is not without its revealing aspects. Ideally one would have liked to know something about his message, but there seem to be no sources for that. The following annotations are, at least, better than just the bare name.[1]

Born in 1861 in Leydenburg, Leshega was a Pedi from Seku-

[1] Material on Wm. Leshaga in National Archives, Pretoria: S.N.A., 1902, 15, 2058, Native Free Baptist Congregational Church. On Leshega's contacts with

kuniland, and had his elementary education at the Lutheran school of Botshabelo. He must have been an enterprising young man, for in 1880 we find him in Pretoria, as a 'boy' in the house of Mr. [later Sir Geoffrey] Lagden. When in 1902 the Boer war came to an end, Leshega discovered that his former boss had become an important figure in the British administration. This was an opportunity not to be missed. On September 20, 1902, Leshega wrote "to The Honourable and Dear. Lord Mr. G. J. Lagden Esq."

I Beg to inform you this few lines hopping this should fine you in held ny Lord as it leaves me in held. I am yours obedient servant which was by you on the 19.9.1902 at 12 oclock name you know very well at the time when I was your servant at Pretoria at this year 1880. You use to call me Ottey its now about 23. years ago So now ny Lord I am very Glad to fine you again & Still alive. I take this work of God in the year 1882 I was an Evangelist of the above Church & at 1890 I was ordain to be a Minister By the Rev. H. T. Cousins Pretoria & the Rev. J. T. Ochse".
"God Save the King".[2]

It is characteristic of certain aspects of Protestant work at the time that Leshega should think or say that he had been ordained in 1890. When his European superintendent later wrote to the authorities, he stated merely that Leshega was "baptized and received in the Baptist Church" on Nov. 20, 1891. His superintendent in the Baptist Church now was Rev. W. E. Kelly. But soon Leshega was left to his own devices. Kelly published a surprising announcement in the Johannesburg papers:

This is to Certify that I, W. E. Kelly, have ceased to be the Pastor of the Baptist Church and have no longer any control over its affairs. 16.4.1902 (Signed) W. E. Kelly.

Leshega had been through the Boer War and found new scope for his activities in the refugee camp in Boksburg; this again is a small, but not insignificant indication of the effect of the war on the Africans: we have already pointed to its

W. E. Kelly's successor, Rev. E. R. Davies, and with American Baptists: S.N.A. 1906, 63, 890; on Leshega's contacts with American Baptists, more especially Rev. D. E. Murff, "Coloured American": S.N.A. 1909, 92, 3643.
[2] The text left unedited.

effect upon some of the other Independent leaders. We know that in 1901 Leshega baptized Paul Mabilitsa (p. 59). In 1903 Leshega tranferred his loyalty to the Foreign Missions Board of the National Baptist Convention of America whose missionary, J. W. Jordaan, recognized Leshega as "an ordained minister"; but at the same time, Leshega also represented the "Native Free Baptist Congregational Church".

For a year or two, 1905–06, Leshega now obviously hesitated whether to carry on under American supervision or whether definitely to strike out on his own. Exemption from passes was a consideration that made white supervision acceptable. In May 1906 the Missions Secretary from Louisville, Kentucky wrote to Leshega's old friend, Sir Geoffrey Lagden, now of Native Affairs Department in Johannesburg, asking for his support regarding Leshega's application for an exemption from carrying a pass. In November 1905, however, Leshega had already established his African Native Baptist Church. It was in his capacity as leader of this Church that he, together with ten other "Ethiopian" leaders, was received by the High Commissioner, Lord Selborne. This was an important delegation—it included J. M. Kanyane Napo, M. M. Mokane and S. J. Brander, all of them great names in the early history of the South African "Ethiopian" movement. So Leshega was in good company. The delegation brought up certain matters which were to become of outstanding importance in this discussion of the privileges of Independent African pastors: letters of exemption; native marriages; educational facilities; railway travel. The petition handed over by the delegation stressed the need for recognition of African Churches. The peroration says: "All Petitions addressed to the Native Affairs Department receive courteous refusals now based on the groundless ground of your petitioners' Churches not being recognized."[3]
To the extent that Shembe received from Leshega some of the basic tenets of his religious convictions—later to be modified under the pressure of the expectations of his faithful—it would thus seem important to take account of his fellowship with Leshega.

[3] Deputation 25.11.1905. Cf. Gov. 1905/50/12. National Archives, Pretoria.

166

To the Mountain, the Zulu Zion

This was the minister with whom Shembe worked during his formative years. In 1911, Shembe established his own Church of the Nazarites. He founded his organization near Ohlange, north of Durban; he called his centre Ekuphakameni, the Elated Place. It was at this time that he had his second mountain experience. He heard a voice telling him, "Go to the mountain Inhlangakazi, and pray there. I will give unto you new power." He did not know the place, and was unwilling to follow the dictates of the Voice; consequently, he decided to go to Harrismith in the Free State instead. But a man approached him on the train, telling him, "As soon as you put your feet on the Harrismith station, you will fall down dead."

So he went to Inhlangakazi after all, in 1912. Later on he was to draw the obvious parallel with Moses. Just as Moses had gone to the Mountain in order to praise God, so he too must go to the Mountain, with his congregation, to bring praises to God. (Dube, 62)

But that first time he was alone, and he stayed on the mountain for twelve days. He was pursued by ferocious people who tried to kill him; he was visited by lions, and by leopards pretending to be angels, and saying, "We are sent by God." But he replied, "No, I am waiting for Jesus." Then he found himself surrounded by a rattling host of the skeletons of the dead, making a noise, *khehle khehle* [a Zulu ideogram of something utterly dry and brittle, collapsing, *Doke-Vilakazi*], as they stood around him. He fell down in terror. But one of the skeletons, who in his lifetime had been a great White evangelist, told him, "Brother Shembe, I am sent by God to tell you of the power which you will receive by coming to this mountain. You are not going to die, but you shall live." Then two angels brought him wine and bread, "a sort of sacrament", heavenly food. He knew that having eaten this food, he would never be his old self again, but a new person.

When he returned from Inhlangakazi he looked like the person he had been before, but he was in fact a different man.

In January 1913, he took his flock with him on a pilgrimage to the Holy Mountain, there to stay together for two weeks, living in temporary shelters, built anew for each occasion. This became the Church's "Feast of the Tabernacles". At our visit in January 1973 hundreds of these huts could be counted. More than five thousand of the faithful were there, we were told, yet there was a hush of awe and expectation in this great crowd. Prayers, preaching and teaching are followed by sacred dance.

We stress the importance of the "Mountain experience" in Shembe's life, and shall bring it up again as we consider the role of the Mountain, "the Zion", in the Zulu-Swazi charismatic movement as a whole.

This was to become the centre of the yearly **January** pilgrimage of the church. As soon as he had been baptized himself, Shembe began to baptize others, sometimes in great numbers. But even more significant, he felt within himself a strange power: he could drive out demons. He visited the Wesleyan congregation at Georgedale and was confronted by people plagued by lunacy and hysteria. To his amazement, he saw that his prayers had power over the demons (Dube, 29). His church grew. Shembe himself felt driven to go on extended evangelistic tours throughout Natal and Zululand, and sometimes much further afield. Soon two great Church festivals established themselves, the January Feast of the Tabernacles on the Inhlangakazi Mountain, and the great July Festival at the Ekuphakameni headquarters. All activity in the Church was determined by the yearly rhythm of these two great festivals. Eventually the Church spread through Zulu Society. At first chiefs had been reluctant, and even hostile, but Shembe the healer won them over. In the end some fifteen chiefs were known to be Nazarites, and the July festival came to include special sessions between prophet and chiefs at which important social matters could be dealt with. The crowning glory came when Shembe was able to give his own daughter Zondi to king Solomon as one of his queens. A precious link between Ekuphakameni and Nongoma, between Shembe and Zulu royalty, had been forged.

The Power of the Prophet

The great Sabbath in the annual July Festival affords a special occasion for Shembe himself to explain the teaching of the Church. In 1969, Johannes Galilee Shembe used Lk. 12:16–23, Jesus' parable of the rich fool with his many barns as his text. This Gospel message, Shembe underlined, applies to all men, and the sermon mainly turned into a review of Isaiah Shembe's life and message.

His whole life is a running commentary on his struggle to follow not the values and customs of men, but the laws of God. You Nazaretha remember his life story.

First he worshipped with the Wesleyans. He went with them and prayed with them and even began to drive out demons, while walking with the preachers of that Church. But then came the time for him to be baptized. Now these people baptize the forehead, but Shembe read his Bible. He read that John the Baptist baptized Jesus in the river with much water, in Jordan. He told the preachers this, and they were irritated by this: "You go then and find other pastors who baptize in water". So Shembe left the Wesleyans because of Baptism. And he was baptized in much water, in Johannesburg, by Leshega who was a Baptist.

But again, Shembe discovered that these people while worshipping in church, sat with their shoes on. He approached the pastor on this matter, for he had found that in the Bible, Moses and Jesus did not wear shoes. Pastor Leshega was afraid, for he had seen that when Shembe lifted his hand to pray for the blind, their eyes were opened. So when Shembe asked him what to do, Leshega answered: "I see that you must follow another road and not take our road." So now Shembe established his own church, where he was different from all other pastors, white as well as black. So he worked out our way of doing things, we of Ekuphakameni. At that time when people wished to become Christians, they had to put on clothes. But Shembe read about Adam and Eve in the Bible. We shall read now in the book of Genesis, at the beginning of Holy Scriptures. Genesis, chapter 3, v. 21.

Until that time the pastors had taught that in order to become Christians, people must shed their *ibeshu* and *izidwaba* and put on clothes. But many of our people refused to accept this, and refused to let their women throw away their *izidwaba*. I do not know from where the pastors and missionaries took their teaching. What I know, I know according to the Bible. When God created our first parents, he made coats of skin and made them put these on. And Shembe said. "Let anybody who so wishes come in *ibeshu* or *isidwaba*."

There is nothing in what Shembe did which cannot be found in the Book. And the things he did and taught, he took out of the Bible.

As regards the bread for Holy Communion, Shembe knew that such bread should have no salt in it. I have seen how they do it in the Church of the American Board. They use ordinary bread. Seated in their Church, I was offered to partake. But not wishing to hurt their feeling, I just said: "No, I wait."

Let us look at Matthew 5. These things are important lest you be cheated by other people. There is nothing greater in the faith than the Bible. So let us read Matthew 5: 17. ["Amen"—from the crowd.]

Many churches, White and Black, claim that we do not believe in Jesus! ["Hmm"] from the crowd.] We do not follow Jesus! ["Hm"] We do not worship Jesus! But let them understand how Jesus is to be worshipped. Is it so that he is worshipped by following his laws and commandments or simply by repeating words with one's mouth? Is it sufficient to sit down until sunset repeating to oneself: "Jesus is the Son of God, Jesus is holy, Jesus is righteous. Jesus is our Saviour, Jesus died for us"? We Nazaretha know that the important thing is to follow his precepts, laid down in the Bible.

This fundamentalist combination of legalism and literalism is obviously experienced by the crowd as solid rock, "Bible truth". The simple argument is easily understood by everybody. Nazareth worship does not exhibit the same rapid repartee as that found in the worship in the majority of Zionist churches. Here the crowd of ten thousand in white—in Paradise—sit quietly listening. But one cannot mistake their interest. They accept this message as food for their souls.

As well as being soft-spoken and reserved, Shembe emphasized certain characteristics which served to set him apart, to suggest that he was a holy man with supernatural powers.

The prophet must avoid any pollution, in order to increase those powers. The Nazaretha have strict rules. A menstruating woman is not allowed to join in meals with others or to shake hands with the pastors or handle their food. A man after emission of semen is polluted. He must therefore go to the river and bathe three times, morning, midday and evening. "When he returns, he is purified." Unless this is done, he must not touch Shembe's clothes or even shake hands with Shembe. Concern with these matters had immediate effects for Shembe's healing power. In order to pray for the sick, he would have to put on special dress, and this had to be handled with particular care by those who were appointed to serve him (Dube, 62, 74, 100, 106).

The same concern for purification was shown by Shembe as he consecrated his first pastors, Petrus Mkayi, Amos Mzobe and Johannes Mlangeni. He took them to the Nhlangakazi mountain. Water was prepared, and Shembe carefully washed their bodies, after which he put on them the special dress appointed for pastors. He then led them down the mountain, and after prayers took oil and anointed their heads. Mlangeni was now entrusted himself to ordain pastors (Dube, 100–1).

People were greatly impressed by Shembe's ability to read their minds and their secret thoughts. The Testimonies offered many examples of this. On one occasion, two women brought him money. Shembe answered, "No, keep it. You have taken this money from your lovers after you have sold your bodies." Somebody brought a sum of money for the Prophet, but Shembe refused it. "No, I can see on that money that you got it from selling a pig" (pork being taboo with the amaNazaretha). One preacher complained that his local congregation did not want him. Shembe looked at the man and said,' "I can see inside your heart a small tin with blood in it. Is that blood from an animal or from a human being?" In the end, the man broke down, confessing that he had indeed killed a member of his congregation, thereby bringing his blood on himself. Again, somebody brought a beast to Ekuphakameni as a gift. Shembe told the man to wait a few hours; then he would be prepared to say whether he would accept it or not. The man was called: "This beast tells me that it is not your property. It belongs to another man, to your brother who at present is away at work. You take it back".

Shembe's sensitivity expressed itself in a deep sympathy with the suffering of nature. He would tell his sons not to cut a branch of a tree, adding: "How would you feel if I were to cut one of your fingers from your hand." He fought any sign of cruelty against animals. His hymn-book has the only example in the history of hymnology in which an animal speaks (No. 213). Shembe met a boy who had caught a monkey and was about to sell it, but the monkey cried out, according to the first verse in the hymn:

Shembe, Mayekisa's son,
Have pity on me.

I have left father and mother
I don't know where I am going.

So, according to v. 4 in the same hymn, Shembe asked the boy how much money he wanted for the monkey, and the reply was: five shillings. Shembe gave him his money with the admonition to let the monkey free at the place where it had been caught.

J. G. Shembe as Healer

Shembe's mysterious power was seen particularly in connection with healing. A patient who turned to him would sometimes have to wait a considerable time. The suspense added to the eager expectation with which the patient anticipated the result.

His son, Johannes Galilee Shembe, is reputed to have inherited some of his father's healing power. In 1941, I attended a healing service. It was one of the most dramatic hours, which I have ever experienced. I shall repeat here some of the observations already published in *Bantu Prophets* (p. 228 ff.).

In the Jamengweni hall at Ekuphakameni a pathetic group of some 250 women had assembled for a service to be led by the Rev. J. G. Shembe. Some had been waiting for this occasion for months or even years. One could feel the urgency of their expectation. All other doctors had failed, and now, hoping against hope, they had come to the "Servant", to be prayed for in order that the shame of barrenness should at last be removed and their suffering come to an end. On a Friday afternoon in the culminating week of the "July-festival", their hour had come. Shembe had invited my wife and myself to attend as observers together with a Zulu theological student. We took off our shoes at the door, and waited for some time. When expectation had reached its highest pitch, a church official in a long blue garment entered and announced that only barren women were allowed to stay, the rest had to leave. Nobody moved, however; they had all come for the same reason.

Now the Servant appears. Dressed in a long black garment with golden embroidery round his neck and with a black veil round his head, he enters the hall. First he removes his shoes, and then courteously comes to me to explain that whenever we want to leave the service, we are at liberty to do so. Then the séance begins.

One or two of the women have begun a sort of continuous hiccough. The Servant stands before the mass of women, stretches out his right hand over the crowd from one side to the other, moving his long nervous fingers while he prays: "Lord, I pray, give them life in their wombs and in their spirits, so that they may bear children."

He unwinds his father's long black veil, charged with hidden powers of life. To me he explains that he has to use a veil in order to cope with the whole clientele in one afternoon. To lay hands on every individual would take far too long. He walks along the rows of seated women and flicks first one, then another with that veil, giving it a rapid jerk, as if cracking a whip.

The effect is astounding. Almost everybody starts, as though receiving a powerful electric shock. One woman, with a top-knot, has been hiccoughing more and more loudly. She is struck by the veil and starts to cry with a terrible loud, shrill voice, and continues crying long after the prophet has left her. Next to her is sitting another woman who also begins to cry. She throws herself to the ground. The prophet touches her, placing his finger-tips upon her shoulders. Then quite unexpectedly he signs for me to approach and explains the case as if he were a professor of gynæcology, but at the same time he is conscious of the fact that in the eyes of these women he has supernatural powers. The history of the woman, the prophet explains, is this: Three miscarriages, the third at the beginning of that same month; now she accuses herself of having murdered her children. Her *indiki*-demon has told her so: "I ate my children" (*ngabadla abantwana bami*), she cries in her terrifying voice. The prophet asks: "Whose children?"— No reply, only streaming tears and crying. "Whose children?" —"Yours, my Lord!" (In this case referring to the supposed fact that she had already once been healed by the prophet and that a snake inside had killed the child). She continues to cry, but the prophet moves on. And then, with a most pathetic effect, the cry of this desperate woman suddenly changes into a lullaby of four notes continually repeated.

Near her sits a diviner in her characteristic attire. The prophet touches her shoulders with both his hands. Some in the vicinity start to cackle like hens and others throw themselves to the ground. One woman runs away when the prophet approaches. He allows her to do so and explains to me: "She will drop down in a moment"—which she does. Another woman kicks out when touched with the veil. The prophet touches her with his fingertips, first upon her shoulders, then in the region of the umbilicus, and at last allows his long veil to rest over her womb. He explains to me: "She cannot get children. I think that she has a snake in her womb."

Another woman becomes as if possessed when the prophet comes close to her. He invites me to listen to her crying. Out of her subconscious mind flows a stream of images and notions. She sees people who try to murder her: "You will bring me back by means of a white snake (*nizongibuyisa ngenyoka emhlophe*). But now I believe in Shembe. He will help me. I will take vengeance on you." At this point it appears that she is addressing her own people at home, who have scorned her because of her barrenness. Her voice becomes hard and harsh: "You hated me because I had no children. But I will return. The Servant will give me children, and I will triumph."

The prophet explains to me: "I remove demons. I am amazed to find that in the case of women, demons take their abode in the shoulders and in the womb. In the case of men, demons reside only in the stomach." Sometimes the prophet shouts, as he hits out with his veil: "Get out, demons! Depart at once!" And as he moves along, the din of cackling, hiccoughing, crying, shrieking, singing, weeping, grows into a tremendous volume of sound. Bitter is their need—and here is their great hope, perhaps their last chance. Can this veil, can this man, can God give life?

The Acts of the Nazarites

Shembe's own message and views are one thing; the reaction and interpretation of his faithful followers is another matter. We are now fortunately in a position to study a collection of testimonies, *The Acts of the Nazarites,* which were assembled on the special initiative of Johannes G. Shembe himself. He entrusted this work to a Church archivist. He expressed his regret to me in 1958: "I have not got anybody to sort this out. I want all these testimonies just as they were told. That is real history, you see. Then people can add their own interpretation later". The Testimonies were typed, and collected in files. The archivist has also for clarity's sake divided the text into verses, just like the *Acts of the Apostles* or the *Acts of St. Thomas* long ago.

It is to be hoped that this collection can be printed. We can only give a couple of brief samples here.

Johannes Ncube's testimony. There was Samuel's wife Mashiwase, born Dlamini. She was very ill and a cripple for a long time. [Samuel] came to God's kraal at Mini, Edendale, asking for prayer for his wife.

The owner of the Iden kraal advised them to go to God's kraal, and the husband took his wife with him. He did not despise the caretaker of Iden. We saw him coming asking for help to get them to God's kraal. One of her legs was very swollen, but this subsided as she was prayed for. She was called by Shembe day after day and the swelling disappeared and the woman was healed.

When the husband saw her walking, he said, "May the Lord of Nazareth be praised. I have seen God in this great trouble of mine. From to-day let my whole house believe. May all my children believe in the Lord of Nazareth." All his children did believe until he passed from this world still believing in Shembe.

Rev. Simon Mngoma's testimony. Mngoma was a member of the African Congregational Church and he was to become one of Isaiah Shembe's intimate friends. He was with him on that fearful May day, 1935, when the Prophet died.

A girl in the congregation had an attack of a hysterical illness (*isipholiyana*). Mngoma realized that people were not healed in the A.C.C. and decided to take her to Shembe.

"In the evening we came to Ekuphakameni. As I entered the gate, I felt as if something fell from my shoulders. I thought that it was my luggage; far from it, no such thing had fallen."

After a while he was called into the presence of Shembe. "As I looked I was amazed. They had told me he was a pastor, yet he was not a pastor, but the Lord." Shembe asked about the ailment of the girl and said, "She will be well."

His presence amazed me. He looked like Jesus, and I was thinking, I am not sleeping, nor am I drunk. Furthermore he was so pleasant, speaking in a friendly manner. I have seen Jesus on pictures. Here only the hair was different from that of Jesus. Later he said, "Let us go." His Jesus-like appearance began to change and slowly disappeared, and now he looked like a beautiful girl, and I have never seen a girl as beautiful as this one was.

As we walked along, people were acknowledging him and I had to ask him, "Did Jesus really come on earth?" He said, "He came for sure, my child, but people did not understand it and they crucified him. Today many do not see him," and he added, "Blessed are those who see him."

Shembe told people to give Mngoma a chair. Mngoma said, "Never shall I sit on a chair, like my Lord who is also sitting on a chair." He then gave me a mat.

In a certain Church service later on, Shembe said, "To-day the witchfinder of heaven (*isangoma sasezulwini*) has come, knowing all the acts which people have committed, good and bad. Some among you do good, others do bad things. I am dividing people according to their acts." Later, Shembe said, "I, Shembe, am leaving with you two prophets clothed in sackcloth; they are the two olive-trees about whom the Book of Revelations (11:4) is speaking. The Lord is leaving and handing over the Church to these two prophets."

In the morning, there was a Church service, and after that the sick ones came. There was a piece of cloth with the help of which the sick ones were prayed for. The Lord gave it to us in order that we pray with it. There was a woman with a bad demon. Then Shembe called those patients and caught hold of the woman who was as dead, lying down. He said, "Her spirit is in heaven!" We were very much afraid as we heard that she was dead, and that her spirit was in heaven.

Then I felt that the work of the Lord at that place was indeed spoiled, because they said they offered human sacrifice at Eku-phakameni, and yet they said about Jesus that he was praying for them with the help of Beelzebul. I saw him looking towards heaven and then to that person. That gave me hope, for now I noticed that the woman began to move: the one who was dead had risen.

Shembe now left for another place. As we approached, an old woman was singing praises and saying, "Now the Saviour has come to liberate me!"

Shembe said, "We have come here to chase away the war from this place." Then he produced the piece of cloth and said, "Let us pray for the sick."

Many people assembled. The time for baptizing people had come. People said, "There are crocodiles in that place where we are to be baptized". They came to a small river. I brought out the word which I did not even know [beforehand] that I was to pronounce. Those who enter this water will find that their sins will remain in it, and the different kinds of illness will remain in that water. Indeed after my sermon, I entered the water and baptized them and these people who had been dragged there by hand-cart were now healed and could walk on their own.

We came from Judia and were on our way to Velabahleke [two different Nazaretha centres]. Near the dip at Emlalazi many came to see Shembe. An old man, Ncwanga, came and said, "Man of God, we are dying, we and our children and cattle are killed by the sun. I pray for rain." The man of God said, "You have your pastors—why do you not ask them?" He replied, "They have no rain" (abanayo imvula). He said, "Whom are you asking about rain?" He said, "I ask you; I see you are man of God, and you will get it."

Only one day passed, and then very heavy rain fell, continuing for two days all over the country. We left and came to Mkhwanazis, walking along praising Jehova on our dancing drum. As we walked along, a miracle happened; a Ndlanzi girl was bitten by a puff-adder. The man of God bowed down and sucked the wound, getting [the poison] out. The girl was healed and she crossed the river, walking easily on her own feet. May the name of Jehova be praised who gave us his Servant so that we should live through him."

The testimonies—the "Acts of the Nazarites"—are a mirror in which one can see the reflected impression of the prophet's personality. Another dimension is the corporate worship of the thousands of the faithful.

Worship

Worship in the Nazaretha Church has a significant and unique note of its own.[4] It is sounded and echoes in the hymns, at the great yearly festivals—particularly the 'July' festival at Ekuphakameni and the 'January' jubilation on the Inhlangakazi mountain; it is heard at the corporate services of Baptism and the Washing of the Feet and Holy Communion.

Most people—Africans as well as Europeans—know Shembe's worship only from the public dances at Ekuphakameni, on the last Sunday in July; and from these, they easily get the impression that the movement is nothing but a nativistic return to traditional Zulu culture. A closer study shows, however, much more of the nature of this original religious corporate experience.

We saw that George Khambule was all the time liturgically creative, for a variety of new occasions shaping services and performing these together with his closed "communitas"-type of a church. The daily contact and co-operation between the prophet and his *communitas* helped to liberate this creativity.

Isaiah Shembe's was a different case. His church was relatively open and of course, much more numerous. At Ekuphakameni it was not only a couple of hundreds—as in Khambule's case—but

---

[4] Cf illuminating studies by H.-J. Becken, 'On the Holy Mountain', etc. in *Journal of Religion in Africa*, 1 (2) 1968), p. 138–156 and idem, *Theologie der Heilung*, Das Heilen in den afrikanischen unabhäng. Kirchen in Südafrika, Hermannsburg 1972; and J. W. Fernandez, 'The Precincts of the Prophet', *ibid.*, V (1) 1973, p. 32–53.

worship of ten thousand and more. This made it impossible for Shembe to experiment with a large number of service forms.

In any case, the fact of his printed service forms, in the Nazarite Hymnbook, must not be overlooked. This book with its 188 pages is introduced by a liturgical section of some 23 pages. This includes *three* different services: I, the daily Morning worship; II, Evening worship; and III, the weekly Sabbath worship. Each of these is divided into brief passages or paragraphs, of two to five lines each, sometimes including a short hymn: I has 44 such passages, II has 37, and III has 56. One common feature in all three is Ps 23. In all three services this Psalm belongs to the introductory material. Apart from this psalm, the message of each of the three services is characteristically different:

I, The Morning worship contains the most uncompromising, unrelenting and persevering exhortation to work, and against laziness, ever to be heard in liturgical form, (this may be a sweeping statement, but I shall be surprised if proved wrong on this point!).

II, Evening: Jehova visits his people in their sleep. You must keep your house well, so that Jehova will not show wrath in the dreams in which he visits you.

III, Sabbath: The duty of honouring parents and the glory of Sabbath: a double theme infinitely variated.

I. The muscular *morning message* against laziness was formulated about the time of the first World War and that of the Natives Land Act of 1913. It is addressed to an agricultural population—industrial development later on lies outside its scope. (21): "Do not be lazy, for laziness is sin. A lazy person is like a dog begging for food from people. At the conclusion of this Prayer take your hoe and dig with it. Thus you shall live and not need to go and beg for food from people." (24): "If the sun is shining—dig ... If it is raining—dig and weed and be on guard (against birds eating the crops). (26): "All the lazy ones will be cast away. Their blood will be exacted out of their hands because with their laziness they pour shame on God. God gave them hands for work ... They pour shame on God."

It sounds very much like an angry farmer's pep talk in a frosty morning. But there is more to it than that. Shembe is addressing his oppressed and despised people. With a prophet's energy he wants them to realize their situation in a land where their land has been taken from them. Here the Zulu must buy the time and seize such opportunities as might still be left.

II. The warm and velvety-soft note of Shembe's *Evening Service* is of Africa, and nowhere else; is of Zululand, and nowhere else. Mother's womb and the world of sleep—here they belong together.

Almighty God
Father of all who worship Thee
Sleep with us tonight
Keep us by thy grace.

(17): "Worship Jehova, the Supreme Being, thy God who kept you in the wombs of thy mothers. And the day when you were born, Jehova did not abandon you". (24): "We were asleep in the wombs of our mothers, the King of kings kept us; and this coming night we have a firm hope that thou will keep us. Indeed, Lord, tarry not, but keep us the whole night."

With this touch, the concluding note follows, read in the hut or house at the flickering light of a candle or a paraffin lamp (35): "For Jehova visits his people in their sleep. You must keep your house well, so that Jehova will not come in wrath to you in your sleep." (36): "Keep us and guard us during this coming night, o King of kings. Be Thou our mat and headreast and cloth us with the sleep of joy, Lord and Father ..."

III. Shembe's *Sabbath service* is the best known of the three. The thousands of faithful, all in white, all seated on their little mats on the ground in Paradise, at Ekuphakameni, hear the service read on their behalf by a church crier with an enormous voice. Occasionally they respond with a swelling, and then slowly dying note of *A-a-a-men*.

This is a Zulu Sabbath. Its message is addressed to the dispersed house of the Zulu. (52): "May the Lord remember the scattered house of Senzangakhona and of Dingaan and gather it together from its dispersion." (21): "Be not like your fathers Dingaan and Senzagakhana, our fathers who hardened their hearts. Jehovah punished them in this matter and to-day we are carrying the burden of their sins. Keep ye Jehovah's Sabbath."

Even in the Sabbath service, the faithful are invited to meditate upon the miracle of sleep and of awakening from sleep: (12) "... so that He may wake you up from the sleep in which you were not knowing whether you were going to wake up again."

It is a measure of Isaiah Shembe's authority and influence that this kind of service still has a seemingly undisputed sway over the minds and hearts of the Church, conveying to the faithful an obvious sense of the Holy.

Without repeating here what has already been said in *Bantu Prophets* (*ibid.* p. 198 ff) on the festivals it is nevertheless important to reemphasize their enormous formative and integrating influence, inducing an atmosphere which surpasses anything else in Nazarite ritual. The great service on the mountain brings them very near to heaven. These sacred gatherings also provide the necessary framework for the total worship of the Church.

In 1958 we attended the birth of a new rite. A brief summary of this service gives some feeling of the special quality of the Shembe worship.

A new temple at Ekuphakameni was dedicated that week, with great expectation and much jubilation. It was in this connection that J. G. Shembe conceived a new "Candle Service". I had the good luck to attend this. Between five and six thousand men and women together went through a most intense religious mass experience. As I was standing on the verandah of the Church looking at that crowd in the moon-light, Shembe told me: "You see, Dr. Sundkler, we have our preaching and teaching. That is alright. But give these people a real mass worship—and they will never forget it".

The service began about 9 p.m. and went on until 12.30 a.m. It was full moon and surprisingly bright. People came into the temple, carrying their candles. They entered, and left, each group through its special door: for chiefs, for ordinary men, for the older women, and for younger women and girls. There were priests burning incense and huge candles in the middle of the Temple. Everybody kindled his or her candle. Then, in a long row, they solemnly danced out, catching now the incessant rising mighty rhythm of the drums. Eighteen big drums, four of them played by women drummers. Their rhythm carried and punctuated the whole performance, endlessly, relentlessly, eternally. Eighteen enormous drums, one beat per second.

The men in their long rows, and the women and the girls all fill in with that slow and solemn beat. I counted some two thousand men and perhaps four thousand women, all in white garments, all in long rows, each right hand holding the lit candle, and the feet following the incessant rhythm: left foot touching; left foot stamping; right foot touching; right foot stamping; touching and stamping the good African soil—for hours and hours on end, without let or leisure.

They did this with an amazing natural spontaneous stage-management, directed one did not know how or by whom. Shembe himself in a shining white long linen garment with golden braids, a round black hat on his head, "a gift of the boys of Durban". He stood there on the verandah with his Swedish visitor. He was distinct from this group—but not for long. With the slightest movements of his right hand he induced all these faithful thousands to raise or lower their candles and to rearrange themselves on the open space below him in the full moon. Now the men ordered themselves in one long row, and the women likewise, facing the men, all the while singing to the pounding and hammering of the drums

Bongani uJehova,
Ngoba ulungile.

Praise ye Jehovah,
for he is righteous;
His mercy
endureth for ever,
for he is righteous.

Then Shembe leaves me standing on the verandah and goes down to join his people. All the while the rhythm of the drums and singing of these thousands is rising and swelling and then fading and dying and rising again, accompanied by the lowering and the lifting of those thousands of candles. Shembe joins the men. I think of King Sobhuza in Swaziland in the middle of his thousands of soldiers. Thus the figure of Shembe melts into the long row of men, still distinct in his shining garment and round black hat. Now they raise high their candles, all the while singing.

Praise ye Jehovah,
for he is righteous.

While dancing, each dancer moves the candle from the farthest reach of his right arm towards the middle, ever repeating, yet never monotonous.

Then Shembe moves over to the women. He speaks to one in the crowd. The woman favoured by his word and all around him kneel, for the Servant is speaking. And the drums go on relentlessly, endlessly, eternally. One drummer has put his candle through the hole in his right earlobe. A practical measure, for he needs both his hands for his drumsticks, as the eighteen mighty drums carry on their beat. Chiefs are dancing, and the lame and crippled with their crutches are dancing, managing crutch and candle together, all the while moving and dancing. All the time the rhythm of the drums is rising and swelling and then falling and fading, in that quiet silvery incandescent moonlight of Africa.

Shembe is now back with me on the verandah, looking out over his faithful, all in white, six thousand with burning candles. He is inspired by the sight and raises his own candle high; the thousands in white respond, each lifting his or her candle with the same quiet gracious gesture of greeting, while the deep dull thuds of the drums are forever carried on.

One old woman cannot control herself, and begins to trill a high note of her own. She moves out of the long row of the women, gently holding her lighted candle, yet still dancing with her entire body, swaying and moving her arms and hands.

Sermon stereotypes

I am fascinated by the way in which *the sermon* emerges in the mind of the leader and among the mass of the people. The most memorable incident of this kind I ever experienced was at the Sabbath service, in July 1958. I was glad to be back among the Nazaretha again, having left South Africa in 1945. Again the ten thousands and more, all in white, congregated in Paradise, at Ekuphakameni. There were some hymns while we were expectantly looking forward to the Annual Message from the Prophet. Seated next to him, I had my notebook ready to take

183

down the words from the Prophet's mouth. The hymn came slowly to an end. The last lingering notes were rolling over the Ohlange hills. Then, unexpectedly, Shembe turned to me and said: "And now Dr. Sundkler, we ask you to preach!" There was no way out, surrounded as I was by this crowd of ten thousand. I also remembered the learned sociologists' phrase about 'participant observation'. Here was obviously an unrivalled opportunity for participation. Fortunately, I had my Zulu New Testament near at hand. Which text? A look at those silent masses seated on the ground, in 'Paradise', and all that they represented of hunger and tiredness and need and alienation, seemed to suggest one passage, and one only: Matt. 11:28–30, the words of Jesus: 'Come unto Me all ye that labour and are heavy laden'.

By some strange happy miracle, my Zulu language came back to the mind and the lips, and I was able to carry on for some twelve minutes, or more, trying to convey the message of that great text.

Then Shembe rose. He preached on that same text for one hour and a half. It was a great occasion and a great message. It gave the younger Shembe his opportunity to interpret the spiritual role of his father, the founder of the movement. He did so through a characteristic interplay of stories and testimonies on the one hand and, on the other, a subtle and sophisticated set of allusions, stating, and yet not stating, the preacher's understanding of Shembe's relationship to God and to Jesus Christ.

We all have our burdens, burdens which we have inherited from our parents, which others have placed on us, and burdens which we have caused ourselves. Jesus does not choose, he receives all. Jesus will lift off your burden and give you rest. No yoke is easy. If it were easy, Jesus would not use the term 'yoke'. There are certain things which burden the heart. The heart can have wounds which no doctor can heal, no *inyanga*, no *isangoma*, neither any purifying water. But Jesus says, Come unto me, with your burdens. Give him your burdens.

There was a girl who became pregnant, and people wanted her to reveal the father's identity. She refused to do so, until in the end she broke down and said, 'Ask father'. Her own father had caused this pregnancy. ("*Hawu*", from the congregation). She had a heavy yoke to carry. Some people hang themselves because of such things. I told her, "My girl, I have no power to lift this off your shoulders. I cannot forgive you. I must not deceive you. I have my owns sins. Only God can forgive you. I leave it to God, and he will forgive you." Jesus said, Come unto me. Jesus did not say, "Throw away your burdens, and then I shall give you sugar and good food and beautiful houses". No, he said, "Come unto me."

When Isaiah Shembe was a boy, he climbed the Boer's peach tree in order to take some peaches. Just then the Boer came riding that way on his horse and stopped under the tree and Shembe said in his heart, "I died today" (*Ngafa namhla—nje!*). But there came a word, saying: "Do not look at the white man; look at me and pray to me". After eternities, the white man rode off, not having discovered the boy in the tree. Shembe climbed down with those peaches in his hand. But for a long time he did not taste them, his heart was still eaten up by fright. But as the fear subsided, he thanked God, "I thank God, thou heard me and saved me from my great need!"

As he was about to die, he told us, "Throughout my life I have worked for God alone. I came with nothing, I leave with nothing." Shembe was born of the Spirit, he was Spirit. So the Scriptures say. "That which is born of the Spirit, is Spirit." Now, the learned people of this earth come with their rulers and scales and they compare their own teaching with that of the others. Shembe was *Thunyiwe ka Nkulunkulu,* "sent by God". All come to Ekuphakameni to receive this teaching. Sweden and England, and America and India [in that order!]—they all see you [who are assembled here]. Shembe was sent to them all.

But when they wished to become Christians they came to the missionaries, but the missionaries said: "Throw off your dirty yokes", and they referred to the *ibeshu.*

No, the yoke of God is always against the thoughts of men. He that loves his father or mother more than me is not worthy of me, or the one who loves cattle more than God. This foreign preacher in our midst had a great message. The young man who came to Jesus was not prepared to go through the narrow Gate. It is Faith which is the great thing. You don't believe just because you are dressed in white. You say this is the dress of Heaven. Don't think that you will reach Heaven just because you have worshipped many years at Ekuphakameni. A white dress cannot remove sin. We are evil and not worthy of being clothed in white. They are the garments of heaven. But Jesus lifts off the yoke. Christ was crucified on the cross with our sins. We crucified Christ on the cross with our sins. But He carried us. He was the Son of God and yet could feel the intense pain as they nailed him to the Cross.

Shembe on the Mountain heard a Voice calling. "Follow Me! You begin to preach now!" He had no house, no shirt, no rest. But he followed the word of God. You listened to the words of our preacher from beyond the seas: "Come to Me, and My burden is light!" This foreigner who is with us spoke briefly because he did not want you to suffer sitting in the sun. I explain to you what he wished to say.

Shembe sat down, and I thanked him. "No," he said, "I thank you. You inspired me." "How?" "Well, Dr. Sundkler, inspiration is a great thing. I had not prepared anything to say today, but your words inspired me to this sermon."

How far this presentation is characteristic of Nazaretha preaching, is difficult to say. There is, obviously, always the main outline of Shembe's life and religious experience to which the preacher can refer. At the same time, the message points beyond Ekuphakameni and Isaiah Shembe to Jesus the Messiah.

"I remember Ekuphakameni"

Shembe's "*Hymns of the Nazarites*", (Izihlabelelo zama Nazaretha), is religious poetry of great beauty. It was born, not at the dogmatician's writing-desk, but in song, carried by the incessant rhythm of drums, shaped in order to be sung while dancing.

Professor G. C. Oosthuizen, of Durban, wrote a study of Shembe's hymns, entitled *The Theology of a Zulu Messiah* (1967), where the author makes this claim: "The *Izihlabelelo* should be considered as the catechism of the movement".[5] We suggest that one should discard such heavy and learned Western panoply and let Shembe walk along as he used to and loved to: moving light, barefoot.

Johannes Galilee Shembe explained to me how Isaiah Shembe, his father, conceived his hymns. He would hear a woman's voice, often a girl's voice, singing new and unexpected words. He could not see her, but as he woke up from a dream or walked along the path in Zululand, meditating, he heard that small voice, that clear voice, which gave him a new hymn. He had to write down the words, while humming and singing the tune which was born *with* the words.[6]

This was, indeed, his strongest motive for learning the art

---

[5] G. C. Oosthuizen, *The Theology of a South African Messiah*, Leiden 1967, p. 6.
[6] Interview with J. G. Shembe, August 1969.

186

of writing. He had remained illiterate until quite late in life, about 40 years of age, but these irresistible songs that would well up from his unconscious had to be grasped, and translated into words and verses.

Johannes Galilee himself had of course quite a different background. He was educated, with a B.A. from Fort Hare and was a teacher at the prestigious Amanzimtoti School when called to succeed his father. While the father was auditive, Johannes Galilee was visionary, and it is characteristic, perhaps, for the school-teacher that he should *see* the new hymn written on the blackboard of the mind, coming down, lowered before his eyes. Then he has to write down the verses straight away—if not, the visually revealed verses are forgotten, and lost.

With Is. Shembe it was the rhythm that moved in him even while sleeping; it was this rhythm that first came to the surface and had to be caught and written down. This rhythm expressed itself in two or three words to be sung to the accompaniment of the beat of drums, and the feet of the dancing faithful. Here he found the chorus, and he built the hymn on this foundation.

> *Phaphamani phaphamani*
> *nina ma Africa*

Waking up from his sleep, he still carried within him the rhythm of what he had heard in the dream-dimension of life:

> Wake up, wake up,
> You Africans.

In no time five short verses, of four lines each, emerge. Two lines in each verse have to be found, and for the first verse, a Zulu proverb will do, while the remaining two lines for each verse are already there, through this chorus:

> *Phaphamani, phaphamani*
> *nina ma Africa.*

On another occasion, he was given a word as if a child's play-word, carried to the dreamer by a girl's voice:

> *Soyana, soyana,*

and the chorus is there:

187

> *Soyana, soyana,*
> *soyana kweli pezulu.*

One cannot find this word *soyana* in Doke-Vilakazi's dictionary, but there was something in the liquid consistency of the particular consonants of the word that made the prophet associate to *"Yizani,"* and *siye, let us go.*—Where? To Ekuphakameni, of course and—the hymn is there!

> *Yizani nina nonke*
> *Siy' Ekuphakameni*
> Come ye all,
> Let us go to Ekuphakameni;
> We shall be richly anointed
> with an ointment of grace.
> *Soyana, soyana,*
> *soyana pezulu.*

Hymn No. 2 (written on the Nhlangakazi mountain in 1913) is composed to the simple rhythm of a repeated word, *Ngisize, ngisize Nkosi yami,* "Help me, help me, my Lord." One can well imagine that, once again, the words and the tune with the rhythm of a lullaby were given to the prophet while waking up on the dangerous mountain: it was his very first visit to that holy place which was to develop into a pilgrimage centre of his church. The rhythm is repeated in the first words of the following three simple verses

> 2. *Ngincede, ngincede …*
> 3. *Ngazise, ngazise …*
> 4. *Namabandla, namabandla …*

Each of the four short four-line verses is concluded with the line, "Amen, Amen, my Lord".

Or again, the rhythm in the dream transfers to him, waking up early at daybreak,

> *Kudumisa wena* (praise thee)

Here is already the recurrent, second and fourth line in a hymn of five short four-line verses. A mighty and moving hymn of praise was born in that fresh morning (No. 78)

> v. 1 The stars of dawn
> praise Thee,
> The joy of the firmament
> praises Thee.

188

v. 4 The moon and its light
     praise Thee,
     The sun and its light
     praise Thee.

But already the prophet is looking towards death:

Stay well, you firmament,
I am leaving you;
I am going to sleep
under the wings of the earth.

It is hard to resist the temptation to dwell on other fine points of the rhythm in this Zulu poetry. One admires, for instance, the sophisticated effects of natural in-rhyme:

No. 103
     v. 1 *Sivumele wena Nkosi*
          Sishumayele izwi lako
     v. 2 line 3. *Zilindele* ...
     v. 4 *Sithumele* ...
          line 3. *Sibuthele* ...

One cannot but be impressed by the sureness of touch of this religious poet. This sureness shows up even more by contrast with some of the additional hymns not composed by him but added to the hymn-book after his death.
No. 243 has the two lines:

Yehla Moya oyingcwele
Ngena wena kiti
(Descend Holy Spirit and enter, Thou, us)

With respect, one cannot but notice that Isaiah Shembe had much too delicate and sophisticated sense of the Zulu language to allow such a combination of sounds as in that second line. It reminds one too forcibly of European hymn-carpentry in Zulu churches!

The words *and* the tune of these hymns were born together. The tunes contribute to make the Nazaretha worship something altogether unique. The difference from the happy, lusty rhythm of ordinary Zionist songs, mostly taken over from Western hymn-books, is revealing. The Shembe tune moves slowly, in long sweeping cadences. Ekuphakameni is situated only three miles from the shore of the Indian Ocean, and these solemn, lingering lines, carried by ten thousand singers, roll over the hills as if waves of the Ocean.

We suggest that Shembe's Hymn-book should be understood, *not* from the outside, from a Western standpoint, measuring its contents according to the standards and ideas of a European catechism, but rather from its own presuppositions. We have already discussed one of these, as we tried to show the hymns as revealed by way of rhythm.

We have already characterized the three services—Morning, Evening, and Sabbath—printed at the beginning of Shembe's Hymnbook. They form, of course, the necessary frame for any study of the hymns. It would be strange indeed to claim to analyse Shembe's hymns *without* reference to this liturgical frame.

Shembe mismanaged

In order to understand the place and role of Shembe himself in his hymns, one must be aware of a fundamental methodological factor. The lack of such an understanding has led Dr. Oosthuizen astray. Oosthuizen starts out with a blunt *a priori* claim that "Shembe I [by which term he refers to Isaiah Shembe] is not only mediator but is Messiah, the manifestation of God". From this, vast conclusions are drawn. We shall hear Dr. Oosthuizen's argument in his book, *The Theology of a South African Messiah:*

The names for God when used in the hymns really refer to Shembe himself. "He associates uMvelingqangi with himself" (12). "The emphasis on 'our uNkulunkulu is a direct reference to Shembe himself." (14) "He (=Shembe) is *uThixo* and in him is the salvation of the world." "Shembe II designates his father as *uThixo*" (17). In a characteristic phrase, Professor Oosthuizen says: "In this Isl. (=hymn) Shembe I keeps himself busy with his own coming to this earth when the stars fell." *Simakade* ... "refers to Shembe I." (19) The term *Guqabadele*, "Shembe I applies to himself" (21). Shembe confesses: *Ngiyakolwa kuyise* (I believe in the Father). This is by Oosthuizen made to mean that Shembe again uses this term to describe also himself (23). And, further, "Shembe is a manifestation of Jehovah" (32).

Most of these names are to be found in one particular hymn, No. 93, *Siyakubonga nguye Onguye.* In fact these five short verses contain no less than ten of these great names of God. Oosthuizen devotes two–three pages to each name and laboriously attempts etymological studies of each name. Thus we are told that *uMvelingqangi* consists of three components *uMveli, ngqa* and *ngi.* Why all this, in a study of Shembe? There is a solemn explanation. Some ancient authority or other declared more than a hundred years ago: "The best solution for the enigma of mythology lies in the etymological explanation of the names for Gods and heroes." (p. 11).[7]

But there is an obvious explanation—obvious to anybody to some extent familiar with Zulu culture. This plethora of God's names is a Nazaretha exercise in *izibongo* to God the King, adapted from the traditional *izibongo* to Zulu kings in the past. But precisely because this is so, this hymn has a totally different meaning from what the author has set out to prove. The whole substance of the hymn itself is lost by this detailed scrutiny of the supposed etymological meaning of each term.

In a chapter on *The Messiah,* Oosthuizen claims that Shembe accepts "fully the position of Jesus Christ" (36). "Shembe as Mediator is pictured as the *iNkosi.*" (39) "Shembe has excluded Jesus as the uMkhululi (liberator)—he is not merely an earthly liberator but is the Supreme Being" (41–42). Again, Oosthuizen recognizes that the place-name Ekuphakameni often occurs in the hymn. What does that mean? "Ekuphakameni *is* heaven." (25)

All this—impressive, and depressing, as it may seem—proves too much. The author has failed to understand the subtle and sophisticated nature of Shembe's proclamations.

To such an extent is Dr. Oosthuizen obsessed with his assumptions that he will constantly misread the most simple and direct statements of faith and trust.

Wangidala Nkulunkulu is one of Shembe's beautiful Paradise hymns, No. 114.

> You created me, God
> Thixo, Lord of Lords

[7] Dr. Oosthuizen's references are to a study about Max Müller who more than a hundred years ago developed the idea of etymological explanation of mythology.

> You placed me in that Garden
> For thy great love's sake.

But then he recalls how man ate of the forbidden Tree and how therefore all his beauty was lost.

> I am in need, my Lord,
> of soap to wash me
> Return me in haste
> to the bliss that was mine.

What does Professor Oosthuizen make of the first two lines of this paradise hymn?

"True to Zulu tradition uNkulunkulu is not described as the one who created the world. He is the first outcomer. Shembe I (=Isaiah Shembe) is also honoured as Creator so that the question arises: Who is the Creator? Shembe is the *uNkulunkulu* of the restored Zulu nation" (15).

We have already quoted Professor Oosthuizen's view of Hymn No 21 (p. 191). It is a prayer on behalf of all Africans and of all men—to *uThixo ka Adam,* the God of Adam, also invoked as *iNkosi ye Sabatha,* the Lord of Sabbath. With reference to this hymn, Dr. Oosthuizen states bluntly that Shembe has "excluded Jesus as the Mkhululi" and on the following page he states that "Shembe is the Supreme Being".

One would have thought that the long debate conducted among historians of religions since the days of Lévy-Bruhl, concerning the concept of "identification", would have served as warning against such brashness and made a European researcher more cautious. I must surmise—there is no proof or argument, only the bold statement—that Professor Oosthuizen takes for granted that the term "the Lord of the Sabbath" automatically refers to Isaiah Shembe personally and to him alone. He does not see that, *firstly,* this hymn plainly and obviously is directed to the God of Adam, Shembe's own noble concept of the God of all men. And, *secondly,* that Shembe's hymns share with those of other creative religious personalities in what Ian T. Ramsey has called "the odd-ness of religious language": there is an ambiguity, a plethora of meanings in the words. In Shembe's case, the words must be understood in the context from which they emerged: in the worship and the struggle of this Nazaretha community.

192

Towards understanding

Two methodological observations are necessary, and Oosthuizen overlooks both of them. (1) One must *distinguish* between
the prophet's own personal faith and expressions of faith *and*
the testimony of his followers. (2) The principle of *ambiguity of
meaning:* there is a constant oscillation in these terms, a double-
meaning which cannot be grasped by stereotype, ready-made
phrases.

(1) We have already seen some of the Testimonies of the
faithful, in which claims to divinity for Shembe are indeed
made. But even in the case of Simon Mngoma's Testimony
(p. 176) it should be noticed that he is awed by Shembe's likeness to Jesus. Instead of the idea of a Messiah we suggest the
Biblical, and, indeed, African, concept of the *eikon,* i.e. the mask,
and in this case the mask of the Black Christ. The African
prophet turning to God's black people is privileged to wear that
mask which they will recognize as of God.

(2) Ekuphakameni, their beloved Zion, is a "heavenly" place,
has its section called "Paradise", and for the festivals the faithful in their thousands will sit down in their white garments, in
the shadow of the trees in "Paradise". But, *of course,* they realize
that Ekuphakameni is also of the earth, earthy, situated 10 miles
north of Durban. Of course, Shembe knew, and all his followers
know, that there is an Ekuphakameni "which is above" (Cf. St.
Paul, Gal. 4:25–26, Jerusalem which now is—Jerusalem which
is above).

Most of these songs are hymns of praise, at least such songs
as are most often sung, or rather performed, in the worship
of the Nazarites. A characteristic and very popular example
is No. 60, *Bongani u Jehova.* Creating his hymn in South Africa,
Shembe gives thanks to God for what he has done for Africa.
In a world surrounded by Whites and by churches following
the strange customs of the Whites, God is praised by Shembe
because he encourages Africans to worship Him in their own
free and natural way, and not according to the heavy, artificial
rules of the Whites. God had gone so far in helping his African
children that he sent his servant Isaiah Shembe to show them
that this worship was in accordance with the Holy Book itself.

Praise ye Jehovah,
for he is righteous,
for his grace endureth for ever,
for he is righteous.

He remembered Africa,
for he is righteous;
He has not forgotten his people,
for he is righteous.

He made that heaven
together with the earth;
it is his handiwork,
for he is righteous.

He remembered his people
with naked hips;
He sent them his Servant Isaiah,
for he is righteous.

In those days
the deaf will hear
the message in that Book,
for he is righteous.

For those who walk
with naked feet
He prepared room
in the Holy Place.

[But] those who shave [their] heads
and continue on each side [of the head]
Those who shave their beard
thus transgressing the laws;

And those who enter carrying shoes
into the house of Jehova,
[all] these turn it into a house of play
by their transgression of the laws.

Free and unhindered, the daughters of Nazaretha can therefore dance and sing. One of the most beloved dance-songs runs
thus (92):

I shall dance full of hope;
I am the maiden of Nazaretha,
I fear nothing,
for I am perfect.

We too trust thee,
In the past [yesterday] we did so;
And we trust thee to-day.

Shembe is close to Nature, and his hymns are full of meditations on man and nature, and how prior to the creation of all
the phenomena of nature, man was there in the mind of God
(71):

Before the mountains were shaped,
Thou my King loved me;
From eternal times thou anointed me,
I am the first-fruit of thy ways.

Before the hills took their form,
Before the sources of the rivers
were streaming mightily,
Before the deeps existed ...

The answer depends on the question, here as always. If the
question is wrong, every conceivable answer will be wrong.
Ask the question whether Shembe follows and fits into some
European Catechism—and you miss the whole thing, his whole
message.

These lovely songs of his must be interpreted, not from the
presuppositions of Luther's catechism or of that of Heidelberg,
but out of their own milieu, on a basis of their own presuppositions, out of the needs and aspirations of the Zulu in the
context of race-ridden South Africa.

It is with this hermeneutical principle as a key that one must
try to open the locks of the shrine.

From this starting-point one will understand that a Shembe
song containing a great number of Zulu names for God is not
meant to be a catalogue of theological definitions but is as
we have already indicated *izibongo*, an act of homage to God
the King. From this same starting-point in the essential needs
and aspirations of the Zulu themselves, one understands why
these songs do not regard man first of all as a sinner—as one
should do in § so-and-so in a catechism—but as a perplexed and
suffering human being, seeking for health and wholeness. European—and, indeed, African—efforts to interpret Shembe's understanding of relationship to the Divine have often been al-

together too clumsy and square, lacking that dimension of "ambiguity of meaning" which I believe to be fundamental here.

To Shembe himself and his followers there was never any hesitation in their realization of the fundamental difference between God and his "Servant". God remains God the Exalted, also to them. But in his mercy, God allows this Zulu Servant of his to reveal to his African children his power and love.

Of course, Shembe's theology was far from being orthodox Christian. In fact, his hymns contain strikingly few Biblical associations. Johannes Galilee Shembe discussed his father's position with us:

Shembe always said, God and Jesus Christ are the same, they are not to be separated. When he said Jesus Christ, he meant God—and vice versa. What Shembe did, he did in the name of God. Shembe believed in Jesus Christ. If you believe—do the works of Christ and the "greater things" which he has promised! When we are told that this is not 'Christian', we are simply not interested. But I know that as a Christian I shall one day stand in the presence of God. I shall have to give account for all my acts and all my sermons. If I have told lies, I shall be judged.

Johannes Galilee Shembe has a right to be believed when he declares emphatically:

Some of our people say 'Shembe is God'. But no, Isaiah never wanted to accept that. He is, perhaps, 'God to the people' in the same way as a missionary (umfundisi) can become 'God' to his people. They speak of Shembe's God, uNkulunkulu ka Shembe, because Shembe brought God to them, and they pray to that God of which Shembe spoke (1941).

I am Shembe's son and grew up with him. I do not know why he came. I do not know where the limits of this end (kaulaphi). Isaiah Shembe himself would say: "Where I am going, I do not know. Whether I go to God or to Satan, to heaven or hell, I do not know. To me, it has been enough to work for God. I came with nothing and leave with nothing". Holy Scriptures say "That which is born of the Spirit is Spirit". Was Shembe of the earth or of heaven? Angazi, I do not know. Shembe was not born as you or I. He was born of Spirit and was Spirit (1958).

It is only one thing for which we must pray, that is: to be given a place in the future world and that our names will be written in the Book of Life (1969).

These indications are necessary as a sounding board for any interpretation of these hymns. They make it impossible for anybody to make that square and unconditional statement that Shembe "claimed" that he *is* God or Jehovah or "the Supreme Being" or Jesus Christ.

Shembe himself sings (91)

> *Sengiya ku Baba ongithumileyo.*
> I am going now to my Father who sent me,
> I leave you.
> I go to my Father,
> May you keep me in hope.

This is a moving declaration, made by somebody, the Servant (*Inceku*) Shembe who was clearly aware of the fundamental difference between himself and the One in whose service he spent his life.

The God of Adam, *uThixo ka Adam,* Shembe called Him. This is a challenging and noble concept and name: the God of all men. This was indeed a meaningful invocation to make in South Africa, for there divisions between men were wide and deep. Some of the learned theologians, trusting in their Hebrew scholarship, knew God as *Hammabdil,* the Divider—didn't Genesis teach, after all, that God "divided" the waters and divided day from night; the fundamental pattern in creation seemed thus to be clear. Division was a divine ordinance. Shembe's "God of Adam" was inclusive.

Two foci

The contents of Shembe's hymns have *two foci: Ekuphakameni* and *the human condition.* There are, of course, other aspects, too, but they are secondary, and do not concern us here.

1. Shembe's *Ekuphakameni*—"The Elated Place"—is the incomparable and glorious Zion of the Church of the Nazarites. Yet, as a centre of worship Ekuphakameni is different from that of the other Black Zionists. To the great majority of these churches, Zion is an object of longing, a projection of hope. Zion is not in Johannesburg, nor in Zululand. It lies far away and high above, in heaven. Theirs is a futuristic eschatology.

Shembe's Ekuphakameni is here and now. Ekuphakameni is realized eschatology.

Some fifty of these two hundred and fifty hymns are devoted

197

to Ekuphakameni exclusively, or in part. Shembe never tires of sounding this great theme of his life and witness. Listen to No. 102:

I remember Ekuphakameni,
where is assembled
the saintly congregation
of the Nazarites.

I remember Ekuphakameni,
where the springs are
Springs of living water
lasting for ever.

I remember Ekuphakameni,
a dew of *umkholongo,* a loudly falling cascade
is the response of the Saints
of the Nazarites.

Ye all who thirst
come to Ekuphakameni,
There freely to drink
from springs of water.

The hymn I personally prefer among all Shembe's hymns is also devoted to Ekuphakameni (101):

Thou wingèd eagle
lift thy mighty wing;
we seek thy shelter,
Thou rock of our fathers.

Fortress we have none
Other than thee
where to find shelter,
we, thy wayward creatures.

Thou glorious hen,
we stand before thee;
It is not only Jerusalem
that Thou lovest.

So love us and hatch us
thou glorious hen,
we stand before Thee,
Hen of heaven.

O, Lord, bring it forth,
this Ekuphakameni,
Like the hen
loving her chickens.

Jerusalem, Jerusalem,
How great was my longing
to gather thy children
under my wings;
But thou would not agree,
Thus I leave you desolate.

All the great power-lines of Scripture meet at Ekuphakameni: from Eden (No. 49) and Sinai (83) and Bethlehem (94),
and the heavenly Jerusalem (100). God Himself wears Ekuphakameni as his cope:

God the King of Kings,
We are Thy poor children.
Turn to us in thy grace,
Thou hast put on Ekuphakameni
as Thy coat.
[*Chorus*] Come, come, Amen.

There is a parallel between Bethlehem and Ekuphakameni:

There came wise men
out of the East
Asking, Where is he,
the King of the Jews?

Then follows the chorus:

So it is also to-day
on the hill-tops of Ohlange.

The fifth verse of the same hymn brings together Biblical
prophecy and Zulu reality:

In no wise art thou least
among the princes of Judah,
For out of thee
prophets shall come forth
who will save
the city of Ohlange.
[*Chorus*]

So it is also to-day
on the hill-tops of Ohlange.[5]

What once happened through Jesus, among the Jews and for
their salvation, is now being re-enacted through Shembe among
the Zulu and for their salvation. God in his wisdom is now
using his Bantu mask as he turns to his Black children.

Ekuphakameni has a miraculous effect on the faithful:

> Those who enter with sorrow
> They leave rejoicing.
> Listen all ye nations
> Come and be saved.
>
> (74)

To enter—but who and how? In order to enter, the faithful
have to pass the gates. The *amasango,* gates, are a key image
in these hymns, just as in Zionist dream-life in general. The
gates of Ekuphakameni are indeed identified with those other
awesome gates of old, those of Eden (49). All the more there
is a holy concern to press on:

> Let me hurry, let me hasten
> to enter Ekuphakameni
> before the Gates are shut.
> [*Chorus*]
> Come, come unto Ekuphakameni
> and listen to its word.
>
> (63)

There is a constant oscillation of meaning here, a correspondence between Ekuphakameni, near Ohlange, Durban,
and the Ekuphakameni which is above. And if one sharpens
one's hearing, one may perceive a wonderful sound in the
heavens:

[8] G. C. Oosthuizen translates this "on the hillocks of uHlanga" and confuses this
with "the bed of reeds from which the first Zulu was broken off". It is embar-
rassing to have to point out a notorious topological fact. Ekuphakameni, North of
Durban is built near Ohlange. One will recall that Shembe's friend and neighbour Dr. John Dube was the Principal of the Ohlange Institute. Oosthuizen
must associate to "uHlanga" in the Zulu creation myth, and attempts to construct
his mythological explanations on these far-fetched and non-existent foundations.
Op. cit., pp. 12 and 143.

We emerge dancing through the gate
of the holy city,
we who were victorious
whilst on earth.
Angels will beat their wings
at our victory.

(100)

2. *The human condition.* The last Sunday of July: all of Durban, apparently, has found its way out to Ekuphakameni. Cars are parked everywhere; large numbers of Europeans are watching the dances and taking photos. Nazaretha women of all ages, young and old, are in a Nazarite variation of Zulu national dress, the *isidwaba* for women. This leaves the breasts bare; the presence of these onlookers may have something to do with this phenomenon: breasts, rich and big, black and beautiful. The eyes of the onlookers have their fill of it all. These Natives seem to have their bit of fun, on a sunny Sunday afternoon.

Meanwhile, the beating of the drums goes on, solemnly, endlessly. The dancers in their thousands—carefully organized in groups according to age and sex—move slowly, ponderously, reflectively. From time to time, they join the music by singing. It is difficult to catch the words. Seated with Johannes Galilee Shembe, I ask him what they are singing. He informs me—and this whole picturesque scene changes radically. For *this* is what they sing:

> *Kufa, wena uyisitha*
> *kubo bonke abaphilayo*

(J. G. Shembe's own hymn, No. 226)

> Death, Thou art the enemy
> of all who live,
> old and young—
> at Thy arrival they cry.
> King or servant [it matters not],
> In the grave they are alike;
> They are dressed the same,
> maggot and epileptic.
> Save me then my King,
> from the second death,
> As the flesh rots
> Let my soul have life.

201

This note is fundamental to Shembe's religion. Death as the fate of all men. "I came alone to the earth, and I shall leave alone", Shembe used to say. He is praying for courage on his own behalf, to face the inevitable.

> I shall go my lonely walk
> into the valley of sorrow
>
> [*Chorus*] Give me then
> that courage of Japhet's daughter.
> Alone I shall enter
> into my own grave.
>
> ——
>
> I shall cry my lonely cry,
> For, poor sinner, I have nobody.
> The road of the grave is frightful
> even if unwillingly walked by many.
>
> (38)

This cry is the cry of all men, and it is our response to Adam's cry in Eden.

> A voice sounded
> at sunset
> in the garden of Eden
> at sunset
> [*Chorus*] Adam, what have you done,
> the earth was injured.
> The voice of the beasts
> that had dwelt in Eden
> cries, Alas, where are we going
> [*Chorus* ...]
> We parted from our fathers,
> The earth is injured.
> Help us, Jehovah, bring out Adam;
> Adam was chased from the garden of Eden.
> [*Chorus*]
> And Adam cried
> as he was driven out through the Gate.
> He said, my heart is sad,
> for I have broken the laws.
> [*Chorus*]
> I was led into sin by the woman
> whom Thou gavest me.
>
> (33)

Adam in Eden becomes the archetype of all men:

> You created me, God
> my God, thou King of Kings,
> You placed me in the garden
> because of that great love.
> I ate from that Tree
> and all my goodness disappeared.
> Therefore, My Lord, hear my need
> of soap to wash me clean,
> So that without delay
> I return to the goodness I once had.   (114)

Sin places a burden on the heart of man, a burden of sadness and tears. No wonder that Shembe sees himself as the "Servant of Affliction" (*isikondzi senhlupeko*). He can direct the sorrowful to drastic help.

> Tongs of heaven,
> come and pull me out
> . . .
> Lover of sinners,
> have pity on my spirit   (31)

In the case of the Africans in the country of South Africa the burden of existence is heavier than that of others.

> You lass of Nazaretha,
> cry like a flowing stream
> because of the shame which is yours
> in your own country.
> You lad of Nazaretha,
> cry like a rapid stream
> because of the shame which has come over you,
> you lad of Shaka (45)

Then again, Ekuphakameni is the solution, Eagle and beautiful Hen, there to hide and to live!

> "I remember Ekuphakameni".

The great majority of Zionist and Apostolic churches have no other alternative than to rely on the hymnbooks of the Whites for their worship. Those of the Wesleyan Church or of the American Board especially contain choruses and songs, the tunes of which could be transposed into exciting and catching rhythms, accompanied by drum-beat or hand-clapping. Paulo Nzuza's church produced its own hymnbook, as closely related to apocalyptic imagery as was George Khambule's liturgical texts.

But as a Zulu poet and hymnwriter, Isaiah Shembe was altogether unique. If ever words and verses were a mirror of the poet's own soul, Shembe's hymns reflect the visions and concerns of this, the greatest of Zulu prophets. He appeared quiet and withdrawn, and he had to be withdrawn and turned-inward, for he listened to that strange voice which forever inspired him to song. Waking up from his sleep or walking along a steep and narrow path in the Thousand Hills, he heard a Voice dictating to him both words and tune:

> *Lezwakala ilizwi*
> *Emthini wokudelwa* (87)
> A word was sounded
> on the cursed tree:
> Today, o sinner,
> I shall be with you in Paradise

The burden of this chapter was therefore to point to the need for caution and care in the interpretation of Shembe's hymns. His was an infinitely subtle mind, and the meaning of Shembe's poetry does not yield to brash and blunt onslaught, least of all to any arrogant attempt to coerce these visions into paragraphs of a European catechism.[9] But, as is the case with any great religious personality, we must ask, What was Shembes's concern? His concern for his Zulu, in race-torn South Africa, was to extol the glory of God—

---

[9] Professor Oosthuizen has produced an article, characteristically entitled "Wie christlich ist die Kirche Shembes?" *Evang. Missions-Zeitschrift*, (31), 1974, p. 129–142. He formulated a set of twenty-seven questions and had an African assistant put these to forty-two persons, about evenly divided between men and women. This is the kind of question asked: (5) "To whom does this church belong, to Jesus Christ or to Jesus Christ and to Shembe, or to Shembe? If the latter, which [Shembe, i.e. Isaiah or Johannes Galilee?]. (10) What is the relationship between God, Jesus Christ, the Holy Spirit and Shembe?"
To the question, "How Christian is Shembe's church?", Dr. Oosthuizen's answer is: "This is a post-Christian movement. One ought not to call it Christian".

Thixo wami uyamangalisa
My God, Thou causes me to marvel
Thy greatness is
a- shining
Look, the beauty of the Throne of Grace (66)

—and to express the need to turn, and to return, to the God of all men. The sight of Jehova, Shembe insisted, had made him into another man, a new man, set aside for a unique task. He was inspired by the visions of the Holy Book, and, for all that, gloriously free to interpret the hunger of his own soul and of that of his people, in genuine Zulu words.

"Praise ye Jehova. Amen." Chalk text on Amos Shembe's door, Ekuphakameni.

6. A Kingdom for Zion

'This is the greatest thing in Swaziland.' With this exclamation—
and exaggeration—a European, ideally placed for observation of
Swazi culture at the beginning of the nineteen-seventies, expressed his amazement at the role of the Zionist movement in present-
day Swazi life. Swaziland with a population of not more than half
a million is after all a small country. Some people who hardly can
identify the place on the map might regard it as insignificant,
compared with its more powerful neighbours.

Yet, Swaziland has an attraction and interest of its own. The
beauty of the country and of the people is striking. The role of
the king, and the relationship of king and people, have traditionally been factors of fundamental importance. At present, the
country is being rapidly industrialized and modernized.

Throughout these dramatic changes, the Zion groups constitute an enigmatic phenomenon. On certain important occasions, the white-dressed church leaders and their followers, complete with cross-staffs and flags, seem to dominate the social life
of the people. These enthusiastic religious groups are very much
part of Swazi society, yet stand out from it as a distinct movement with a variety of signs and symbols. What do they stand for?

Traditional Swazi society was hierarchically structured with the
king and the queen-mother (*Ingwenyama* and *Indlovukati*) as head
and centre of the whole. Traditionally, all conditions and relations could somehow be derived from the king and be regarded
as functions of Swazi kingship. Dr. Hilda Kuper sums it all up:
"The king and his mother hold positions of unique privilege and
authority. They are the central figures of all national activities;
they preside over the highest courts; they summon national
wealth, take precedence in ritual, and help to organize important
social events".[1] The Swazi year is punctuated by certain public

[1] H. Kuper, *An African Aristocracy* (1947), p. 54.

206

festivals, particularly the great drama of the *Incwala:* "The first and foremost actor in this drama is the king; where there is no king, there is no *Incwala*".[2]

Remarkably, this fundamental traditional pattern was preserved not only in Protectorate times, but also in what is now referred to as 'modern Swaziland'—after 1968. As leader of the *Imbokodvo* National Movement, the king asserted himself as the virtually unopposed political leader and on September 6, 1968, was sworn in as head of state of the independent Kingdom of Swaziland. Modern agriculture and forestry, industry, business and tourism are rapidly changing the map and face of Swaziland. Yet, underneath all this sudden modernization, the mystique of traditional kingship is there. The *Incwala* 'play of Kingship' (Kuper 1947, 225) is re-enacted every year, as vigorously as ever.

At Christmas 1972, I attended the *Incwala* and saw the King, once again, in traditional dress and with his red feathers dance with the long rows of his warriors. I saw the *lusekwane* boughs from the sacred tree; and was present at the great moment when the king lit the fire. By the use of firesticks, one male, one female, he started a spark by friction and the huge pyre burned, destroying all filth and dirt, bringing 'rain and blessing to the people and the nation'.

I followed the sacred ceremony from a corner, together with a distinct and distinguished group of onlookers: some fifteen Zionist bishops in white and blue uniforms. They explained the ritual to me. A huge pyre was built in the royal cattle kraal. The king, they told me, would place the fire at the four cardinal points of the pyre, East and West, North and South: "This is our traditional altar, as in the Old Testament. And the altar is facing East, just as at a burial, when the corpse is placed facing East." An old traditional warrior came up to my Zionist friends: "We celebrate our Christmas here", he said, with a gesture towards the abundant green *lusekwane* twigs to be seen everywhere.

The total pattern of Swazi life was, and is, dominated by kingship. Zion in Swaziland is one component in this multicoloured pattern.

---

[2] *Ibid.*, p. 197.

Tree of Swazi Zion

In the following pages I attempt to give, albeit in outline, a comprehensive survey of the Independent Church movement in Swaziland. The word "comprehensive" is used on purpose. For in the comparatively limited sphere of the Swazi it is possible to attempt what obviously is not feasible for the parallel situation in the Republic of South Africa. For the Swazi situation, one can at least attempt a total view of the movement as such, yet emphasizing the individualities of leaders and particular churches.

But through it all one must keep in mind that all-pervading and integrating influence of Swazi kingship.

The very manner of the introduction of Zionism into Swaziland was nothing if not providential. About 1913 a young lady teacher, no ordinary woman, by the name of Johanna Nxumalo, became the first Zionist convert. She belonged to one of the most influential families in the realm and was in fact a sister of Lomawa and of Nukwase, both successively Queen Mothers. From the very beginning, this relationship was bound to forge a link between Zion and King in Swaziland.[3]

The Nxumalo family represented a distinguished line in the early missionary occupation of Swaziland. When in one of the tribal tumults of the 1860's the Methodist missionary Allison had to flee from Swaziland, he took a trusted Swazi, Nxumalo, with him. Allison settled for some time at the Methodist stronghold of Edendale in Natal, where Nxumalo's children, among them

---

[3] I am aware of the possibility that there may have been some other individual Swazi who, prior to Johanna Nxumalo's baptism in 1913, became Zionists. It is also possible that her husband, the Rev. P. S. Kumalo, in his letter to me (March 18, 1960) may have post-dated Johanna's baptism. He thinks that she was baptized by Zion in 1915. Generally-held tradition in Swaziland claims that it was in 1913. Kumalo joined Zion in 1909, and Johanna may possibly have followed his example not very much later. But these are minor considerations compared with the important symbolic fact that Johanna Nxumalo, sister of the Queen Mothers, *was* the first Swazi Zionist. Rev. P. M. Masangane, in an interview 1958, stated that the first three Zionists in Swaziland were 1. Johanna Nxumalo 2. Zaccheus Dlamini 3. Andrea Zwane—the latter we shall meet later. Cf. report by J. H. de Wet, Bantu Commissioner, Wakkerstroom 29.1.1960, H.O. file 1798/214 and J. H. de Wet letter 10.4.1960 to the present writer. Ref. No. N 2/3/2.

Johanna and a brother Benjamin, were educated. Methodism here—as always—gave these gifted young people a chance. Johanna was trained at the Teachers' Training School of Inanda, and Benjamin at the neighbouring Ohlange, the two centres of higher learning for Bantu, a unique opportunity for progressive intellectuals. Benjamin was to become the King's trusted councillor in Swaziland, and the first President of the new Swazi Progressive Association from 1929. He died in 1942.

Johanna was for some reason sent to help her aunt in the Transvaal about 1907 and while teaching there, at Wakkerstroom, she met her destiny in the group of the Zion faithful. There she was baptized by the African leader, Daniel Nkonyane, who himself originated from Swaziland and insisted that he was a Swazi.[4]

There she also met her future husband, Rev. P. S. Kumalo. She died in 1930. Thirty years after her death, the widower testified about his Johanna (answering certain questions which I had put to him):

She prophesied and prayed for the sick and for barren women in order that they might get children. With the sick she would see how they could be healed. Yes, she had the Spirit to a high degree. She worked with the power of the Spirit of God. I, Paulos Kumalo, and she helped each other to perform these miracles. Yes, it was this Johanna Nxumalo who prophesied with veils, and then followed it up with sticks. She led people, using both sticks and veils, following those who taught them the function of these. Yes, she trusted that the sticks would help the sick.

It was Johanna Nxumalo who introduced the Nkonyanes to Swaziland. She was herself baptized by Daniel Nkonyane, but he soon delegated his Swazi interests to his brother Andries who be-

[4] D. Nkonyane's Form of Application to Zion, Ill., U.S.A., dated 4.6.1913: "What nationality are you? *Zwaze*" (In the spelling of the American Zion preacher in Johannesburg at the time, H. M. Powell). Archives, Christian Catholic Church, Zion, Ill., U.S.A. Sources: (*a*) Letter March 18, 1960 from the Rev. P. S. Kumalo (Johanna's husband) to the author. (*b*) Interview June 1958 with Mrs. Edith Mngabi, Johanna's sister, a distinguished-looking old lady of about eighty, had first been a Methodist, like her parents and brother and sister. Married to a Roman Catholic, she was at the time of the interview a member of his church. She sympathized with Zion though: "They are doing a great work, as there is so much illness about."

came the virtual Church father of Swazi Zion. Only very occasionally could Daniel manage to leave his headquarters at Charlestown, or his work on the Rand. Andries was his right hand in far-off Swaziland.

The Nkonyanes cultivated their relationships with royalty. Johanna Nxumalo's close contact with the royal house was only one factor in this development. The fact that it was the Zion of Wakkerstroom and the Nkonyane group which became her spiritual home was the other factor, and was almost as important. For this meant that for the next few decades Swaziland—although blessed with a rapidly rising number of different Zionist groups—would largely be related to the leading Zionist Nguni church under the leadership of the Nkonyanes (and of certain offshoots from them). In order to understand the whole genealogy of Swazi Zion we shall therefore consider the Nkonyane line as the main and central tradition.

"All church work in Swaziland was started by the Nkonyanes", Zionists will claim with a sweeping gesture.

The first act of healing was performed when the then Queen Mother—who after a serious crisis had been temporarily blinded —was prayed for by Daniel Nkonyane. Her sight was restored: "Never shall I abandon a Church that has helped me thus", was her promise, to which she adhered loyally and royally. Stephen Mavimbela, while still one of Nkonyane's lieutenants—he was later to form his own church—added even more to their treasury of virtue, for he went to the Royal Residence itself and 'prophesied' the presence of a hidden dangerous container, a horn, in the thatched roof of the Residence itself. Thereby he was everywhere and for ever reputed to have saved the royal house from a catastrophe. Dramatic occurrences—healing as well as this particular kind of 'prophecy'—made the Zionist influence felt, not least with people of very high rank in the realm.

The Zion image in the Republic of South Africa is complicated and sometimes confusing. By comparison the development in Swaziland is easy to follow and can be reduced to a few main branches. Yet, there is perhaps a temptation in the Swazi case, to draw too sharp and clear outlines which in this present case would be misleading. In this field we must always allow for the

210

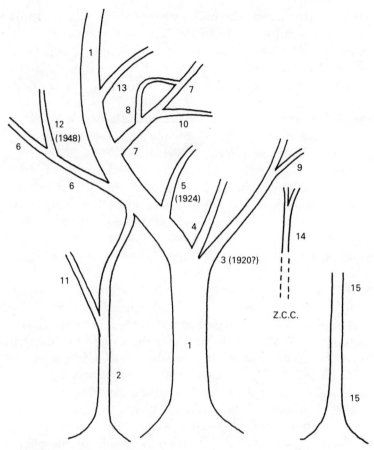

Tree of Zion.
See references in the text, pp. 212–219.

surprising, the spontaneous and the unforeseen, for we are dealing with movements of men and women who were conscious of
one thing above all: they felt carried by the wind of that Spirit
which, as Scripture reminds us, bloweth where it listeth.

The main configuration of the Zion development can be
rendered in terms of a genealogical tree, or cluster of trees, in-
dicating the main lines and connexions. The details can be filled
in later.

1. Daniel and Andries Nkonyane, representing the main trunk of Zulu Zion, fed by the "Living Waters" at Wakkerstroom and Charlestown. The first Swazi convert was Johanna Nxumalo, in or about 1913. Through her and her sister, the Queen Mother of Swaziland, the royal link between Zion and King was secured.

2. About the same time, another prominent Swazi, claiming to be a son of the royal family, Prince Solomon Madhevu Dlamini, appeared on the religious scene of Swaziland (1898–1962).

He was not technically a Zionist and should rather be characterized in general terms as a Swazi mystic and nationalist. By his family connections he was in a position to befriend and promote Swazi Zionism, pointing to its faithfulness to royalty. As a young man he was trained as a teacher at Amanzimtoti, near Durban and thus one of the very first in the country to receive higher education.

In 1915, apocalyptic visions transformed his life and world. He gathered his own community, called "The Christians", *ama Krestu.* In his Church Constitution, packed with Bible references, chiefly from the New Testament, he also uses the name "The Church of Swaziland". This denomination obviously had a deeper meaning; his church had originated not with foreigners but from Swazi soil, the core of the Church consisting largely of members of the Royal House and of chiefs of the realm.

A fervent Bible reader, he knew what Isaiah of old and the other prophets were referring to when they spoke of "Babylon": obviously this meant the Whites and their rule and their customs.

> Go ye forth of Babylon
> – – –
> Say ye, The Lord hath redeemed
> his servant Jacob (Is. 48: 20).

In this vein, he pleaded for Swazi custom, including polygamy, and the levirate and is reputed to have practised what he preached, also in this respect. He advocated Swazi dress. Yet, in his preaching he would combat the "shades" (*amadlozi*). He was a creative writer of hymns, particularly of national anthems. One of the best known was

> *Hlaba Nkosi Tinhliziyo yeNdlu yaka Ngwane*
> Pierce, o Lord, the heart of the House of Ngwane (=Swaziland)

Influenced in a broadly "ecumenical" spirit ("not Churchianity, but Christianity") by the "Church of Christ", Prince Madhevu was to become the main influence in the so-called 'Good Friday movement'. His position as a "Prince" gave him and his message a special prestige. He made a bid to run a Bible school for Swazi preachers (at Sihlahleni in the South), but this enterprise lasted only a few months.

Generous and emotional, he was regarded as a great preacher, and this royal evangelist was not above accosting people in the streets of Mbabane with his evangelical message.[4a]

3–4. While the main form of Zion in the country was that initiated by the Nkonyane group, two other original Zion branches from the Republic were also represented, although neither had much influence. Mabilitsa's Zion had a local leader in Marko Mtetwa (9) and the John Philips and Mathew Khoza brand of Zion found Swazi disciples.

5. In 1924, Daniel Nkonyane's group experienced a secession. Whatever the real reasons for his break-away may have been, Petros Hlatshwako claimed that he had to start on his own because Daniel Nkonyane, without proper authorization, changed the very name of his Church; in 1922 he had added the powerful words of "Holy Spirit" to the long list which formed the name of his denomination. His church was now led by Frank P. K. Moagi, residing on the Rand. Hlatshwako († 1953), who originally had come from an "Alliance" Mission, in South Swaziland, founded the Zulu Apostolic Church in Zion. In those early years one could without risk use the "Zulu" name in Swaziland; Swazi nationalism would soon make this unadvisable.

6–7. More serious were the Zwane and Mavimbela secessions, the Swazi Christian Church in Zion, dating from 1937. It was, as often happens in the case of these Zion churches, the death of the leader and the question of succession that caused this Swazi church crisis. After Daniel Nkonyane's death in 1935, his son

[4a] Interviews with J. S. Mavimbela and J. J. Nquku and letter from Khanya-kwezwe H. Dlamini—Prince Madhevu's son—14.6.1974 to the author.

Stephen became the leader, as a matter of course. In the beginning, the young man's authority was not established in distant Swaziland—and Zwane and Mavimbela grasped the opportunity. The moment was auspicious. This was the time when the European missions lost most of whatever influence they had had in Swaziland. There was a period of vacuum and a groping for a Swazi consciousness and Swazi nationalism. If the conclusion is not *too* sweeping, one might say that there was at that moment a disenchantment with both the *abafundisi abamhlope*—the white missionaries—and with the Zulu Zion leader at Charlestown.

The latter must have found this paradoxical, because at that very moment he made an imaginary bid to overcome his supposedly foreign origin. Called to become the new leader, he recalled that his forefathers did indeed hail from Swaziland. He therefore revived his Swazi heritage when in his episcopal regalia he attended the Incwala, in 1938. The *outsider* had returned to the fold. In the long run, this daring initiative was to become a model for all Swazi Zion leaders.

At that particular time, however, Nkonyane still carried the stigma of being a foreigner, and Zwane and Mavimbela, in a spiritual vacuum, discovered the Churches' one foundation in Swazi kingship. From now on the "Good Friday" conventions were to become the national movement of the Churches.

6. The observant Swazi nationalist Mr. Mfunza Sukathi characterized Andrew Zwane (†1957) to me as "a man's man, but uneducated". His mission background was with the "South African General Mission", and in 1916 he was baptized as a Zionist. He must have been a loyal character, for he kept to one particular branch of Chicago Zion, under Snelling, as far as possible. They gave him one pastor's certificate in 1921—in the margin of his copy there is the startling claim: "There is a great God in Apostate churches", Ps. 99: 2—and another certificate, "No. 25", from 1930. In addition just to be on the safe side, perhaps, he was also ordained by Daniel Nkonyane, in 1927.[5] Zwane's successor was Jonah Dhlamini.

---

[5] Papers with Mr. Joseph Zwana—A. Zwana's son—at Lobamba, and interviews with him in 1958 and 1972.

7. Stephen Mavimbela (1860–1948) was perhaps the most interesting of all Swazi prophets, more impetuous and sensitive, of a more nervous disposition than his colleague Zwane, and more visionary than most preachers. The turmoil of the Boer War snatched him from his relatively quiet milieu in Swaziland, and he fought for the British during the war. After the war he became a policeman, but had trouble with hashish until one day he heard a voice: "Go to Mahamba [a Methodist centre in South Swaziland]; there you will be told what to do". He met the well-known Methodist pastor Daniel Msimango, and was received into the Methodist Church in 1902. When Msimango's son soon afterward formed his Independent Methodist Church, Mavimbela followed him, and was sent by him as a preacher to Mozambique. In 1920 he joined the Nkonyane Zionists. He proved to be highly acceptable to the King and the Queen mother, not least because of his eminent gift of "seeing" things (*ukupholofitha*). His standing in Swazi society can be judged by the fact that when in 1945 an official Swazi delegation was sent to Pretoria to welcome General Smuts home, Mavimbela was included and appeared in his clerical collar in a photograph of the group.

When in 1944 Zwane and Mavimbela decided to unite, Mavimbela insisted that Zwane become the President, while he himself was satisfied to be Vice-President. King Sobhuza often referred to this impressive example of a prophet's humility.

Mavimbela's section was carried forward by the present leader, J. S. Mncinah. This choice was all the more logical as Mncinah's wife was of the Khambule clan, just like old Mrs. Mavimbela.

The fundamental Swazi principle of inheritance was thus adhered to: power was acquired by men, but transmitted by women (Kuper, 1947, 91). It was loosely explained to me by my informants as the *gogo*-line, *gogo* meaning grandmother.

Bishop Mncinah—a powerful man, a successful builder, often employed in building royal residences—was to occupy an increasingly central position in the whole movement. He is now the influential Secretary of the League of Zionist Churches.

In connection with Zwane and Mavimbela, we should also mention Luka Ziyane. At his headquarters at "Antioch", his agricultural activities became a fine example to the whole Zion movement. As is typical for a number of Zionists, Ziyane was the chair-

215

man of the local Farmers' Association. Mncinah the builder and Ziyane the farmer set the tone for industrious Swazi Zionists. They became church leaders who—according to a well-known pattern in other parts of the world—through their hard work and obvious worldly success proved to their fellow-men that God had blessed their religion.

8. Luka Lushaba contested Mncinah's leadership for a whole decade, 1949–58, until King Sobhuza coerced the two to unite.

9. In a report of 1945 to the District Commissioner, Manzini, the Mabilitsa groups claim a Swazi membership of 4064, under Marko Mtetwa. However, this claim must have been exaggerated, even if there seem to have been Mabilitsa groups in four different places. J. J. Dube also joined the Mabilitsa branch.

10. While Mncinah and Lushaba were struggling for the leadership of the same Church, the situation was aggravated by the fact that a third President, Joshua Nyembe, made the same claim. For some years there were thus three contenders. Nyembe's position was made less complicated by the fact that he claimed Swazi supremacy not in Swaziland itself, but from the relative safety of far-off Johannesburg. There was no more devoted Swazi royalist than this bishop in Orlando, signing his letters "Royal Crown 8193, Orland West". He was a charming and warm personality, proud of the imaginary recognition which he believed that "Pretoria" had awarded his church. Originally a Roman Catholic, he joined Nkonyane's Zion when Daniel Nkonyane consented to bury his brother, who had died in prison. He had left the Catholic Church about 1913, but as late as 1958, when we visited him, there was still a vestige of the old values left in him. He was assured of his episcopal position *because,* he said, he himself had been consecrated by Bishop Johannes Twala, who in his turn had been consecrated by J. Md. Hlongwane of the Bantu Methodist Church. One felt that one was faced here with a more or less unbroken line of succession, although it did perhaps not reach very far back. He did not extend his episcopal claims to Swaziland itself, but was satisfied with his own "Royal kraal", as he put it, in urban Orlando.

11. Rev. Isaac Ngwenya's organization is called the Church of Christ, and his background was a mission church with this name. Like most of the other Zion leaders, he could not afford to work full-time for his church, but worked as an assistant in an Indian haberdashery in the Republic.

12. By far the most exotic of all Zion prophets in Swaziland at present is Bishop Eliyasi Vilakathi, at his "Jericho" head-quarters. He is a broad, friendly, self-assured person with a genial and generous smile. The visitor to the annual Good Friday meetings at Lobamba will notice that the majority of Zionists appear in white or blue. There is, however, a particularly vocal group dressed in red and black, sometimes in sackcloth, some of the leaders festooned with chains and padlocks and keys; this is Bishop Vilakathi's "Jericho" group. He was a member of Zwane's church but soon branched out on his own, forming his Jericho Christian Church in Zion. He had special authority for doing so. On April 15, 1948, he received the Holy Spirit, while in jail in Johannesburg. His was the usual offence in that part of the world, some passport infringement or other. The enforced solitude in jail induced visions. He was visited by three angels flying with mighty wings, who carried him through the three heavens: the first heaven for "all people"; the second one, where Jesus dressed in red, resided; and the third, that of the Father on his throne. He was shown great numbers of people and he knew that: "All these people will pass through me (*ukudlula*). I must preach to them".

He returned to Swaziland. There he claims that he spent three years on the Umnyambe mountain, living on a diet of soil and grass and water. Much of the time was spent in grottoes in the mountain, where he preached to a strange tribe of "small people"—*abantu abafishane*—living permanently in these mountain grottoes of Bishop Vilakathi's. For a language they used ordinary *isiSwathi*, but Vilakathi could only communicate with them while speaking in tongues.[6]

He soon established his own Church headquarters in the beau-

---

[6] M. J. Field, *Search for Security*, 1960, has recorded similar ideas in rural Ghana. They were called *mmoetia* there. *Ibid.*, pp. 17, 82, 222, 241.

tiful "Jericho" valley below this mountain. The place is well marked by nine flagpoles with flags. Here he has built his church and his home and receives a number of patients. The padlock and the keys signify that the Bishop has been given the Power to Lock and the Power to Open.

When we visited him he was already far ahead with the building of a new Church. He showed his plans to us. It was in keeping with the whole situation that he gave the most eloquent demonstration of the correlation social body—human body that we have yet come across: In that direction was to be the gate or as he said, "the mouth of the church", and he underlined this by forcibly protruding his nether lip.

We do not need to stress that Bishop Vilakathi is regarded as something of an outsider by the other Zionists. His colour scheme, in particular the red and black, with the sashes on which is embroidered the name "Jericho" seemed all wrong; the right colours, of course, are white and blue. He therefore had difficulty at the beginning in establishing himself in the house of bishops. But his success in winning followers impressed his episcopal colleagues, and he now seems to be fully accepted by the others, in the Lobamba Good Friday meetings. (See also *Appendix,* p. 324).

13. E.E.C.H.S.A.C.Z. is the string of letters on the brooch of Barnabas Sibiya's Church at Kwaluseni: *E*dwaleni *E*kusindiseni [On the Rock, In Salvation] *C*hurch, *H*oly *S*pirit *A*postolic *C*hurch in *Z*ion. No wonder that this must be abbreviated to a more accessible term, also inscribed on the brooch: *"Tongo Tongo"*. As such this Church is more widely known. This name, as every good Swazi knows, was that of one of King Sobhuza's aunts and underlines the special responsibility that Sibiya and his group felt for royalty. This Princess Tongo-Tongo was not herself a member of Zion, Sibiya explained to me, but she was famous, and the *umcwasho* ceremony was performed for her and her colleagues in the Royal Kraal. Healing is one of the main activities of this Church. There are three different ministries in this medical field: the *umbonisi,* the seer or diagnostician, 1 Sam. 9 being the Biblical authority; the *umpholofithi,* or the prophet; and finally the *umazisi,* the herald or announcer. Various methods can be applied to different ailments. For mental disorders, a

cord is fastened round the head, with a cross hanging in front on the forehead. Water-drinking and vomiting follow. In praying for pregnant women the prophet dips a cord of wool in specially treated water; the cord is then tied round the prophet's waist, while he continues praying.

14. Comparative late-comers into Swaziland are the selfassured messengers of the Z. C. C., Lekganyane's church from Northern Transvaal. These activities fall outside the scope of our study. Suffice it therefore to say that it is also in Swaziland a dynamic group. Its healing performance is experienced as helpful: the green woolen cord round the patient's waist and wrist is sure to be effective. Hitherto barren women for instance have been known to testify to its power.

15. *Apostolics.* In Swaziland, too, Apostolics are a category of their own among the Churches of the Spirit. St. John's Apostolic Church with its headquarters at Evaton, Johannesburg, under the leadership of Ma Nku, has a local representative in Alphaeus Msibi. He is Swazi, born at Mahamba in the South, where his parents were members of an offshoot from the [Congregational] American Board Mission. We have followed him for some twenty years, and feel that his contribution deserves special attention here.

For years—"seven years", he thinks—he was haunted by a frightening, ever-recurring vision. A big star would come rushing toward him, and he avoided it only at the last split second. In the end, he went to Mrs. Nku at Evaton to be prayed for (p. 80). But even then, in the Temple, the Star pursued him, chasing him, almost killing him. He rushed out of the building and ran and fell. This time the star did not miss him. As he gaped at this terror-inspiring shining globe, it went down his mouth and into his stomach.

On another occasion, in a dream, he saw himself with a big key, about to fit it into the opening of a door leading to Bethesda, a room with water. Then he heard a voice, telling him to go and preach, at home in Swaziland. He took the next train from Johannesburg to Piet Retief and found himself sitting under a tree, at home. Then he knew that he was at last healed from his fear and that life was about to begin anew. He was baptized in a river by Lazarus Nku, Ma Nku's husband. From 1951 he began his work at Kwa Luseni, Swaziland. There he has managed to establish his Swazi Bethesda, not far from his Swazi Jordan, the river otherwise known as the "Little Usuthu".

Broadly speaking he appears to the researcher as one of the many Swazi Zionists, with similar concerns against pollution and exhortation to purification and healing. Yet, he is anxious to draw a sharp line between his movement and the world of Zion. "Zionists who have no sense". The Zionists for their part are just as careful to distinguish themselves from the *aba Postoli*.

This was his difficulty *and* his opportunity when in the 1950s he set out to build his Bethesda. The difficulties were great. Although a Swazi he appeared to represent a foreign element, and this during a time of intense Swazi nationalism. "I am Msibi's enemy No. 1", a prominent Swazi Court official told us in those years. Without clear legal rights he had settled at Kwa Luseni, one of the projected residential areas, and his first loyalty was, at that time, to a Sotho-speaking woman, Ma Nku on the Rand.

Yet he managed to establish himself. In a limited way he is perhaps an illustration of a development which Mary Douglas in her book *Purity and Danger* calls "The System Shattered and Renewed." His particular brand of Spirit-religion was different from the ways of Zion, and therefore seemed foreign and maybe dangerous. Well, emphasize and dramatize that foreignness—and you will soon be accepted, but now on your own terms. So, hundreds of little Swazi children and hundreds of Swazi men and women were purified or baptized in the Usuthu River, in the name of the Father and of the Son and of the Holy Spirit, using not Swazi but the Sotho language: '*La Ntate lela Mora lela Moea ohalalelang*'. His bishop on the Rand, Petros Masango, also a Nguni (Zulu) visits Swaziland from time to time, and he uses the same linguistic effect, often mixed with one or two English or Afrikaans phrases. The use of the Sotho language here had a two-fold function: it established a spiritual contact with the great Mother, Ma Nku, in distant Johannesburg, *and* the foreignness of sound helped to intensify the sacredness of the experience.[6a]

[6a] On Ma Nku, see p. 80–85.

Novelty and foreignness in a new movement could therefore, even in traditionalist Swazi society, be turned into an advantage, an evangelistic opportunity, and Msibi apparently has managed to do just that. He has established a Church colony, with fine buildings, dominated by the Bethesda with five doors, as a real Bethesda should have (John 5). He has a number of patients: "This is not a church, this is as hospital", he says. He has the power to look through people and he can diagnose illnesses, particularly TB and mental cases. One girl with a hysteric disorder (*isipoliyana*) had spent two years in the church colony. He would give her special food and *isiwasho*—in this case, water mixed with ashes—in order to remove the *isimnyama* and the *isiphosiso* (blackness and transgression) which were the causes of the complaint. In cases of transgression of God's commandment about sex, ashes and Sunlight soap were mixed with the water. The ashes were of really choice quality. Outside the church Msibi had built an altar—the exact measurements had been laid down in Ex. 30 and 38. For the sacrifice he would use selected cattle which, prior to slaughter, had been "baptized" by the prophet himself. The water used in this connection must be taken from below a rock. The prophet prayed for the person, laying hands on his, or, perhaps more often her, head, smearing it with ashes and soap.

The emphasis in St. John's Apostolic Church is on the purifying effect of water. At Ma Nku's temple at Evaton or Bishop Masango's at Natalspruit there is a very considerable consumption of holy water carried home from the church in bottles and large containers. Msibi at Kwa Luseni, Swaziland, has followed this example. An important activity in his colony is fetching water for the services, but as a progressive person he was looking forward to acquiring an automatic water pump which would lighten this particular burden.

Msibi has developed what could be termed a "water mysticism" and thereby possibly deepened the message first conceived by the Mother at Evaton. On a Saturday evening we heard him give an address at Kwa Luseni, in preparation for purification services the following day. His Bible text was John 5, on the pool of Bethesda, "having five porches".

Water is a great thing, a very great thing [he began]. *Aakuthula* (Peace [the congregation automatically responded with "Amen"]). When Jehovah created everything, he did so from out of the waters, the Primeval Waters. The work of water is great. Jehovah is in the Water. Water is the great work of God. Now for tomorrow you must be prepared to bring your bottles. They must be *clean and nice*; there must be no *dart* [dirt; these words rendered in his English]. So you must be very careful in looking for the kind of water you need and pour into bottles or jars or jugs carefully prepared.

Because remember, it is not water you are going to drink tomorrow. You are going to drink Jehovah. *A-Akuthula* [*Amen*]. You are going to drink Jehovah, who created everything from out of the waters. When you were born, you were cleansed with water. When you are going to die, you will be cleansed with water. When Jehovah created everything in the beginning, his light shone on the surface of the Primeval Waters. Thus he created heaven and earth.

Now some people do not believe this. They are like Nicodemus [!]. It is the same with you, perhaps. But if you do not believe in the water of Jehova, you will burn (*nizosha*).

So remember, to-morrow we shall drink Jehovah.

A-akuthula [*Amen*]

An Afrikaans hymn, particularly popular, I think, with the Mother, was sung, *"Ons sal saamgaan hemel-toe"*, "We shall go together to heaven."

What had happened here was of course nothing less than the emergence, or the birth of a sacrament. Msibi confided to me, as one theologian to another, that he found the use of wine in Holy Communion problematic. Basically, he thought, the Bible taught water. No wine was used at the Passover of the old Covenant, he thought. In 1 John 5:6, the reference to "water and blood and Spirit" showed, he said, that "water is the Blood of God". Jesus sweating blood in Gethsemane (Luke 22:44) meant, he insisted, that "water is the blood, full of God's Spirit". More fully, perhaps, than other Apostolics, he interpreted a collective experience of his Church: in a filthy world of all kinds of threatening pollution and illness and death, a new sacrament of purity and life had been born.

The following day we witnessed this. On the table in the midst of the Bethesda Temple were white water containers, a washbasin, and dozens of small glasses filled with water. Young and old, men and women and children came up to the table, where

Msibi and Bishop Masango presided. Some were as if in a frenzy, shaking and gyrating, most would perform that particular sharp sudden jerking movement with one leg as if the knee had suddenly given way, the Mother's special mannerism in Johannesburg repeated here in Swaziland by thousands who had never seen her.

Later in the day, there was a long procession to the River. Only Bishop Masango himself came by car, in his impressive white-and-blue Chevrolet. A Zulu himself, he preached in Zulu, and, very strangely, this was interpreted into Sotho: "Not all can baptize in water. Only the ones who are sent. We have come to the land of the Lion (i.e., the King). We shall see to it that the Law of the Waters will fulfil the Law of Kings".

Clearly, what was involved here was a bid to identify this particular church and message with the Swazis in attempting to fit the message and the ritual into the Swazi context. But there remained an emphatic foreignness, in the extraordinary measure of having the message interpreted into Sotho.

King and Zion

Research into the history of Swazi society may reveal certain peculiar tensions in the 1930s. It is not our task here to try to uncover these; we can do no more in this context than hint at them. There were numerous cases of accusations of *ubuthakathi,* such as Rex v. Mampendensi Mngomezulu; Zionist prophets were called upon to 'prophesy', or smell out, who was the originator of this particular trouble. In Chief Maloye's ward a Zionist prophet was brought all the way from Ermelo to help out in a similar crisis. In 1937, a number of Africans were evicted in the Hluti area because they had been singled out as witches or wizards by Zionist preachers. Swaziland in the 1930s thus provided parallels to simultaneous developments analysed by Audrey Richards for Northern Rhodesia.[7]

Neither should one forget the positive aspects, however. It was also in 1937 that Chief Pahla of Stegi after a particularly bad spell of lightning in the district invited a band of Zionists

[7] Audrey I. Richards, A Modern Movement of Witchfinders, *Africa* (8) 1935.

to pray at his kraal in order to avert a second visitation of lightning.

It was at this time also that a new impression of Zionism as an unruly army of numerous competing prophets suddenly came to be formed in Swaziland. Until that time Nkonyane and his co-workers seem to have wielded fairly unopposed authority. But in about 1937 both Andrew Zwane and Stephan Mavimbela launched out on their own. This was by far the most notorious breakaway at this time. After this, the Zion scene became increasingly multiform. In little Bremersdorp alone (now Manzini), the Native Commissioner reported in 1937 to Government Secretary, Mbabane, that there were four different branches of Zionists (February 4, 1937).

The situation seemed to call for an effort at amalgamation and unification. The King himself took part in this constructive venture. In 1939, the "National Swazi Church" was formed, with an ex-Methodist, John M. Dube as Chairman. This organization attracted mainly non-Zionist Independent groups. It soon proved to be a largely abortive attempt, but it must at least be mentioned here as a forerunner of greater things to come. Dube also informed me that in these pre-war years the King, speaking to prophets and pastors, presented the challenging idea of building a National Cathedral of Swaziland. It was all very logical: England had its "Church of England", Germany was represented abroad by its German Mission.'" So we in *Ngwane* (the traditional name for Swaziland) ought to have a Swazi Church and a Swazi Cathedral."

Dube's organization originally held itself aloof from the Zionists and, as we have already indicated, had difficulties in getting started. There seemed to be much greater hope—and of course much greater need—for Zionist amalgamation. Nkonyane's ex-lieutenants Andrew Zwane and Stephen Mavimbela took the lead. In the process they arrived at a gentlemen's agreement—missionaries called this sort of thing "comity". They conceived a plan which would lead to the least friction between them. They therefore divided all of Swaziland between themselves, Zwane taking the South and Mavimbela the North as their special spheres of interest. This seemed to solve, at least for the time being, their personal problems and tensions.

It was the King himself, ever active and resourceful, who suggested the approach. Just before the war, in August 1939, a
meeting was held. The appeal to the Nation, signed at Lozithalezi
Royal Kraal, was formulated by Zwane and Mavimbela:

The meeting of uniting the churches by The *Ingwenyama* [the Lion,
i.e., the King] to all churches. In this meeting the ways and laws [were
discussed] to carry this church which is united by *Isilo* [the Beast, or the
Lion which is another colourful reference to the King] of the Swazi
people and the [British] Government. All full members of Zion
[should] join this meeting which is called The Swazi Church in Zion
of South Africa. This name was proposed by the Ingwenyama who
spoke with the Government to represent this Church, on Aug. 8, 1939.
The *Isilo* proposed the Church's name to the Zion that they see this way
of uniting Churches is right ... All members of this church are notified
that during Good Fridays [they] must come to the Royal Kraal to meet
and worship God with the Ingwenyama ..."

In 1942, they were prepared to form an "amalgamate
Church". A "Constitution and Deed of Trust" was worked out.
The introduction reads:

Whereas it has been found fit by Swaziland [British] Administration
to take a vigorous step and to exterminate the existence of the very
many Separatist group[s] of Zionist[s] and that after such interma-
tion [*sic*] has been received by the Paramount Chief, Sobhuza II, to
summon these separatist groups, with the object of drawing their attention to the step thus contemplated by the Adminstration.
A meeting was therefore held, with representatives from all these sec-
tarian groups whereat it was unanimously resolved "to amalgamate all
sects of the Zionist movement into one consolidated and constituted
body ... [to] be called *The Swazi Christian Church in Zion of South Africa.*"

Stephen Mavimbela with characteristic humility stepped aside
and himself proposed that Zwane become President for life,
while Mavimbela was elected Vice-President. They even went to
the extent of visualizing the "Creed and Tenets of faith" of the
Church. This was to be "embodied in the Catechism of this
Church", a literary and theological venture which unfortunately
never materialized.

In the nature of things, this amalgamated church was a loose
federation. The leaders were, as can be seen, unfamiliar with the
niceties of bureaucratic protocol. Yet they were carried forward

225

by a common concern and spirit, yes, by "The Spirit", as they would claim. In the long run, this group, related to the King *and* to 'Good Friday' when they were to meet the King, proved to be a strong body.

The parallel organization was different. The non-Zionists under John Dube consisted of ex-Methodist groups mainly from the Southern part of the country. Towards the end of the war, the King had expressed dissatisfaction with the name of Dube's church, National *Swazi* Church. What about the Zulus and all the other peoples? The horizon had widened in those years. So when Dube and his group met at Gege on October 7, 1944, they decided to call the new, or re-organized church, "The United Christian Church of Africa" (UCCA), a name which, again reputedly, was the King's invention.

If the Zionist group seemed to be lacking in secretarial efficiency and finesse, the UCCA had both in abundance. For now an interesting personality appeared on the scene of Swazi church politics. John J. Nquku, a Zulu by birth, had been a school-inspector from 1930–42. He was also active in Benjamin Nxumalo's Progressive Association; this was where he conceived what was to become the radical Progressive Party which in the early 1960s was to make an abortive bid for political leadership and power. At this early time, Nquku was in the King's confidence and was asked to be his advisor on school and church affairs. Although himself still an Anglican and not a member of the UCCA, he became its General Secretary. Active, boisterous, irrepressible, short in stature but loud of laughter and speech, Nquku took the lead in the group. Here was a constitution maker and a writer of appeals and complaints who for some years by sheer propaganda and persuasion, rather than by any noticeable achievement was going to place the UCCA on the map of Swaziland.

From then on things moved quickly. Zephaniah Kunene, an ex-Independent Methodist from the Methodist stronghold in the South, Mahamba, was given the Presidency of the United Church, at the end of 1944. In March 1945, Nquku applied to the Swaziland Government for recognition of the Church—thereby introducing an administrative problem in that corner of Southern Africa that had hitherto been spared this particular kind of application. He was informed by the Protectorate Government in the same month "That there is no provision for registration of Churches in Swaziland". This reply was the kind of challenge that roused Nquku's energies. He managed to play off the African Government against the local representatives of Westminster, and persuaded King Sobhuza, in March 1946, to write to the Government Secretary in Mbabane that the UCCA "has presented to us its Constitution which has been accepted by us".

It was also without any doubt Nquku who formulated the paragraph on doctrine in the Church's constitution—thus a formula, it should be noted, which was worked out by a non-member of the Church. The broad and sweeping generosity of this formula reflects the interested intellectual layman rather than the churchman.

> Its foundation is indigenous and its doctrine adaptable and adoptable to all environments and peoples. Tolerating all national customs so long as they are not inconsistent with Christian principles and for its aim so far as possible intends to Christianize such customs, so as to make them conform to Christian doctrine ... The policy of our Church in its doctrine means to grant full liberty to all men to worship God according to the dictates of their own consciences.

This generous openness with regard to doctrinal position could not always be maintained when it came to the internal power politics of the Church. At its inauguration, in October 1944, the UCCA elected Zephaniah Kunene as its first president; but less than four years later Nquku had to inform the Government that Kunene's licence had been withdrawn, and, again, "these men are manufacturing faked appointment certificates which are signed by Rev. Z. Kunene" (June 1949).

A schism had occurred in the Church. For a number of years this caused considerable confusion. The anti-Kunene party was now under the leadership of J. Dube, the same man who in 1939 had formed the Swazi National Church. These internal struggles weakened the organization to such an extent that it lost what little influence it had had. On the other hand, the administrative aspects of this controversy afforded Nquku the opportunity for a wide variety of propaganda. When a government official seemed to side with Kunene, Nquku, as "the chief leader and founder of this Church", retaliated (Aug. 8, 1949): "Even if this Church is only a native Church it ought to receive the respect it deserves".

The Swazi 'Good Friday movement' is a function of nascent Swazi nationalism. It began to find its form towards the end of the 1930s. We have referred to the schism between Stephen Nkonyane and his two Swazi lieutenants, Zwana and Mavimbela. It happened, paradoxically, at the same time as Nkonyane aligned himself with Swazi nationalism by appearing at the *Incwala* ceremony. Mavimbela rationalized his stand in the crisis by stating that Nkonyane took good Swazi money out of Swaziland —an accusation which was often voiced concerning European missions at the time, as a reaction against their efforts towards financial self-support of the churches.

It was in connexion with this crisis, in 1937, that the "League of Swazi Churches" was formed. The Good Friday movement is an outcome, the most significant and important result, of the League. At the very outset, there was an interesting co-operation over the Good Friday conventions between two men from an 'Ethiopian' Camp—AME Church—and Zion. The AME were a relatively educated élite with men such as Rev. Pepete and Rev. Sibiya. These two men joined forces with Stephen Mavimbela, who represented Zion, and the group were in close contact with the King.

To the King, the League was an instrument for uniting the churches, or for creating a National Church. It inspired him to the extent of spontaneously formulating a watchword of the movement. As he addressed one of the meetings, possibly in 1944, the King called out: *"Hambani—funani unyawo luka Jesu"* —"Go ye and look for the footprint of Jesus!" There was a secret overtone in that watchword. Just as a century earlier old King Somhlolo had challenged his people to consider the new faith, (cf. p. 238), so now King Sobhuza called the nation. This might have been a powerful soundingboard for the King's pious watchword.

He appointed councillors to prepare a Constitution of the League and to advise the League generally. Three men formed the first group of Church councillors: Prince Solomon Madhevu Dlamini, Benjamin Nxumalo and Alpheus Hlope, all three

228

closely related by blood to the King and the Queen Mother. When Nxumalo died in 1940, a successor was found in the person of J. J. Nquku. The latter, while wielding an influence in the parallel UCCA movement, did not have the temperament to take Zionism seriously. In the group of three councillors it was Prince Madhevu who was to become the real power.

As an organizer he was assisted by another preacher, close to the Swazi throne: M. P. Masangane-Sithole. Masangane had been baptized by Andries Nkonyane in 1927, and might have remained an ordinary local preacher if it had not been for the happy fact that, in 1930, he married into royalty. His young wife —herself baptized as a young girl by the same omnipresent Andries Nkonyane—was the daughter of Mbandzeni, the late Paramount Chief, and his wife La Msibi.

Because of this relationship, Masangane was to act as a king-pin in church matters, for the whole Zion organization. Officially he was subordinate to Stephen Nkonyane who in the 1950s became known as 'Archbishop'. However, the real power rested in Masangane's hand. He told one of my informants: "Nkonyane could do nothing without me here in Swaziland". Masangane was the one who would confer with the King and the Queen Mother and was the liaison officer between Royalty and Zion. As the son-in-law of Royalty—*"umkwenyana we bukhosi"*—he was fully trusted, and knew his power. He was invested with the two leading administrative offices, being elected as President of "the Federation of Churches in Zion" *and* of the "League of Swazi Churches"; in fact these two organizations tended to overlap to such an extent that for all practical purposes they could be regarded as identical. Nkonyane himself had to tread circumspectly in his relations with Masangane. Sometimes he would remind Masangane of his subservient position, thereby implying that he, Nkonyane was, after all, the head.

In July 1958, I interviewed the two men in Masangane's home near the Royal Lodge. It was a hot afternoon, and while I was discussing with Masangane, Nkonyane as the important person, seated on Masangane's fine sofa, felt that he could go off to sleep in order to preserve his strength for a vigorous display of *uMoya* in a meeting late in the afternoon. I asked Masangane about Zion's response to the fine initiatives taken at that time by the

[Protectorate] Agricultural Department. With justified pride Masangane told me of his growing rice fields and his sale of rice. This roused the Bishop from his afternoon nap and he turned to his host: "*Mfundisi,* you have not sent me your tithe of rice this year". He then leaned back again on the sofa.

The annual conference of the church is also related to the royalty of the Dhlamini clan. In the case of especially privileged groups the contact may become particularly strong. Here, as a matter of course, the Nkonyanes score above all the others. Pastor Masangane-Sithole mused to himself: "All in our Church are Dhlaminis. This Church is their England". (It was probably the supposed identity of royalty and the Church of England that provoked this remark.) The last weekend of July 1958 was in fact a "royal weekend", the Saturday being the Queen's day and the Sunday the King's day. From afar, a thousand or more of the Nkonyane Zionists had arrived. Archbishop and Mrs. Nkonyane had come all the way from Charlestown in their white-and-blue Chevrolet, and stayed with Pastor and Mrs. Masangane during the meeting. Hundreds had come by bus from Johannesburg or from Natal.[8]

On the first day the crowd congregated at the Queen's Royal Kraal, Lobamba. There had just been a disaster; one of the royal huts had burned down, and it was taken for granted that it had been a case of arson. This was to lend a special note of concern and sorrow to the hymns and prayers.

A bell was rung, the signal for all to find their "holy sticks" and to set out for Lobamba. The lady wardens (*emagosa*) bore flags and led the way. The women with sticks, while marching, would walk in circles, *kuhlehla*. This was the term used for warriors or age-groups when giving a dancing display before royalty. Eminent people in the Swazi hierarchy would lead the way, thus pastor Masangane and one or two other preachers, well versed in court etiquette, would *hlehla* in front of the others, applying also in the Church the discipline of *umbutso* (the realm). The effect of the crosses in their hands added to the sacredness and

---

[8] In the 1960's a Bishop's Lodge was put up in the grounds of the Royal residence. This was a wooden house where the Zion leaders could stay and congregate while preparing themselves for their attendance at National festivals. In 1972, I held my interviews with some fifteen bishops at this Lodge.

power of the ceremony. *"Emandla ase ndukwini"*, the power is there in the stick.

The crowd assembled in a wood of Eucalyptus trees, waiting for their leaders. Nkonyane himself arrived by car. All wore robes and careful instructions were given about the removal of shoes before touching the holy ground in the courtyard of the Royal kraal where the service was to be held. Masangane gave the marching order: "Ministers first, according to rank, and then evangelists (*Befundisi pambili edilezini yabo*)", but there had to be a long wait, for Mrs. Masangane herself was late. During the preceding night she had had to attend to the queens, as only she could. She was after all not so much a "Pastor's wife", or *"Make"* —"Our Mother", as pre-eminently *Umnthfwanenkosi,* a princess, and a princess she remained to all, even her husband, who had to render to her the respect due to her as a royal person.

At last she appeared in her Zionist uniform with cruciform staff. Some five hundred people moved through the gate into the Royal Kraal, women marching on the men's left. For a while women with flags would *kudlalisa*—dance and wave flags. The Queen Mother with the other royal women were seated outside in a row. Benches were brought in so that the ministers could sit down. The men were placed in front, facing the Queen Mother, with the women behind. Opposite the Queen Mother the leaders, including Nkonyane and Masangane, were placed in a crescent line. The royal family appeared in tribal dress.

Bishop Nkonyane opened with prayer and a hymn and a brief address, referring to the fire and suggesting that they as Zionists were going to bring their *intelezi* (protective medicine), i.e. the Word of God: "Long live the Lioness and the Lion and the whole House of Ngwane [Swaziland] and the land of our forefathers!" This was followed by short speeches given by three pastors. This part of the ceremony took only some forty-five minutes. Then the Queen Mother rose and went into the Indhlunkulu enclosure accompanied by two of her attendants, and followed by the leading ministers (and an African female sociology student, our informant). This was an occasion for Nkonyane and three other preachers to pray for the Queen Mother's health.

That Sunday morning afforded special blessing for three of the ministers. Up to now they had carried simple wooden staffs but were now promoted into a higher class, into the elite with brass staffs, one of them being a prince (a classificatory brother of Mrs. Masangane). A great number of ordinary people received ordinary wooden staves of various patterns according to "prophecy".

One can surmise that they could now face the event of the day with greater dignity. This was the day of meeting the King, at the Lositahlezi Royal Kraal, some five miles from the scene of the previous day (at the Queen Mother's residence). The crowd now numbered some 1,300 people, with a slight predominance of men over women. The procession found the King seated with a number of Queens on his left side. One of the pastors recited the "Lion's" praises. The group paraded twice before the royal group and then sat in a crescent formation, with the Zionist leaders opposite the King. Nkonyane and three pastors addressed the King and the meeting as a whole, Bishop Nkonyane dwelling again on the lamentable fire in the royal place. One of the non-Swazi Sotho-speaking ministers declared that he loved Sobhuza because he combined kingship and religion; as a king he was submissive to the King of Kings. A characteristic change in the programme was the appearance of a prophet from Southern Swaziland, one Mota, who was reputed to have performed miracles of healing among members of the Royal family. Now Mota rushed forward roaring and shouting; it was felt that he had seen a vision which he wanted to broadcast.

A woman's choir sang a popular song: "Ezekiel called out and said: Ye bones come together" (with reference to Ezekiel, ch. 37). To the nationalist Swazi mind, this song had happy overtones of seeing all Swazi in Swaziland as well as the scattered Swazi beyond its borders, gathered together as one army of salvation, for Sobhuza II.

It was now time for the King's reply. He wished to contradict Bishop Nkonyane who had been down-hearted because of the fire: "This is rather a challenge to you Zionists. You can now show your strength. With your weapon of faith and prayer you must be confident that you will conquer". Fourteen hundred Zionists answered *"Bayete"*. As the King took his leave and went to Lobamba, Nkonyane, Masangane and other leading ministers followed, in order to pray for the King. A list was also made of those who had special visions and dreams and a record of these was handed over for further study.

The King will be kept regularly informed about the internal problems of the Churches. Sometimes he finds it necessary to interfere, in order to settle some problem of ecclesiastical power. This happened in the 1950s in the Swazi Christian Church in Zion of South Africa, the official name of Bishop Mncinah's Church. Here there was a conflict between the forceful Mncinah, who had been elected Bishop, and L. Lushaba, who had for a long time been a prominent figure in Zion affairs (p. 217). Mncinah did not have the genealogical advantages enjoyed by his predecessor Masangane, who, as we know, had married into royalty. All the more, Mncinah would attempt to use modern means of communication in order to establish himself. On December 8, 1956, he published a rousing article in *Izwi lama Swazi:*

God bless our Lion Sobhuza II!
May God bless our Swazi King, the son of Mahlokohla. May he grow until he is [so old that he] will have to walk stooping. To me, Sobhuza II is [like to] Solomon of old in wisdom, and [his father] Mbandzeni I compares with Moses of old in Israel.

This comparison with King Solomon of the Old Testament was to reappear in a speech by Sobhuza himself, less than two years later. At this time the conflict between Mncinah and Lushaba had taken on significant proportions. The King called a public meeting. A lively article in *Izwi lama Swazi* (17.5.1958) gives the whole scene. It also conveys the extraordinary place and role of the King among his people and of his genial involvement in a matter of this nature. A few quotations are therefore not out of place.

After being greeted by the crowd with cries of *"Bayete!"*, the King spoke:

There has appeared a noisy conflict in the Church because of [two leaders] not wanting to show one another mutual respect. Therefore I have scrutinized your votes—as you know Church-work is run according to votes.—I put in the one who got the majority of votes, Mncinah. But I have noticed that since then Lushaba is roaring about on the mountains and in mischief. I wonder why, as it is well known that according to church laws there may be changes in leadership after five years. I sent my commission, consisting of A. K. Hlope, S. A. Sibiya, Rev. P. M. Masangane together with Mr. Nquku and they returned a report to the effect that, "Oh, Mncinah is hiding in the grass. He says, As that Lushaba never respects Kingship, why should I respect it?" Now do you wish to settle this matter on your own or do you wish the King to adjudicate? A thunderous *"Bayete!"* followed, and Rev. Zeph. Dlamini (for Mncinah's group) answered. "Thou Lion of the Swazis, we look to Thee alone to judge." So he turned to Lushaba with the same question, and he replied: "I too am looking to the King".

The King then said: "I see that you are at loggerheads because of money, so I shall take it away from you and appoint a Church steward.

There was a thunder of *"Bayete"* so that every fish in the waters dried up. The King went on to tell the story of King Solomon and the two women each claiming to be the mother of a child. He then turned to the whole church, once founded by Stephen Mavimbela: "No, children of Mavimbela, I am not going to cut you in two. Come together in one place and be united and one as the late Mavimbela left you. I am going to give you a Superintendent [of funds].

The *Bayete*! roared as if even the fish in the Sutu and Mtilane [rivers] were going to rush to the fountains, full as the ocean (*zakhuza ulwandle*). We men rejoice at being healed by our King.

The King's own involvement in the formation of a Swazi National Church, at a time of increasing pressure from the outside world, aimed at the preservation of church unity. His generous and authoritative interventions in Zionist church conflicts in the 1950s were steps in that direction. His first Minister of Education, Dr. Gamede, in an interview in July 1969, emphasized the same point. "Secessionism", he told us, "the divisive trend in Protestantism, came from the West. The denominational differences expressed in the various Church uniforms were the result of Western influence." He had a suggestion. They should do away with all these different uniforms. Let the Bible be the one authority *and* let all Christians put on the same uniform. He also hoped to see the establishment of one Swazi Bible School for all the churches.

For some years in the 1950s it seemed as if this surge of religious nationalism would find its culmination and apex in a Swazi National Cathedral at Lobamba. Here again, there was close co-operation between royalty and Zion. The foundations of the Temple were laid in 1953. Great financial efforts were made, particularly by the various Zionist churches. The latest official statement of accounts which we have seen showed that no less than £2,735 had been collected for the purpose.[9] Walls were raised on the foundation, and the National Cathedral was expected to be finished by 1960. After that, from time to time sporadic efforts were made, but so far without results.

Another indication of the strength of the Zionist movement at this time was the lively debate about the building of Zionist schools and a Zionist "College". J. S. Mavimbela, the son of the Zion leader Stephen Mavimbela, and himself later to become a Senator, was the chief spokesman for this enterprise. It stirred the imagination of people for some time. The local paper was full of articles on the subject. Not all were as progressive as Mavimbela himself. Some good Zionists were sure to point out that neither Jesus nor the Apostles—nor Joseph or Mary, for that matter—were learned people. In those far-off days the ministry was never a vocation for which one prepared by study. It was all a matter of being filled by the Spirit.[10]

Good Friday Movement

On Good Friday the Churches worship together with the King and the Queen Mother; they sometimes also do so on Easter Day. An Easter service may include ten speakers, each dealing with a special Easter text. Easter Monday was generally reserved for a more technical Bible exegesis in the presence of the King himself, regarded as the final arbiter as to the soundness of the opinions expressed.

Towards the end of the 1950s a routine had been established. Months beforehand the committee of three drew up a programme. For the 1958 meeting the following problems of Bible exegesis were selected, and speakers chosen to explain the texts.

(1) *Dan 8: 14:* He said unto me: "Unto two thousand and three hundred days; then shall the sanctuary be cleansed". Explanation of the purity of the Holy Place in the Old Covenant.

(2) *Rev. 20:* the thousand years and the resurrection of the dead.

(3) *Math. 16: 18:* "On this rock I will build my Church"; compare 1 Cor. 3: 4, 10–11.

[9] *Izwi lama Swazi,* 14.4.1958, 26.4.1958.
[10] *Izwi lama Swazi,* 14.12.1957, 4.1, 11.1, 1.2, 8.3, 22.3, 12.4, 19.4, 12.7, 15.7.1958.

(4) *Gal. 3:4; Rom. 7:4–12:* The New Covenant and its basic laws, given by Jesus Christ to his Disciples.

(5) The prophecy and vision of Prince Madhevu Dhlamini.

As a rule, only trusted and well-known preachers could act as speakers. On this particular occasion a Jehovah's Witness, F. Matsebula, was asked to explain a problem dear to his flock: the Millenium. It was discovered, however, that while Matsebula was a fluent speaker, the radical view of earthly powers taken by his particular group might imply a critical attitude to Swazi authorities, and Matsebula was not asked again.

For the 1959 meeting two major themes had been selected: (1) What teaching should the Swazi follow in order to be saved? (2) Which commandment must be obeyed? On this occasion, the first subject was treated by a Seventh Day Adventist and the second by Prince Solomon Madhevu himself. Each had elaborate charts painted on calico, illustrating his message. Efforts had been made to invite the great Zulu preacher, Nic. Bhengu, who willingly had accepted, but because of overseas engagements had to send a substitute. He could not have chosen a better man, for it was none other than John Nxumalo, himself a Swazi, the son of a chief of the Queen Mother's clan, and, as one must expect from a pastor of Bhengu's church, an effective Bible student.

Also on this occasion Prince Madhevu managed to put across his basic concern: the wrongness of dogmas and denominations ("not Churchianity, but Christianity"). The Swazis must find out for themselves what Christ meant by his teaching and pursue this.

One can follow this line of thought through Swazi discussions for decades: in fact, as we have already indicated, from the 1930s. It was the ideology of Prince Solomon Madhevu Dhlamini, and therefore the common denominator for the activities of the Good Friday movement, in spite of the apparent differences between the various Zion groups. The cyclostyled agenda for the Good Friday Bible Debate in 1957 has this aim in view: "It is our purposive wish that the meeting should, if possible, arrive at the vividly right and perfect religious footprint which is first to be taken and followed by the Swazi as a Nation. See St. John 17:20–21." No Swazi could overlook the reference here to the religious watchword of the King himself: *"Funani unyawo luka Jesu,* Go ye and look for the footprint of Jesus". And here the King's word was corroborated by the well-known prayer in the Fourth Gospel.

The Prince was joined in this concern, as on so many other points, by his supporter in the Good Friday movement, Rev. P. M. Mkwanazi. For the 1958 meeting he suggested—with a reference to the prophecy of old King Somhlolo—that the churches throw away their distinctive names and build together "the one Church of the Father and of the Son and the Holy Spirit".[11]

Mkwanazi came from Barberton, Transvaal. No Good Friday conference could be held without new and fresh songs composed by *La Mangundwini,* the song-writer's pet name. The simple songs had a rhythm which made them immensely popular. He would arrive with a bunch of hand-written copies, distribute these to a choir, and Mkwanazi himself would start conducting community singing. Two examples will suffice:

> *Singama Krestu nje, Singama Krestu nje*
> *Enkosini ye Zulu uJesu*

We are simply Christians, nothing but Christians;
And Jesus is in his Kingdom above.
Let us not part, then; Let us not hate, then;
For that is not done in heaven.

Let us unite then, in the only name
of the Lord Jesus and of his Father.
Let us unite then, all of one herd;
and let us all break bread together.

Jesus, united with Father and Spirit!
They are united and love one another.
They do not part, they are One only.
Well, whom do we copy?

Wake then, believers and be united
With God and Jesus and the Spirit;
Let us copy those who are united
Being one with Jesus and the Father.

The following hymn has become very popular with the Zionists:

[11] *Izwi lama Swazi,* 16.11.1957.

My spirit says Yes, my spirit says Yes,
And Jesus to his disciples:
Let us go to Galilee.

My Spirit says Yes ...
Send thou me, my Lord;
Send thou me, my Lord.

My Spirit says Yes,
Let me live where thou art;
Let me live where thou art.

My Spirit says Yes,
Let us go to the next world;
Let us go to Galilee.

The Churches and Swazi cultural unity

Watching the long rows of happy, swinging and singing Zionists
in the Good Friday processions at the Lobamba Royal Kraal, one
could not but face up to some fundamental questions.

For fifty years and more the European missionaries had been
at work in Swaziland; yet, they were not to be seen here in the
jubilant crowds at Lobamba. One thought of some of their
achievements in the context of a small country in which individual
missionary contributions could stand out. English Methodists had
begun work in the South of Swaziland, bordering on Zululand,
by about 1880, after a dramatic but unsuccessful early attempt
in 1847. Those were the days—long before any effective contact
with the Europeans—when old King Somhlolo had a vision. He
saw foreigners arriving with an *umculu*—generally translated as a
"scroll" and by the missionaries interpreted as meaning the Holy
Book—and *indingiliza*, thought to be the equivalent of money. He
exhorted his people to honour the former and eschew the latter.

The Methodists were soon followed by a number of "Holiness"
and "Alliance" groups, with their particular message and methods. Southern Swaziland attracted missionaries of this particular
type and formed the image of what missions were. The
Nazarenes, from 1909, were of a similar type of radical Evangelical piety, although they were to make a special contribution
through medical service, under the leadership of Doctors David
Hynd and Samuel Hynd and their colleagues.

The little groups of Anglicans were part of the Diocese of Zululand, until the first Anglican Bishop of Swaziland was consecrated, in 1968. German Lutherans had established themselves at about the turn of the century. Two World Wars hampered their efforts. In 1914, the Roman Catholics arrived, and in Swaziland, too, they were to lay strong foundations, not least through an energetic and far-sighted educational programme.

But it was now late in the day. There was no longer any time nor interest for a neat and polished objective chronology of mission history. Surging through Swazi society was a constant, severe process of critical re-interpretation of the European presence, including that of the missionaries. This re-examination on the part of vocal representatives of Swazi culture was one of the dynamic factors in the rising Swazi nationalism at the time.

They looked at the missions. With the "older" ones, there had obviously been a case of "too little too late": Swaziland to them had become something of an outpost in a forlorn corner, not always remembered when it came to staffing and when the needs of Zululand and Natal seemed to represent more pressing priorities.

The Methodists, particularly, lost out to dissident African groups: The African Methodist Episcopal Church established itself; there were a few scattered groups of the Zulu Congregational Church and—later—the African Congregational Church. The most serious breakaway from the European-led Methodist Church was the Independent Methodist Church, formed in 1904. Its leader was Joel Msimang († 1935), son of Daniel Msimang, the very cornerstone of the first-generation Methodists in Swaziland. From his headquarters at Makosini, near Mahamba, Joel Msimang seemed for some time to dominate the scene in Southern Swaziland and Northern Zululand. With his characteristically Methodist background and educational ambition, he established his own school, up to Standard IV, which was high at the time. Powerful and attractive, he exercised a wide influence, independent, and yet, as a matter of course, representing something of the best in Methodist piety.[12]

[12] Interview with his son, the well-known journalist Selbie Msimang, Edendale, Pietermaritzburg, 14.1.1973.

And the radical Evangelicals with their numerous little centres in the South? Benjamin Simelane commented on their role. He had himself been an evangelist in an Alliance mission until 1946 but was now an independent farmer and a King's counsellor, a sane and solid man. "The faith is finished (*inkolo isipelile*) among the people," he told us in 1958. The first generation of missionaries whom he had known proclaimed that Jesus was to return to-morrow. "We had fear then, and the mission had great success." But the apocalyptic fervour subsided. One or two Watch-Tower preachers would still suggest various dates for the Return, but those dates came and went. After the apocalyptic expectations there was only emotionalism left, or a flickering memory of it. *That* side of religion Zionists could of course handle much more effectively, as one could notice when watching those happy Good Friday processions.

A new, articulate generation expressed criticism of missions in the period of rising Swazi nationalism. They had a litany of complaints against the missions. By fencing in their tracts of land, certain missions had committed a serious offence. And the mission schools? On the one hand, they had tended to alienate good Swazis from their traditional culture; on the other, missions had failed to push educational standards fast and far enough. Neither had they produced Swazi graduates to meet the needs of a new age. They had been concerned to teach Africans how to pray and to sing, but in a European way. Above all, Western missions, in communal Swazi society, were individualistic and divisive. The traditional Swazi family system was breaking down, because of their laws and their emphasis on monogamy.[13] The missions did not induce their people to respect Swazi culture. The faithful were advised not to participate in Swazi national ceremonies.

It was on this last point that the comparison between the missions and the Zionists was revealed most clearly and critically. If, as we have suggested, a spiritual vacuum developed in the

[13] The Zionists, on the other hand, while in principle favouring monogamy, at least as far as the preachers were concerned, took a more large and generous attitude to the problem when it might affect more prominent converts. Bishop Joshua Nyembe told me: "We are not concerned with the *inyama*-side (the flesh) of Chiefs and Kings, only with their religion, and *that* we care for".

1930s, this was filled by the Zionists, particularly through the imaginative decision of Bishop Stephen Nkonyane to attend, in his episcopal garb, the national *Incwala* festival and similar great occasions in the life of the nation. The debate over participation in the national festivals went on year after year. Thus the University Seminar on Swazi culture, at Luyengo in May 1969, insisted that all young people participate fully in "the recognized National Ceremonies", including *Umcwasho,* the puberty ceremony for princesses and other girls.

Only a very few Christian parents were prepared to contest this demand. A notorious criminal case, No. 1/72, June 30, 1972, at the High Court of Appeal concerned the refusal of one Harry M. Msibi, a Jehovah's Witness, to allow his daughters to participate in the *Umcwasho* ceremony. The case took on great proportions and seemed to engage the whole traditional system of government, in modern dress. His Majesty the King himself had proclaimed a comprehensive "explanation" regarding *Umcwasho* in a Royal Speech to teachers on November 8, 1969, and the Permanent Secretary for Education stated on December 1, 1969 that it was "extremely important that all teachers should know exactly the procedure with all matters connected with the *Umcwasho* custom" (Ministry for Education, Circular No. 124/69).

While admitting that *Umcwasho* was a Swazi custom, the defendant made an interesting point as he "wanted to know whether custom is the law in Swaziland". There the President of Appeal Court (Feb. 23, 1972) held that "the King is empowered to make orders. Therefore according to law the King made an *umcwasho* order", and Msibi was guilty of an offence. The appellant had thus broken the order of the King.

After an appeal, the President of the Higher Court of Appeal, on June 30, 1972, devoted himself to profound Bible study and prepared a conclusion, stating that "Christianity and Tradition are both of permanent importance". But when the Msibi girls did not "take part in the National activity on the ground that they are Christians", the President of the Higher Court of Appeal went on to say: "It must be remembered, however, that our Lord Jesus Christ encouraged the then Christians to follow their traditions but warned them in turn to worship God. (Matt. 22: 15; Mark. 12: 13).[14] This Court, too, wholeheartedly encourages every child to worship God while it warns [the child] not [to] follow an act of communism. According to the will of God, Kings shall be there to keep law and order, i.e., to advise their subjects and such subjects shall follow accordingly (Romans 13: 1–14)".

The Higher Appeal Court upheld the judgment, finding Msibi "guilty of criminal offence for contravening the *Ingwenyama's* order of *umcwasho* and thus fined him R[and] 120 or seven months' inprisonment".

We are dealing with Zionists in this study, and it can be safely taken for granted that no Swazi Zionist or Apostolic would query the decision of this Higher Appeal Court. The Jehovah's Witnesses, as in the Msibi case, seemed anyhow to be outlaws. We discussed the case with a leading 'Apostolic' preacher. Twenty years earlier he had himself had to overcome an initial impression of being a foreigner. All the mote he now emphasized the wisdom of the Court. The guilty person, he informed me, in Swazi interspersed with English, had in fact stated that Swazi custom was "no good to God". As if reprimanding the culprit, he turned around and asked an imaginary respondent: "What did you say?" The mere suggestion of a possible conflict between religion and order now seemed to him outrageous. He, like his numerous colleagues had conformed happily.

On the surface it seemed as if the concern of the leaders was the preservation of Swazi culture as such. This was the ideology, this was the message of those in high places. The articulate leaders of Swazi nationalism in the last few years of Protectorate regime varied this argument. At present it often appears in the newspaper articles and in Assembly debates. An example was the debate in 1972 over the proposed introduction of a second Casino in Swaziland. Senator Mekiseni Dhlamini knew that he represented a vast opinion when in that debate he said, "What

[14] As will be remembered, the two Bible verses quoted here by the highest legal authority in the land, read as follows: "Then went the Pharisees and took counsel how they might entangle him in his talk" (Matt. 22: 15). "And they sent unto him certain of the Pharisees and of the Herodians, to catch him in his words" (Mark. 12: 13). Cf Umcwasho Circular No 1/69, Lobamba National Office 29.10.69. The Harry Msibi case, in Court of Appeal, Case No 12/71.

I mean is that we should do away with other peoples' traditions and stick to our own".[15]

Yet, it was not so much Swazi culture, as the unity of Swazi culture, that was the real concern and it is on this point that missions seemed to be at fault while Zionists, possibly, might provide a solution. Not only had the missions failed to identify with Swazi national ceremonies, but also—and this was the real danger—by their own divisions they seemed to undermine the national unity. The Zionists on the other hand through their programmatic identification with kingship seemed to strengthen this unity—at least, up to a point. Beyond *that* point, some of the finest minds in the rising generation of Swazi politicians recognized that the lack of education on the part of the Zionist leaders and their followers was bound to jeopardize their contribution.[16]

[15] Swaziland Senate, Official Report (*Hansard*) 17.11.1972, p. 189.
[16] The relationship in modern Swazi society between a first generation of Zionists and a second generation of politicians and civil servants is a fascinating theme. We can no more than hint at it here. A fine example is that of the already mentioned prophet Stephen Mavimbela (p. 215). In his sermons he must, according to accepted Zion dogma, on numerous occasions have referred to the aspect of mysterium tremendum in Holy Baptism. As a prophet he would enter the pool in order to purify his people by baptism, but as he did so, he would first have to drive away any lurking reptiles, perhaps dangerous crocodiles, from the pool; only then baptism could begin. Cf. *Bantu Prophets* (1961), p. 205–206.

His son is now a Senator in modern Swaziland. In 1972, the Senator was faced with an intricate problem of whether or not to accept the introduction of a second Casino into Swaziland where they had already experienced something of the dubious blessings of a first Casino.

The Honourable Senator J. Mavimbela, according to Senate Hansard, Nov. 20, 1972 (p. 200) rose to speak in the Senate debate: "Mr. President, I would liken this Bill to a dam or pool of water. People do make a living out of this water. [It is] necessary to provide water for human consumption and for the fields. But there may be crocodiles or snakes or any other types of animals that might kill people. The only remedy, Mr. President, would only be to try and cure and sort of retain our Swazi way of doing things … In conclusion, Sir, I would like to ask the Honorable and Learned Attorney-General to ask the Government to find ways and means of getting rid of the crocodiles and other animals I have referred to above. Thank you, Sir."

7. Missions and Zion at Ceza

Perspective is everything. Zion and its local influence must be seen in perspective. To some extent this may be provided by comparison with the role of established Mission-related churches. For Zululand we need an interpretation of the total situation of the Church, a study that goes beyond mere Church statistics, Church administration, constitutions and the like, to a comprehensive understanding of the life of the church at the present time, the function of the local congregations and the aspirations and inspiration of the individual. We know in fact very little about these fundamental dimensions of the Church's life in South Africa at present.

To arrive at such an understanding and insight, a comprehensive programme of research needs to be undertaken. Local studies of Independent Churches could well be, at least to some extent, integrated into this more ambitious and far-reaching enterprise. Only then shall we be in a position to evaluate the significance of the total Christian witness, including the Zionist contribution and challenge.

This brief chapter has a much more limited scope but gives at least an indication of some of the problems involved. We present here a local church situation in Zululand with which we were closely associated for some time. I was myself a missionary at Ceza, Northern Zululand, in 1940–42 and was daily faced with the challenge of Zionist presence and practices. We shall be concerned with the interplay of Lutheran mission and Zionist influence at Ceza.

This chapter deals with the church communities at Ceza, situated mainly in two Zululand magisterial districts, Mahlabatini and Nongoma, and to a certain extent in two Natal (farm) districts,

Vryheid and Louwsberg. The population covered by the mission in the area and its outposts is computed to some 30–40 000. On the Zululand side of the border the population is divided into two chiefs' wards, that of Buthelezi and that of Ndebele, the central mission station being situated in Ndebele's ward.

Lutheran mission work began in 1903, and Pentecostal mission work in 1921. A Lutheran missionary was placed at Ceza in 1905–07 and from 1910 onwards. The outreach of the ordained missionary and the catechists soon extended as far as the coal mines near Vryheid. In 1920, the outposts in this new sector were detached from Ceza and formed a new congregation of their own. This accounts for the temporary downward trend about 1921 in the diagram on p. 247. At present, the congregation has more than three thousand members.

In 1915 the first ordained Zulu pastor was posted to Ceza, as an assistant to the missionary. In 1942, the period of ordained European missionaries was at an end, and a Zulu pastor was for the first time put in charge of the whole work with his headquarters next to the mission station.

Both the Ceza central station and the nine outposts lie far from the beaten track. The first roads into the district were built both by the mission and, in the interests of the gold mines near Johannesburg, by the Native Recruiting Corporation. A clinic was opened by the mission in 1910. In 1938, the first medical doctor was placed at Ceza and the hospital at present has five doctors, 36 trained nurses and a capacity of 270 beds, with an African nurses' school. There is now also an adjacent T. B. hospital with a doctor and some 160 patients. The first elementary school was opened at the central station in 1910 and such schools *cum* catechetical centres were established with various degrees of success at the outposts. The school system advanced rapidly after 1945, and now includes a well-established Secondary School (leading to Junior Certificate) at Ceza itself and Primary feeder schools in the district.

The diagram of expansion and regression in the life of the Lutheran group at Ceza is constructed from the figures of catechumens, adults baptisms and infant baptisms alone. It shows the rapid transition from an evangelistic group to a settled African congregation, and indicates dramatic changes. There is a

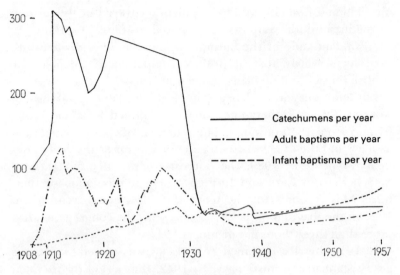

Expansion and regression at Ceza 1908–1957.

sudden initial climb and expansion in the first five years. This level is maintained in the following period of fifteen years. The catechumens were then between 250 and 300 annually. From 1929 the trend goes inexorably downwards. This development was closely connected with a breakaway movement under the leadership of a Zulu pastor.

Church and Society

The Ceza congregation was founded in one of the most agitated periods of the dramatic history of the Zulus. Only a few years earlier, in 1898, King Dinuzulu had returned from exile on St. Helena. He had been "on the island"—as the Zulus said—for nearly a decade, sentenced to imprisonment because of his war with another chief, Zibebu. On his return he was given to understand by the Natal Government that he was no longer Paramount Chief but simply a Government headman. In connexion with the Zibebu affair, too, the Zulus had to pay a large tract of land to their then allies, the Boers. North-East Zululand was cut up into White farms and became the 'New Republic'.

Zululand proper was drastically reduced. Ceza was situated

246

next to the New Republic. The precarious land problem of the Bantu was forced upon the population of Northern Zululand in a way which nobody could overlook. Zulus who had hitherto lived under the authority of their own chiefs and headmen suddenly found themselves living as landless squatters on European farms, having to adjust themselves to new and unfamiliar conditions. Some of the first Lutheran evangelists had been farm workers until they could stand the conditions no longer and moved over into the fast-shrinking and overpopulated Zululand reserve. The outposts of the Christian congregation were placed both on farmland and in Native Reserve, and hence the church workers had to establish their groups of adherents under very different circumstances, dependent upon either Boer farmer or Bantu chief.

On Dinuzulu's return to Zululand in 1898, and later, headmen and kraal-heads in the Ceza area and from other parts of Zululand often paid their homage to Dinuzulu at his kraal which was situated only some twenty miles north of Ceza. After a few years hopes of national freedom and greatness were definitely quenched in the Zulu Rebellion (the "Bambata Rebellion") of 1906; Dinuzulu himself was charged with high treason and deported to Transvaal, where he died in 1913.

The Swedish missionary at Ceza registered popular opinion: "There was a tremor of joy among the Christians in these parts when they heard the words from Dinuzulu's death-bed: 'Let my people turn to God'. A general conversion of the whole people was expected. Chief Shibelika [Ndebele] now allowed some of his sons to learn to read".[1]

These political developments are not without importance for the attitude of the Zulu population to the missionary approach at Ceza about 1905–1910. Much of the subsequent history of Ceza can be understood in terms of Zulu opposition to White land-grabbing. The first Swedish missionary met with hard resistance over the land question. Embittered men told the catechists in 1905 that the missionary had in mind to "steal their country".[2] The mission station which was established in 1910 eventual-

---

[1] J. Sandström, *Bland svarta kristna,* Stockholm *1935.*
[2] *Ibid.*

ly extended over no more than ten acres (for church, hospital, school and manse). The fate of the Zulu kingdom and the drastic reduction of the Zulu country cannot simply be relegated to some general background of Ceza Church history or of Zulu Church history as a whole—it influenced at that particular time, and much later, the reaction of the Zulu population both to the religion of the Whites and to the presence of the missionary and his Zulu co-workers.

This can be gauged by the rôle played by the dethroned and deceased king in the realm of ideas and dreams at Ceza. Eselina Zulu Simelane told me she was allowed by her father to visit the church only because it became known that the Christians in their holy house prayed for Dinuzulu and his return to Zululand. Andelina Nyandeni, leading *umsizikazi* at Ceza, in 1925 had a dream of heaven, in which she was shown Dinuzulu, the beloved king.[3] During the second world war it was still rumoured that Dinuzulu was alive and that he might one day return in power.

At Ceza, the relationship to the white man's political power was possibly more complicated than in most other parts of Zululand at the time. In the 1890s the local chief of the ruling Zulu house was deposed, and the Government appointed a hefty policeman at the magistrate's office in Nongoma as the new chief. This man, Shibelika Ndebele, knew only too well that he was not a chief of the blood but of the book, i.e., a Government-appointed official (*induna yasebukwini*, an official in the Government book). He had to move cautiously in order to manage the situation. (The tension between 'Zulu' loyalists and Ndebele adherents still occasionally flares up to-day into recurrent faction fights.) His political acumen was tested over the mission issue. What was to be his attitude to the missionaries and their new ideas?

When the chief's eldest daughter reported that she wanted to be baptized, he thrashed her until she became well-nigh demented. When two of his sons reported their intention to join the white man's religion, Ndebele went to the Native Commissioner at Mahlabatini to get his advice. As this was positive, the two young men received their father's permission to be baptized.

[3] *Umsizikazi*, Lutheran prayer-woman.

He was himself attracted to the new community. About 1903 a Swazi foreigner, Benjamin Dlamini, had fled from his own country and 'surrendered' (*ukuzinikela*) to Chief Ndebele. The two men became close friends, a friendship which was not weakened when Dlamini became evangelist at Sidakeni, next to the chief's main kraal. Shibelika had in fact very happy relationships with both Dlamini and Stefano Mavundla, the first leader of the local catechists. Dlamini called the chief "my father", and the chief's sons (of whom two became leading pastors) and Dlamini called each other "brothers". Stefano, who was not always a great diplomat, managed to nurse the contacts with chief Ndebele with great care. He wrote the most famous of all the Ndebele *Izibongo* (praise-songs to remember his great achievements in war and peace). Ndebele responded to these promptings. When he held lawcases in his hut, he placed Stefano at his right side. They left the hut together and the catechist went next to the chief. These courtesies were not lost upon the Zulu men at that time. "The chief protects Stefano like a shield", they said, and they were not surprised when Ndebele sent word that they must not hinder Stefano's work.

The teaching and personal example of missionaries and catechists exerted its influence, and Ndebele in 1928 felt he should no longer resist the faith, but aware of his position, he went to the Native Commissioner at Nongoma for advice. The commissioner supported Dlamini and the missionary. The chief, now seventy-five years old, was prepared to accept baptism—but on one condition. He may have been a Government-appointed official rather than a chief of the Zulu royal house, but he had been one of King Cetshwayo's warriors and he wore the head-ring (*isicoco*) which he had received from him. So when at the baptism he was asked: "Wilt thou be baptized to this faith?" Ndebele replied: "Yes—but I shall never remove Cetshwayo's head-ring." And *with* the head-ring he was baptized in the name of the Father and the Son and the Holy Ghost.[4]

[4] An interesting sidelight on missionary attitudes at that time is shed by a remark —under the heading: "the Power of the Word of God in the Soul of Men"—in one of the books written by the first Swedish missionary at Ceza. During a visit to one of the outstations he discovers Job Mtetwa, baptized as one of the first in the Ceza area. "There sits old Job. What power in the world except of God could have

Missionaries and African Local Leaders

A Zulu congregation of the type represented by the Lutheran group at Ceza is to a certain extent formed by the objectives and example set by the missionaries and their African co-workers. Our study will show, we think, that these objectives were constantly modified and re-interpreted through the fundamental religious needs of the particular African group. But in order to understand these modifications it is necessary first to know the evangelistic and ecclesiastical programme and example of the missionary and the understanding of this programme by the local African leaders.

There was a succession of five White missionaries at Ceza in the years 1905–42, all of them Swedes. In that latter year, an experienced and highly esteemed Zulu pastor, Thomas Luthuli, took charge, and the work has been under African leadership ever since. We shall here call the Swedish set of five missionaries: "I" through "V".

The first Swedish missionary at Ceza, I., who served there 1905–12, 1936–40 and again for brief intervals in 1941 and 1943, regarded himself as a faithful exponent of evangelistic Swedish 'church pietism'. In a number of popular books in Swedish, of an autobiographical character, he discusses the reactions of the Zulu to the preaching of the Gospel, defining the overall goal of missionary work only incidentally. Sometimes the threatening competition of the Independent Churches makes him face the ultimate issues of missionary outreach in South Africa. "Our aim is of course an African Christian National Church", he says, "with which eventually the Lutheran National Church must merge, with the particular gifts and blessings that have been bestowed upon her. But will we get the time to reach our first goal", he asks, "a strong, self-supporting and self-propagating Lutheran Zulu Church, before the development overtakes us and the Natives' own National Church builds its walls higher and higher, attracting the masses perchance by concessions with regard to polygamy, church discipline etc.?"[5]

prevailed upon him to remove the headring, the pride and glory of Zulu men ... And yet, the Word of God had overwhelmed him." Josef Sandström, *Från Sydafrika, rasmotsättningarnas land.*

[5] J. Sandström, *Tjugo års missionsarbete i Sydafrika*, 1926, 158.

In accordance with this general programme his main concern was to train a group of African co-workers. There was Stefano Mavundla from a German Lutheran mission. In the upheavals of the Boer war he had on his own initiative began evangelistic work in the Ceza area, which was in fact his home country. As the Swedes decided to concentrate on Ceza, the two Lutheran missions arrived at an agreement. Stefano was "handed over to our [Swedish] mission"—as the paternalistic expression ran in those early times.[6]

Marko M. was another evangelist. He also came from a German station which had been abandoned on account of the Boer war. Soon there was a personal feud between Stefano and Marko. As the latter took a second wife, he was dismissed from his Church service, an indication of the initial difficulties encountered.

In the period of 1905–12, while the missionary was absent from Ceza for long periods in order to look after another congregation further South, Stefano was virtually in charge of the mission work; the newly appointed assistant catechists, all of them recently baptized, were responsible to him. What was more, although only a catechist, he was entrusted with the administration of Holy Communion. He regarded himself as superior to his African colleagues, not least to the Rev. Andreas Mbata, who came to Ceza later than Stefano. Mbata, a real pastor of souls, was preferred to him for the theological school, and he soon returned as an ordained pastor. This was a blow from which Stefano never recovered. In 1941, when he was to retire and the present writer thanked him for his long service, Stefano declared, perhaps not without a certain amount of self-esteem: "I know I am No. 1 in the Book of Life above. I am 'Revival' (he used this English word) until I die." During the whole period he was in constant strife with Mbata and with the other catechists. He had been the first to accept the message of the White teacher and he was prepared to go through hardship and sacrifice in order to help to build the new religious community. But he was touchy and far from tenacious in the planning of his work.

His family connexions are important. His wife, a woman of

[6] J. Sandström, *Första Kärleken*, p. 7.

deep personal piety and great natural dignity, was endowed with a gift for visions and dreams which sometimes brought her close to the Zionist groups.

The discussion in the group of Swedish missionaries on evangelists' training sheds interesting light on the circumscribed world of this particular Lutheran mission at the time—in the first years of the century. Their African co-workers were too weak: "Repeated cases have happened when our evangelists have come up against better trained evangelists of other creeds and were left nonplussed without being able clearly to give account of the more important points in the teaching and doctrine of our Church". Doctrine and precision in doctrinal statements were to save Africa—this was the self-evident presupposition. They had to be all the more careful. Could they join with other Lutherans such as Norwegians and the Berliners? No, "for then one would not have guarantees for what they were going to learn". They go on to say: "Furthermore experience has shown that they would in many respects become alien to us and our work if we were forced to train them at foreign seminaries". By being trained at a "Swedish" seminary "they would grow into the doctrine and order of our Church". A dominating Swedish die-hard patriarch had in his theological studies picked up a German nineteenth century phrase which now was supposed to summarize all wisdom: "Union is the worst enemy of union".[7]

The ideal of the "African Christian National Church" does not seem to have played any obvious rôle in the programme of the first missionary. He was succeeded by "II", who for twelve formative years, 1914–24, assisted the growth of the young congregation. A strong, weighty personality, an excellent Zulu linguist, an indefatigable organizer and, above all, a solid teacher of the Gospel, he did more than any other to lay the foundations of the young Church. His main interest was directed to the development of local African leadership and of a certain

[7] Swedish Missionary Conference, July 20–26, 1901, in Minute Book, Swedish Missionary Conference. Church of Sweden Mission Archives, Uppsala.

The debate unfortunately high-lights the denominational and national narrowness of some of the missionary groups at this formative stage of the young Church's development.

decentralization of the church district; already in 1920 a strong outpost was established as a district of its own.

A serious crisis occurred in 1928 under his successor, III. The African leadership issue and the question of local responsibility were mixed with African nationalist aspirations. The break occurred over a local matter. A young well-trained Zulu pastor was placed at one of the Eastern outposts of the district. The confirmation candidates from all the outposts were as a rule finally examined by the missionary prior to confirmation; they therefore had to walk long distances once or twice a week in order to attend the confirmation class and the final scrutiny at the mission station. The young Zulu pastor felt that he should have the final say whether the candidates from his outpost could pass muster for confirmation. This resulted in a show-down with the Mission system of that time, and the Zulu pastor, Ph. Mkize, left joining a Lutheran Separatist group under P. Lamula. After a few years he was again to break with Lamula in order to form his own church, the African National Church, the creed and liturgy of which are identical with those of his Lutheran "Mother Church". The defection of Mkize resulted in a dramatic decline in the work of the three Eastern outposts of the Ceza Lutheran group (see diagram, p. 247).

The missionaries who followed after 1930 found the strength and outreach of the Ceza congregation tragically reduced by this crisis.

No. IV, 1930–36, was an American of Swedish descent. He had come to Zululand from Tanzania and appeared to prefer the Chagga to the Zulu, so the Zulu reacted by preferring others to him. He found the Zulu language difficult and was very much an uneasy alien in a strange situation, in lengthy reports lamenting the lack of spirituality around Ceza. In the years 1936–40, No. I, now an old man, returned to Ceza.

No. V, 1940–42, was really the strangest of the lot. He only spent two years at Ceza but in that short time managed to confuse things very thoroughly. He represented another generation of Africa missionaries who had taken an interest in social anthropology combined with a belief in the importance of liturgy. As he suggested new and richer forms of celebrating Easter, Absalom Butelezi, the solid old evangelist, felt called to protest.

Attempts at introducing new ritual proved that there was no stability—and in a world of change, stability obviously was the good Lutheran principle. "Now one missionary introduces one law", he complained, "and the next comes along to change it, and so on. So we do not know where we are."

But this was only the beginning. Much more surprising was the fact that this same Swedish missionary showed a positive interest in the Zionists at Ceza. There had existed an unwritten rule that these were not to be befriended. Now, to the amazement of good Church people, the missionary himself seemed to go out of his way to contact the prophets. And the Lutheran Church building at Ceza, hitherto a refuge "for Lutherans only", was thrown open to meetings where hundreds of Zionists in white garments and with wooden crosses were invited to friendly and lively dialogues with Lutherans on themes such as Baptism, the Holy Spirit, Salvation and Healing.

It is the Church's teaching on the family, not theoretical speculations on God, heaven or hell, which here leads to an existential spiritual struggle. Absalom Ndebele, the most impressive evangelist in these Northern parts of Zululand, himself a family man and a brother of the regional chief, expressed this struggle in lapidary words: *"Abafo wethu ba nabafazi abaningi. Kepha mina ngimkhethile uKristu",* (Our brothers have many women, but I have chosen Christ.)

Recent reports show a tendency towards polygamy which automatically leads to placing the men under Church discipline. Church attendance and other activities is largely a women's affair. It is often noted that Zionist congregations tend to consist mainly of women; it should not be overlooked that this applies also to most Mission-related Churches.

At present two Zulu pastors, eight catechists, some 30 churchwardens and nearly 140 prayer women (*abasizikazi*) carry most of the burden of the local Lutheran work. Together they constitute a splendid group of Christian workers.

The close contacts between the structures of the Church and of Zulu society showed in the predominance of local leaders—as pastors or catechists—from the Butelezi and Ndebele clans: they seemed more obviously acceptable as local leaders than men of various other clans. For more than thirty years now leadership in Church administration and evangelism has been exclusively African, thus fulfilling in this particular locality the avowed long-range programme of missions: an indigenous and self-governing Church. Yet, the established mission influence in worship and hymn-singing was adhered to with surprising loyalty—or, was it perhaps a less surprising conservatism? This was the case as much in this particular Lutheran community as in certain neighbouring Anglican or Wesleyan congregations. In fact, it is in itself a hitherto neglected research task to study and interpret the way in which otherwise live and active Mission-related congregations acknowledged and endured forms of worship originally shaped for very different times and climes. In the heavy European forms of expression they probably felt a sense of worthiness which was much too easily accepted as expressions of a Zulu sense of "style", but which on a deeper level was quite possibly just as much an emotional means of adjusting to a dominant alien culture.

Here, Zionist forms and rhythms of life and worship served as a response to a deeper urge of the heart.

The Lutheran mission hegemony at Ceza was seemingly threatened by the arrival on the scene in 1922 of Pentecostal missionaries from Scotland and the United States. John Guthrie, the Scot, represented the Full Gospel Church. He worked closely with American and Scandinavian Pentecostals, one of these F. H. Burke, who later was to lead the well-known All Africa Bible School at Witbank, Transvaal; another the Norwegian Kaare Hansen. They settled nearby, on the Ceza mountain. According to their claims, various miracles happened at Ceza as results of their ministry, more especially some spectacular cases of healing and a mighty downpour of rain: as a response to eager Pentecostal prayer "a heavy rain came immediately".

It is necessary to underline that Pentecostals—Black and White —were united in condemning Zionist activities. The above-mentioned Guthrie reported for the benefit of his constituency "back home" in New Jersey about the situation at Ceza. It reflects Pentecostal attitudes to Black Zion. "The phenomenal rise and continuance of the sect amongst us known as Zionists proves [the need for a well trained Native ministry]. The great pity is only that, having thrown off white supervision from amongst them, they have let hatred of white evangelists enter, with the result that Satan has not been long in seducing [them] from the truth and naturally to-day very much error is manifest in their doctrine and their lives." This danger, Guthrie felt, could "only be counteracted by a native ministry true on every side to the Pentecostal message, the full gospel according to God's revealed word".[8]

Even in this acute form, the gospel apparently had its problems, for the first local leader, Joseph K. "fell into sin", and had to be dismissed. Instead, there was one Mizraim Dlamini—"of a line of chiefs"; the name suggests that he might have been of Swazi origin. He became the real builder of a Pentecostal congregation at Ceza.

Above all was he anxious to secure tight control of his flock. Members were not allowed to marry men or women from other churches, Lutherans, Catholics, Zionists or whatever: the pure Pentecostal strain had to be preserved. It is a measure of Dlamini's strength as a local leader that his attempt could be adhered to for such a long time. In recent years, however, it has been discontinued. With rising education and wider contact the younger generation was determined to have a mind of its own. Even Dlamini's strong sanctions on beer drinking are nowadays not always easily controlled among the Pentecostal members.

Sometimes, too, the Pentecostals may have felt that high-ranking clans needed extra care and consideration. Khehla Zulu was a prominent member of their congregation, all the more important because he lived in the ward of Chief Ndebele whose rights to chieftainship were, as we have seen, questioned by the 'Zulu' party. The Pentecostal leader, M. Dlamini pleaded Khehla Zulu's case in the Pentecostal assembly in Durban. It was a special case, for Khehla Zulu according to Dlamini "had three wives and was a very good Christian". Dlamini wanted him to be accorded a leading position in the local church, and this apparently was supported by Dlamini's white colleague at the time. It was Job Chiliza of Durban who in the meeting turned the assembly against this large-heartedness of Ceza. He asked: "How can a man who has three wives to look after, speak the truth? He must speak

---

[8] *South African Evangel* (Newark, N.J.), Vol. 1, No. 1. 1931, pp. 10–11.

three words, three truths and thus not be able to speak the truth".

In recent years the related Full Gospel Church, also under white leadership, has used spectacular modern methods in their approach to isolated Ceza. The missionaries will arrive on the scene by light aircraft, a case of *propheta ex machina*; Gospel tents are pitched, and considerable interest is attracted, for a while.

Compared with these organized missionary efforts, Zionist invasion into Ceza was spontaneous, accidental, contingent on a great number of circumstances. Although the first Zion prophets appeared quite early, the Swedish missionary reports a sudden influx about 1932: he combines this with changes in farm policy in Natal. Those were the years of the Great Depression, and farmers were determined to get rid of "undesirable elements", among whom Zionist prophets were prominent. These found their refuge in the chiefs' wards in the Reserves, and Ceza was as good a refuge as any.

Some of the local Zion pastors were members of leading clans. Bishop Mdlalose [see p. 70] had a personal interest in developments at Ceza, for his wife in her old age lived there, a charming and humourous lady, full of wisdom. It is characteristic of Mdlalose's royalistic attitudes that he supported the first Zion representative—from about 1924—in the Ceza area, David Zulu, although the latter insisted that his allegiance was to Nkonyane, rather than to Mabilitsa. Pastor David Zulu belonged to a special line—that of "Egazini"—within the Royal house. This background made it all the more easy to define David Zulu as "the fountain of Zion in Ceza country".[9]

Somewhat later, Mdlalose's local representative was the Rev. Enoch Butelezi, thus a member of the second most important clan in the area. One cannot speak too highly of this gentleman. An ambitious, hard-working builder and brick-layer, he was a fine representative of the energetic, clean-living type of people whom Mdlalose's group had fostered. His son, Johannes Butelezi, was trained as a carpenter at the Evangelical Teacher Training College, Vryheid. Together, father and son managed to put up a

[9] Rev. Lyon Mthembu, Jan 15, 1974 to the author.

fine church building. It had an altar with altar cloth and candles —an influence on Zion from the Lutheran milieu, I would think. Altogether, this family and their group was an example of the social role of Zion. In Zululand of the twentieth century it represented the same Puritan lever as Methodism had done for eighteenth-century England and Pietism for nineteenth-century Sweden.

It seems necessary to emphasize this point. While it would seem that in certain other parts of the subcontinent "the Zionist and like movements appear at the bottom of the social heap, the educated from the established churches at the top" (A. Mafeje, "Religion, Class, and Ideology in South Africa", stencil. n.d.), this is really no longer so, at least not exclusively so, in Zululand, nor, as we have suggested, in Swaziland. The role of Zion in fostering the growth of a hard-working lower-middle class and middle-class community of artisans cannot be ignored at Ceza or at Manzini.

Another Butelezi, Isaac, was the headman in the Esikwebezi valley. He had first joined Paulo Nzuza's Church of the Spirit but was now a local leader in a "Church of the Spirit", under a Bishop Vilakazi.

It is impossible to follow here the fortuitous local ramifications of various Zion break-aways from these local Ceza leaders. All the more we stress that with widening opportunities for Bantu education, there was also at Ceza a recent tendency for the younger generation to abandon the Zion of their fathers and to join established churches with educational opportunities. At the same time, recent resettlement schemes all the time tend to bring in new Zion prophets.

We have, of course, not attempted to map out this invasion into the microcosm of Ceza, and must be content with the general statement that besides the two main Zion branches of Mdlalose–Mabilitsa and Nkonyane, a great number of unspecified Zion groups found their way into the district. It is more important to perceive the general influence of the Zion movement in an area largely dominated by Lutheran and Pentecostal (together with Anglican, Wesleyan, Roman Catholic) influence. I have come across a summing up of the situation at Ceza in 1940, in a yearly report by the then missionary—myself. It might serve as an example of the missionary's involvement in the total situation.

"Zionism is the Ceza problem above all others. Not only because the life and forms of faith also within our Lutheran congregation are threatened by an overwhelming influence from this direction. To possess the Spirit or not, to speak with tongues or not, to be able to pray quickly and with many words in a 'spiritual' manner or calmly and slowly and unspiritually in the Lutheran manner, to be baptized in a river or to be sprinkled on the head—these are theological problems of the first order in this district, and this raises doubt as to the efficacy of the Lutheran forms of worship (for this, of course, is what is expected here from a sacrament or a prayer, namely that it be efficacious)".[10]

Resistance and Alienation

There were at least two levels of resistance against the influence of the Mission at Ceza. There was one on which the first pioneers, European and Zulu, were engaged sixty years ago: the sullen and determined aversion to the White man's religion and the White man's laws, that foreign and fearful power which seemed to undermine the whole fabric of Zulu society. This reaction was sharpened because the first encounter coincided with the political development at the time when the whites removed Dinuzulu, the Zulu chief, from Zululand.

Some of the best-known of the first local church leaders, the young catechists of Ceza, were strangers to Ceza and formed something of a foreign legion. They had either been placed there by the missionaries or had sought refuge in the chief's ward, away from the Boer farms on the other side of the border. As foreigners they were not popular at that time. "Kaffir" (*ikafula*) was the epithet which the kraal-heads at Silanda used against the catechist Titus Mtshali. When he put up the first church building a rumour spread from kraal to kraal: "Mtshali is bringing the White man here." The initial resistance of the Zulu men was directed against the White man's political power, which

[10] Yearly Reports; Missionaries; 1940. Ceza: Church of Sweden Mission Archives, Uppsala.

threatened the two fundamental values of Zulu society: kingship and land.

But at first the women were even more determined in their resistance than the men. "Our mothers", the combined woman-power in polygynous households, withstood the new religious ideas cherished by young men and girls, their pressure being directed particularly against the young girls joining the new community which emerged in their midst. The technical term for this transition to the dangerous foreign realm of the church was not very flattering: *ukundinda* (to prostitute oneself) was the Zulu word used by "the mothers". When it was discovered that a young girl had managed to break through the social control of the kraal in order to visit a church service, "the mothers" had a word for it: "The prostitute has gone to her lovers." Sometimes the girls did not return; they found refuge at the mission station, having taken the definite step over to the new community. There was at Ceza, as in other parts of Zululand, a technical term for this flight of individuals from Zulu society over to the community around the mission station. It was called *ukweqa,* to jump. The mothers in the kraal were determined to see to it that there should not be too much *ukweqa.*

Today, sixty years later, the centres of resistance are to be found elsewhere than among the groups of old women and men. In fact, the new converts are nowadays mainly to be found among the widows and the old women. Neither do the old pagan men constitute a power of open resistance any longer. Mrs. A. N., the personable widow of an excommunicated evangelist, said about them: "All the men believe [i.e., in God] now—but they do not wish to be baptized. When we have a prayer meeting in a kraal, the men sit and listen humbly and thank us afterwards. They know the Lord's Prayer by heart and they all read it aloud. I can sit quiet myself and listen to them saying our Christian prayers in chorus. But they do not go any further than that." Polite benevolence—but not transition to the new community until in danger of death. The great majority of baptized adult men at Ceza after 1940 were received *in extremis.*

If we compare the proportion of men in the Ceza congregation in the first decade with later developments—keeping in mind the general socio-economic development in South Africa, with rapid emigration of able-bodied men from Zululand and other homelands to the economic centres at the mines—we find that in the period of 1904/05–1914 there were 600 baptized, 178 of these being men, whilst in the years 1931–40 there were 369 adult (above 14 years of age) baptisms, of whom 69 were men. The percentage of baptized adult men has thus decreased from 29 % to 19 %. In the first decade the congregation register gives (in the case of 60 men) reliable information on age at the time of baptism. Their average age was 25 years; only a very few were older than 40.

In the period of 1940–49 there was a total of 837 baptisms at Ceza, including men, women and children, the latter forming the great majority. Of these only 71 were men, of approximately 18 years of age and above. Of the 71, half were cases of emergency baptisms *in extremis* (28) or in very old age (8); the remaining 35 were apparently able-bodied men at the time of baptism, although it is now reported that some of them were baptized because of illness.

Interchange and Challenge

The first Ceza Christian, Marko M., who was baptized in 1901, served as an evangelist for some years, but took a second wife in 1907. After having been excommunicated he took up the two best-paying jobs then known at Ceza: carpentry and dispensing native medicines. The sons of at least four of the first leading evangelists at Ceza followed in Marko's footsteps, taking more than one wife and dabbling in *inyanga* medicines. This was often referred to in church council sessions, but no effective remedy was found. When Mrs. A. N., herself a daughter of a Zulu *inyanga* and a determined Christian worker, criticized the evangelists for not looking after the education of their own sons and for allowing them to become herbalists, one catechist made a pithy Zulu remark on her courageous criticism:

> The pastor begat a herbalist
> The herbalist begat a pastor.
> (*umfundisi uzale inyanga*;
> *inyanga izale umfundisi*)

The *inyanga* sometimes extended his influence fairly deeply into the Christian congregation. Catechist B. D. was about to die. The mission nurse visited the kraal and wished to bring him to the hospital for better care. His wife, a member of the Lutheran *abasizikazi* (prayer women) group, hesitated, for the *inyanga* was busy with his cure. "Why don't you let us help him?", the nurse asked the wife. She was quiet for a while and then replied: "Because both God and Satan are so strong, we thought it might be better if they could cooperate."[11]

Some of the men who after baptism have taken more than one wife were very keen churchgoers. At Ekukhanyeni, Meshak B., with four wives, acted as a kind of unofficial churchwarden. He was excommunicated, as the term goes, and could not be readmitted to full membership. Therefore he was not allowed to give the annual church fee, but made this up tenfold by generous church contributions. He looked after everything in the church building, and the evangelist called him 'his right hand man'. But such men are exceptions. The polygamous men form a dead-weight in the Ceza church. In not a few cases these men have been turned into enemies of the congregation by the disciplinary application of the church laws on marriage. Premarital sexual relationships among the young, leading to a high illegitimacy rate, should be mentioned in this connexion. The increased social mobility from Ceza to Durban and Johannesburg has made the disciplinary arm of the Church fairly ineffective, a fact brought out rather vividly in the minutes of the Ceza Church Council. The secretary, Pastor Philemon Ndebele, was one of the most gifted in the group of local leaders and he knew some English. He does not fail to show this in his minutes, for the numerous cases of a breach of the sixth commandment (in the Lutheran catechism) is simply abbreviated to the person's name and "C.D. 6." Thus: "X.Y., C.D. 6.," meaning X.Y. has transgressed Rule No. 6. in the Church Discipline. If the offender, after being under church discipline for a year or two and having been forgiven, repeats the same sin, the note in Philemon Ndebele's paragraph is a brief and factual "X.Y., 2.C.D. 6."

[11] Anna Skarin, in *Svenska Kyrkans Missionstidning*, 1958, 215.

Some Zionists act as a modern witch-finding movement and are as such regarded as being of great value to society. Recent visits to Lutheran and Zionist church services in the outlying parts of the Ceza district have convinced me that the Zionists also score heavily because of the form of their worship. Their catchy songs and rhythm are more attractive than the slow-moving and difficult tunes of European hymns.

There is a constant interchange, a give-and-take between the churches. There are occasions when, if at all possible, all must come together in the village, from the various congregations. Weddings and, more especially, burials are such opportunities. But what Mia Brandel-Syrier has noticed for the churches on the Rand is also true of the rural congregations at Ceza. There is a general sisterhood of the Christian women which is stronger than all the divisive paragraphs of Western doctrine. At Sizana, Mrs. Sibisi's little grandson, aged 7, was old enough to start going to school. It was a great event in his life, but almost as memorable for Mrs. Sibisi. Thus she invited all the Christian women far and wide to a tea-party to celebrate: Lutheran *abasizikazi* in black and white, Wesleyan *manyano* in red, black and white, Zulu Congregational ladies with their fur hats and the Zionist women in white and blue and green and yellow. There was tea and milk and then Mrs. Sibisi had baked various kinds of wheat bread, the one more delicious than the other. They sang together, and on occasions like these it is taken for granted that the lively hymns of the American Board and of the Wesleyan Church will be sung by all.

Much more important are the cases of men and wo-men—particularly women—who balance on the borderline be-tween the Mission Church and Zion. We do not even mention here the numereus cases of those who officially insist that they are altogether faithful to the Mission Church of their fathers but who in a case of their own illness or in that of members of the family will secretly resort to the Zionist prophet's pravers and purifica-tion rites.

We think rather of those who officially are Lutherans or Angli-cans or Wesleyans—as the case may be—but whose temperament makes them search for a kind of worship where Zion seems to afford a possible model.

The best example I know at Ceza was Kaolina Magwaza–Mavundla. She was a foreigner at Ceza, being born near Melmoth. Even as a young girl she saw visions and it was such an event which made her understand that she must become a Christian. She saw the sun and the moon fall down from their places on the firmament—and she was frightened.

She married Elias Mavundla and came with him to Ceza. Elias, like his first cousin Stephen Mavundla, the first Lutheran evangelist, had "fled" from the Boer farms in Natal to find a refuge and a future at Ceza. Kaolina thus shared the first years of building up of the Lutheran community.

But she did not feel altogether at home with the catechism and the heavy Lutheran hymns. Being sickly and of a nervous disposition, she felt in the 1920s that she had become "filled with Holy Spirit". She was led from time to time to put on white garments instead of the Lutheran black. The Word ordered her to go to the pastor and Mrs. Madide to inform them that the Lord had placed her on the Throne of Glory, distinct from the ordinary 'prayer-women' in the congregation. She would sometimes exclaim "Hallelujah" during a hymn or a sermon, and the new Swedish missionary—No. III in our list (p. 254)—took her to task over such unseemly extravagance.

It was the malaria epidemic around 1932 that brought things to a head. "Death was rampant" (*kukhulu ukufa*), and she was one of the elect to take up the Sword of the Spirit against the threat of destruction. Now she was led to put on red garments, with a yellow band round her neck. She had visions: they would come in a state of giddiness or in a dream, and she felt that the Spirit filled her whole body. In her prayers she would see the Angel flying in white garments and would excitedly tell her listeners of the marvellous things which she saw. She gathered around her a group of women followers also in red, smearing white clay on their faces. "As we were praying, I saw a jersey in red—it was thus not in a dream. I was to pray with this jersey on, and to wrap my patients in material of this colour." She managed to keep this group of faithful women followers: "I am their Superintendent." She was obliged to take even stronger measures against the hysterical illnesses which she had to treat. She would use gall from cattle, mixed with water, or she might use blood: "I purify with blood." Sometimes she would feel that placing her patient in the water under a waterfall would have the full purifying effect.

All this seemed to be in full accordance with Zionist healing practices. But Kaolina insisted: "I am not a Zionist. I am a Lutheran with Spirit"—a rare combination, to be sure. Her sympathies for Zion were not strengthened when her daughter was killed because of their drastic "healing" methods. The young girl had consulted a prophet, who forced ashes down her throat, and she was suffocated.

Her husband was bewildered by all this spiritual activity and preferred to withdraw from all churches. When he was dying in 1957, he was brought to the Mission hospital. Therefore, after his death Kaolina told the Lutheran pastors: "You bury him, for he died in your care." The Zulu pastor in charge decided that Elias had not in fact been a member of his congregation, so the request was refused. Kaolina went on: "So I buried him, with prayers and hymns".

It is difficult to know how far Kaolina represented a more general tendency, even at Ceza. However, what is obvious is that she had a spiritual urge and concern which was not taken care of in her own Church. There was a serious spiritual authority and resolve about her which had to find an outlet of its own. That she refused to follow the ways of the majority and instead managed to create forms of her own is an important indication of the resources of spirituality in the huts and hearts of Zululand.

And there is another factor of very great importance: the promptings of Zulu *dream* life. Asked why he left the Lutherans or Anglicans for the new group, a Zionist will often reply: "I was shown this in a dream"—and details of the dream will follow. The pathetic importance of this dream activity is only caught when comparing the manifest dream contents reported by Zionists today with accounts of the manifest dream contents at Ceza more than a generation ago. At that time certain Zulus, who joined the Lutheran Church, apparently did this because they had been told by God in a dream to do so. It is obviously impossible to show now the approximate percentage of conversions prompted by dreams. But we have been impressed by the number of cases with which we came into contact. And, interestingly enough, the colour-scheme in these dreams is always the same. As a girl, Eselina Zulu Simelane, now a Lutheran *umsizikazi*, had heard catechist Stefano Mavundla threaten his hearer : "You are all going to burn in hell."—"Then I dreamed about white clothes and asked to be received in the baptismal class." Simon Xaba told me he had seen in his dream a sudden white light. It took form and was Jesus standing on short green grass, and exhorting him to be converted. Under the heading "A Rescued Soul", the first missionary at Ceza writes about one Johannes Zwana who three days prior to his death on September 20, 1908, had a vision: "I have seen Jesus' home, it is beautiful, green as fresh grass. There are many believers there, all in white clothes."[12] To the first generation there was one obvious interpretation of these symbols: "green" stood for the green pastures of heaven, and "white" for baptismal garments and a holy life (*ubumhlope*). What happened? The Lutherans put their men and women in black, the colour of the uniforms of pastor, catechist and prayer woman. The Zionists appropriated to themselves the white and green colours and put on white garments with green sashes and cords. The luminary visions in Zulu dream life— which seemed to resolve the hidden moral problems of the heart and soul—found a new, generally accepted point of reference: the Zionist prophet group attired in white.

And whether Lutherans or Zionists, one can be sure that it is at the dream level of life that these people experience their deepest conflicts and somehow try to come to terms with them.

Grace M's life story is, we think, characteristic of the situation. She was the daughter-in-law of one of the first Lutheran leaders. She is a charming woman, petite, with rapidly moving eyes and a rapid flow of speech. Her husband, instead of following in the footsteps of his catechist father, practised as an *inyanga,* and Grace felt this as a shame, yet could not protest. "My husband has deceived me before God. My spirit is tired. It is as if I were ill, yet I am not ill. All this weakness has come over me because my relationship to my Church is bad." She had had nine children and was now expecting the tenth. Her mother had died when she was an infant. Her father was a member of the Salvation Army. As a young girl she had joined an "Ethiopian" off-shoot from the Lu-

---

[12] J. Sandström, *Första kärleken,* p. 34.

theran church. She used to be a promising member of the *ama-joina* (youth group) of that Church, and in her dream she still saw herself preaching and she heard a voice—characteristically referring to light: "Do not put your candle under a bushel". "But it is only a dream." This dream had been a help against a hysterical illness (*amantindane*) which used to plague her. The symptoms of this illness were that in her dream she saw beasts trying to catch her. Native medicine had removed those dreams.

Now she sees a recurrent dream. "I am far away, in a place with soft green grass. There is a house with five doors. I try to enter the first, and then the second, and so on, but I am always told to proceed to the next door. At the fifth door somebody shows me a crowd of people inside. Their faces are all alike. I hear a wonderful song. The One at the Door points to my mother. She died when I was small, I don't remember her, but people have described her to me, her eyes and her face, and there was no mistake. I recognize her just as she was. The One at the Door says: 'There is your mother.' Mother stretches out her hand. I reach out mine to grasp hers—but then, the One at the Door tells me, *Pindela emva,* go back."

This dream, she felt, was concerned with her Christian faith. The doors may have represented her earlier multiple church affiliations. The association of her mother's image with the Divine presence suggests what Grace was seeking in her religion, yet she felt that her personal situation constantly deprived her of finding the refuge that she sought.

In the same way, father-figure and mother-image appear in this dream-world at Ceza, among people striving for personal identity and wholeness.

Burial and Remembrance Rites

The Christian preachers at Ceza claimed that their God gave new life. However this may be, what was obvious and beyond doubt was that the white religion preached a new death. The first leading evangelists, particularly Stephen Mavundla and Titus Mtshali, preached the terrors of hell-fire as the great motive for conversion—"you must believe if you are not to burn" (*ukusha*) —and a Christian burial as the great reward for a virtuous

267

Christian life. The death and burial of the Christians possessed a very strong power of attraction. A large number of first-generation Christians, when interviewed in 1941 and 1958 on the reasons for the conversion of the first Ceza Christians, mentioned Christian burial as the primary reason. "Christians were not afraid to touch the corpse; they did not cry at the burial but sang hymns of victory and about heaven. This was something beautiful and it attracted people to the Christian community."

The great concourse of people at burials of leading members of the Church tended to become a social occasion of great importance. Fifteen years after Chief Ndebele's burial, people told the minister who officiated on that occasion that that particular burial service had done more to draw people to the Church than most other activities. A local headman, Khehla Zulu, distantly belonging to the royal clan and a member of the Pentecostal group at Ceza, told me that pastors of many different churches visited him and prayed for him. "There will be lots of pastors in my kraal on the day of my burial", he mused, and he was unmistakably pleased at this bright prospect. In her study of Swazi culture, Dr. Hilda Kuper interpreted death in aristocratic Swaziland as "an index of rank".[13] This pattern is not absent from the Christian groups in adjacent Zululand.

One category was especially attracted by the Christian burial. Women who had not borne sons had a special reason for joining the Church. Without a son, a woman had nobody to bury her; but if she joined the Church, the Christian group would see to it that she was properly buried. The remarkable and paradoxical fact that women would be given the same honour as ordinary men at burial was highly attractive to the women. Two *abasizikazi* were more specific. Their mothers, who had no sons, had joined the Church because, they said, the Christians would "wash with a goat or a beast". In traditional Zulu religion a goat is killed one day after burial in order to wash away any ritual impurity from the tools used in connexion with the burial, and from the people who had touched the corpse. My informants would not admit that they shared this traditional belief, yet they used the traditional Zulu terms, albeit in a somewhat altered sense: the killing

[13] H. Kuper, *An African Aristocracy*, 1947, 177.

268

and the ceremonial eating of the goat or beast had a general cleansing effect on those who took part, they claimed.

The sense of solidarity expressed by the Christians in their coming together to the burial has in itself been a strong evangelistic factor.

In traditional Zulu religion, the *ukubuyisa idlozi*-ceremony (bring back the shade of a deceased person) is of great importance for the clan. By this ceremony a deceased kraal-head is finally incorporated into the group of ancestors. The rites are performed two to four years after his death. An ox is killed as a sacrifice on behalf of the deceased, special care being taken over the gall bladder of the sacrificial beast, as gall is particularly delectable to the spirits. Gall is scattered over the feet of the sons of the deceased. The chief's son is given the gallbladder of the spirit-beast; this has to be worn on the wrist. The smell of gall will attract the spirits, who will then surround his bed in order to guard him against all lurking dangers of the night. The *ukubuyisa*-ceremony guarantees the help of the deceased not only for the chief's son but for the whole lineage.

To the first Ceza missionary anything which had to do with this rite was as a matter of course unacceptable in the Christian Church. The first catechists, on his instruction, argued against any adaptation of the rite, "for the soul is already in heaven, and the Gospel is against any such ceremony of remembrance" (thus according to my Ceza informants in 1941 and 1958, who obviously may not have been able to render correctly the actual words used by catechists about 1910). The quoted reference to the abode of the soul in heaven does, however, reflect the attitude taken by the first church leaders at Ceza.

Soon, however, there was a change. About twenty to thirty years after the first beginnings of the Church at Ceza the *ukubuyisa*-rite was already definitely re-adapted as a Christian *ukubusisa*-ceremony (*ukubuyisa* means 'to bring back' [the shades]; *ukubusisa:* to bless). One of my informants—a catechist's widow— told me in 1958 that when the change took place they felt they had the blessing of one of the most influential lady missionaries, a nurse and midwife. "It is only remembrance of the burial", she is reputed to have told her Zulu friends, as there should be remembrance ceremonies of the days of baptism and of con-

firmation. It is impossible to ascertain how far the religious influence of independent churches, Ethiopians and Zionists, has
contributed to the development on this point. The fundamental
factor is certainly to be found elsewhere; the void left in the
minds and hearts of the people by the repression of the *buyisa*-
rite simply *had* to be filled by some content which could be
described as "Christian". The need created an adapted and
Christianized ceremony.

We relate here in some detail a typical example of the *isibusiso*-
ceremony. Eselina's own clan was Zulu. She was a cousin of
Mlokotwa Zulu who, because of blood relationship, could have
been the chief of the area. Eselina's husband, Simelane, died in
1956. In 1958, she set about to perform the *isibusiso*. She had to
take the initiative herself and arrange everything, having "no
brother of the same mother". The preliminaries started as she
left for the coast in order to visit her husband's grave in Durban.
Her eldest son, who worked in Durban as the father had done,
followed her, and they prayed together at the graveside. The
isibusiso, however, could not be performed in the city. It had to
be done at home, at Ceza, and in winter after the ploughing
season. The whole ceremony took two days in July. On the first
day a brother of her husband, and thus of the Simelane clan,
went into the cattle kraal and chose a beast to be slaughtered.
At about 4 p.m. this ox was killed by Eselina's own sons. As the
men were engaged with the slaughter and skinning, Eselina took
three women of her husband's clan and went with them to the
river. Eselina wore the black frock which she had put on as a sign
of mourning on the day of the burial two years earlier, and
which she had since worn constantly; one of the Simelane
women carried her new dress. At the river the Simelane women
helped her to take off the black frock; they tore it to shreds and
buried these in the mud near the river. Then the Simelane
women cut Eselina's hair—"the hair I had when my man was
still alive"—and buried it in the mud. "We do all these things
which were performed in olden times, for Jesus did not come to
destroy but to fulfil", Eselina added. Now she was prepared to
enter the water, and the Simelane women helped her to wash her
body and afterwards to put on the new dress. The little group
of women then returned to the Simelane kraal and prayed there.

On their return after dark they found that the meat had been prepared and sat down to eat "*inyama yokuhlambulula*" (the cleansing meat) of the beast from the Simelane kraal. They drank beer and *amahewu* (light beer) with it. Next day, Eselina passed the Ivungu river and the Lutheran mission station—about a mile— and went to see her cousin, Mlokotwa Zulu, to inform him of the business. He went into the cattle kraal, picked out a suitable beast and gave it to her. She drove this beast back to the Simelane kraal, where it was slaughtered. This was an important moment. "When Mlokotwa Zulu's beast was slaughtered and we ate the meat, I could at last eat sour milk [traditionally, sour milk (*amasi*) had ritual significance among the Zulus] and enter the cattle kraal again, which I had not been allowed to do during the whole period of mourning. In this way we purify with blood" (*hlambulula ngegazi*). The purification rite included a detail of some interest. Gall and chyme (*umswani*) from the beast were poured into water and Eselina and the others—who two years earlier had handled the corpse—washed their hands.[14] In the meantime the Lutheran pastor, together with an evangelist and some fourteen prayer women in their black and white uniforms, had come together. There was a simple service including Bible reading, prayers and some singing.

There exist, of course, modifications of these ceremonies. Lina Khumalo Dlamini, widow of catechist Benjamin Dlamini, gave her version. She insisted on the importance of the *isibusiso,* and referred to one of the widows in the congregation who had performed the rites with meticulous care. "She had shown her deceased husband great respect (*hlonipa kakhulu*) and we all look up to her." Lina was somewhat more specific than Eselina Zulu about the material of the dresses to be worn. When the black dress had been torn to shreds and buried at the river, the new dress was to serve for a year and should then be given away and an ordinary dress put on instead. The 'German' dress must not be torn to pieces, but given to some old woman beyond child-bearing age. "We must not give it to a younger woman who can bear children for then she would be regarded as stained."

---

[14] *umswani*, chyme; stomach contents of a beast, consisting of chewed grass and herbs, of considerable ceremonial significance at times of marriage, death, etc. Doke-Vilakazi, *Zulu–English Dictionary*, 772.

Lina Dlamini told me that at the first day's ceremony near the river she had not been assisted by women belonging to the clan of her deceased husband, as the husband's Dlamini family were in fact strangers (from Swaziland) in the Ceza area. This service was performed by the widow of the late Chief Ndebele, a Lutheran *umsizikazi,* because the late Chief and her husband, the late cate-chist, had been close friends. After the dress-changing ceremony at the river, there followed, as a matter of course, the same kind of feast which Eselina had prepared. Lina explained this in a char-acteristic Zulu phrase. *"Kuya khunyulwa ngenkomo na ngotshwala nangamahewu."* "The mourning dress is laid off by the help of [the slaughtering of] a beast and of beer and of light beer." She also referred to these ceremonies with the Zulu verb *ukugeza,* to wash. It is the *"isimnyama"* (blackness) of the dead body that must be washed away, and this refers to both the people and the tools which they used in connexion with the burial.

Lina and Eselina can safely be taken as typical of the great majority of an older generation of loyal church women at Ceza, and throughout Zululand; in these parts the local congregations consist mainly of women, since the men are away in the cities and in mines. There are exceptions. A. N. was one. He had been the trusted station evangelist at Ceza from 1917 until 1922 when he took a concubine and was excommunicated. He earned his living as a builder in the district but was never allowed to return to full membership of the Church. He forbade his family to perform the *isibusiso*-ceremony after his death, and his resolute first wife shared his conviction in this respect.

There are, particularly among the Zionist groups at Ceza, in-teresting re-interpretations which tend towards a more and more pronounced Zulu adaptation, breaking through precisely on this point which was, and is, the great concern of traditional Bantu religion. Zionist groups recognize the important con-nexion between the *isibusiso*-ceremony and the physical well-being of the surviving family. If there is sickness in the kraal, the Zionists 'prophesy' (=diagnose) that it has struck because an *isibusiso,* or the right and proper *isibusiso,* had *not* been performed on behalf of the deceased, an argument which appears totally convincing and logical at Ceza. They have a speciality which ap-pears to be attractive. They do not wear black, but must have a white dress with sashes of varying colours. In May 1958, I paid a visit to Kaolina Mavundla. Her husband had died the previous year. She wore the right kind of mourning dress, shown her by the Spirit: navy blue with yellow bands, the yellow colour being particularly effective against malaria. She was busy assisting at *isibusiso* ceremonies in the different kraals near the Ceza mission station. "I use water and gall and chyme and I purify all, both dead and living in the home, so that the shadow of death (*isithunzi sokufa*) will cease. I wash the feet with water mixed with gall, and therewith the whole body, as written in John 13."

Recent modifications are, we think, mainly terminological. Traditional *Ukubuyisa* is now referred to as *umsebenzi* (work) by the non-Christians; the Christianized rite is, on the other hand, simply called *umkhuleko* (prayer), and "most of the Christians, more especially the Zionists, believe that with their pastor they come to remove the darkness of death and to bless everything" (a letter, 1973, from a Zulu pastor at Ceza). This change in wording is believed to accommodate the tender feelings of the pastor, for he must be there to read the word of God, to pray and to bless. Large crowds congregate in happy unison, Lutherans and Pentecostals, Anglicans, Catholics and Zionists.

Certain combinations of old and new may be carried on without the pastor being in a position to do very much about it. A recent "prayer" in remembrance of a man of the "ruling house" gave examples of this. The deceased was described by the pastor in a somewhat generalizing term: he had "belonged to the Christian circle". The pastor and his flock came to do their part. Walking out of the gate of the kraal, they met with a group of men carrying some sticks which the pastor in this case was observant enough to notice. It was explained to him that the sticks were to be "thrown" in the veld (*kuyojikijelwa*), thus adopting traditional ritual. The experienced Lutheran pastor adds this reflection to his report: "It appears as if, where a member of the kraal died as a Christian in the home of non-believers, both procedures are followed, and it is difficult for anyone to give a ruling here".[14a]

[14a] Cf. H. Häselbarth, *Die Auferstehung der Toten in Afrika* etc., Gütersloh 1972 and F. Kollbrunner, "Auf dem Weg zu einer christlichen Ahnenverehrung?', in *Neue Zeitschr. f. Missionswissenschaft*, 1975, p. 19.

The point about these adapted burial and *isibusiso*-rites is the constant mutual interplay of give-and-take between Christian ritual and traditional re-interpretation.

On the Border-line between Past and Present

We are aware of the fact that, throughout Southern Africa, Zion has lifted great numbers of people from their traditional background and given them a new feeling of health and hope. Yet, there are numerous Zionists at Ceza and elsewhere who are no longer sure that Zion is the solution for them. They feel pulled between Zion and the Past, and they may yet decide that security and "health"—for these matters are what they are looking for—do after all belong with the shades of the Past. Instead of generalities we shall quote one particularly revealing case from Sidakeni, Ceza. If nothing else, Samson Mbata's story introduces a dash of realism into a world of beautiful theories connected with this field.

Samson is 29. His father is an *isangoma* with two wives. The elder of these, Samson's mother, is now demented and according to Samson she is "hated" by her *isangoma* husband. As a little child Samson was brought by his mother to the Lutheran Church and baptized there. As he grew up, he fell ill and joined Ndlovu's Zionist group. This did not prevent him from also consulting the Lutheran hospital on numerous occasions and he had an operation for some abdominal disease. The hospitals could not help him, but more seriously, Zion failed to give him the help he had hoped for. They put a white dress and blue sash on him. They gave him *isiwasho* (usually a concoction of water, ashes and blue soap) to drink. They prayed for this fluid and Samson took large draughts of it. It had an enema effect—yet "the heart was not satisfied; I did not feel well". Another complaint he had against them was that "they never sacrificed anything". It was well known at Ceza that Zionists would sacrifice a goat or a head of cattle in order to remove possible ill omens caused by the "shades". In this particular case, Samson thus felt that they had been negligent in this important respect.

This negative opinion may however have been caused by the new urge that he felt within himself. Basically, he was unhappy because of his alienation from his *isangoma* father. He deeply wished to earn the father's respect and love.

I found him as a patient in Dr. Barker's Nqutu hospital and had repeated interviews with him there. He felt torn in his heart, he said, between two spirits that were trying to "come up and come out" in him: "the Spirit of Zion" and the *isangoma* spirit which was about to *thwasa* (become possessed).

"I don't know where to turn. I am just a thing (*Ngi yinto-nje*)." But he was becoming sure that he would "never be well in Zion", nor at the Nqutu hospital. The deepest cause of this was the dissatisfaction of his father with these foreign ways of attempted healing. "Father was always against my Zion worship." "I now believe that the *isangoma thwasa* will heal me." The only snag was that an old *isangoma* whom he had consulted claimed two goats for sacrifice on his behalf, and he did not have that bounty. "*Ngihlupeke kabi*"—"I am very unhappy."

That *ukuthwasa* was now in fact the way for him was proved by a recurring dream. He had seen the same dream three times at home at Ceza, and now once in the Nqutu hospital. In the dream a pitch-black *mamba* snake approached. He got so afraid that every time he had to rush out of his hut to vomit in the gate of the cattle kraal. But now, the fourth time, in the dream in his hospital bed, the snake finally revealed its identity to him. It spoke to him: "I am not a snake. I am a man. I am the shades of the forefathers who died in a war [Which war? we interrupted. No, he had not been told]. I am he—Do not be afraid. I am a man. When you were ill all those years, I was there close to you." —"He wants to help me. I now only need those two goats. He will heal and purify me with herbs related to this trouble of mine. To *thwasa* as *isangoma* will heal me. And Father will be happy. He wants me to be as he."

But there are further modifications leading right back to the old spirits again, making the full round of the cycle of ideas. "Rt. Rev. Elliot Butelezi", of the Sabbath Zion congregation at the Ekukhanyeni (=in the Light) outpost can be cited here. He started as a Lutheran and had four years in the Ceza mission school. With this academic background he soared to leadership among the Sabbath Zionists. He was haunted by the spirits of the deceased, he told me. "These spirits (*abaphansi*=those below)

275

appear as angels, they come in the night, and place themselves on the chest and take a grip around the neck. I am not sure whose ancestral spirit this angel is. I try to see it, but as a rule he hides away a little. To be on the safe side I therefore prepare sacrifice for all the spirits." They had to be appeased. The Holy Spirit in a vision showed him some goat or beast to be sacrificed. "I take chyme and pour it with blood in water and stir. Then I purify with this all in the kraal." He needed assistance for this important work, and got it from his pagan father. "I can do nothing without him. The angels visit me in the dream, and I pray to heaven for the beast to be sacrificed. But it is father who prays to the angels in the cattle kraal. He uses our prayers of old [=of our Zulu religion] and concludes with Our Father."

Laduma Michael Madela. Madela is easily the most widely known personality in the Ceza area. Scholars have broadcast his fame far and wide. Professor Otto Raum and Dr. Wolfgang Bodenstein— the latter for some years working at the Ceza Mission Hospital —made a fine study of him under the title 'A Present Day Zulu Philosopher', published in *Africa,* 1960. Dr. Katesa Schlosser of Kiel followed this up by a weighty and impressive volume (some 470 pages!) in German, *Zauberei in Zululand, Manuskripte des Blitz-Zauberers Laduma Madela* (Kiel 1972).

These two studies were built on Madela's own voluminous notes written in an alphabet which he has made for himself. In the same strange hand he wrote two most valuable notebooks for me—in Zulu of course—and I shall repeatedly have to refer to these notes in his own hand. We have also had long inter-views with him, more especially in 1958.

Madela has a burden which he shares with many Zulu of his generation. The whole Zulu culture had been despised, destroyed and forgotten. And Madela was the one who was called by *uMve-linqgangi* himself to recapture it and bring it to life and impor-tance again, for the benefit of the Zulu nation, but at the same time for mankind as a whole. Of course, he realized that it is the onslaught of Western civilization that caused this destruction. But in Madela's eyes, the real culprits are to be found much closer to home. All this "was destroyed by the soldiers of the King of the royal clan 'Zulu'". He is aware of a historical tension between the 'Zulu' clan and his own clan of Madela. "The Kings of the 'Zulu' clan committed great sins in killing people." This is a guilt which lies on the people, and "we must find forgiveness for those sins".

Because of these sins the nation had become like a man with two legs, where one leg is rotten. The "black leg" of Zulu cosmology and mythology has become putrefied and no longer gives any support to the body. The "white leg" of the Bible and of Western knowledge functions well, but that does not help the body as a whole. He must for ever go on limping and failing and falling until both legs are equally strong and healthy.

They are made to fit and to function together. They are like "*Elofa*" and "*Seven*", i.e., like the letter "L" and the figure "7". They are meant to correspond and to co-operate. He was fascinated by the symbolical potentialities of these signs of the alphabet and of the series of digits. Madela has built up a complex system of cosmology and mythology. Christian faith and Zulu mythology must go together. Sometimes they did so in his dreams. "I always dream of the forefathers. Now lately I dreamed of a priest together with a man in *ibeshu*. That spells luck, for the two 'legs' walk together."[15]

He had his Bible, and the names and personalities in the Bible present to him daring but obvious parallels to certain signs and names in Zulu mythology: Eden—Ekudeni, Noa—Noa, Satan—Sita; *ingelosi* (angel)—*idlozi* ('shade' of the forefathers); Jehova or Jesus—Emajukujukwini; The Wise and Beautiful Woman in *Proverbs* and *The Song of Songs*—Nomkubulwana, the Zulu 'Princess of heaven'; the Cross—the Cardinal Points. "I am in love with everything in the Bible", he continued, obviously prepared to work out in more detail the happy correspondence between the two worlds that had split and parted, the one from the other. They belong together, and this Ceza philosopher was anxious to bring them together.

Madela was born about 1908–09 at Makitika, a place which

[15] I realize that the version which Madela gave to me differs somewhat from the one imparted to Dr. Schlosser. In her presentation, Madela's aversion to Christianity is stressed (*ibid.*, p. 38). If he emphasized co-operation and synthesis in his talks with me, it is an interesting commentary on the communicative gifts of this many-sided personality.

Laduma Madela, of Ceza, relates how he was baptized and received his Christian name [Michael]. He has never attended school and his hand-writing is unorthodox. Original with the present author.

when he grew up became one of the more important out-stations of the Ceza Lutheran congregation. His mother was a Madide and thus a "sister" of the Lutheran pastor Andreas Madide at Makitika, later to be placed at the main station of Ceza. His father was an *inyanga,* medicine man, and Laduma was charged with carrying his father's bag of herbs and bones. He therefore could not be sent to the little Elementary School at Makitika, as his sisters were. He acquired the art of writing from them, but developed his own characteristic alphabet. "I have not lost one penny on schools", he exclaimed with a delighted smile to me; he knew as well as anybody else that schooling for Africans is not free, but an expensive luxury. His father trained him to become an expert smith and a lightning doctor.

In 1930 he decided to join one of the Zulu Churches, *"Ohlangeni"* (of the Reed of Origin) which is in these parts the Zulu name for the Zulu Congregational Church (Z.C.C.). This is an organization of the "Ethiopian" type, formed in 1896. Madela was under the impression that it was particularly favoured by King Solomon of the Zulus. This obviously was a strong reason for him to join this particular group. He had seen visions which intimated that he was ill. He knew that he *had* to be baptized. The local pastors of this church practised immersion, and Madela's baptism was experienced by him as a dramatic event.

It took place in a river pond near Ceza, and the deep waters were sure to be crawling with pythons and other lurking monsters.[16] While the other catechumens on that occasion were immersed only once, Madela was treated to it three times: he felt that he had probably more sins than others and therefore needed this extra purification, but he was never given a satisfactory explanation for the special care afforded him. "I am a Christian—my name is Michael", the name given to him on that numinous occasion.

But, he would go on to say, "I am not a Zionist." Madela had made sure that he was not to join any of their groups. He had two main objections to them. Women were permitted to preach —which is "very bad", and—this was his "second" reason: women go to wake-services at night, leaving their husbands at home. This was all very unnatural, and definitely not for Laduma Michael Madela.

Joining the Zulu Congregational Church in 1930 had not made him a very fervent Church member. "I am just sitting, but I belong to ZCC and can go there any day." They caused him problems, however. They were against his concern for the "shades" of the ancestors, so he could not feel at home there.

This Zulu philosopher at Ceza represents a concern which is, we feel, more widespread in Natal and Zululand than is generally realized. John Thusi and his *Amakhehlane* (The Old Men) Church present, for example, structural similarities, although Thusi retained much more of the Biblical imagery.[17] Fundamentally, Thusi, too, looked for a synthesis of traditional Zulu religion and the God of the Bible: "We pray to God through the 'shades' (*amadlozi*)." Placed at Amanzimtoti near Durban, Thusi had a wider horizon than ethnocentric Madela at Ceza. Thusi would therefore use a more generous list of mediators: Shaka, Jesus, Queen Victoria and Mary, among others. "We cannot really make a choice between these." Neither was it for him necessary to be that selective. "God Himself knows in whose

---

[16] *Bantu Prophets*, (1961), p. 206.

[17] My interview with Maphithini Thusi (or Mfene), July 1958, at Amanzimtoti and with his successor Hlongwane in Dec. 1972, at Kwa Mashu. Also Notes by T. W. S. Mtembu, with B. Sr. Cf. Brian M. du Toit, Religious Revivalism among Urban Zulu, from *MAN: Anthropological Essays presented to O. F. Raum* (ed. E. J. de Jager), Capetown 1971.

name He will listen to John Thusi or his followers." He knew as well as Madela that "all my departed are before God". Madela felt as keenly as Thusi that his religion was related to "the God of my Fathers". That was the beginning and the end. In a world of revolutionary change, affecting Ceza as well as Durban and all other places, both of them found their identity and meaning in looking not to the future, but to the past. "In my beginning is my end."

Ceza is of course no more than a microcosm of Zululand but our Ceza story is possibly more representative of the religious situation than most White observers—or Zulu church leaders, for that matter—would care to admit. While Zulu members of Mission–related churches would officially claim that there exists a reassuring abyss between them and Zion, my own observations over the years show that there are numerous footbridges across the depths and that there in fact is traffic day and night over those bridges.

Clan relationships were fundamentally important here. "Blood is thicker than water", and—to quote only one example, well known to everybody in the district—the fact that Mrs Henrietta Madide, the Lutheran pastor's wife, was a Butelezi—"Ma Butelezi"—made her, sociologically, a "sister" of the Zion leader, the Rev. Enoch Butelezi.

By conceiving the relationship in terms of two distant parties separated by an abyss the observer may perhaps give himself away as an outsider. The insider—inside the kraals and clans at Ceza—tends to look at things in another light. In that kind of situation, religion must answer the real questions of real men and women, and must satisfy the pressing needs of sickness and anxiety, of separation and loneliness. Just as the need was shared by many, the solution tended to be looked for in terms common to most.

8. Unknown Unsure Unrecognized

"The Magistrate knows me only through wine", he insisted.

This was a surprising statement, but I took it down in my note-book verbatim just as he put it.

Our words are not always self-explanatory. They are expressions of a milieu and form part of a context. Without the context and the milieu they can be misleading and misunderstood.

I could think of a fitting milieu for those words: *M. le maire* and his friend, the *curé* in a little French town, both of them busy men, manage to meet sometimes in the evenings over a good glass of wine. The *curé* could—at least for argument's sake—refer to his friendship of theirs in words not very different from those just quoted.

Yet, the statement I heard was not in French but in Zulu— *iMantshi uyangazi ngewaini kuphela*—and the place was Dannhauser, a coal mining village in Northern Natal, in 1958. My friend, Pastor Jonathan Sibiya, head of the National Zulu Lutheran Church and Vice President of African Ministers Independent Churches Association had invited a few local Church leaders to meet me. We discussed the eternal problem in these Independent churches: how to secure Government recognition. One of the benefits of such recognition then was that the Church President automatically could receive a permit for buying wine "for sacramental purposes". The practical Sibiya tried to show his fellow pastors that Holy Communion need not be less holy if non-alcoholic wine were used. But Pastor Ngubeni, of Bishop Mdla-lose's Zion, insisted: "The Magistrate knows me only through wine. My only chance of being known to Government—as an individual and as a local Church leader—is through these regular visits when I can come along to the Magistrate's Court asking for a wine permit. Without wine, I am unknown. We must make obeisance to Government (*sikhotamele uHulumeni*) and my sole opportunity of so doing is these occasions." His colleague, the Rev. Majola, supported him: "As we apply for wine, we are known. I want to be near to Government."

This was, in fact, a South African situation, imaginable only in that kind of country.

The discussion is of some significance. Once all the bridges between the races had been pulled down, the African Church had to find some makeshift in order to contact the White world. The "Ethiopian" who knew the Whites only too well also realized that he could and would manage without them. The barely literate Zionists were much further away from the Whites in culture and education. Yet the further away they were placed, the more ready they seemed to be to approach this White world and its ways. Red Communion wine, once a symbol of sacrifice in the service of unity, had in a split culture become a symbol of group status, of being noted by the powers of the Whites' State.[1]

Crisis of "recognition"

The Tomlinson Report of 1954 had drawn the blueprint of *apartheid* society. It dealt with African life in all its aspects and thus affected the future of Independent Churches, as well.

Some of the architects of the new society—Verwoerd, Eiselen, C. W. Prinsloo and de Wet Nel—followed developments in this particular field with some concern. The seemingly wasteful multiplicity of the churches was an affront to the plan of society. In 1955, the Zulu politician A. W. G. Champion met Dr Verwoerd at Nongoma. Champion made a pious plea on behalf of the thousands of Churches, with an elegant reference to the Founder of our Faith: "The harvest is plentiful"; the many churches thus ought to be recognized.[2]

This was indeed the point. The whole machinery of Church

[1] The situation occurred in 1958. Three years later, the Liquor Amendment Act of 1961 made provision for the erection of bottle stores in Bantu-populated areas. Liquor, including wine, was thus from that time available also to Africans in South Africa.

[2] Interview June 1958 with A. W. G. Champion.

recognition had obviously been thrown out of gear, and Government was seeking a new approach. The broad principle of separate development was related to the problem by Dr. Eiselen:

I wish to inform you that the Department, in principle favours independence of Bantu Churches from European control when the ability of the office-bearers designated to administer the affairs of the Church in an efficient manner, has been established. The Department will therefore consider sympathetically the further recognition of the Church when transfer of Moderatorship to a Bantu office-bearer takes place.[3]

The Tomlinson report associated itself with this principle in stating:

"It regards the acceleration of ecclesiastical independence among the Bantu as essential".[4]

The commissioners felt that the time had arrived for a new approach to the problem. It thus recommended that

"all churches and missionary societies at work among the Bantu, be registered *de novo* by the State" and

"except in very exceptional cases, the State should for an indefinite period grant recognition to no new churches".[5]

In 1957, Government issued far-reaching amendments: "Churches having in South Africa a following of a million or more souls of all races" were automatically qualified for church sites: this applied to Methodists, Anglicans and Dutch Reformed. Other churches would have to show that they had a following of at least one hundred baptized members over the age of fifteen. The new rules also implied that pastors had to show that they were employed by a recognized organization.

In February 1959, this was followed by instructions more specifically affecting the Independent Churches: by December 31, 1960, church sites occupied by unrecognized Churches in urban locations had to be vacated. The new rules hit almost all the Independent churches, and threw them into a severe crisis.

The crisis was part of the general influx of Africans into urban areas in the late fifties. On many occasions, Government ministers, particularly Dr. Verwoerd and de Wet Nel, expressed con-

---

[3] Dr. Eiselen 17.2.1953 to Rev. C. J. Lucas; letter with the late Rev. Job Chiliza.
[4] Tomlinson Report, Summary ed., (U. C. 61/1955), p. 201.
[5] Ibid.

cern over the ever-rising number of "non-recognized Bantu Churches". "It is quite impossible"—this was a recurrent argument in official statements at the time—"to provide, say, 1 000 Church sites in a township layout embracing 10 000 resident sites and as you are probably aware, the number of Bantu Churches already far exceeds that first figure quoted." The total of Bantu Churches in South Africa was then estimated as 2,200. A soothing little statement was added here: "Of these 81 are recognized." This gave the happy impression that, after all, a considerable number of African Independent churches had been awarded that privilege to which these thousands were longingly looking forward.

It was for the churches to fend for themselves, as best they could. But Government, too, was ready with advice. At the Nongoma encounter in 1955, Dr. Verwoerd had discussed with the above-mentioned Zulu leader, Mr. Champion. That Africans could break away from Europeans, he could understand, Dr. Verwoerd said, "but I cannot understand why they split among themselves." A few years later Dr. Verwoerd suggested that the many Independents should unite into five churches.[6] The whole problem could presumably be more easily handled by the administrators in that way. But the Independent Church leaders did not, of course, appreciate this point.

The effect was one of alarm, each Bishop and President trying to find such refuge as he best could. In 1958, I listened to Rev. T. W. S. Mthembu challenging some of these churches in his inimitable way: "You are a sinking ship!" was the warning he addressed to Zionist leaders. "You better hurry up in joining now with somebody already recognized."

The situation for two thousand little churches, and some of them not so little, became critical, even desperate. The reaction was sharp. From Durban came a move "to boycott all European-controlled Churches." Government's measures were condemned as discriminating against African religious organizations. This appeal seemed to win the favour of many alienated churches.

Certain Zionists sought affiliation with the Assemblies of God, still others approached Job Chiliza's African Gospel Church. Doctrinal considerations weighed less than ever in these tem-

---

[6]   *Ilanga lase Natal* 25.1.1958 and 12.7.1958.

porary unions. An indication was the affiliation of the Archbishop Brander's relatively old Ethiopian Catholic Church in Zion with the "New Church", under Obed Mooki. The latter, an African version of the Swedenborgians, was relatively small and had rather less than 10,000 members, but it was connected with White fellow-believers and recognized by Government.

Pastor Mooki insisted that a group joining his "New Church" must undergo theological training into the more fundamental aspects of our faith: "that the Bible was originally written in Hebrew, and such things."[7] Brander was one of the Church Fathers of the Ethiopian movement. Born into the Wesleyan Church of his parents—"His Grace was born by Christian parents", the Church was to attest in its Constitution—he soon joined the Anglicans and was made a catechist. In 1890 he joined first M. M. Mokone's Ethiopian Church, and then, A.M.E., only to form, in 1904, his own Ethiopian Catholic Church in Zion—a nice comprehensive name.[8]

Brander's Church, founded in 1904, was an interesting attempt to combine Zion with 'high-church' ministerial claims. Its membership was at least three times that of the "New Church". The marriage between the two unequal partners did not prove very happy but helped to tide this particular Zion Church over what seemed to be the threat of extinction.

In this study of the 'Spirit' Churches, we cannot discuss the entire problem of the recognition or otherwise of the Independents.

It was of course the Bulhoek tragedy of 1921—when one hundred and seventeen of Enoch Mgijima's "Israelites" were fatally wounded— which occasioned the appointment of a Government commission that in 1925 was to propose certain methods of recognition of "Native Separatist Churches". Bulhoek and all that needs to be studied anew. At least as far as J. C. Smuts is concerned there are indications showing this need for further research.[8a]

[7] Interview with Rev. O. Mooki 21.12.1972, and on numerous other occasions, through the years.

[8] E.C.C.Z., file 5/214, (Nat. Affairs Dept.) now National Archives. Pretoria.

[8a] I have come across an important letter from J. C. Smuts 13.12.1920 to "My dear A. H. Frost" (Sunnyside, Waverley, C. P.) where he says: "I am most anxious to avoid unnecessary bloodshed. The application of force to the Israelites will

It is notorious that the machinery of Government recognition of churches, initiated in 1925, was discontinued about 1965. We refer here to our *Bantu Prophets* (p. 65). For the purposes of this survey suffice it to say that from 1900 only eleven Independent Churches were recognized—one of these moreover, the Ethiopian Church of South Africa, was struck off the list in 1953, the total number thus being reduced to ten. Out of these, only four were recognized after 1925, i.e. in the period regulated by the rules of the Native Affairs Commission laid down in 1925. These four are Bantu Methodist Church of South Africa, 1933, African Congregational Church, 1937, African Orthodox Church, 1941, and finally, African Gospel Church, in 1948.

It is an interesting commentary on the role of these *African* organizations that in the case of at least four out of the ten, recognition was awarded to churches somehow connected with Europeans: Kanyane Napo's The Africa Church, sometimes called New Africa Church, is loosely related to the so-called "Church of England" in South Africa, i.e., the remainder of Bishop Colenso's faithful. This African group attends the White Synod and its members looked upon themselves as bound by the laws of the Church of England![9] The Lutheran Bapedi Church and its hanger-on, The Lutheran Bapedi Church of South Africa, are historically related to the breakaway from the Berlin Mission in the eighteen-nineties of a disaffected German missionary, J. A. Winter. When Job Chiliza applied for recognition of the African Gospel Church, at the end of the 1940's, he did so in conjuction with and supported by the already mentioned American revivalist C. J. Lucas, D.D.

Official statements quoting the number of recognized Bantu

probably mean the loss of many lives, as those people are religious fanatics whom extreme measures would make quite mad. Bloodshed on a large scale at the present juncture would have the most lamentable political effects in many parts of South Africa ... I am therefore for proceeding cautiously and giving time for the present effervescence among the Natives to calm down. I want to impress on you and on other friends the urgent necessity of dealing very wisely with the present situation." 420/13F/387 (Israelites); National Archives, Pretoria.

Cf. W. K. Hancock, *Smuts*, (1968), II, pp. 89–110 and Sundkler, *Bantu Prophets*, p. 72 f.

[9] Alan Ewbank, Vicar-General of "The Church of England in South Africa", Dec. 14, 1940 to the author.

Churches as eighty, were more ingenious than ingenuous, for the figure 80 refers to *all* churches and missions working among the Africans, the great majority of which have White leadership: such as Church of Scotland, Church of Sweden Mission, Hanno-verian Evangelical Lutheran Free Church Mission, the Roman Catholic Church and the Salvation Army, etc.

Zionists and comparable organizations were less fortunate. Not one of them was recognized. Not that they did not try. All of them, throughout their history, were intent on this one thing: to be recognized by "Pretoria". They all produced their Church constitutions, such as they were, hired lawyers such as *they* were, made their personal appearance before officials in the Bantu Affairs Department and arranged group deputations. The story was the same after 1948 as before that year. They received a stan-dard answer, with the phrase that there was "no objection to the conduct of *bona fide* religious work among the Native people, provided law and order are observed." A Registration number was affixed to the statement: for each of these two thousand and more churches there was a special file with a number in the Government office. In very many cases the "registration" was in-terpreted as a "recognition". Even scholars writing on this subject have been known to confuse the two terms, yet there was of course an abyss of difference in the significance of the two terms.

All the more easy it was for various organizations which pur-ported to serve the interests of these Churches, to give the impres-sion that they had been successful in obtaining the coveted recog-nition for their credulous clients.

There is one famous exception to this rule of Zion alienation: Lekganyane's "Z.C.C.", the Zion Christian Church, in Northern Transvaal. It is the most successful of all Independent Churches in Southern Africa, with a membership of well over 200,000, and still growing rapidly, a highly organized and tightly dis-ciplined body. Its annual festivals at Zion City Moria where fifty thousand and more members congregate for days are great public events.

It represents tremendous actual and latent African power. Any Government takes account of power when it sees it; so also in this case. More than any other Independent Church, the Z.C.C. has been favoured with Government's positive and constructive interest and sympathy. The official version of the Church itself is that it was "recognized by Government before 1964".

Be that as it may, the Z.C.C. has by immense vitality and wise engineering established its position as a power in the land, and—ordinary administrative procedures could be dispensed with.[10]

A number of union organizations were formed in the nineteen-sixties—some of them carrying forward earlier initiatives—with a view to giving advice and help to the Independent churches. Some of these had White advisers, others had purely African leadership.

Union Associations with White Advisers

There were four associations, each with a White adviser, three of them claiming each four hundred member churches, most of them small and, even in African terms, powerless. There, the similarities between AICA and PMCA end. The difference was obvious: the former well organized, highly endowed through overseas contributions: in the peak year 1970, with an overall expenditure of some Rd 50,000.[11] Inner tensions and some money-grabbing brought the downfall of the Association, in 1973. PMCA, existing on a shoestring, was held together by the sacrifice of the African brethren.

"AICA"—*African Independent Churches Association,* is well known because of its contacts since 1965 with Dr. Beyers Naude's Christian Institute. For that very reason the big and influential Independent Churches kept away: they were not to be politically tainted by something potentially risky. An exceptionally competent European staff helped AICA in its outreach and propaganda. The African leadership of AICA was weakened by power struggles on various levels. The most imaginative contribution of AICA was its theological programme, including for a few years a small Theological College at Alice and an ambitious

---

[10] We repeat that we only deal with Zulu and Swazi churches. The Z.C.C. thus lies outside our limited field. We refer however to the historical note on p. 66 relating the Z.C.C. with the early history of Zion in Lesotho, and with the church drums of Natal.

[11] Martin West, African Independent Churches in Soweto, unpublished Ph. D. thesis, Capetown 1972.

correspondence course reaching out to preachers. There is also a WAAIC, Women's Association of the African Independent Churches.

By contrast to AICA's particular position, RICA, the *Reformed Independent Churches Association* describes itself as "a non-political organization to promote the Church work among the Bantu on separate lines to the honour of the Kingdom of God and to work in harmony with the State", according to its Constitution. Here a Dutch Reformed minister, Rev. N. van Loggerenberg, was the adviser.

A gallant effort, on another level altogether, was made by Rev. Archbishop J. H. Abel, a European who in 1947 helped to form the *Pentecostal Mission Churches Association* (PMCA). Some four hundred churches, Zionist and Apostolic, are claimed to be members of this Federation, itself an illustration of the general situation. J. H. Abel, now 68 years of age, recently retired from a job with the South African Railways. He is thus all the more ready to devote himself to the instruction of his African friends. For they need instruction, he feels: before he took over in 1947, "there were", in the Archbishop's own version, "a few anomalies and stumbling blocks to overcome. Among others, their wearing of uniform, unchristian practices and the animosity against them as Separatist Independent Bantu Churches; and also the Zionist cult." The Archbishop "took the matter to the Lord in prayer", and has since had encouraging contacts with his African Bishops.

He claims to have played a certain role, on a wider scale: "It was me who never left any stone unturned until I persuaded the Department of Bantu Administration and Development to allow the Bantus more religious freedom".[12]

Of late, Rev. Brian Brown, Methodist minister and co-worker of the Christian Institute, has taken the imaginative step of accepting to serve as an adviser of this group. This bodes well for the future of the Federation.

Archbishop Abel teaches his members theology. He had made a theological discovery of his own. "To obtain my degree I had to write a thesis about the various dogmatics, theologies, and functioning of different denominations. This drove me in a corner

[12] J. H. Abel 14.7.1974 and on numerous other dates to B. Sundkler.

and eventually I found the only solution: I represented God as the greatest DOGMATIC THEOLOGIAN. Producer of dramatic history which coincided with prophecy in a figurative manner and finally confirmed God's purposes, consistent with his perfect will and "EVERLASTING GOOD PLEASURE".[13]

He was thus all the more anxious to transmit this theology to his charismatic African friends. No doubt this effort was appreciated by those involved, the instruction being very much on a level with that of the students. The Federation has as a characteristic feature common to all these organizations and churches, an extensive Constitution. As the first of the "Administrative Rules" is to be found 1. *High Priest*: "The officially recognised Spiritual Head of the Federation P.M.C.A., its corporate bodies and member Churches is our Lord Jesus in his Spiritual capacities as personal Saviour, Redeemer, King of Kings, Lord of Lords, Righteous Ruler, Judge, High Priest, after the order *of Melchizedek*—Amen."

We saw that AICA and PMCA each claimed to serve some four hundred churches. Almost the same number—but not the same groups!—is reached by the *All Africa School of Theology* at Witbank. Led by an American Pentecostal, Fred H. Burke, and his devoted staff, it is organized as a correspondence Bible School.

Burke started his missionary career in the Ceza mountains at the beginning of the 1920s, and thereby came in contact with Zionism in Zululand and Swaziland. The intention of his Witbank School is to discourage "the outward manifestation of the Holy Spirit". "As a Pentecostal missionary, I feel that part of my ministry is perhaps to lead some of them back into reality in place of the outward frenzy which exhibits itself in the beating of drums and dancing and various contortions." At the same time, the deeper Bible study, on an "undenominational" basis, and the annual Bible conventions are designed to foster co-operation and unity. More than seven hundred ministers, mainly in Southern Africa but also in other parts of the Continent, were trained by the school. "Simple basic English" is used, and the material is translated into six Bantu languages, including Zulu and Swazi. Extensive use is made of picture-charts, cartoons, etc. A certain

---

[13] Ibid. Statement left unedited.

apocalyptic system is propagated, with Millennium and Rapture, and Lake of Fire, and an almost imminent Doom. Time is short. Therefore: "Where will you spend your eternity? If you are interested in further Bible study, please write to us, Box 263, Witbank, Transvaal."[14]

Distance Overcome

One must not exaggerate the feeling of distance between the African churches. In various ways, the innate feeling of African unity does tell and expresses itself in the relationships between the churches. Sometimes this is a development at the local or regional level. As an example, the annual United Service on May 30th in Port Elizabeth should be mentioned. Here Zionists meet together in prayer and praise with all other churches and feel accepted and thoroughly at home.

Even more important is, on the Rand, the underground, *Sephiri* (secret) prayer movement. It took form in the nineteen-forties during the years of the Second World War. It is a uniquely and characteristically African approach to the unity of the Church. Whites meet—if they meet at all—in Faith–and–Order debates on "validity" of ministries and sacraments and such like. They sit together in the afternoon and discuss round a table. In Soweto, there are the Faith Healing "Fountains" which draw people together, in the night.

Nobody is asked whether he or she is Anglican, Catholic, Lutheran, "A.M.E." or Zionist. At the Fountain, "The Lake of Peace", all are alike: the same anxiety about health and wholeness; the same trust in that blessed water which they are given to take home. In July 1969, we visited Motsikari, supposed to be the leader of the secret prayer movement: a heavy, collected, concentrated man with an enormous head; impassive eyes at first— while still under the impression that the White man had come "to spy". Soon however those eyes glisten with a friendly glint, as if close to tears. The man, without formal school education; supported by his active and enterprising wife, who with her Standard V diploma is the educated person in the family.

[14] F. H. Burke to the present writer 5.11 and 13.12.1972. Interview at Witbank December 1972. Copious school material.

An interview with an Anglican priest, holding a leading position in the *Idamasa*, confirms the impression, that this movement helps to foster a new piety, a Biblical mysticism with African signature. As a rule, Zionist preachers were less educated than others, and they felt a certain inferiority when meeting with other Churches. This was experienced as a problem in IDAMASA and the enterprising secretary of the association, Rev. A. L. Mncube (Methodist) took the initiative in 1965, forming a new organization, AZASA (Apostolic and Zionist Assembly of South Africa) for these alienated groups. In 1967, some one hundred and eighty churches were affiliated to AZASA. Mncube managed to have AZASA attached to the South African Council of Churches. When he left the Assembly, about 1968, the new movement lost most of its impetus and strength.[15]

African Union Associations

The *African Ministers' Independent Churches Association* has since its inception in 1934 had a fine succession of impressive Zulu church leaders, including S. Shibe of the Zulu Congregational Church, the redoutable P. V. Lamula and J. L. Gwala. In 1956, Ephraim Zwane (b. 1906), himself head of the Zulu Congregational Baptist Church with some two thousand members, became the President. Zwane had had a Std VI education, with a Std VII diploma through the Efficiency Correspondence College. In this Union endeavour he was increasingly to feel the "Zulu" epithet in his church's name as a limitation, and attempted to have this changed, in view of his connexions with other churches of mainly Sotho and Bhaca background. Churches of both Ethiopian and Zionist lineage are members. Attempts have been made to send the younger ministers of the Association to Bible Schools at Sweetwater and Witbank, and Zwane was known for continually trying to secure Government recognition for his member churches.[16]

A busy leader of Church deputations to Pretoria was President

---

[15] Dr. A. I. Berglund, South African Council of Churches, August 5, 1974, to B. Sundkler.
[16] Interviews with E. Zwana July 1958 and with J. M. Sibiya, Vice President, numerous occasions 1958, 1969, 1972.

L. L. Ndziba, (b. 1887), head of the *Bantu United Ministers' Association* which more than Zwane's organization specialized in Zionist groups. They claim some 250 churches as members. Thus the Mabilitsa–Mdlalose Zion was a prominent member of this organization, and Ndziba spent much time in the 1950s in papering over the cracks in that organization.

Ndziba, a personable church leader, began in Mzimba's Presbyterian Church of Africa, where he felt at home because of its preponderantly *Hlubi* membership. In 1940 he formed his own Free Church of Africa, but returned to Mzimba in 1958, the attraction to that Hlubi fold being too strong: *"Hau,* I am a Hlubi from toe to head!" he told us in an interview in 1958. He specialized in arbitration of conflicts within and between churches and in representing churches before Bantu Affairs Department. He made regular trips to Bantu Affairs Department in Pretoria and felt well received by the Government official in these matters: "Potgieter is my friend". If this friendship did not lead to recognition for any of the churches that were members of his Association, this did not seem to matter: the main thing was the regular representation in Pretoria.[17]

A rapidly growing organization was the AICM, *African Independent Church Movement,* a breakaway from AICA (p. 289) in 1973, under the enterprising and energetic leadership of Bishop C. J. Bengeza, Durban. AICM is as a large collection of small churches. The latest claim has some 460 member churches, thus with a nominal membership size at least comparable to better-known organizations. Comparing itself with the White-inspired association from which it seceded, AICM emphasizes African initiative and leadership throughout. It takes an "ecumenical" attitude and wants co-operation for a so-called "South African College for Independent Churches" and—looking further ahead —possibly for an overall umbrella organization of *all* the Union associations. Here, Bengeza has so far the personal support of the influential Bishop Isaac Mokoena, of RICA.

By comparison AMASA, *Apostolic Ministers Association of Southern Africa,* with its twenty members is still small. It is claimed, however, that numbers were about a hundred member churches in

---

[17] L. L. Ndziba, Interview, August 1958.

1970, although some of these churches were rather on the small side, sometimes with less than twenty individual members each. The present number (1975) of twenty churches is thus the result of some local canvassing and of smallscale amalgamations. The present leader is Bishop J. A. Njikela of the New Jerusalem Faith Mission Church of South Africa. The great majority of the member Churches are under Zulu leadership.[18]

"Zion Combination Churches in South Africa" was another— combination. For Zionists to combine, strong pressure was needed. This was provided by the threat in the nineteen -fifties to their existence. In 1956–57, a Government official dealing with Information urged Stephen Nkonyane and related churches to unite—the possibility of recognition was held before them as a bait—and in February 1957, the new organization was formed, eventually to bring together twenty-eight Zion Churches.

Most of the groundwork for this union had already been done by the women in the churches. Grace Tshabalala's *Zion ka Baba* (p. 78) formed the basis of the endeavour. She was herself the wife of a pastor in Nkonyane's Zion, and Stephen Nkonyane of the Christian Catholic Apostlic Holy Spirit Church in Zion became the Chairman, while S. G. Shange of the Zion Congregational Church acted as one of the most energetic supporters. Nkonyane had been provided with a car by his Church, and he and Shange went together "from door to door all over the Union", to solicit new members. "Without Nkonyane's car it would have been impossible."

Their main activity consisted in finding places in Bible Schools for their younger aspirants. It was recognized that the training of the ministry was basic in order to secure what was the driving force for their union: to obtain Government recognition. In an interview in 1958 they were hopeful about their future. Their churches were influential, they felt, and thus much superior to a Natal competitor, Titus Msibi's African Zionist Ministers' Association. That one consisted of *"ama-scrapes nje"*, as one of my informants put it in his combination of English and Zulu.

---

[18] Axel Ivar Beglund, S.A.Co. of Churches, 23.12.1974 to the present writer.

Union Federations with African Advisers

Two of the best-known among these purely African union organizations were led by Bishop W. M. Dimba and Dr. E. M. Gabellah.

Walther Makhobosi Dimba (1902–1973) was one of the most complex and colourful personalities ever to be connected with this movement.

By instinct a political animal, he was recognized as by design a Government supporter. He was a preacher without a church of his own, yet he claimed to be a bishop and somehow directed the policies of many hundreds of other men's—and women's—churches, insisting that he be regarded as their sole spokesman before the Government. *"Uyangizwa kambe? Ngi jule kakhulu mina, man"*, he would tell me. "I am very deep"—and one had to agree with him there.

Dimba was born at Groutville and thus, as he would always proudly point out, hailed from the birthplace of other prominent Zulu: Albert Luthuli, Gardiner Mvuyana and J. Mdelwa Hlongwane—the two latter founders of Independent Churches. He would claim that he came from "a wealthy sugarcane family" at Groutville. The American Board Mission gave him his initial educational opportunities: he studied at Ohlange and Adams, both prestigeous school centres in Natal at that time. Gardiner Mvuyana, however, broke with the American mission in 1917 and formed the African Congregational Church, and young Dimba eventually joined this body. After that he went to Anderson College, Indiana, U.S.A., from 1926 to 1931.

There he studied theology—graduating B. Th. and Collegiate Dipl. B. Th.—but, more important, he found out how some of the American Blacks managed their Whites at that time. This he was not slow to learn. He developed and perfected an irresistible role: that of the voluble and volatile, roly-poly Black who when required could instantly turn into the serious, burdened statesman, preferably making solemn statements on national and world issues: "Moon rockets are a death threat to the earth and could lead to war." (*Ilanga lase Natal,* 24.10.1959).

Such characteristics of statesmanship were added later. He did not display them in the boisterous, near-riot clash with his own African Congregational Church. On his return to South Africa in 1931, he discovered that the ACC had in his absence established a "company" in order to take care of its considerable property. As this company was managed by people other than himself, Dimba broke with the ACC. He was assaulted by the other party and spent weeks in the hospital as a consequence of this ecclesiastical difference of opinion.

He now formed his own "Gardiner Mvuyana African Congregational Church". He issued an appeal: "We let the Zulu know that here is his home now. Gardiner Mvuyana is risen from the dead. Hurrah!" (*Uvukile u G. M. kwabafileyo. Halala.*)

Two years later he was excommunicated by his own church and/or broke with it. He consequently formed a counter- church, now called, for a change, "African Congregational Church Ibandla lika Mvuyana." This connection did not last long. He now disappeared for a few years, reputedly devoting his energies to the United States and/or East Africa.

With this broad experience he was the obvious person to organize a *Federation of Bantu Churches,* and he did so in 1943. At this early time he claimed some sixty member churches. (In Johannesburg I followed the early development of the Federation about 1945, and, as I now see from my notes, I was invited by Dimba to become what he called the "figurehead" of the Federation, but as a modest person I resisted the temptation).

The crucial fifties were relatively uneventful for Dimba's Federation except for some occasional initiatives, mostly abortive. Thus from 1952 he was reputed to run classes for pastors. These were supposed to last two years. He had from the beginning twenty-six students. Ministerial training was devoted to bookkeeping and how to bank church-collections, in itself of course very useful. The membership grew, along with the claim that they alone would be in a position to provide what all these churches were seeking: government recognition. Dimba bided his time and while he tried to keep open his political contacts in different directions, he remained pragmatic enough to draw his own conclusions from the fate of more outspoken contemporaries. He also found opportunities for rather unorthodox business connections and activities; one ingenious device was to tuck a consonant to his Bantu *isibongo* (surname); thereby his name seemed to take on a definitely lighter hue. But this was only for a time.

It was the crucial show-down for the "non-recognized churches" in 1959 that afforded Dimba his real opportunity: By the end of 1960, Church sites occupied by unrecognized churches in urban locations had to be vacated.

He staked his future on this. Commuting in those weeks between Durban and the Rand, he spoke strongly against the desperate boycott threat from Durban and managed by force of his personality to avert this (*The World* 14.11.1959). In his opinion there was one main problem, and the African churches had better take account of it: "Municipalities lost revenue by the large number of churches. Church sites were not charged for."

Ever resourceful, Dimba also had a solution this time. Government should allow "perhaps in every location, one site for a hall which would be used by all unrecognized churches in turn." This idea proved, of course, that Dimba, himself without a church, was more interested in a temporary administrative device than in the worship of such churches as he claimed to represent. To Government his idea seemed good. Dimba received a letter from the Ministry of Bantu Administration, November 23, 1959, stating that "this Department has already requested all local authorities to consider the possibility of a Church hall or halls on one or two sites for letting in turn to church bodies who have substantial following and for whom sites are not available".

Bishop Dimba naturally regarded this as a victory for his line of approach. He could now feel and claim that his Federation had the blessing of the powers that really mattered.

He had a vision of his Federation providing social amenities, such as ambulance and fire brigade services in the locations, as well as a Bible school for the training of the ministers of the Federation. In his exuberant mood, making great promises for the future, he would say: "We are going to call a big campaign. We are going to baptize location by location from the age of three years. I can dry all these churches if I want to. Once the Federation goes into action there will be no future for white churches in the Bantustans and homelands. Our ultimate aim is a National church. I have one weapon to topple all these so-called Christian Churches and that is the formation of a National Church." (Interview 4.6.1960.)

He felt he was in a strong position now. He could act on behalf of all the Independent churches: "There is no more need for the delegates to proceed to Pretoria, until such individual churches shall have been able to comply with the conditions as set out by the Bantu Administration and Development Department. It shall then suffice to let you know that at present we do have a chance to be allotted the use of Class rooms in the locations." Dimba 13.11.1959 to J. T. Mokhati.

The time had now come to spell out the political standpoint of the Federation, speaking in the name of some 750 churches which were enlisted by the Federation. Again Dimba had a plan of his own, applied to the political situation as a whole.

"We as leaders of the Federation of Bantu Churches in South Africa are in favour of all the Government policies etc." What was lacking, however, was real information. The Federation "blames the Government for not having had first created a body of trustworthy men among the Africans to interpret the Government's laws as they should have been explained to these poor unfortunate creatures."

After statements of this kind he would comfort his Zionist bishops gathered in Dimba's mammoth meetings on the Rand: "The world and the state will respect you if we respect ourselves, and you will all get your rights. Are you going to respect yourselves? Are you going to respect yourselves? Hallelujah (Amen). Hallelujah (Amen). If you promise me that you will respect yourselves you are going to see halls in which to worship. Hallelujah (Amen)." (Orlando 28.5.1960.)

As head of the Federation he was engaged in drawing up constitutions for member churches, all on the same pattern and with identical wording—a fact which of course lightened the burden but diminished the value of the effort. They were treated as prestige documents by the organizations concerned. Dimba also issued ordination certificates for pastors, documents which in times of influx control could be of a certain value.

In this and hundreds of similar cases, the impression was conveyed that a particular church had been recognized—which as a matter of course was not the case. Impression was the thing, and impression held the Federation together and strengthened it, as long as Bishop Dimba was there, ever volatile, ever boisterous.

He had his worries, however. Really rich and influential

churches refused to join the Federation. His ambition was to win the Lekganyane's and the Limba's and the MaNku's. But no, they were big enough, and wise enough, to keep to themselves. Among the 750 member churches he could however count Nkonyane's Zion, and he received some financial and other support from J. G. Shembe.

A few years later, Bishop Dimba climbed to a more solid platform, carpentered as it seemed to suit him sell. This was the African Foundation of South Africa, with Mr. Lloyd N. Ndaba as Managing Editor and Dimba as chairman. It served to bolster apartheid and Bantustans. The first issue of *"Africa South"*—the publication of the Foundation—had a significant article by the learned Mr. Ndaba: "Whenever Africans (Negroes) are living side by side with any other racial group, be it Europeans or Indians or Arabs, racial strife ensues. There must be a biological or generic anthropological reason for this strange phenomenon." In this review one could learn that Bishop Dimba, together with Ndaba, was one of the Foundation members of the Zulu Bantustan Party, otherwise called Zulu National Party.[19]

What was the secret of the influence of this man who for many Zionists appeared as a helper in their dire need? He was not, after all, without enemies. Many African Church leaders and other leaders loathed him. Yet he carried on as if unscathed by the suspicion and the opposition around him.

In saying that he had a more powerful, or overpowering, personality than most people, we have of course only shifted the question, for one would like to understand wherein this "power" consisted. His bullfrog voice helped him. It put off thoughtful people but impressed those whom he wanted to enlist in his endeavours. "I am the Gate", he could blurt out. This meant, "only through me will you be able to obtain what you are after —Government recognition for your church."

He could turn the merest little act into a big occasion. In Boksburg there had in 1960 been a quarrel between two competing groups within Nkonyane's Zion. There was a struggle over the

---

[19] *Africa South,* vol. I, No. 1, p. 3.
The political symphathies of Dimba's African Foundation naturally led to questions. In 1967, Dimba told a meeting: "I want to make clear now that we are not stooges." *The World,* 14.2.1967.

keys to the door of the temple. Dimba somehow got hold of the keys, invited Nkonyane to come from Charlestown to a great ceremony on the Rand, and handed over the keys with a characteristic peroration: "Brother Nkonyane, I give unto you these keys in order that you will open, so that when you open, nobody will shut, and when you shut, nobody will open". The keys were lifted up high and shown to the masses. Cries of 'Hallelujah' and 'He is holy' were heard from the crowd. The allusion to the key passage in the Book of Revelation was not lost on this particular congregation.[20]

In the same way, meetings of the Federation were preferably staged as "mammoth" assemblies—a word he liked—with mighty processions through the streets, with hundreds of Bishops all led by the genial Dimba. Shembe gave him a new Ford car, and Bishop Nkonyane white garments: "The Angel had criticized," (ingerosi iya sora), Nkonyane insisted, "that their great leader appeared in black", the right colour of course being white.

And all this generosity with a view to passing through this "Gate" to Government at Pretoria and the longed-for recognition of their Church. But—had not the whole machinery of Government recognition come to an end by this time? Did he not know this? The point was that his Zionist clients did not know and could not know.

Government might change their policy, but Walther Makhobosi Dimba did not. He did not always like change, particularly not small change.

An interesting Durban parallel to Dimba's Rand-based Federation was Dr. E. M. Gabellah's *Bureau of Bantu Churches*. Here again, church politics on the level of Independent groups was in the hands of a colourful personality. With all its sharp and sudden changes, Gabellah's personal development mirrors the frustrations of the African intellectual in Southern Africa. Himself a Zulu (born in 1923) with Anglican background, he established

---

[20] *Ilanga lase Natal* 30.4.1960 and 18.6.1960. Very rich material on W. Dimba in the African Congregational Church files, 54/214, now National Archives, Pretoria, and the files of the African Congregational Church Gardiner Mvuyana, 521/214, *ibid*. See also Minute Book of the ACC 1923–1957, in ACC Headquarters, Durban.

early contacts with the famous 'Hosannah' Church—John Masowe's Apostles—in Port Elizabeth. Being one of the few literate men in that movement, he started in 1953 a day-school for children combined with a night-school for adults. But educated as he was, his position in a group of this kind was precarious, and he was thrown out of the tightly-knit community.[21]

He joined an American Church organization in Durban, but his healthy reaction to the peculiar policy of the pious made him join a Muslim group for some time.[22] He managed to move around in the world a great deal and when he eventually turned up again in Durnan in the 1960s, he had a long string of impressive academic letters to his name:

"D.D. Midwestern Grad. B. S. Advanced Divinity 1961
SMAE. Inst. Medical Electricity
Indian Inst. Hon. Fellow, Kumbakonam
Northern Inst. of Massage
International Inst. of Naturopaths
Dr. of Homeopathy"

[21] Numerous personal interviews with Dr. E. M. Gabellah 1958 and 1969.
E. M. Gabellah, "The Story of Shoniwa, called Johane Masowe", 71 pp.+6 pp., with the author. This is a remarkable document. Gabellah joined the Masowe 'Hosannah' movement at the beginning of the nineteen-fifties. He claims that he "invented" the official name of the Masowe Hosannas: *"Apostolic Sabbath Church of God"*. In his account he shows a fine eye for the changes that took place over the years both in Masowe himself and in his movement. Various questions are presented, such as the economic rights of the individual in a movement that in principle was a kind of Christian "Communism"; celibacy v. polygyny; Masowe as "another individual" than Shoniwa (the prophet's name prior to his revelation on the mountain); Gabellah also discusses a change from an initial anti-education attitude to an interest in at least an infant school in the Church: "this was the effort of a certain E. M. Gabellah who was at that time the second right hand man" in the movement, mainly attending to communication with Government officials. But Gabellah himself was an educated person and his position in the movement was to that extent delicate: soon he was dismissed by Masowe. He then moved from Port Elizabeth to Durban, where he could engage in activities open to an enterprising African, i.e., in the medical and religious fields. Thus he started his Bureau.

[22] We must be more specific on this point. Dr. Gabellah had learned that a famous Western evangelist was to preach in Durban. He expressed his desire to listen to the great man. "Of course, dear brother", his missionaries said, "you can attend

Another interesting effort of Dr. Gabellah, the intellectual, was his ambition to publish an African *Who's Who* with some 4,000–5,000 names, an initiative that soon proved abortive.

In June 1969 he told me that extensive study had made him accept the Christian fellowship again. He felt it as his duty to return to the Christian fold. This time he was connected with the African Orthodox Church, where he in 1967 became Bishop Elect for Natal and Zululand, and a Vice-Chancellor and Patriarchal Administrator.

In 1962 Dr. Gabellah formed his Bureau and he eventually claimed 500 member churches—a good round figure. This was important also for the *Azasa* (cf p. 292) as he was Vice Director of this organization for some time. There was thus a personal union between the Bureau and Azasa. With such a vast number of churches on his membership list he felt that one should not press doctrinal requirements too hard. "We arrive at the Bible in a mild way", he suggested. The annual conference included a Refresher course lasting one day, a full day, with Bible study, practical demonstration of how to preach, personal evangelism, although "on a small scale", and finally a United Service. Dr. Gabellah himself, in the impressive ecclesiastical garments of a Bishop Elect in the African Orthodox Church, was the inspiring leader.

As practical aims of the Bureau, the Doctor specified assistance to the churches with their applications for Government recognition, the writing of such applications being one of the major industries of some of the churches. In the end, Dr. Gabellah rather suddenly disappeared from the Durban scene, and as is well-known, has of late devoted his vibrant energies to more ambitious, political moves in Rhodesia.

All these organizations, White and Black, were supposed *inter alia,* to help the Churches to secure Government recognition. The results in this respect were modest, as we have just seen. What then was the ordinary local Zion preacher to do?

It slowly dawned upon him that recognition was out of reach.

---

the meeting. We will put you behind a curtain so that you will not be seen". It was to the great credit of Dr. Gabellah that he reacted against this kind of thing.

"Pretoria" had been a concept loaded with expectations and longing, but clearly it was not for him. In the city where during the week he had a job in industry or as a driver or a waiter, he would call his little flock of faithful together in a neighbouring garage or school room, yet longing for the day when in thousands they would congregate for the Annual Festival, perhaps on a Mountain top, on their own Mount Zion. Endless years of busy constitution-making and application-writing had not brought him any closer to recognition.

I can still hear in my ears the ringing of a Zion pastor's indignant protest. He was an ambitious and successful builder and a good and solid preacher: a splendid and upright specimen of a man. He had a Std VII education and spoke to me in his English. With his higher education he felt all the more the slights and the injustices that *are* the African's lot and ration in his country. Why should he not get his right? he asked. Why was his church not recognized? "Am I like a dirty thing? I am not a dirty thing. I am a person".

9. An Interpretation

"The one who calls others a sect is a sect himself"
T. W. S. Mthembu, (p. 332).

In the preceding pages I have on occasion referred to that earlier book of mine, *Bantu Prophets in South Africa,* the first edition of which appeared in 1948, and a second in 1960. Since that time much water has passed through the Zulu and Swazi Jordans. Over the years the book has evoked agreement from some and disagreement from others. Our own position has changed on certain essential points, and we shall open this concluding "Interpretation" by trying to define our present standpoint vis-à-vis that earlier debate.

"Bantu Prophets" discussed

1. *Causes and Effects*

Some concepts die only slowly. They are formulated and broadcast and they seem to attract people's fancy, more perhaps than ever asked for, and it is not easy to modify or eradicate them.

I experienced this with regard to a conclusion in *Bantu Prophets* of 1948, where I had interpreted the syncretistic group—"nativistic Zionism"—as the bridge over which Africans are brought back to that traditional religion from which they had once emerged (*op. cit.,* p. 297). At the time, this conclusion was carefully formulated on a basis of our local encounter with certain forms of Zionism at Ceza, Zululand, at the beginning of the 1940s. I believed there was ample evidence in support of this view, see *Bantu Prophets,* pp. 238–264.

Yet, this conclusion as formulated in the nineteen-forties became misleading in that we had come to generalize our local daily observations at Ceza (1940–1942) to represent Zulu Zion as a whole. As early as in the second edition of *Bantu Prophets,*

1960, we made amends for this and emphasized a very different point of view.

The mistake was not so much the observation that such regress did sometimes take place but rather that I had overlooked a methodological consideration of prime importance. *From the point of view of those involved,* Zion was not turned to the past but to the future, and was their future. In some of its forms at Ceza it may indeed have appeared to the Westerner to be definitely "syncretistic", whatever that term might mean. But that is not really the point. To those in the movement, Zion meant newness of life, health and wholeness, a new identity. If it was a bridge, it appeared to them as a bridge to the future.

Some of my critics have made their case too easy in ascribing to me a simplistic understanding of the *causes* of the Independent movement. It is claimed that the author of *Bantu Prophets* recognized only two causes of the emergence of this phenomenon: colour-bar in the church and denominationalism between the churches. Let me quote the book referred to. *"The two main reasons for secession from Mission churches* are the colour-bar of white South Africa and Protestant denominationalism" (*op. cit.* p. 295). This is of course a very different matter. A large part of my book was in fact devoted to an analysis of the causes of African breakaways from other African leaders; I refer to the Index of subjects, *Causes* of Secession, p. 379 in the book quoted.

A new, possibly controversial, consideration in this debate on "Causes" is provided by the first chapter in the present *"Zulu Zion"*. Much ingenious thought had been devoted to guesswork about supposed traits and tendencies in what was called "Zulu character" or "Swazi character". These traits were intended to explain some of the strength and depth of Zion influence among those people, as compared with the Xhosa or Venda. The fact of a sustained Zion missionary effort, in the first formative years, under White leadership, can now no longer be overlooked, and must be integrated into a general framework of causation.

2. *Types*

A serious point of criticism concerned my typology. Those looking for universally recognizable categories were of course put off

305

by the rather simple-looking dichotomy between "Ethiopian" and "Zionist" churches. (For a reference to these terms, see p. 15–16 in this book.) My defence is that these terms were obviously viable when in the 1940s I tried to establish some kind of order in a seemingly chaotic situation among what were then called "Native Separatist Churches". If these terms have survived in a rather surprising way, this would seem to indicate that they have remained comparatively useful tools.

Various suggestions for a new classification have been made. They all have good points and are worth considering except perhaps the one suggested by Dr. Oosthuizen. In his case it suffices to quote verbatim, for this is what he says:

"The following classification is proposed, namely:

a) *Churches*. Some of the groups which are described are churches, such as the African Methodist Church, the Bantu Methodist Church etc.
b) *Christian Sects*. Under a sect is here understood Jesus Christ plus something else, especially adult baptism or the Sabbath.
c) *Nativistic Movements*. While most of the Christian sects are literalistic and fundamentalistic in their interpretation of Scripture, the nativistic movements again are also fundamentalistic, i.e. they wish to restore aspects (at least) of the traditional African religion."[1]

I am fully aware that both "Ethiopian" and "Zionist" must be understood as comprehensive terms. Some Ethiopians are today on much the same level in policy, leadership and educational ambition as certain Mission-related churches, which, after a period of devolution, are now under African leadership—with perhaps some European support in men and money.

The term "Zionist" is much more debatable, and the second chapter in this book develops a broad spectrum of differences in theology and ideology between a number of charismatic groups, loosely referred to as "Zionists". We emphasize here that Job Chiliza, after a spell as a convinced Zionist, formed a church closely connected for a time with a Western charismatic church, The Full Gospel Church, and that Chiliza himself was to become

[1] G. C. Oosthuizen, *Post-Christianity in Africa* (1968), p. 71–74.

very critical of the Zionists as a spiritual influence among his people. This did not prevent his group from displaying some of the outward signs of charismatic worship that are commonly identified with the larger group of Zionists. Chiliza himself would in later years rather align himself with a Pentecostal type.

There are differences of course within the charismatic, or Spirit, movement as a whole. The Apostolics regard themselves as different from the Zionists—"we clap hands, the Zionists beat drums"—and they emphasize even more than the Zionists the therapeutic efficacy of water; thence the use of hundreds of buckets and bottles of blessed water from the Fountain of the prophet or prophetess. The "Gospel" churches and the Pente-costals, on the other hand, regard the activities of Zionists as a threat to the purity of the Gospel message. And all these are determined to draw a sharp line between themselves on the one side and Shembe, Lekganyane or Limba on the other.

With all this in mind we nevertheless do emphasize certain broad features and overriding concerns common to them all.

In a world of disintegration, danger and disease, they all claim to function as a refuge of health and wholeness. Healing is the need of their fellow-men, and this they all attempt to provide. With this, they give to uprooted and lonely men and women the warm fellowship and loving concern—not seldom by way of tactile expression—which they are seeking.

The majority of these churches—I do not say all–seem rather as units within one great Spirit movement than separate or-ganizations. There are, of course, Spirit groups which disclaim the epithet "Zionist". Nzuza's sober men in black do not wish to be confused with the swinging white-uniformed Zionists. And as we have shown, there are much more fundamental ideological rea-sons for this distance. Nzuza is regarded as a unique source of revelation, as the *Mqhalisi* (Originator). Again Shembe, as we have shown, is just as original and unique. He cannot of course be char-acterized as a Zulu Zionist in the strict sense, and all Zionists would emphatically insist on this point.

In spite of these limitations, the term "Zion" is a useful one in the context of Southern Africa as applied to Nkonyane and a thousand others in the strict sense, and to Zulu and Swazi char-ismatic Spirit-groups in a wider sense.

The terminological ambition is limited: I speak of these movements in Southern Africa in terms understood in Southern Africa. By this I do not, of course, for a moment argue against the need for a more comprehensive terminology capable of being applied to the charismatic Spirit-movements over the continent as a whole (Aladura, etc.) or to "New Religious Movements" on a world-wide scale.

Before leaving the Ethiopian and Zionist theme, it remains to be said that the *trend in membership and appeal* has, since 1948, been one of increasing Zionist pressure, while the Ethiopian churches have been losing ground. This observation must be set against the broad development in South African political life. As long as there was some room for legally tolerable political expression on the part of the African, this could take its form in the Ethiopian protest. After 1948, the Zionist church became a refuge, providing for an emotional outlet and, in an apartheid system which the prophet accepted, sustaining the Utopian dream.

A much more controversial term is that of *"Messianic"*. Very cautiously I referred in 1948 to certain tendencies towards a "Black Christ" idea in Shembe, and devoted rather less than ten pages to this theme. Very cautiously again, in 1960, I took the step of speaking of "a third, Messianic type", along with, and distinct from, Ethiopians and Zionists. As I did this, I insisted at the same time that this term could be applied only to *"perhaps one per cent* of the [then] 1.500 Zionist churches." It was suggested at that time to recognize four Zulu Messiahs: Cekwane, Khambule, Nzuza and Shembe; from the other parts of South Africa one would have had to add Lekganyane and maybe Limba, and a few others. It was necessary then, and it is necessary today, to emphasize the numerical point—one per cent only—against a tendency in the rapidly expanding Western literature on the subject to lump the whole Independent church movement together as *"Messianisme africain"* or *"Messianische Kirchen und Sekten"*.[2]

---

[2] To the discussion of the Black Messiah concept, see B. Sundkler, "Messianisme Zoulou?," in Les missions Protestantes et l'histoire, *Actes du II colloque* (4–9) *octobre 1971*, Montpellier, p. 75–82. and *idem*, "Messies Bantou?" in Studia Geo Widengren, *Ex orbe religionum*, Brill, Leiden 1972, p. 246–251.

I have become even more hesitant now to apply the term of "Messiah." As sometimes happens, the caricature of a thesis can point up certain weaknesses in the argument.

In my earlier writings I had drawn vast conclusions *e silentio* from Shembe's hymn No. 164

> I believe in the Father
> and in the Holy Spirit
> and in the communion of saints
> of the Nazarites.

I took this to be the *summa fidei* and creed of Shembe's church, and went on to say: "Here there is no room for the Son ... His place has been usurped by another" (*Bantu Prophets*, 1960, p. 283.) In our discussion of Shembe's hymns and of later studies of them, we have now found that these conclusions were "too Western, too dogmatic". This view was thrown into sharp relief by outrageous claims made by later writers proving that they had misunderstood Shembe altogether. I refer to Chapter V in this book.

As mentioned in the chapter on Nzuza, my former view on this point was challenged by Nzuza's son, Rev. Peter Nzuza. He told me that he and his church queried the idea of placing Paulo Nzuza among Zulu Messiahs: "That is a blasphemy," he told me in 1969, and I promised to quote this and to make the necessary readjustments with regard to an interpretation of Paulo Nzuza's role.

It must be emphasized that even in spite of the protestations of leaders of a younger generation, the scholar must retain his freedom and responsibility to draw his conclusions in appropriate terms. Nevertheless, I feel, as shown in the chapter on Shembe, the need for an understanding of the *ambiguity* in the Zulu religious terms. Even while the prophet refers to his special role as healer and helper, he is at the same time and as a matter of course, dialectically aware of God and his Christ on the Throne in Heaven: Shembe knows that he himself, having come with nothing and leaving this life with nothing, will indeed stand before the judgement seat of God.

We have previously emphasized the role of the prophet at the Gate of Heaven (*Bantu Prophets*, p. 323). It is necessary to add to this idea a general Nguni thought-pattern:

309

In hierarchical Zulu society, a visitor could not approach the King directly. He had first to turn to a certain number of *izinduna* and servants whose task it was to introduce the visitor to the ultimate authority. In the belief of the Nazarites, this is what Shembe in heaven does with regard to the King of Kings on the Throne of Heaven. Thus the mediating role of the Zulu prophet does not, at least, exclude the Jesus of the New Testament. There may be a syncretistic element in this ambiguity— and we shall return to the matter of syncretism presently.

I have suggested the idea of role-taking and the concept of the *eikon* or the mask. It is a New Testament (1 and 2 Cor., Col.) image, and it fits certain aspects of the view of the faithful with regard to one or two of the Zulu prophets. Shembe was as convinced as Khambule that Christ was in his heaven and that Christ was to be the Ultimate Judge. Shembe's hymn No 34 relates the Bethlehem story, that of Incarnation. But the chorus runs:

> *Kunjaloke namhlanje*
> *Emagqumeni as'Ohlange.*
> So it is today
> on the hillocks of Ohlange.

And George Khambule in his own fashion quotes Deut. 30: "Therefore—come to be shown this foundation. Neither is it in Heavens nor is it in overseas, but just here".

Long ago and far away Jesus revealed God in Judaea and its capital Jerusalem. Here and now, God appears to the Zulu through this Man, this Mask, at Ohlange or at Telezini. There is no conscious attempt to minimize the revelation of Jesus. Sermons and testimonies underline that Jesus is the Ultimate Authority and Final Judge. But, as has been suggested, the Zulu Servant of God has revealed himself in the life of his people, as Healer and Helper and thus of an extraordinary quality.

The Search for Identity

Discussing in general terms the situation of "the African" in today's South Africa, reference is always made to the uprooted individual, torn from his traditional tribal milieu and placed in the turmoil of the city. While this is a valid consideration, one should not forget the other dimension of the alienation crisis among the African masses: the experience of being deprived of their land, suddenly finding themselves landless and forced to serve as squatters on Boer farms. In the case of the Zulu, this was one principal consequence of the Zulu war of 1879 and the partition of Zululand. Twenty years later, there followed the Boer War—and I have suggested that there is a connexion between the Bantu Refugee Camps after that war and the flaring up of apocalyptic visions in the very first Zulu Zion community (p. 44).

I have not even tried to explore the social provenance of the group near Stanger who on June 17, 1917 went with Paulo Nzuza into the Church of the Spirit, nor of those who followed Timothy Cekwane into the Church of the Light. I fall back on certain generalizations of social psychology which, as it happens, may be at least as relevant as other hypotheses.

Those were all deprived people. They were sons and daughters of proud Zulu clans with a famous past, related to royalty and martial glory. Now suddenly, they had lost that identity and found themselves without any earthly hope as miserable serfs on Boer farms. The Natives Land Act of 1913 had a traumatic effect. A. W. G. Champion, the Zulu politician, told me in 1958: "As from 1913 we knew one thing—there is no God with the White man."

It was in this situation, in the city, on the farms, and in the reserves, that a Search for a New Identity went on. This was the opportunity for the Mission-related Churches. Baptism, most often in a white dress, and the new Biblical Name signified that this individual was now a new person, with a new identity.

Yet, the struggle was more fundamental and went deeper than the missionary ever knew. For the individual it was fought out through sickness and the struggle for health and also in his or her dream world. *"Ngaphupha"*, I dreamt, is the constant answer to the question why he or she became a Zionist. Here the dream showed the way of Light along which this search for identity could lead to an integration of personality. That search at first created a sense of insecurity, but the visions and auditions in the dream helped to recapture the wholeness which once had been lost. The luminary visions in Zulu dream life formed a new and obvious point of reference: the Zionist group in white.

311

Here again there was something else in the Zionist worship and style of life, which helped to strengthen this integration. The individual was not alone in his search: he was just a small person without much importance. But the Prophet, the Leader, or the Mother showed the way.

There were certain gestures or mannerisms of the Leader which became determinative for the individual follower. The identification with the leader required the individual's repetition of these quaint mannerisms (at least, they appeared quaint to the onlooker). But to the faithful they were part of that new "dress" with which the church enveloped them.

The rigid jerking movement of the Cekwane group, suddenly kneeling for a moment and then swiftly lifting the right hand to the face; the jerking, limping rhythm while dancing in Ma Nku's church, and the expressions in her Sotho language in a Nguni church (p. 221); the swaying of the body when moving to and fro in the dance of the Khambule group: all these mannerisms are of necessity different from one church to another; but within the group they are closely followed and repeated. Here is an identification with a Leader who may have died years ago or whom one has perhaps never seen; yet, that Presence is there, re-enacted in that peculiar rhythm, in the tune of that enrapturing song. And this identification with the Prophet helps to build and strenghten the integrity of the insignificant individual, until then lost in a harsh and inimical world.

This identification with supposedly religious mannerisms of the Leader can of course be related also to a Westerner.

At Ceza, one could hear the Pentecostal pastor who when preaching would intensify the religious efficacy of his message by distorting his fine Zulu vowels "o" and "u" as if he were indeed from Indiana, U.S.A. In Chiliza's morning service in Durban I noticed an old little lady who intermittently and without any relation to what was happening in this Zulu worship as such would exclaim *"Jesus"*, in English. I presume that decades earlier she had heard some missionary lady making religious noises of that kind, and she obviously was edified by her identification with this refined example.

The Western onlooker (I was one of them) saw only the signs of the Past and thereby had his hypothesis confirmed: this religion was a bridge and a return to the past; were not traditional values and visions and patterns given an honoured place in the worship and dream world of this or that particular Zionist group?

To the Zionists these things appeared in an altogether different light. With their prophet they had gone into the New Land marching towards Mount Zion. They were constrained and carried, as it were, by the Spirit. The prophet's own personal authority stood for that Newness which was experienced as breaking with the Old Life and walking into a New Existence.

Zion and Mount Zion

In a massive volume of some six hundred large, tightly-packed pages, Professor Otto Raum has concentrated the result of a lifetime of research, as he analyzes *The Social Functions of Avoidances and Taboos among the Zulu* (Berlin and New York 1973). It is not without importance for our particular problem. In fact, every page of that book is related to a basic concern of the Zionists, that of purification. One wishes that it would have been possible to illuminate the whole complex of Zionist avoidances and taboos with the help of this research. Only then would we be in a position to understand the obsession of Zulu (and Swazi) Zionists with danger and purification, functioning as a modern movement of witch-finding, i.e., combatting magic and witches. In the meantime, I refer to the chapter on "Worship in 'Bethesda'" in *Bantu Prophets*.

Purification, too, is closely related to the new Identity of the believer. The *rite-de-passage* is Baptism, and more specifically total baptism, i.e., "not only of the forehead"—which is the custom of the Whites and therefore identified with "the Mark of the Beast", in Revelation 13—but "in much water", and preferably "in living water", of a running stream or of a river. Uncleanness and the "mystical gloom" of the past are thereby washed away, and the new identity of the believer emerges; or is emphasized and strengthened. The river with its pool or fountain had of course its traditional background. The ritual significance of rivers was well-known among Zulu and Swazi as well as among others such as Pondo or Xhosa.

It is the sacred Mountain as a focus of purifying power

which is the new contribution of Zionism, and without which it would not be—Zion. Fountain and Mountain belong together. Their functions are partly different, yet at the deepest level congruent. (Cf *Bantu Prophets,* p. 155).

It was on a mountain that Shembe as a young man had his first vision. When he returned from that experience, he did not work for a time. He said, "I have seen Jehova". As a Moses, he came to another mountain, Inhlangakazi, where he had strange visions. When he returned, he was a *"different man"*. Here he eventually ordained his first pastors. This became the holy mountain of the Church and the high destination for the yearly pilgrimage with its Feast of Tabernackles.

The Nazarites are related to *two* mountains. Ekuphakameni may not topographically be much of a mountain, but in the eyes of faith it is "the Elevated Place which enlightens all the nations" (Shembe's hymn No. 160, *chorus*), and the Church centre there is acclaimed as "a city built on a mountain" (ibid, v. 5). The high Inhlangakazi is a very impressive mountain, and inspired both Isaiah and J. G. Shembe to song (Nos. 162, 196, 223).

It was on the Mountain that Khambule found some of his sacred stones with which to sanctify his people. Some of his stones were from the river bed, purified and baptized by water. Others came from the mountain top, near to God, filled with life-giving power. In Swaziland, Elias Vilakazi lived for three years on the Mountain, preaching to a tribe of "small people". Again, it was on the Mountain, in the Drakensberg that Timothy Cekwane and his congregation saw a star with a long tail that almost touched them. This mountain ever afterwards became the centre of the annual pilgrimage.

Both the Nkonyane and the Mabilitsa traditions of Zion confirm that the leader used to take his people for a time of seclusion onto a mountain. They would fast there for a number of days and return with renewed spiritual strength.

Ordinary Zionist preachers discover anew the Holy Mountain in their Bible. They know that the holy words refer to them and their church.

> Remember ... this mount Zion
> wherein thou hast dwelt (Ps. 74: 2)

The two great experiences inspired by the high Mountains are, firstly, the sense of nearness to God, a realization of His presence; and, secondly, the ascetic aspect. The time spent there is regularly one of fasting and purification. Khambule felt that he returned from these mountain meditations filled with renewed strength. To the ordinary follower in the crowd, the Mountain fast, along with the Fountain plunge, served to integrate the personality, the more so that he or she had often encountered Mountain and Fountain in the realm of the dream.

The mountain experience was accompanied sometimes by the strangest phenomena. That unmistakeable apocalyptic Sign inscribed in bold letters on the Heavens—the Whites referred to it in their cold and uninvolved way as "Halley's Comet"—was a terrifying warning. We hear of it in the life of one of the prophets, and as such it is of merely passing interest. But when seeing that at least five of them—Enoch Mgijima of the Israelites, Isaiah Shembe, Timothy Cekwane, Job S. Mtanti and Philemon B. Sibiya, and for all I know many more—regarded "the Star with a Tail" as an especially important Messenger, it is an indication of the role of cosmic events for the emergence and the trend of the movement; and this at a time when people still lived closer to nature than in an urbanized society.[3]

A sacred place, a Zion, as in the Old Testament—this was what they were longing for, in the land of the Whites where they no longer had any right to possess land. It was sometimes overlooked that *this* was the decisive point for the Israelites under Enoch Mgijima at Bulhoek, in that fatal month of May, 1921. They had no legal right to establish their Holy Place but refused to be moved from there. In the end, 117 men of Enoch's Israelites fell to the machine-guns of the police. Smuts's Administration has been blamed for this massacre. In the light of history, it is interesting that Smuts was determined to avoid bloodshed. There was at least one European administrator, by the name of Clement Gladwin at Middledrift, who recognized the need for a "Zion" to be placed at the disposal of this religious group. Two months before the Bulhoek incident, Gladwin—in the liberal tradition that was

---

[3] As to Isaiah Shembe in this connection, see G. C. Oosthuizen, "Wie christlich ist die Kirche Shembes?" in *Evangelische Missionszeitschrift*, [XXXI], 1974, p. 131.

once characteristic of the Cape—had written to the Secretary of Native Affairs: "It seems to me that if it be possible this opportunity should be taken to allow the native mind to expand along its own line of thought, but most certainly not in defiance of the law ..."

[They should be given] "say two morgen of land for the erection of their Tabernacle which land they could treat as holy ... Hoping that my report will not tire you, Clement Gladwin."[1]

Mount Zion and Zulu Mountains

Is "Zion" then a form af *syncretism?* First of all, our plea for distinction here must be repeated. There are a number of Independent churches which are just as Jesus-oriented as are the Mission-related churches. More precisely, there are a number of Zionist churches which in intention and confession are as loyal to Jesus the Christ as Mission-related churches. Proof is provided—for anybody who cares to listen and manages to attend —by the most vital experience and expression of faith in these churches. I refer to the day-and-night services in Holy Week— from Good Friday to Easter Morning, including two nights of vigil. These services show an intense identification in witness and song on the part of almost every man and woman present, with the drama on Calvary and with the Man of Sorrows. Nobody has the right to cry "Syncretism" here, whatever the peculiar denominational paraphernalia may have been.

There remains a certain qualified residual, the Shembe's and the Khambule's and a few others.

An attempt at understanding must of course avoid the danger of romanticizing these New Religious Movements.

When referring to Syncretism it sometimes seems to be implied that there had been a studied, *deliberate* effort on the part of the prophets at combining certain elements from the traditional religion with those of the new religion. This view can be dismissed as far as the South African case is concerned, for here there was an initial, fundamental experience of a prophetic call which, most often against his will, forced the elect out of his or her

[4] C. Gladwin 8.3.1921 to Secr. Nat. Affairs (E. E. Barrett); 420/13 F/ 387 (Israelites), National Archives, Pretoria.

old milieu and set him on the road towards the future. The dynamic was the urge to obey the dictates of Jehova as in Shembe "I have seen Jehova today"—or to follow the will of Jesus—Khambule in his heavenly vision—or again to be led by the Spirit, together with the Initiator, *Mqhalisi*, to serve God in the newness of that Spirit.

It goes without saying that patterns and pressures of the past were to condition certain structures of that new faith. This must be taken for granted, for this is what the phenomenology of religions demonstrates in relation to all cultures. It would seem all the more necessary to emphasize that the intention of the Zion prophet was to establish a *new*, Christian community. From his fundamentalist, indeed literalistic view-point he was convinced that his approach was "more Christian" than the others: perhaps that it was the only real Christian approach.

From his point of view he had taken an infinitely decisive and radical step, away from the Past, baptized to the new life, walking henceforth towards the New Land.

On the other hand, it may well be asked what right we have to question the good intentions and the sincerity of others who claim Jesus Christ as the focus of their faith. We cannot prescribe the manner in which others must behave in order to be acceptable as Christians.

There must always be a dialectical tension here, not so much between established forms and wildly spontaneous, new expressions of faith and worship, as between "Old" and "New", the question being how the New is related to the Old and vice versa. When attempting to assess these particular movements we must realize that the problem of "Syncretism" is double-edged. It must not be taken for granted that syncretistic tendencies are a temptation of the new religious movements exclusively while more or less established churches in the West or the East would automatically be regarded as being above such suspicion.

This leads us finally to the Ecumenical perspective and task. The Church of Christ is not uniform but Universal.

This universality or Catholicity stimulates full freedom for the local expression of faith, thus representing what the great Epistle of the Church Catholic calls the "multi-coloured" wisdom of God, Eph. 3.10.

A Future for Zion?

Taking a closer look at the situation for Zion, one discerns two different trends.

A tendency towards an accommodation of the church to modern conditions is being strengthened (cf *Bantu Prophets*, p. 307). There is an increasing emphasis now on higher education for the young as well as a readiness to resort to hospital and medical services. All this would seem to accentuate the accommodation of the charismatic group to the conformative patterns and pressures of modern society and to more established forms of churchmanship.

Another process is, however, going on simultaneously, possibly counteracting this accommodating tendency. The cities attract also the illiterate young people. Thus on the beaches of Durban or in the open fields adjoining Soweto one can, on a Saturday or Sunday afternoon, study how *ad hoc* Zionist groups are being formed around budding prophets, recently arrived from country places into the maelstrom of the city. Lacking in educational opportunities, they find in the Zionist family worship an outlet for their leadership urge. With some luck they may some day emerge as healing prophets as charismatic and attractive as Daniel Nkonyane or Ezra Mbonambi were regarded in Zion's spring time.

Bearing in mind these two competing tendencies, it is of course not easy to predict what developments might take place in the next twenty-five years, between now and A.D. 2000.

Speaking in sociological terms—as if they were the only ones!—one might also point to the Zionist group's role of a social lever: the hardworking, clean-living builder-brick-layer in Swaziland and Zululand; the shopkeeper in Kwa Mashu or Soweto; the bus-owner in the district of the Thousands Hills. All these cases, in their microcosm, go to prove in Zululand and Swaziland of today Max Weber's theory on Protestant ethics and the spirit of capitalism in Puritanism.

But there is more to it than that. There are now already two generations to judge from, and the development, at least in some families, raises more fundamental issues.

The Gospel, also in its Zion garments, was not only "pie in the sky". It had a liberating effect, setting man free, free from fear, fear of witches and the power of darkness, but above all confer-

318

ring a freedom to take a stand and to be a person, freedom from inner dependence on European tokens of grace or favour, to aim for higher things and a finer sensitivity.

In a second generation of charismatic families there is emerging a new élite: the Chilizas and the Mabilitsas and the August-Nkus are indications of this tendency.

To the distant onlooker, the loud and lively Zion worship seemed like an escape into Utopia. Yet, at least in some of these men and women something had happened—and happened through Zion—which made them more prepared for the next phase and stage in the struggle for the liberation of man. There was a new realization of selfhood and worthy identity in these men and women because of their discovery, in and with Zion, of the richness and relevance of their own religious and cultural expressions. This led some of them to readiness for cultural creativity and social involvement which in any society must be given high priority.

Among modern African intellectuals there are two different, in fact, opposite views whether the Zionist movement has a future or not.

The Ethiopian group or the Zionist Utopia are sometimes interpreted as potential centres for political protest. The political scene in Southern Africa is undergoing rapid change and radical upheavals may hit South Africa sooner rather than later. In such an emergency—including a general strike, for instance—one could visualize some of the Independent Churches as centres to which Africans might turn for prayer, inspiration and other help.

African intellectuals in South Africa, cannot spare much time for *ama Zioni*. They judge the Independents with harsh realism just as much as they condemn the Mission churches. Njabulo Ndebele wrote in 1972:

"Thus, the many sects we see are a perpetuation of bondage. The blacks must obliterate all these sects. On the other hand, the blacks must turn their backs on all the Western Churches; they have been shorn of all emotional content. A genuine religion will spring out of the blacks' own circumstances, just as a genuine philosophy of life should. It should be a religion that will find God through man; and not man through God."

319

From this vantage point, a decisive question in South Africa of today is the extent to which not only Zion but the Church as a whole offers a possibility of that "finding", finding God through man.

The seriousness of the situation was brought home to me in a conversation with an African church leader at, or rather outside Eshowe, Zululand. He was not an "Independent" but a highly placed Zulu church official in one of the most respected churches in the land, a man acclaimed everywhere else but in his own country. He told me: "Our greatest problem is this: never for one day to be treated as a human being."

Dr Gabriel Setiloane, in quoting this, deepens my own observation by a searching comment. Listen to this vital African pastor and theologian: "It really means that the Independent (and the African in general) is attempting to fit his theology of Man (learning from mother's knee) to his life's everyday experience which denies his humanity".[4]

In the South Africa of apartheid and of legally condoned radical discrimination, the problem of personal identity and the meaning of "hominisation"—to use Teilhard de Chardin's term—takes on a fundamental urgency for both Black *and* White. What has White South Africa, as a people, not lost by discarding the enormous personal resources of their great African contemporaries!

I remember a testimony by one of the Swazi Apostolics. Pastor Alpheus Msibi, representative of Ma Nku's St John's Apostolic Church delivered a long meditation on the mystique of water. He praised the purifying qualities of such holy water as had been prayed for by the prophet, supporting his sermon by a long sequence of Bible quotations, from the first chapter of Genesis to the last verses in the Book of Revelation. In the middle of all this—a two hours' display interspersed with lively *"Amens"* and *"Hallelujahs"* from his flock—he announced: *"Umuntu ung umuntu ngomuntu"*: man becomes man through Him who became man".

---

[4] Cf. Gabriel M. Setiloane, "The Independent Church Movement in South Africa: its significance for the Church", Paper, Univ. of York, 1973.

Appendix

The very first Black Zion: Additional Material (to pp. 43–46)

Some statistics: In June 1902 there were in Transvaal 38 Native Refugee Camps with 54000 Africans, and in Oranje Freestate 28 camps with 56000 Africans. In June 1903, the Secr. Native Affairs, Natal, instructed his counterpart for Transvaal and the Magistrates of Klip Rivier and Newcastle—both important districts for our story—to give notice to all Native Refugees that they must return to Transvaal or to the Free State at the end of June 1903.

The Pietermaritzburg Provincial Archives provide more detailed statistics. In this connexion, instruction was given by Major Lotbinière to the Superintendent, Nat. Refugee Dept. to arrange four centres for the refugees, at Upper Tugela, Ladysmith, Newcastle, and Harrismith. Of a grand total for Natal of 5492 (later expanded to 6648) no less than 2445 were in the Newcastle district.*

From Wakkerstroom, Le Roux would go on evangelistic tours in Northern Natal and Eastern Transvaal. The statistical result of his influence can to some extent be indirectly ascertained by a Register which he kept between 1905 and 1914 of the number of "children consecrated to God"; one must surmise that these were children of parents baptized on such occasions by Le Roux. 1905: 149 children from Wakkerstroom and "Slang rivier" to Utrecht and Ermelo; from the last-mentioned place, he registers 41 children thus consecrated on May 21, 1905. In 1906 the total was 66, now including Standerton, relatively far away from headquarters at Wakkerstroom. 1907: 93; 1908: 36; 1909: 46; 1910: 19; 1911: 13; 1912: 77; 1913: 25; 1914: 41. For 1907 partic-

---

* S N A 9, 1170; 9, 1211; 1441. National Archives. Pretoria.

G. J. de Lotbinière telegram 21.8.1902 to Locations, Bloemfontein. I /1/ 297, and *ibid.* 2948/1902 Provincial Archives, Pietermaritzburg.

P. L. Le Roux, Baptismal register. Archives, Apostolic Faith Mission, Johannesburg.

ularly his right-hand man Daniel Nkonyane. Contributed to the large number of that year.

The perspective on Zion and the Rebellion could be widened beyond Zion to Zulu charismatics in general. There were personal ties and affinities, sometimes with supposedly supernatural sanctions, between Rebellion leaders and Zulu prophets. The outstanding example is Isaiah Shembe's role in connection with chief Messen Qwabe, one of the outstanding supporters of Bambata, the nationalist hero. After Messen's death, Shembe announced at the chief's grave: "I am going to revive the bones of Messen and the people who were killed in Bambata's Rebellion". Cf. Sundkler, *Bantu Prophets,* p. 313.

Le Roux and the Zulu leaders naturally observed limits and border lines which were not always recognised by one or two of the younger Zion missionaries in far-off Basutoland. Under Le Roux's chairmanship, the Executive Council in Johannesburg was to express somewhat later "strong disapproval of the practice of kissing between White and Native which has sprung up in the work in Basutoland and in future discountenances the continuance of the practice as being highly inexpedient. 1. Cor. 6: 12 and 10: 23".

Exec. Committee Minutes, Ap. Faith Mission: March 7, 1914. Six months later the missionary couple Saunders were instructed to leave Basutoland, and, likewise, the Sotho leader Edw. Lion told to appear before the Council in Johannesburg to answer charges against him. Ibid., Sept. 30, 1914.

"White Zion" in Durban

I have of course not covered the whole of the White Zion' story in South Africa. A leading part was taken by John Taylor, of Scotland, who having been "converted" in 1895 went to Natal, South Africa, to work in a law firm in Pietermaritzburg. He took his "final examination" in Law in 1899. In 1897 he came across copies of *Leaves of Healing*, Dr. Dowie's paper, in the Soldiers' Home and in the YMCA in Pietermaritzburg. From that time he believed in Divine Healing, and as the Boer War broke out he actively preached this message to soldiers arriving in Durban. He was joined by John Thomson, leader of a "Zion Gathering" in Johannesburg. In December 1899, John Taylor went "with the Gospel" to the front. In 1900, he definitely joined the Christian Catholic Church in Zion. I presume that he was active in the first white Zion group in Durban. J. Taylor's own report in *Leaves of Healing*, Sept 6, 1902.

Constitution of the Church of Christ,
the Congregation of All Saints of South Africa
(G. Khambule)

This church of Christ is based, raised on the foundation of the Bible through God prophets and Apostles the message from our Lord Jesus has instructed us to go all over the world preaching that they should resign themselves and keep strictly to the faith of this message by which only the way inherit the everlasting life of the Kingdom of God. Every nation and every Christian individual should keep away from all hatred and grudge one to another, and be bound to unity in Christ as he himself is with his Father God.

Here under are some principles prescribe[d] as the message, which all nations should follow closely. Church of Christ is based on the same principles actually stated by Jesus himself; that all should abhor all evil bodily appetites for all such is enmity towards God: Covetousness, envy, adultry, fornication etc. Rom. 8. 1–8. All who are predominated by the desires of the flesh are not confidential to God, because they are jealous, commit adultery, curse and backbite and do all sorts of evil which is against the Holy one like drinking wine and all other intoxicating drinks. Jehovah says be apart from all that so that ye may be given the all power of healing.

This church does not participate in evils such as mentioned above; does not eat animals' blood; drinks nothing except water. Does not use tobacco of any kind;—Does not eat pork.—She lives only on God's spirit. St. Math. 10: 1. Does not get reward or bear any purse for silver or gold. But the only reward she longs for is the "Heavenly Reward".

She does not baptise with water but through service of Ashes St. Math. 3: 11–12. Acts 19: 1–4 and verses 18–19. Heb. 9: 12–15 Acts 1: 4–5 and v. 8 and 2: 1–4. She does not partake the Holy

Communion but the passover. St. Math. 26 25–29, Is. 28 6–8, Jer. 6. 10.

Does not greet or salute by hands—but only saying—Peace be unto you. Hands are not laid upon the sick, but all those who confess their sins are empower[ed]. G.M. K[ambule]. St. Math. 10: 8–13. St Luke 10: 4–5; 2 Kings 4: 29; Acts 19: 6.

The Bishop of this church is Jesus Christ—to whom it is founded, all which is done is according to his will. Eph. 2: 19–22 and 1: 22; St. John 10: 1–8. All who join this church are sanctified first and blessed to receive the Holy Ghost which purifies their hearts. 1 John 3: 3–10. St. John 14: 14–17. She is built up from the foundation of the prophet Daniel 2: 44–46. This stone is her foundation base. All nations should come and see the mountain where G.M.K. God put his new covenant, Isaiah 2: 2, 3.

Therefore I am ever waiting for everyone, who feels Christ like, to come to be shown this foundation where this church is laid upon. Deut. 30: 11–15. Neither is it in Heavens nor is it in over seas, but just here.

The Church Services: −
Sundays from 6 a.m. to 11 a.m. to 3 p.m. to 7 p.m.
Tuesday and Friday are services for the sick from various places.

Service is held on the mountain, where they last three days and three nights without food. Here the followers of Christ are spiritual.

This church is against beer drinking nor any other of this sort which is against to what is said in the following:—1 Peter 4: 1–3, 2 Cor. 6: 14–18, St. Math. 19: 10–12, 1 Cor. 7: 2, 7, 9, 17, St. Luke 20: 34–36. On Good Friday we visit all parishes of this Church.

Everything was revealed to me. I am sent forth to all who are still in darkness and in the shadow of death to bring them light. I am to work at his disciple. Fuifilling all what he has ordered me to do among all the nations. Making them act accordingly so as to be saved. Act[s] 26: 17–18, Isaiah 35: 6–10 and 42: 6–9 and 44: 6–9, St Luke 1: 79, St. John 8: 12, 2 Cor. 4: 4. 1. Tess. 5: 6, 2 Cor. 6: 14–18. Heb. 5: 4–6. Ye may be Bishops and such without a call, but ye still need milk, see Heb. 5: 12, 1 Cor. 1: 19, 27–29, St. John 7: 36–39, St. Math. 11: 25–27, St. John 3: 30–32. How then shall they preach except they be sent—How shall they pray to him G.M.K. whom they have not hea[r]d. Blessed are the feet of those who bring good [t]idings of good things of truth. Rom. 10: 13–15, St. John 3: 8–11. I know whom I am preaching unto you, and whom I witness. G.M.K. This Church was established in 1923. The [l]ame healed. The dumb spoke and praised the Lord. Demons were cast out, native herbalist[s] left their drugs and repented, blind were given sight and those without children got children. All these mentioned above were manifested at Telezini Nqutu District, Umsinga, Nondweni, Talane near Dundee, Mpemvaan near P. P. Burg (Paulpietersburg), *Septzikop* at Edudusini, Benoni, Witbank and Johannesburg.

All who have joined this church are regarded as her members; they are 1.046 in number.

She has her own apostles and priests who are earnest and willing workers for Jesus Christ our saviour.

I am
The Superintendent and Nazar.
GEORGE M KAMBULE
Ekupakameni home Surrey school Dannhauser

Bishop Elijah Vilakathi

The balance in our rapid survey of Swazi churches (p. 211–223) did not allow a detailed report from our interviews with Elijah Vilakathi, but some of this material should be set out here.

The Bishop's considerable self-assurance has supernatural sanctions. "If God gave me, Vilakathi, the Spirit, it must be realized that I had teeth in my mother's womb and was born thus. I came out with those teeth."

His colour scheme is—as we have pointed out—unique for Swaziland. His Jesus appears in red—this was related to His Blood. God the Father usually wears a robe of gold but sometimes appears in a brown garment, his Face shining as the sun. This God it was who told Elijah Vilakathi to wear a golden armlet for the left wrist (this was in a dream; in the harsh world of wake-fulness this was for practical reasons modified to brass).

His Jericho Church joins all of Swazi Zion for the Good Friday national festival but Christmas is celebrated at Jericho. The Methodist hymnbook and the Gospel Trumpet (in Zulu) is used. Here the Spirit advises them what hymn to choose. Most of the time, however, they can carry on singing the two well-known words "Amen, Hallelujah", with variations. This has the advantage of the participants not needing to resort to a book.

E. V. himself is supported by the presence of Angels. "They are numerous, for I have a great work to perform", while ordinary people have just one angel. E. V. can call upon one particular angel for Healing, another for Speaking with Tongues, one again for Interpretation of Tongues. The language of the Angels being incomprehensible to human reason, E. V. communicates in Tongues with them.

The Church's centre is called Jericho—this name was given through an archangel, Michael himself: "Thy Church shall be called Jericho. Blind shall see there, and their eyes will be opened."

Occasionally, the Twelve Apostles with St. Paul visit E. V. They are then on an inspection tour: "They come to examine (hlola) whether my work is proceeding well and if I am well."

Related to the Angels is another vision, mentioned in the printed Constitution of the Church. "I saw our old Departed Ones, they told me to slaughter a goat. So I did, and everything succeeded."

On occasions a high and holy company arrives from over there, from the East, walking as if on clouds: "The Pope, and Mary and Joseph, and the forefathers (okhokho)." Last time they said: "We come from Rome", and then they left.

The Bishop's uniform is red with a pectoral cross in brass and three small padlocks sown to the uniform: this signifies the special power bequeathed to E. V., "the power of the keys". His brass staff is crowned by a brass soldier with a gun. This image symbolizes his power to fight illnesses: It is with this power-loaded staff that he touches his many patients—and not only African patients. He also has a three-tongued wooden staff: almost as effective when placed on the sick part of the patient's body.

326

The Bishop also has a gown made by sacking with red bands and padlocks fixed to the material. There are in fact a number of other gowns in the vestry in his main house, "the House of Jesus Christ". The patterns and colours are all from the Bible of course. The Constitution of the Church (printed in 1968 in isi Swathi) says: "This Church wears all the worship garments spoken of by Jehova." The Bishop wears a crown of brass with the figures of a fish (for luck, when healing) and a lion (for power and strength, also for healing).

Patients stay at Jericho for periods that may vary between just a few days and four to eight months. It is all very logical: The patients may have been plagued by their illnesses for a number of years: the healing must of course take a corresponding number of months.

Vilakathi tackles a number of illnesses: mental cases; headache; ear pain; barrenness and "when the power is finished down here" (with a massive gesture to the nether parts).

Mental cases are brought to the river. They are also treated with ashes. "I tie a sash round them if shown by the Spirit. I do not use the power of reason, but the Spirit who reveals himself both in dreams and in visions in broad day-light."

Headache: tied with a sash of any of the following colours: red, green or white.

Barrenness: patient brought to the river, tied with sashes; laying on of hands, round the waist and stomach.

"I just say 'By the power of God', or 'By the power of Jesus', and that holy power enters easily (*kalula*) into the person."

A special device is a round wheel, more than a yard in diameter. It consists of grass, tied with cloth. The patient touches this, or the Bishop encircles him or her with the wheel. "The power enters easily—because I am well. Thus I serve as a conductor of the strength of God. But, of course, in order to be healed people must believe." This power-wheel is suspended from the ceiling of the church.

Shembe debated

Shembe has been studied by Western scholars. Dr. Katesa Schlosser, of Kiel devoted a large part of her book on *Einge-*

borenen Kirchen in Süd- und Südwest Afrika (1958) to a meticulous presentation of Ekuphakameni and the activities of the Church.

As early as 1954 Dr. Absalom Vilakazi wrote an M.A. thesis on *The Church of the Nazarites,* presented at the Kennedy School of Missions, Hartford University, Connecticut. As this study (117 pp., cyclostyled) was never published, it has unfortunately remained almost completely unknown. Only in 1967 was I made aware of its existence (through Dr. Oosthuizen's book), and I managed to borrow a copy in 1973. Dr. Vilakazi is a Zulu himself and is therefore in a privileged position to understand the movement. He has brought out certain Zulu concepts, particularly in the medical field, which had not been noticed before. He has also emphasised the concept of the Covenant in this Church, and has brought out the otherwise overlooked significance of the Ark of the Covenant. He takes a broad and generous view of the "chief aim" of the Nazarites being that of "the regeneration of Zulu society"—a most valuable point of view.

A specific study of Shembe's hymns has been made by Professor G. C. Oosthuizen of Durban. The title of his book gives the whole thesis of the study: *The Theology of a South African Messiah.* In the preface the author underlines that his German professor had suggested that he should treat Shembe's hymn-book "as the catechism of the Nazarites". This the author accepts, and he goes on to say: "The Izihlabelelo should be considered as the catechism of the movement and gives insight into its theology." After this overture the Zulu thought-world and imagery of Isaiah Shembe are pressed into the following categories: the Supreme Being; the Messiah, Man and the Supernatural World; The Community —including (A) The Congregation, (B) The Building, (C) The Scriptures, (D) The Commandments, (E) The Festivals, (F) Numinous power in the Congregation, (G) Sin and Sinners, (H) Baptism, (I) Miscellaneous (1. Decoration. 2. Dancing)"; and finally, "Eschatology".

Sources

National Archives, Pretoria. For our *Bantu Prophets* we had the privilege of consulting in 1945 and 1958 the rich material with Native Affairs Department, containing at that time towards a thousand files under the number "214", relating to each individual church. Together with our interview material mainly from Ceza, Zululand, these official files in fact formed the foundation of our research in the 1940's.

The Transvaal (pre- 1910) files with the National Archives have yielded rich material, consulted in 1969 and 1972, particularly on the beginnings of the Independent Church movement.

The Provincial Archives, Pietermaritzburg, and the Native Commissionar's archive, Johannesburg, were consulted.

The Swazi Government Archives, Mbabane, and those of the Magistrate's office, Bremersdorp-Manzini must be mentioned in this connection.

Church Archives of special importance for our research were those of the Dutch Reformed Church, Pretoria; the Apostolic Faith Mission, Johannesburg—particularly important for Ch. I —and that of the Full Gospel Church, Irene, Transvaal. I am particularly grateful to Dr. and Mrs. F. P. Möller of the Apostolic Faith Mission, for their help and hospitality. Dr. W. Bodenstein, Pretoria, placed at my disposal valuable notes on a visit in August 1958 to the annual festival of Cekwane's Church of the Light.

Family collections of letters

My conviction has been for a long time that important private collections of correspondence etc. could be uncovered with the second and third generation descendants. This was abundantly confirmed in the cases of both Whites and Africans. The descendants in South Africa of Le Roux, Büchler and Mahon have co-operated generously. Tenacious search over the North American continent eventually resulted in the valuable material kept by Mr. Daniel Bryant, Los Angeles, California, the son of the Rev. Daniel Bryant.

Similar efforts were made with regard to correspondence kept by descendants of the African Church Fathers of the movement: the Nkonyanes, the Mabilitsas and the Mahlangus.

The Rev. J. C. Shembe kindly allowed us to make use of the church archive which he is in the course of establishing: we have used this for the *Acts of the Nazarites* (p. 175).

As far as Nzuza's Church of the Holy Spirit is concerned, we studied its hand-written *Book of Prophecies* in other circumstances.

Bibliography. We must limit ourselves to references in the footnotes. Fortunately we can refer to a remarkable tool. R. C. Mitchell and H. W. Turner have published *A Bibliography of Modern African Religious Movements,* Evanston, N.W. University Press, 1966, listing no less than 1319 books, articles etc. in this field. Their bibliography is regularly brought up to date in the *Journal of Religion in Africa.*

Illustrations. First four pictures between pp. 48–49, from the Bryant collection, Los Angeles. The Nzuza group picture facing p. 49, and the following, by Mr. Ulf Carlson, formerly Dundee, Natal, now Gothenburg, Sweden. The picture of W. Dimba, facing p. 141, by courtesy of the Editor, *The World*, Johannesburg. Cover picture, by Mrs Constance Stuart, Johannesburg. The Swazi church pictures taken by Dr Ludo Kuipers, of Holland.

Interviews

To a large extent the material for this book consists of personal interviews with Zulu and Swazi church leaders, apart from extensive correspondence with some of the leaders and their descendants.

My personal notebooks from interviews with Zulu and Swazi Independent Church leaders contain for

1958: 16 notebooks: *1 800 pp.*

plus 5 notebooks by African assistants

mainly T. W. S. Mthembu and P. Mp. Mkize 400 pp.
  1969: 15 notebooks: *1 500 pp.*
  1972/73: 10 notebooks: *920 pp.*
Prior to 1958:
  10 notebooks: *1 100 pp.*
  African assistants (1941) *470 pp.*
    P. B. Mhlungu 100
    K. Msomi 110
    T. W. S. Mthembu 170
    A. Xakaza 30

A rich find was that representing George Khambule's Church. I have been gathering material on his church over a period of thirty-five years. In 1941, some fifty pages were thus written on that Church by a young Lutheran theological student from Khambule's village Telezini. His name was Paulos B. Mhlungu, now the Lutheran Bishop in Natal. He had observed this religious group ever since his first school days in 1919 when his teacher in the elementary school, J. S. Mtanti, suddenly saw strange visions.

In 1958, Mr. Zuma, a Zulu student in the Sociology Department, Durban, was sent to the headquarters of the Church. He secured a photostat copy of one of Khambule's main diaries. I gave instructions for the original to be returned to the rightful owner, the Church itself. Not until 1969 I was in a position to follow this up. My personal visits to the headquarters brought me into contact with the last remaining Archbishop, M. Sikakana. He made it possible for me to take photostat copies of the hand-written library of Khambule's diaries and liturgies (see p. 160). That this find was thus copied was just as well, for after half a year Archbishop Sikakane himself was dead and only a few weeks later the whole place war burned to the ground. Nothing was left of the unique archives—except for the fact that it was all reproduced and kept in the Uppsala collection.

I was assisted by two contact-men, without whose help such communication as was achieved could not have been reached. They were both Zulu and Lutherans, but otherwise very different. Rev. T. W. S. Mthembu, born about 1915, assisted me in 1957 and

1958. He had served as a Lutheran pastor but was out of work and looking for any odd job. Exuberant, genial, and full of humour he was ideal for contacts with chiefs and prophets. We were old friends. As a missionary it had been my task for a few happy weeks in 1941 to teach him and his fellow-students some Church History. Questions for a "Term Test" had to be worked out and I asked the conventional things. At the end of the list there was this one: "African sects in South Africa." I have forgotten what the others replied but well remember Mthembu's answer: "The one who calls others a sect is a sect himself." From that moment we became great friends. His cheerful approach was a help in getting unwilling Zulu dignitaries to open up. In 1959 he was found dead, hanging from a tree near Durban. The many-levelled complexity of his relationships had earned him not only friends but enemies, too.

From 1958 onwards, Mr. Peter Mp. Mkize, (b. 1927), earlier Church secretary, then Bank Supervisor, African dept., has arranged contacts in 1958, 1969 and 1972–73 for me on the Rand and in Swaziland. Conscientious, precise and meticulous he won the confidence of African churchmen and we spent very many weekends together with Zionists and Apostolics. For ten years he also made newspaper clippings for me from the African press. Nine large volumes of clippings contain that material.

The following newspapers were consulted, some (in italics) throughout the years. [*Bantu*] *World;* Bona; *Drum;* Grace; *Ilanga lase Natal;* Imvo Zabantsundu; *Izwi lama Swazi;* New Age; *Rand Daily Mail; The Star;* Sunday Times.

A small Matsushita National tape recorder was a useful adjunct. On most occasions it was used openly. I explained its use and function, and played some of it back to the performers, who enjoyed the technological miracle almost as much as I did.

Index

DATE DUE